Financial Accounting
Study Guide and Selected Readings
Fourth Edition

Belverd E. Needles, Jr.
DePaul University

Edward H. Julius
California Lutheran University

Houghton Mifflin Company · **Boston** · **Toronto**

Dallas · Geneva, Illinois · Palo Alto · Princeton, New Jersey

Senior Sponsoring Editor: Donald J. Golini
Senior Development Editor: Jane W. Sherman
Ancillary Coordinator: Elena Di Cesare
Manufacturing Coordinator: Holly Schuster
Marketing Manager: Karen Natale

Cover photograph by Keller/Peet Associates.

Copyright © 1992 by Houghton Mifflin Company. All rights reserved.

No part of this work may be reproduced or transmitted in any form or by any means, electronic or mechanical, including photocopying and recording, or by any information storage or retrieval system without the prior written permission of Houghton Mifflin Company unless such copying is expressly permitted by federal copyright law. Address inquiries to College Permissions, Houghton Mifflin Company, One Beacon Street, Boston, MA 02108.

Printed in the U.S.A.

Library of Congress Catalog Card Number 91-71970

ISBN: 0-395-59405-7

ABCDEFGHIJ-HS-998765432

Contents

To the Student

This Study Guide is designed to help you improve your performance in your first accounting course. You should use it in your study of *Financial Accounting,* Fourth Edition, by Needles.

Reviewing the Chapter This section of each chapter summarizes in a concise but thorough manner the essential points related to the chapter's learning objectives. Each learning objective is restated and its page reference given for easier cross-referencing to the text. All key terms are covered in this section or in the Testing Your Knowledge section. Where applicable, a Summary of Journal Entries introduced in the chapter is also presented.

Testing Your Knowledge Each chapter contains a matching quiz of key terms, a short-answer section, true-false statements, and multiple-choice questions to test your understanding of the learning objectives and vocabulary of the chapter. This Study Guide also contains eight crossword puzzles to test your knowledge of key terms.

Applying Your Knowledge An important goal in learning accounting is the ability to work exercises and problems. In this section of each chapter, you can test your ability to apply two or three of the new principles introduced in the chapter to "real-life" accounting situations.

Readings Most chapters include one or two current readings to provide you with a broader understanding of the accounting profession, careers in all fields of accounting, and current issues.

Specimen Financial Statements The Financial Report from the 1990 Annual Report of Coca-Cola Enterprises Inc. is provided as a real example of the financial statement of a major, well-known corporation. This complete set of financial statements, management's discussion and analysis, notes to the financial statements, report of the independent accountants, and other information are provided for students to see the end product of the accounting process. They may be used by instructors and students for discussion and illustration of the concepts, techniques, and statements presented in *Financial Accounting*, Fourth Edition.

Answers The Study Guide concludes with answers to all questions, exercises, problems, and crossword puzzles. All answers are cross-referenced to the learning objectives from the chapter.

CHAPTER 1 ACCOUNTING AS AN INFORMATION SYSTEM

Reviewing the Chapter

OBJECTIVE 1: Define accounting and describe its role in making informed decisions (pp. 3–6).

1. **Accounting** is an information system that measures, processes, and communicates financial information. **Bookkeeping,** a small but important aspect of accounting, is the mechanical and repetitive recordkeeping process.

2. The **computer** is an electronic tool that rapidly collects, organizes, and communicates vast amounts of information. The computer does not take the place of the accountant. However, the accountant must understand how it operates since it is an integral part of the accounting information system.

3. A **management information system (MIS)** is an information network that takes in all major functions of a business, called subsystems. The accounting information system is the financial hub of the management information system.

4. Making a decision involves (a) setting a goal, (b) considering alternatives, (c) making the actual decision, (d) taking action, and (e) using feedback to evaluate the results. Accounting assists in planning, control, and evaluation by providing useful financial information to the decision maker. **Planning** involves setting a course of action, **control** is the process of comparing actual operations with planned operations, and **evaluation** is the process of studying the decision system to improve it.

OBJECTIVE 2: Identify the many users of accounting information in society (pp. 6–10).

5. There are basically three groups that use accounting information: management, outsiders with a direct financial interest, and outsiders with an indirect financial interest.
   a. For a business to survive, **management** must make satisfactory earnings to hold investor capital (called **profitability**) and must keep sufficient funds on hand to pay debts as they fall due (called **liquidity**). The company will have other goals, such as improving its products and expanding operations. It is management that directs the company toward these goals by making decisions.
   b. Present or potential investors and present or potential creditors are considered outside users with a direct financial interest in a business. Most businesses publish financial statements that report their profitability and financial position. Investors use these financial statements to assess the strength or weakness of the company, whereas creditors examine the financial statements to determine the company's ability to repay loans.
   c. Society as a whole, through its government officials and public groups, may be

viewed as a financial statement user with an indirect financial interest in a business. Specifically, such users include tax authorities, regulatory agencies, economic planners, and other groups (such as labor unions and financial analysts).

6. Managers within government and within not-for-profit organizations such as hospitals, universities, professional organizations, and charities also make extensive use of financial information.

OBJECTIVE 3: Distinguish between financial and management accounting, define generally accepted accounting principles (GAAP), and identify the organizations that influence GAAP (pp. 10–13).

7. A distinction is usually made between **management accounting,** which focuses on information for internal users, and **financial accounting,** which involves the preparation, reporting, analysis, and interpretation of accounting information in reports for external users.

8. Accounting theory provides the reasoning behind and framework for accounting practice. **Generally accepted accounting principles (GAAP)** are the set of guidelines and procedures that constitute acceptable accounting practice at a given point in time. The set of GAAP changes continually as business conditions change and practices improve.

9. The financial statements of publicly held corporations are **audited** (examined) by licensed professionals, called **certified public accountants (CPAs),** so that the statements can be made more believable to the user. Before the audit can take place, however, the CPA must be **independent** of the client (without financial or other ties). Upon completion of the audit, the CPA reports on whether or not the audited statements "present fairly, in all material respects" and are "in conformity with generally accepted accounting principles."

10. In 1973, the **Financial Accounting Standards Board (FASB)** succeeded the Accounting Principles Board as the authoritative body in the development of GAAP. This group is separate from the AICPA and issues Statements of Financial Accounting Standards.

11. The **American Institute of Certified Public Accountants (AICPA)** is the professional association of CPAs. It was instrumental in developing GAAP, mainly through the Accounting Principles Board (APB), from 1959 to 1973.

12. The **Securities and Exchange Commission (SEC)** is an agency of the federal government. It has the legal power to set and enforce accounting practices for companies that are required to report to it. Generally, these are companies whose securities are traded by the general public.

13. The **Internal Revenue Service (IRS)** enforces and interprets the set of rules that govern the assessment and collection of federal income taxes.

14. The **Governmental Accounting Standards Board (GASB)** was established in 1984 and is responsible for issuing accounting standards for state and local governments.

15. International accounting organizations include the International Accounting Standards Committee (IASC) and the International Federation of Accountants (IFAC), which was formed in 1977.

16. There are other organizations of accountants besides the AICPA. The Institute of Management Accountants (IMA) was organized to deal with cost and managerial accounting, the Financial Executives Institute (FEI) is interested primarily in financial accounting, and the American Accounting Association (AAA) is concerned chiefly with accounting education and accounting theory.

OBJECTIVE 4: Explain the importance of business transactions, money measure, and separate entity to accounting measurement (pp. 14–16).

17. To make an accounting measurement, the accountant must answer the following basic questions:
    a. What is to be measured?
    b. When should the measurement occur?
    c. What value should be placed on what is measured?
    d. How is what is measured to be classified?

18. Accounting is concerned with measuring transactions of specific business entities in terms of money.
    a. **Business transactions** are economic events that affect the financial position of a business. Business transactions may involve

an exchange of value (for example, sales, borrowings, and purchases) or a nonexchange (for example, the physical wear and tear on machinery, and losses due to fire or theft).

b. The **money measure** concept states that business transactions should be measured in terms of money. Financial statements are normally prepared in terms of the monetary unit of the business's country (dollars, pesos, etc.). When transactions occur between countries with differing monetary units, the amounts must be translated from one currency to another, using the appropriate **exchange rate.**

c. For accounting purposes, a business is treated as a **separate entity,** distinct from its owners, creditors, and customers.

OBJECTIVE 5: Describe the corporate form of business organization (pp. 16–20).

19. The three basic forms of business organization are sole proprietorships, partnerships, and corporations. Accountants recognize each form as an economic unit separate from its owners. A **sole proprietorship** is a business owned and managed by one person, a **partnership** is a business owned and managed by two or more persons, and a **corporation** is a business owned by stockholders but managed by a board of directors.

20. The corporation is the dominant form of American business because it makes possible the accumulation of large quantities of capital. The stockholders of a corporation are liable only to the extent of their investment, and ownership (evidenced by **shares of stock)** can be transferred without affecting operations.

a. Before a corporation may do business, it must apply for and obtain a charter from the state. The state must approve the **articles of incorporation,** which describe the basic purpose and structure of the proposed corporation.

b. Management of a corporation consists of the board of directors, who determine corporate policy, and the officers, who carry on the daily operations. The board is elected by the stockholders, and the officers are appointed by the board.

c. Some specific duties of the board of directors are to (a) declare dividends, (b) authorize contracts, (c) determine executive salaries, (d) arrange major loans with banks, and (e) appoint an **audit committee** to serve as a channel of communication between the corporation and the independent auditor. Management's primary means of reporting the corporation's financial position and results of operations is its annual report.

OBJECTIVE 6: Define financial position and show how it is affected by simple transactions (pp. 20–28).

21. Every transaction affects a firm's financial position. **Financial position** is shown by a balance sheet, so called because the two sides or parts of the balance sheet must always equal each other. In a sense, the balance sheet presents two ways of viewing the same business: the left side shows the assets (resources) of the business, whereas the right side shows who provided the assets. Providers consist of owners (listed under "owners' equity") and creditors (represented by the listing of "liabilities"). Therefore, it is logical that the total dollar amount of assets must equal the total dollar amount of liabilities and owners' equity. This is the **accounting equation.** It is formally stated as

Assets = liabilities + owners' equity

Other correct forms are

Assets − liabilities = owners' equity

Assets − owners' equity = liabilities

22. **Assets** are the economic resources of a business. Examples of assets are cash, accounts receivable, inventory, buildings, equipment, patents, and copyrights.

23. **Liabilities** are debts of the business. Examples of liabilities are money borrowed from banks, amounts owed to creditors for goods bought on credit, and taxes owed to the government.

24. **Owners' equity** represents resources invested by the owners. **Equity** is described by the FASB as "the residual interest in assets after deducting the liabilities."[1] Because it is equal to assets minus liabilities, owners' equity is said to equal the **net assets** of the business.

---

1. *Statement of Financial Concepts* No. 3, "Elements of Financial Statements of Business Enterprises" (Stamford, Conn.: Financial Accounting Standards Board, June 1, 1982), par. 43.

25. The owners' equity of a corporation is called **stockholders' equity** and consists of contributed capital and retained earnings. **Contributed capital** represents the amount invested by the owners, whereas **retained earnings** (broadly) represent the accumulation of the profits and losses of a company since its inception, less total dividends declared. **Dividends** are distributions of assets to stockholders from past earnings; they appear in the statement of retained earnings.

26. Retained earnings are affected by three types of transactions. **Revenues,** which result when services have been provided, increase retained earnings. **Expenses,** which represent costs of doing business, decrease retained earnings, as do dividends. When revenues exceed expenses, a **net income** results. When expenses exceed revenues, however, a **net loss** has been suffered.

27. Every transaction changes the balance sheet in some way. In practice, companies do not prepare a new balance sheet after each transaction. However, it is important for accounting students to understand the exact effect of each transaction on the parts of the balance sheet.

28. Although every transaction changes the balance sheet, the accounting equation always remains in balance. In other words, dollar amounts may change, but assets must always equal liabilities plus owners' equity.

OBJECTIVE 7: Identify the four basic financial statements (pp. 29–32).

29. Accountants communicate their information through **financial statements.** The four principal statements are the balance sheet, income statement, statement of retained earnings, and statement of cash flows.

30. Every financial statement has a three-line heading. The first line gives the name of the company. The second line gives the name of the statement. The third line gives the relevant dates (the date of the balance sheet or the period of time covered by the other three statements).

31. The **income statement,** whose components are revenues and expenses, is perhaps the most important financial statement. Its purpose is to measure the business's success or failure in earning an income over a given period of time.

32. The **statement of retained earnings** is a labeled calculation of the changes in retained earnings (defined in paragraph 25) during the accounting period. Retained earnings at the beginning of the period is the first item on the statement, followed by an addition for net income and a deduction for dividends declared or a net loss. The ending retained earnings figure that results is transferred to the stockholders' equity section of the balance sheet.

33. The **balance sheet** shows the financial position of a business on a certain date. The resources used in the business are called assets, debts of the business are called liabilities, and the owners' financial interest in the business is called owners' equity.

34. The **statement of cash flows** shows much information that is not present in the balance sheet or income statement. This statement discloses all the business's operating, investing, and financing activities during the accounting period. Operating activities consist mainly of receipts from customers and payments to suppliers and others in the ordinary course of business. Investing activities might include selling a building or investing in stock. Financing activities might include issuing stock or paying dividends. The statement's bottom line will indicate the net increase or decrease in cash during the period.

OBJECTIVE 8: Describe accounting as a profession with ethical responsibilities and a wide career choice (pp. 33–37).

35. **Professional ethics** is the application of a code of conduct to the practice of a profession. The accounting profession has developed such a code, intended to guide the accountant in carrying out his or her responsibilities to the public. In short, the accountant must act with integrity, objectivity, independence, and due care.
   a. **Integrity** means that the accountant is honest, regardless of consequences.
   b. **Objectivity** means that the accountant is impartial in performing his or her job.
   c. **Independence** is the avoidance of all relationships that could impair the objectivity

of the accountant, such as owning stock in a company he or she is auditing.

    d. **Due care** means carrying out one's responsibilities with competence and diligence.

36. The accounting profession can be divided into four broad fields: management accounting, public accounting, government and other not-for-profit accounting, and accounting education.

37. An accountant employed by a business is said to be in **management accounting.** Though decision making is the function of management, the management accountant must first provide relevant data and then help management make the best decision. Management accountants may certify their professional competence by qualifying for the status of **certified management accountant (CMA).**

38. **Public accounting** is a profession that has gained the same stature as law and medicine. Certified public accountants (CPAs) are accountants licensed by the state. To become a licensed CPA, one must pass the uniform CPA exam and meet educational and experience requirements. CPAs perform a number of services, most of which are classified as auditing, tax services, management advisory services, or small business services.

    a. An auditor is a public accountant brought in to give an independent professional opinion as to whether a company's financial statements fairly show its financial position and operating results. Auditing, or the **attest function,** makes it possible for users to depend on the statements as a basis for their decisions. The auditor must, of course, gather sufficient evidence before he or she can give an opinion.

    b. Public accountants perform **tax services** by preparing tax returns, making sure of compliance with tax laws, and bringing tax considerations into the decision-making process.

    c. **Management advisory services** consist of any recommendations that the public accountant can make for improving a company's operations.

    d. Many CPA firms offer small business services. In this area they provide such services as setting up an accounting system and preparing financial statements.

39. Government and other not-for-profit accounting is practiced by thousands of accountants in various capacities. Here, accountants are concerned not with profitability, but with the proper and efficient use of public resources. For example, government accountants prepare financial reports and audit tax returns for many agencies, such as the FBI, the IRS, the General Accounting Office, the SEC, the Interstate Commerce Commission, and the FCC. Hospitals, colleges, foundations, and other not-for-profit organizations also employ accountants.

40. Accounting instructors are needed in both secondary schools and colleges. In either setting they need to meet certain educational qualifications. In many schools, holding the CPA, CMA, or **CIA (certified internal auditor)** certificate will help an instructor advance professionally.

Testing Your Knowledge

Matching*

Match each term with its definition by writing the appropriate letter in the blank.

H _ 1. Accounting

F _ 2. Bookkeeping

O _ 3. Computer

R _ 4. Management information system (MIS)

W _ 5. Management accounting

N _ 6. Financial accounting

S _ 7. Public accounting

C _ 8. Dividend

J _ 9. Certified public accountant (CPA)

V _ 10. Sole proprietorship

I _ 11. Partnership

B _ 12. Corporation

U _ 13. Generally accepted accounting principles (GAAP)

E _ 14. Balance sheet

I _ 15. Income statement

Q _ 16. Statement of retained earnings

M _ 17. Statement of cash flows

T _ 18. Separate entity

D _ 19. Money measure

G _ 20. Asset

A _ 21. Liability

P _ 22. Owners' equity

K _ 23. Contributed capital

a. A debt of a business

b. A business owned by stockholders but managed by a board of directors

c. A distribution of earnings to stockholders

d. The standard that all business transactions should be measured in terms of dollars

e. The statement that shows the financial position of a company on a certain date

f. The repetitive recordkeeping process

g. An economic resource of a business

h. An information system that measures, processes, and communicates economic information

i. A business owned and managed by two or more persons

j. An expert accountant licensed by the state

k. Representation on the balance sheet of stockholders' investments in a corporation

l. The statement that shows a company's profit or loss over a certain period of time

m. The statement that discloses the operating, investing, and financing activities during the period

n. The branch of accounting concerned with providing external users with financial information needed to make decisions

o. An electronic tool that processes information rapidly

p. The balance sheet section that represents the owners' economic interest in a company

q. The statement that shows the changes in the Retained Earnings account during the period

r. The information network that links a company's functions together

s. The branch of accounting that deals with auditing, taxes, and management advisory services

t. The accounting concept that treats a business as distinct from its owners, creditors, and customers

u. The guidelines that define acceptable accounting practice at a given point in time

v. A business owned and managed by one person

w. The branch of accounting concerned with providing managers with financial information needed to make decisions

*Note to student: The matching quiz might be completed more efficiently by starting with the definition and searching for the corresponding term.

Short Answer

Use the lines provided to answer each item.

1. The accounting profession encompasses four broad fields. List them.

   _____

   _____

   _____

   _____

2. On the lines that follow, insert the correct heading for the annual income statement of Alpha Corporation on June 30, 19xx.

   _____

   _____

   _____

3. Briefly distinguish between bookkeeping and accounting.

   _____

   _____

   _____

4. What five steps should be followed in making a decision?

   _____

   _____

   _____

   _____

   _____

5. Briefly define the terms below, all of which relate to the accountant's Code of Professional Conduct.

   a. Integrity _____

   _____

   b. Objectivity _____

   _____

   c. Independence _____

   _____

   d. Due care _____

   _____

6. What three broad groups use accounting information?

   _____

   _____

   _____

7. What two objectives must be met for a company to survive?

   _____

   _____

8. List the four principal financial statements and state briefly the purpose of each.

   Statement

   a. _____

   _____

   b. _____

   c. _____

   _____

   d. _____

   Purpose

   a. _____

   _____

   b. _____

   _____

   c. _____

   _____

   d. _____

   _____

Circle T if the statement is true, F if it is false. Please provide explanations for false answers, using the blank lines at the end of the section.

T F   1. Financial position can best be determined by referring to the income statement.

T F   2. The IRS is responsible for interpreting and enforcing GAAP.

T F   3. Planning, control, and evaluation are essential when making business and economic decisions.

T F   4. One form of the accounting equation is assets − liabilities = owners' equity.

T F   5. Revenues have the effect of increasing owners' equity.

T F   6. The existence of Accounts Receivable on the balance sheet indicates that the company has one or more creditors.

T F   7. When expenses exceed revenues, a company has suffered a net loss.

T F   8. The measurement stage of accounting involves preparation of the financial statements.

T F   9. Dividends appear as a deduction in the income statement.

T F 10. The current authoritative body dictating accounting practice is the FASB.

T F 11. A sole proprietor is personally liable for all debts of the business.

T F 12. The statement of cash flows would disclose whether or not land was purchased during the period.

T F 13. The statement of retained earnings links a company's income statement to its balance sheet.

T F 14. The IASC is responsible for setting guidelines for state and local governments.

T F 15. A corporation is managed directly by its stockholders.

T F 16. Internal auditing is a service provided by public accounting.

T F 17. Generally accepted accounting principles are not like laws of math and science; they are guidelines that define correct accounting practice at the time.

T F 18. Net assets equal assets plus liabilities.

T F 19. The major sections of a balance sheet are assets, liabilities, owners' equity, revenues, and expenses.

T F 20. A business transaction must always involve an exchange of money.

T F 21. A management information system deals not only with accounting, but with other activities of a business as well.

T F 22. The income statement is generally considered to be the most important financial statement.

T F 23. A business should be understood as an entity that is separate and distinct from its owners, customers, and creditors.

T F 24. The status of CMA is sought mainly by those engaged in public accounting.

T F 25. Economic planners are accounting information users with a direct financial interest.

T F 26. The essence of an asset is that it is expected to benefit future operations.

T F 27. Auditing is also referred to as the attest function.

_____

_____

_____

_____

_____

Multiple Choice

Circle the letter of the best answer.

1. Which of the following accounts would *not* appear on the balance sheet?
   a. Wages Expense
   b. Common Stock
   c. Notes Receivable
   d. Wages Payable

2. Companies whose stock is publicly traded must file financial statements with the
   a. FASB.
   b. APB.
   c. SEC.
   d. AICPA.

3. One characteristic of a corporation is
   a. unlimited liability of its owners.
   b. the ease with which ownership is transferred.
   c. ownership by the board of directors.
   d. dissolution upon the death of an owner.

4. Which of the following is *not* a facet of management accounting?
   a. Budgeting
   b. Public accounting
   c. Computer systems design
   d. Cost accounting

5. Which of the following statements does *not* involve a distinct period of time?
   a. Income statement
   b. Balance sheet
   c. Statement of cash flows
   d. Statement of retained earnings

6. The principal purpose of an audit by a CPA is to
   a. express an opinion on the fairness of a company's financial statements.
   b. detect fraud by a company's employees.
   c. prepare the company's financial statements.
   d. assure investors that the company will be profitable in the future.

7. Collection on an account receivable will
   a. increase total assets and increase total owners' equity.
   b. have no effect on total assets, but will increase total owners' equity.
   c. decrease both total assets and total liabilities.
   d. have no effect on total assets, liabilities, or owners' equity.

8. In a partnership,
   a. profits are always divided equally among partners.
   b. management consists of the board of directors.
   c. no partner is liable for more than a proportion of the company's debts.
   d. dissolution results when any partner leaves the partnership.

9. Which of the following is *not* a major account heading in the balance sheet or income statement?
   a. Accounts Receivable
   b. Owners' Equity
   c. Liabilities
   d. Revenues

10. Payment of a liability will
    a. decrease total liabilities and decrease total owners' equity.
    b. decrease total assets and increase total owners' equity.
    c. decrease total assets and decrease total liabilities.
    d. have no effect on total assets, liabilities, or owners' equity.

11. Which of the following is not a specialization within public accounting?
    a. Management advisory services
    b. Auditing
    c. Financial accounting
    d. Tax services

12. The purchase of an asset for cash will
    a. increase total assets and increase total owners' equity.
    b. increase total assets and increase total liabilities.
    c. increase total assets and decrease total liabilities.
    d. have no effect on total assets, liabilities, or owners' equity.

Applying Your Knowledge

Exercises

1. Lindlay Steel, Inc., always publishes annual financial statements. This year, however, it has suffered a huge loss and is trying to keep this fact a secret by refusing anyone access to its financial statements. Why might each of the following nevertheless insist upon seeing Lindlay's statements?

   a. Potential investors in Lindlay

   b. The Securities and Exchange Commission

   c. The bank, which is considering a loan request by Lindlay

   d. Present stockholders of Lindlay

   e. Lindlay's management

2. Randi Corporation had assets of $100,000 and liabilities of $70,000 at the beginning of the year. During the year assets decreased by $15,000 and owners' equity increased by $20,000. What is the amount of liabilities at year end?

   $_____

3. Following are the accounts of Acme TV Repair Corporation as of December 31, 19xx.

Accounts Payable	$ 1,300
Accounts Receivable	1,500
Building	10,000
Cash	?
Common Stock	14,500
Equipment	850
Land	1,000
Retained Earnings	3,000
Truck	4,500

   Using this information, prepare a balance sheet *in good form*. (You must derive the dollar amount for Cash.)

   Acme TV Repair Corporation
   Balance Sheet
   December 31, 19xx

   Assets

   Liabilities

   Stockholders' Equity

   ---

4. Following are the transactions for Johnson Paints, Inc., for the first month of operations.
   a. Walt and Carol Johnson invested $20,000 cash in the newly formed corporation.
   b. Purchased paint supplies and equipment for $650 cash.
   c. Purchased a company truck on credit for $5,200.
   d. Received $525 for painting a house.
   e. Paid one-half of the amount due on the truck previously purchased.
   f. Billed a customer $150 for painting his garage.
   g. Paid $250 for one month's rental of the office.
   h. Received full payment from the customer whose garage was painted (transaction f).
   i. Sold a company ladder for $20. The buyer said he would pay next month.
   j. The company declared and paid a $200 cash dividend.

In the table below, show the effect of each transaction on the balance sheet accounts by putting the dollar amount, along with a plus or minus, under the proper account. Determine the balance in each account at month's end. As an example, transaction a has already been recorded.

| Transaction | Assets | | | | Liabilities | Stockholders' Equity | |
	Cash	Accounts Receivable	Supplies and Equipment	Trucks	Accounts Payable	Common Stock	Retained Earnings
a	+ $20,000					+ $20,000	
b							
c							
d							
e							
f							
g							
h							
i							
j							
Balance at end of month							

Crossword Puzzle
For Chapter 1

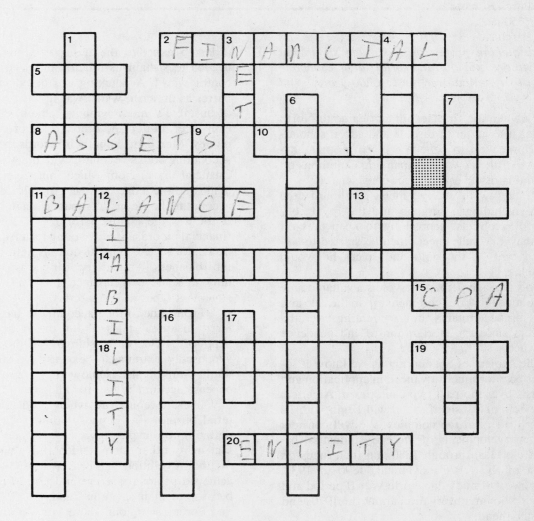

ACROSS

2. Accounting mainly for external use
5. Former principle-setting body
8. Resources of a company
10. One to whom another is indebted
11. _____ sheet
13. Professional organization of accountants
14. The language of business
15. Branch of public accounting
18. Measure of debt-paying ability
19. Data-generating network
20. Separate _____ concept

DOWN

1. Professional accountants
3. _____ income
4. Branch of public accounting
6. Measure of business performance
7. Form of business organization
9. Regulatory agency of publicly held corporations
11. Recorder of business transactions
12. Debt of a company
16. Ownership in a company
17. Professional certificate

Reading

The Accountant in Our History: A Bicentennial Overview

The accounting profession has made significant contributions to the industrial and economic growth of America over the last 200 years.

Exactly when the first accountant came to North America is a matter of dispute and adroit scholarship. If we wish to believe a recent popular description of the crew accompanying Columbus on the famous discovery voyage, consider this:

"There were forty men . . . aboard the flotilla, including a surgeon and the royal controller of accounts, sent along to keep tabs on Columbus's swindle sheet when he started to figure the cost of the gold and spices he would accumulate."

This passage perhaps serves as a suitable note to introduce this brief commentary on the role and impact of accountants and accounting over the 200 years since the Declaration of Independence was issued.

The subject of accounting as we know it today has become much advanced in application and emphasis over the past two centuries in America. Our review of its significance will begin with its uses by leaders in the colonies. We will consider also the developments of the early industrial period of the U.S. through 1880 and then focus on the era of the CPA movement, 1890 to 1930. Finally, we will study the World War II period and conclude with an observation about the 1970s and the years ahead.

The Colonial Period

Our Founding Fathers made good use of the rudiments of what today is a highly specialized professional pursuit. In setting out the uses of accounting or "bookkeeping methodiz'd" as it was known, consider the lifestyle of the times. In 1776 almost all (95 percent) of the estimated 2½ to 3 million American settlers lived on farms. The population hugged the seacoast and waterways in

Source: Article by Gary John Previts. Reprinted with permission from the *Journal of Accountancy*. Copyright © 1976 by the American Institute of Certified Public Accountants, Inc. Opinions of the authors are their own and do not necessarily reflect policies of the AICPA.

order to expedite the transportation and trade needed to sustain its relationship with the Eurocentric world. Accounting was based as much on barter as on cash, which was in short supply and of unstable value. Payments came in the form of rum, beef, butter and other forms of commodity money. Merchants kept their records in a series of accounting books beginning with the wastebook (a financial diary) from which journal entries were made and the ledger posted. Apprenticeship in an accounting house or "computing house" of a merchant was the common form of learning about financial records. Mostly young men from well-to-do families were apprenticed thus before being set into business. Annual reporting was only beginning to achieve acceptance and was not of the statement type we know today.

From time to time accountants have encountered historical tales about the documentation supplied by George Washington in support of his supposedly extravagant expense accounts. Benjamin Franklin also is known to have relied on his expense account to pay for his gay and occasionally libertine court life while conducting ministerial business in France. Perhaps we think this deflating to our past revolutionary heroes, but in fact many other such incidents involving leaders of the revolution indicate that some patriots achieved personal success and political influence because of their savvy in "accompts."

Foremost among these was John Hancock who inherited the business fortune of his uncle, Thomas Hancock, the Boston merchant prince. John might have been less blessed had it not been that "Thomas knew as much about his own affairs from an accounting standpoint as was possible in mercantile capitalism . . . [but] John was . . . swamped."[1]

George Taylor, who signed the July Fourth document as a representative of Pennsylvania, came to America as an indentured servant bound to the owner of an iron works. He was sent to work as a furnace cooler but it was thought that he was too weak for the job. Because he had a better education than most youths of those days, he was

1. W.T. Barker, *The House of Hancock* (Cambridge, MA: Harvard University Press, 1945), p. 22.

given a job in the business office handling transactions and accounts. Indeed, Taylor had an accountant's flair for opportunity, for, when the owner of the works died, Taylor married the widow and became owner of the works.

Perhaps the wealthiest of the signers, Charles Carroll of Carrollton (because at least three other Charles Carrolls were prominent in Maryland at the time, he signed himself "of Carrollton") is known for both his longevity—he survived until 1832, the last of the signers to succumb—and for his keeping "meticulous books."

Thomas Jefferson also maintained extensive financial records, as was customary for plantation owners—including an entry in his account books for July 4, 1776, noting a purchase of two items and a donation to charity.

Another signer, Robert Morris, was instrumental in aiding the cause by providing the means of financing for the new Congress. Morris, later acting as superintendent of finance, administered the funds for Congress and, with the backing of Haym Salomon, is noted to have "introduced system into financial accounting" related to the new government. Salomon, called the "Good Samaritan of the Revolution," lent over $200,000 to the United States. He died at the age of 45, and the loan was apparently not repaid.

Henry Laurens, president of the Continental Congress in 1777 and a signer of the Treaty of Paris, used accounts to maintain a record of his personal financial affairs with the state government of South Carolina during the 1770s; and in 1780, his neatly drawn "Statement of Account with the United States," dated January 20, indicates the customary importance placed on such records in early government transactions.

America's New Industrialism

Through the 1790s and early 1800s several hundred business incorporations took place. As the turmoil of the American Revolution and the War of 1812 were replaced by a stable political environment, Americans set out to restore their trade and expand their holdings of new lands west of the Allegheny Mountains. Technical inventions and their labor saving efficiency tended to reduce costs and as turnpikes, canals and then railroads appeared, new markets were opened for goods which, in turn, induced specialized manufactures and early forms of mass production. Industry and commerce became rooted in the midst of a predominantly rural society. By the 1840s the first modern textbook on accounting was written by

Thomas Jones, an accountant and commercial teacher in New York City. Jones focused on the statements of accounting as the outcome of the double entry system and relegated the accounts themselves to a support role. He, along with other pioneer educators, such as S. S. Packard, instructed those seeking to learn the mysteries of what was now being called "scientific bookkeeping" by some and the "science of accounts" by others. Packard was a leader in commercial education for nearly half a century, from the 1840s to the years preceding the passage of CPA legislation. As a proprietor of a Bryant and Stratton Business College—universities were not disposed to include commercial subjects in their curriculums—Packard was one of many who trained young persons to go forth into the new adventures of corporate business.

One such young man, later called "a bloodless . . . bookkeeper" by a wildcat oilman he had visited, was trained in the points of scientific accounting at Folsom's Business College in Cleveland in 1855. When a group of money men from Cleveland sent the prim 21-year-old bookkeeper, John D. Rockefeller, off to assess the prospects for the commercial future of oil in Pennsylvania, a chapter of American history was begun.

In the decade before the War Between the States, over a dozen public accountants were listed in the New York City directory and by 1895 there were nearly 150.

Perhaps no better idea of the popular image of accounts could be obtained than by reading a short piece appearing in *Harper's Weekly* on January 3, 1857:

"We are a nation of shopkeepers, and none the worse for that . . . It is very important, then, for us to sustain a good commercial name; and to do this, we must take care that the debit does not overbalance the credit account in our ledger. If we allow too large a margin for our expenses we shall be sure, whatever may be the profits of dry good and hardware, to fall short in the final account with our creditors or our conscience."

Although America's early philosophers may have shunned the commercial life, some of them were not adverse to using the tools of the accountant in their private lives. Henry Thoreau, for example, found that a simple system of accounting helped him achieve a spartan and self-reliant life at Walden Pond in the mid-1800s. It was necessary, he wrote, that an account of stock be "taken from time to time, to know how you stand." He added: "It is a labor to task the faculties of a man—such problems of profit and loss, of interest, of tare and tret, and gauging of all kinds in it, as demand a universal knowledge.''

Some scholars have noted discrepancies in Thoreau's accounts despite their apparent meticulousness. Author Charles Anderson, for example, observes of Thoreau's summary of food expenses (''Yes, I did eat $8.74, all told'') that ''it is probably not a coincidence that this figure tallies with one claimed as a possible food budget . . . in the *Young Housekeeper* (Boston, 1838).'' Also, it is noted that ''pecunary outgoes'' of $61.99 ¾ were erroneously totaled as $60.99 ¾ in Thoreau's original working manuscript. But Thoreau has the good sense, early in the pages of his book *Walden,* to issue this disclaimer: ''My accounts, which I can swear to have kept faithful, I have, indeed, never got audited, still less accepted, still less paid and settled.''

In contrast to Thoreau's relaxed approach to justifying his account records, businessmen of his period were becoming more sophisticated in their application of accounting to industrial operations. During the 1850s, Paul Garner notes in his history of cost accounting, industrialism was beginning to have an impact on the character of account keeping. For the first time, many authors began to consider accounts related to factory and production costs. John Fleming's *Bookkeeping by Double Entry* published in Pittsburgh in 1854 included several changes to reflect cost accounting considerations. Fleming changed the name of the merchandise trading account to ''factory account'' and also attempted to determine the appropriate treatment for factory buildings. Whether these adjustments truly reflected a general need for cost system information because of the many iron and steel mills near Pittsburgh can only be speculated.

The post Civil War steel boom developed in response to the demands of the westward drive of the railroads. At that time, as Ernest Reckitt, an early CPA leader, later recalled, a businessman named Andrew Carnegie ''was one of the first pioneers in the introduction of cost accounting, maintaining a considerable staff in his cost department and [attributing] his great financial success to his knowledge of his costs in the steel industry.''

The public's familiarity with keeping accounts, as suggested in the popular columns of *Harper's Weekly* and as used in the financial tool kits of Rockefeller and Carnegie, indicates that accounting was becoming one of the skills needed for small business and in commerce and the home. All this was before the most significant episode of all—the ''professionalization'' movement which took shape at the close of the century, beginning

with the passage of the first CPA law in New York in April 1896.

Enter the CPA

When the first CPA candidates gathered for the first examination in Buffalo and in New York on December 15 and 16, 1896, they were probably unaware of the many thousands who would follow in their footsteps. Within a year the New York State Society of CPAs had been formed, with 24 members. These first few probably also could not have predicted that by 1947, a half century later, this society would number over 5,000 and that today it would have over 20,000 members.

For this reason, we focus on the emergence of the CPA as the central point of development for the accounting profession. The CPA movement, which spread throughout the country during the quarter century after the New York law, laid the foundation for increasing the competence of accountants through education, testing and experience. Financial statements and the ratios evolving therefrom were becoming the essence of the economic and business decisions made throughout a society which for the first time found a majority of the population in cities facing the urban realities of industrialization. As the center of the world capital market shifted from London to New York, the United States became a capital exporting nation. In 1928, E. H. H. Simmons, president of the New York Stock Exchange, noted:

''Since the war . . . not only has the United States become an international lender instead of borrower, but the comparative shortage of capital in this country has been turned into a surplus.''

The characteristics of the corporations using capital had also changed as the CPA era developed. Corporations were rapidly merging so that by the turn of the century ownership and management of major business enterprises were separated, necessitating financial reporting of a dimension and frequency not envisioned in the proprietary years of closely owned and managed corporations.

By 1917, having survived a clash with Congress on the matter of federal licensure of accountants, members of the national CPA organization cooperated with government agencies to prepare a document—*Uniform Accounts*—which, when released, received wide circulation and is acknowledged as the first attempt to present a set of national standards for accounting practice. The 1929 revision of these early rules and the rules themselves, however, were all too little and too late to play a role in the ''casino-like'' atmosphere which pervaded trading in the stock markets of the 1920s.

The catastrophe which followed throttled the capital markets and nearly crippled the economy. While earlier attempts to make inroads into the secrecy and "private ledgers" associated with large concerns had been made by leaders in the profession, not until the Securities Acts of 1933 and 1934 was there sufficient legal leverage for the CPA to make progress in identifying the form and content of financial statements and the principles underlying them. For while the controversy over the need for and effectiveness of the Securities Acts continues, there is no denying that these laws reflected a potent political response which established the dimensions of action for the next generation of accountants—including the pressure for more frequent, more consistent and more detailed presentation and analysis of corporation accounts and business activity.

Early Professional Leaders

Among the early CPAs were a significant number who gave of their time not only for the benefit of professional self-interest but also in service to their country and their communities. During World War I accountants served in several key positions. R. H. Montgomery, an early author, teacher and founding partner of the firm now known as Coopers & Lybrand, worked under Bernard Baruch at the War Industries Board, accepting a field rank commission. Joseph Sterrett, of Price Waterhouse & Co., was decorated for his service on the Dawes Commission, the agency charged with settling the problems of Germany's reparation payments. L. W. Blyth, of Ernst & Ernst, responded to the request of Newton D. Baker, secretary of war, and took on the task of establishing the accounting system for the Ordnance Department.

In their own communities, early accounting leaders were instrumental in moving accounting education from the level of proprietary commercial education into universities. Arthur Andersen, James Marwick, S. Roger Mitchell, Allen R. Smart, Arthur Young and other CPAs were prominent in supporting the successful development of the School of Commerce at Northwestern University in 1908. They were preceded by a group of New Yorkers led by Charles Waldo Haskins, cofounder of the firm of Haskins & Sells, who acted as a formative influence in establishing the School of Commerce, Accounts and Finance at New York

University, which opened October 1, 1900. Haskins also served as the first dean.

If these contributions seem modest, it must be remembered that they represent only a few examples and do not take account of the many significant roles and activities of the other prominent professional leaders of the time, such as Charles E. Sprague, Arthur Lowes Dickinson and Henry Rand Hatfield, each of whom contributed significantly to professional education and practice in the first decades of this century. These men and 32 others have been accorded the honor of membership in the Accounting Hall of Fame, which was established in 1950 at the Ohio State University.

During the early 1900s, as people drew closer together to live and work in cities, comprehensive municipal accounting systems were developed, including the necessary budgetary accounts. Under the leadership of accounting educators, such as Frederick Cleveland and Lloyd Morey, new systems were effectively put to use early in the century. Popular contact with accounting was not limited, however, to such distant although important matters as municipal finance. The levying of a federal income tax before World War I caused individuals, as well as businesses, to seek advice on how their taxes might legitimately be minimized. As a result, there was an increasing focus on how earnings were to be measured. The average person's perplexity with this subject might best be represented by this poem written at the turn of the century by a leading American poet:

> Never ask of money spent
> Where the spender thinks it went
> Nobody was ever meant
> To remember or invent
> What he did with every cent.
>
> Robert Frost
> "The Hardship of Accounting"[2]

We also find that American speech was absorbing accountants' parlance. By the 1920s, it was common practice to evaluate a losing business as "in the red" and a profitable one as "in the black."

Aiding the War Effort

George O. May, the practitioner's counterpart to Professor William A. Paton during the classical

2. "The Hardship of Accounting" from *The Poetry of Robert Frost* edited by Edward Connery Lathem. Copyright 1936 by Robert Frost. Copyright © 1964 by Lesley Frost Ballantine. Copyright © 1969 by Holt, Rinehart and Winston. Reprinted by permission of Henry Holt and Company, Inc.

years of formative CPA accounting theory, noted the significance of accounting during the World War II years as follows:

"The importance of the part played by accounting in our economy of today requires no demonstration. We see daily how rules of accounting become in effect rules of law. Within wide areas value is recognized as being dependent upon income; the measurement of income is an accounting process. . . ."

With these words, May acknowledged what had been heralded by D. R. Scott a decade earlier. Scott held that our society, indeed our culture, depends on financial data for its operation, maintenance and continued prosperity. Accounting makes the difference between economic communication and economic chaos.

The World War II effort again drew important talent from every rank of the young profession. Paul Grady headed the Navy's cost inspection service under Admiral Baldwin. Arthur Carter assisted Secretary of War Robert P. Patterson, becoming a major general in charge of fiscal matters for Army Service Forces. When the federal government undertook to plan its accounting, auditing and financial reporting functions through the Hoover Commission efforts of the late 1940s and early 1950s, again CPAs worked on key task forces. J. Harold Steward, a partner of Arthur Young & Company, for example, headed the second Hoover Commission's Budget and Accounting Task Force in 1953.

CPAs grew in number rapidly after World War II. At only 9,000 in 1945, AICPA membership rolls spurted to 38,000 in 1960, 74,000 a decade later, and now exceed 120,000. As early as 1933, A. A. Berle, Jr., in an article entitled, "Public Interest in Accounting," wrote: "It becomes plain that accounting is rapidly ceasing to be in any sense of the word a private matter."

Actually, the stock market crash of 1929, following a spate of public criticism of the "easy" financial practices and reporting that had become rife in industry, was a major factor in spurring required audits of listed companies and therefore growth of accounting as a profession. In his book *Main Street and Wall Street,* Harvard Professor William Z. Ripley cited "the docility of corporate shareholders permitting themselves to be honeyfuggled." George O. May, in response to Ripley's criticism of then current reporting practices, said, "The time has come when auditors should assume larger responsibilities, and their position [should] be more clearly defined."

In 1932, the New York Stock Exchange required listed companies to agree that their financial statements would bear the certificate of accountants "qualified under the laws of some state or country." That same year AICPA President John B. Forbes named May chairman of a special new committee on accounting principles. In the wake of Institute efforts to achieve voluntary action to deal with some of the problems, Congress passed the Securities Acts of 1933 and 1934.

Arthur H. Carter, then president of the New York State Society of CPAs, had recommended before Congress that financial statements should be examined by an independent auditor who should express his opinion on their fairness. Carter said it would be impractical for a government agency to perform such examinations. The 1933 act contained an audit provision, but it wasn't until after the 1934 act created the Securities and Exchange Commission that machinery was set up for audits by independent public accountants. Carman G. Blough, CPA, was appointed the first chief accountant of the SEC.

As John L. Carey, former administrative vice president of the Institute, wrote in the *Journal* in September 1969: "The influence of the SEC on accounting and auditing standards and practice was tremendous. Without doubt the securities acts strengthened the position of independent auditors in insisting that clients follow sound principles and make adequate disclosures. The commission's requirements also greatly increased the volume of auditing engagements. And it must be conceded that the SEC's goad prodded the profession to make improvements both in accounting and auditing that otherwise might have taken longer to achieve."

The Countdown of History

Since the 1930s, the business world has become more complex, and the role of the accountant has necessarily expanded. Taking a bicentennial perspective, over the past 200 years more than 90 percent of the population has left the farm to work in the big city. Since 1876, American private foreign investment has increased tenfold; in the past 30 years, the United States has supplied more than half of the industrial world's need for capital. And the CPA must now venture into this intricate world of multinational decision making made even more complicated by political action and foreign regulations. For this reason the typical accountant today is better educated than his predecessors so he can help clear the financial fog that can surround statements. Over the past two decades whether required by law or not, most

CPAs have had a baccalaureate degree in accounting.

CPAs now serve in increasing numbers as chief executive officers and chief financial officers in business and industry. Since World War II many CPAs have held important posts in the Cabinet, at the World Bank and on the New York Stock Exchange. Most recently, a CPA, L. William Seidman, was appointed by President Ford as a special personal adviser. A CPA, Kenneth S. Axelson, is also engaged in assisting the mayor of New York, himself a CPA, to develop a sound plan for the city's finances.

The accountant can look back at the profession's history and how it has complemented the growth of industry and the economy and realize that the assembly line could hardly run without a balance sheet and an income statement to back it up. We have entered an age of "popular political accountancy" in which our idiom has become the password. To paraphrase Paul A. Samuelson, "The bottom line—that's what it's about."

Reading

The Bottom Line on Ethics

Is good ethics good business? Ninety-seven percent of the business respondents to a recent *Dallas Times Herald* survey said yes. But the same survey also showed 75% of all respondents believed businesspeople would bend the rules to achieve success. Sixty-eight percent of businesspeople said there were unethical practices in their industries.

Business ethics is not a comfortable topic. Some managers believe acting ethically makes a business vulnerable and places it at competitive risk. In fact, evidence suggests the reverse is true: Strong ethics equals high performance. Why, then, don't more businesses emphasize ethics?

Many organizations do not consider ethical issues when making decisions. In addition, American companies historically have been reactive when confronted with criticisms and accusations about their ethical standards. If this attitude is to change, business leaders must understand the importance of an ethics program and what is necessary to make one work.

Understanding Ethics

In a study of ethical, high-profit companies in the United States and Great Britain, the Lincoln Center for Ethics at Arizona State University used this working definition of ethics developed by Dr. Mark Pastin, author of works on ethics: "The ethics of an organization (person) is the set of ground rules by which the organization (person) operates and evaluates."

The same definition is used in this article. It assumes the ethics of individuals or organizations is based on how they respond when faced with ethical issues, not what they say. By describing the steps, procedures and tasks undertaken in response to ethics issues, the outcomes are observable, comparable and subject to modification, not theoretical or difficult to apply.

In attempting to evaluate what relationships, if any, exist between ethics and the performance of excellent organizations, the Arizona State study found that "ethics does play a crucial role in the

Source: Article by Larry L. Axline. Reprinted with permission from the *Journal of Accountacy,* Copyright © 1990 by American Institute of Certified Public Accountants, Inc. Opinions of the authors are their own and do not necessarily reflect policies of the AICPA.

interactions between a firm and its external constituencies and in internal social contracts." While there was no guarantee of outstanding economic performance for organizations adopting and implementing a strong ethical stance, substantial evidence exists that an ethical framework provides "innovative perspectives." The investigation also suggested ethics is becoming increasingly important to organizations—especially those often subject to scrutiny and criticism from the media, regulators and wide-ranging public interest groups. In fact, evidence strongly suggests that some highly regulated companies can turn a compliance problem into a competitive advantage.

Profit Considerations

What about the bottom line? Does good ethics really translate into increased profits? There is evidence that it does.

Ethics author David Freudberg has written about a study that analyzed the relationship between public service and long-range corporate profitability. The companies selected had been in business at least 30 years and had a written set of principles on their public service policies. Among the 15 publicly traded companies (with accountability to shareholders), the average growth and profits over the 30-year period ending in 1982 was 11%. In contrast, the Fortue 500 companies during about the same period showed growth and profits of 6.1%. This suggests there is a long-term financial payoff for ethical management.

Of course, some conflicting studies show that organizations with ethical codes often have more ethical problems and receive more scrutiny and criticism. However, based on the author's experience, several of these studies have flaws in their basic investigative approach. Specifically, some organizations establish a code of ethics after they have been criticized or charged with wrongdoing. Research shows that increased ethical awareness (such as adoption of a code of conduct) sometimes results in increased reporting of ethics problems. People frequently are testing themselves and others to determine the degree to which they are out of compliance with new standards. This is a short-term result and usually is linked to a more candid environment and increased willingness to discuss ethical considerations.

When a code of ethics has been developed with the involvement of all concerned and when ethical considerations are integrated into the decision-making process (rather than treated as after-the-fact considerations), the organization is much better equipped to cope with ethical dilemmas that would otherwise seem insurmountable. It is important, then, to observe not only what organizations do about ethics but also when they started doing it.

The Human Factor

While experts generally agree ethics can't be taught to adults, it is possible to encourage an environment in which the right questions are asked at the right time. Business ethics weighs ethical arguments and alternatives in a manner that considers the rights, privileges and anticipated responses of all "stakeholders" (that is, persons and groups likely to be affected).

The stakeholders concept is important to developing a better understanding of business ethics. Most ethical problems arise because what seems right—and is right—to one stakeholder is wrong to another.

Businesses must remember to take the human element into consideration or new technologies may be rejected. Organizations may be heading for trouble if decisions are based soley on technological improvements, production schedules and perceived markets. Markets are not the same as customers. Internal talent often is wasted in the quest for a competitive edge. When trust is betrayed, stakeholders get even.

Considerable effort and commitment are required to create a strong ethical climate. Our practice suggests that effective ethical management is a process of asking timely and appropriate questions rather than merely identifying and solving problems. Leaders must ask why an action is being taken and who will benefit or suffer as a result. Most ethics complaints are based on miscommunication and more than half of the related problems concern the handling and management of people. Performance appraisals and consistency of supervision (within and across departments) are the most frequently cited areas of ethical conflict within organizations. If employees do not feel they have been treated fairly, an ethics program probably will fail. Employees get even by waging organizational war or quitting. Some quit but stay on the job.

Alienated customers get even, too. "As few as 4 out of 100 dissatisfied customers complain to the business. Those who don't complain to the business do complain—loudly and frequently—to as many as 20 or more other people," according to Jack Parr Associates Inc., a customer service and management development company. An undeniable link exists between effective ethical management and genuine customer service and support.

The interests and needs of stakeholder groups must be thoroughly and sincerely identified and addressed. Customers and employees are critical stakeholders; others are suppliers, regulators and the media.

Defining a Mission

Vital elements in any organization are the purpose and mission, which describe how the people of the business act and make decisions, or at least how they say they do these things. According to Dr. Pastin, "Purpose gives a company a sense of what it is, where its goals come from and why trying hard matters." Purpose and mission statements may be thought of as one, as long as the mission statement covers all interests served by the organization.

Thomas R. Horton, president and chief executive officer of the American Management Association, has written that "the best mission statement is a concise description of what business the company is in or what business it realistically wants to be in and how it serves its customers' needs." He specifically recommends evaluating management's ethics and the corporate values on which employee behavior is based. By so doing, many other stakeholders' interests are brought into the mission.

If all managers and employees are responsible for the organization's purpose, they can no longer excuse marginal ethical conduct. There can and should be an alignment of individual and organizational ethics. Business ethics also can be linked to other themes and priorities in the organization, such as quality, safety and customer service. However, piggybacking ethics on another program can be risky—especially if the other program is in trouble and its credibility has been questioned. For example, Total Quality Management is a statistically and fundamentally sound program, but its effectiveness can be sharply curtailed in a company in which trust and ethics are given low priority.

Another potential threat to the success of an ethics program is lack of follow-through in employee training. Sometimes, organizations provide managers with awareness training and then expect them to train all their employees without adequate professional support. This approach frequently fails because supervisors often are responsible for other forms of training (such as technical standards, quality, safety, etc.) and because many managers and supervisors are not effective presenters of training sessions on "soft issues." Outside involvement in a companywide training program can be expensive, but the lack of follow-through can be even more costly in terms of the overall effectiveness of an ethics awareness program.

Important themes such as candor, true commitment to quality and customer service and increased sensitivity in performance evaluation are often integrated into a well-designed ethics awareness training program. All these issues can be linked under an overall business ethics theme. It ties the otherwise competing priorities together and makes them coherent and manageable.

Candid Discussion

The *Harvard Business Review* quotes Sir Adrian Cadbury, chairman of Cadbury Schweppes PLC, as saying, "Actions are unethical if they won't stand scrutiny. Shelving hard decisions is the least ethical course."

Organizations must allow and encourage employees to discuss tough questions and difficult ethical problems. Most ethical problems are solvable if they are discussed. If an organization does not allow for candor, there may well be an "unaccrued liability" in the business, no matter how favorable the financials look. If an ethical crisis besets the business (a crisis which could have been prevented through candor and questioning), the impact on the financial status of the business can be staggering. "Unaccrued liabilities" of this type often exist. CPAs have no acceptable methods to account for them.

Managers must remember there is a big difference between a strong corporate culture and an ethical environment. Culture simply describes the way things are done—good or bad. If employees and executives have functioned in a culture that permits or encourages unethical acts, an effective business ethics program will be impossible to implement unless allowances are made for safe-harbor disclosures of prior acts. Because such disclosures can be risky, organizations must carefully consider the degree of violation permitted. Organizations must be very cautious in implying am-

nesty for prior illegal acts or existing illicit practices. Even though many ethical problems are not necessarily legal problems, this issue and the handling of it should be carefully reviewed by legal counsel.

Hard Questions

To determine what changes are necessary to improve an organization's awareness of ethics, leaders must understand how problems currently are being handled. Here are some questions they can ask themselves to decide where their organizations stand:

- Do we inadvertently make false or inflated claims about our own products or services when comparing them to those of competitors? Also, do we misrepresent the competitor's effectiveness or knowingly create questions in customers' minds when we know a competitor's products or services are sufficient for their needs? Are the public's interests given priority?
- Do we place implicit pressure on employees to bend the rules and engage in actions that wouldn't stand up under scrutiny? Even when we don't exert such pressure, do we monitor employee behavior adequately? Are we fair in evaluating and compensating our people or is our opinion based solely on volume and bottom-line results? Have we properly and effectively identified the stakeholders affected by our actions? Are their concerns integrated into our decision-making process?
- What other ethical questions and issues must be resolved to place the organization in a proactive—rather than a defensive—position? Are we willing to tackle these questions and issues? What is the cost? What is the cost of not tackling these issues? If the problems aren't resolved today, will they return in the future to weaken or destroy the business?
- Is top management committed to implementing a code of ethics that reflects all significant stakeholders' interests? Is the organization able and willing to commit the resources for a companywide training program to ensure proper implementation of the code?

These questions focus leaders' and managers' attention on important issues. Promoting the necessary discipline and commitment within organization leadership to address ethical issues and act responsibly is the next important step in the process.

Action to Remain Strong

Although many organizations talk a great deal about ethical behavior, leaders must take action to demonstrate their commitment to stated values.

Business ethics is the bedrock of organizations and industries. A breakdown in this area often is an indication of other problems. If a firm or company is to remain strong, its leaders must understand that good ethics is good business.

CHAPTER 2 MEASURING AND RECORDING BUSINESS TRANSACTIONS

Reviewing the Chapter

OBJECTIVE 1: Explain in simple terms the generally accepted ways of solving the measurement issues of recognition, valuation, and classification (pp. 60–62).

1. Before recording a business transaction, the accountant must determine three things:
   a. When the transaction occurred (the **recognition** issue)
   b. What value should be placed on the transaction (the **valuation** issue)
   c. How the components of the transaction should be categorized (the **classification** issue)

2. A sale is recognized (entered in the accounting records) when the title to merchandise passes from the supplier to the purchaser, regardless of when payment is made or received. This point of sale is referred to as the **recognition point.**

3. The **cost principle** states that the dollar value (**cost**) of any item involved in a business transaction is its original cost (also called historical cost). Generally, any change in value after the transaction is not reflected in the accounting records.

OBJECTIVE 2: Define and use the terms *account* and *general ledger* (pp. 62–64).

4. Every business transaction is classified by means of records called **accounts.** Each asset, liability, owners' equity component, revenue, and expense has a separate account.

5. All of a company's accounts are contained in a book or file called the **general ledger** (or simply the **ledger**). Each account appears on a separate page, and the accounts generally are in the following order: assets, liabilities, owners' equity, revenues, and expenses. A listing of the accounts with their respective account numbers, called a **chart of accounts,** is presented at the beginning of the ledger for easy reference.

OBJECTIVE 3: Recognize commonly used asset, liability, and stockholders' equity accounts (pp. 64–68).

6. Although the accounts used by companies will vary, there are some that are common to most businesses. Some typical assets are Cash, Notes Receivable, Accounts Receivable, Prepaid Expenses, Land, Buildings, and Equipment. Some typical liabilities are Notes Payable, Accounts Payable, and Bonds Payable.

7. The stockholders' equity section of a corporation's balance sheet contains a common stock account and a retained earnings account. Common stock represents the amount of capital invested by stockholders, whereas retained earnings represent cumulative profits and losses, less cumulative dividends declared. Dividends are distributions of assets

(generally cash) to stockholders and may be declared only when sufficient retained earnings (and cash) exist.

8. A separate account is kept for each type of revenue and expense. The exact revenue and expense accounts used will vary, depending on the type of business and the nature of its operations. Revenues cause an increase in retained earnings, whereas expenses cause a decrease.

OBJECTIVE 4: Define *double-entry system* and state the rules for debit and credit (pp. 68–71).

9. The **double-entry system** of accounting requires that for each transaction there must be one or more accounts debited and one or more accounts credited, and that total debits must equal total credits.

10. An account in its simplest form, a **T account,** has three parts:
    a. A title that expresses the name of the asset, liability, owners' equity, revenue, or expense account
    b. A left side, which is called the **debit** side
    c. A right side, which is called the **credit** side

11. At the end of an accounting period, **account balances** are calculated in order to prepare the financial statements. If using T accounts, there are three steps to follow in determining these account balances:
    a. Foot (add up) the debit entries. The **footing** (total) should be made in small numbers beneath the last entry.
    b. Foot the credit entries.
    c. Subtract the smaller total from the larger. A debit balance exists when total debits exceed total credits; a credit balance exists when the opposite is the case.

12. To determine which accounts are debited and which are credited in a given transaction, one uses the following rules:
    a. Increases in assets are debited.
    b. Decreases in assets are credited.
    c. Increases in liabilities and owners' equity are credited.
    d. Decreases in liabilities and owners' equity are debited.
    e. Revenues increase owners' equity, and are therefore credited.
    f. Expenses decrease owners' equity, and are therefore debited.

OBJECTIVE 5: Apply the procedure for transaction analysis to simple transactions (pp. 71–78).

13. To record a transaction, one must (a) obtain a description of the transaction, (b) determine which accounts are involved and what type each is (for example, asset or revenue), (c) determine which accounts are increased and which are decreased, and (d) apply the rules stated in paragraph 12 a–f.

OBJECTIVE 6: Record transactions in the general journal (pp. 79–81).

14. As transactions occur, they are recorded initially and chronologically in a book called the **journal.** The **general journal** is the simplest and most flexible type of journal. Each transaction **journalized** (recorded) in the general journal contains (a) the date, (b) the account names, (c) the dollar amounts debited and credited, (d) an explanation, and (e) the account numbers, if posted. A line should be skipped after each **journal entry,** and more than one debit or credit may be entered for a single transaction (called a **compound entry**).

15. When constructing a ledger in practice, the **ledger account form,** rather than the T-account form, is used. The four-column type is illustrated in your text.

OBJECTIVE 7: Explain the relationship of the general journal to the general ledger (pp. 81–82).

16. Each day's journal entries must be posted to the ledger accounts. **Posting** is a transferring process that results in an updated balance for each account. The dates and amounts are transferred, and new account balances are figured. The Post. Ref. columns must be used for cross-referencing between the journal and the ledger.

OBJECTIVE 8: Prepare a trial balance and recognize its value and limitations (pp. 82–85).

17. Periodically the accountant must double-check the equality of the debits and credits in the accounts. This is formally done by means of a **trial balance.** When more increases than decreases have been recorded for an account (the usual case), then its balance (debit or credit) is referred to as its **normal balance.** For example, assets have a normal debit balance.

18. If the trial balance does not balance, one or more of several possible errors have been made in the journal, ledger, or trial balance. The accountant must then locate the errors to put the trial balance in balance. It is important to know, however, that it is possible to make errors that would not cause the trial balance to be out of balance (that is, errors that would not be detected through the trial balance).

19. Ruled lines appear in financial reports before each subtotal, and a double line is customarily placed below the final amount. Although dollar signs are required in financial statements, they are omitted in journals and ledgers. On ruled paper, commas and periods are omitted, and a dash is frequently used to designate zero cents.

20. To summarize, proper accounting procedure requires that certain steps be followed (additional steps will be introduced in subsequent chapters):
   a. Journalize transactions as they occur.
   b. Post the journal entries to the ledger accounts when convenient.
   c. Prepare a trial balance periodically to test the equality of debit and credit balances.

Summary of Journal Entries Introduced in Chapter 2

A. (L.O. 5) Cash   XX (amount invested)
       Common Stock   XX (amount invested)
         Investment of cash into business by owners

B. (L.O. 5) Prepaid Rent   XX (amount paid)
       Cash   XX (amount paid)
         Advance payment for rent

C. (L.O. 5) Art Equipment   XX (purchase price)
       Cash   XX (amount paid)
         Purchase of art equipment for cash

D. (L.O. 5) Office Equipment   XX (purchase price)
       Cash   XX (amount paid)
       Accounts Payable   XX (amount to be paid)
         Purchase of office equipment, partial payment made

E. (L.O. 5) Art Supplies   XX (purchase price)
       Office Supplies   XX (purchase price)
       Accounts Payable   XX (amount to be paid)
         Purchase of art and office supplies on credit

F. (L.O. 5) Prepaid Insurance   XX (amount paid)
       Cash   XX (amount paid)
         Advance payment for insurance coverage

G. (L.O. 5) Accounts Payable   XX (amount paid)
       Cash   XX (amount paid)
         Payment on a liability

H. (L.O. 5) Cash   XX (amount received)
       Advertising Fees Earned   XX (amount earned)
         Received payment for services rendered

I. (L.O. 5) Office Wages Expense   XX (amount incurred)
       Cash   XX (amount paid)
         Recorded and paid wages for the period

J. (L.O. 5) Cash   XX (amount received)
       Unearned Art Fees   XX (amount received)
         Received payment for services to be performed

K. (L.O. 5) Accounts Receivable   XX (amount to be received)
       Advertising Fees Earned   XX (amount earned)
         Rendered service, payment to be received at later time

L. (L.O. 5) Utility Expense   XX (amount incurred)
       Cash   XX (amount paid)
         Recorded and paid utility bill

M. (L.O. 5) Telephone Expense   XX (amount incurred)
          Accounts Payable   XX (amount to be paid)
              Recorded telephone bill, payment to be
              made at later time

N. (L.O. 5) Dividends   XX (amount paid)
          Cash   XX (amount paid)
              Declared and paid a dividend

Testing Your Knowledge

Matching

Match each term with its definition by writing the appropriate letter in the blank.

_K_ **1.** Original (historical) cost

_F_ **2.** Account

_Q_ **3.** Debit

_O_ **4.** Credit

_B_ **5.** Account balance

_G_ **6.** Ledger

_A_ **7.** Posting

_M_ **8.** Prepaid expenses

_L_ **9.** Accounts Payable

_S_ **10.** Common Stock

_J_ **11.** Retained Earnings

_R_ **12.** Double-entry system

_E_ **13.** Trial balance

_N_ **14.** Journal

_P_ **15.** Post. Ref.

_H_ **16.** Footing

_C_ **17.** Compound entry

_I_ **18.** Unearned revenue

_D_ **19.** Dividends

a. Transferring data from the journal to the ledger

b. The amount in an account at a given point in time

c. An entry with more than one debit or credit

d. A distribution of assets to stockholders, resulting from profitable operations

e. A procedure for checking the equality of debits and credits in the ledger accounts

f. A record that occupies a page of the ledger

g. The book that contains all of a company's accounts

h. Adding up

i. A liability arising when payment is received prior to the performance of services

j. Cumulative profits and losses, less dividends declared

k. The proper valuation to place on a business transaction

l. Amounts owed to others

m. Amounts paid in advance for goods or services

n. The book of original entry

o. The right side of a ledger account

p. The column in the journal and ledger that provides for cross-referencing between the two

q. The left side of a ledger account

r. The method that requires both a debit and a credit for each transaction

s. The account that represents ownership in a corporation

Short Answer

Use the lines provided to answer each item.

1. Proper accounting procedure requires that certain steps be followed. List the three steps covered in this chapter.

   _____

   _____

   _____

2. Given the following journal entry, indicate which part of the entry applies to each measurement issue listed.

   July 14   Cash   150
                    Accounts Receivable   150
                    Collection on account

   a. *Recognition issue* _____

   b. *Valuation issue* _____

   c. *Classification issue* _____

3. Describe a transaction that will require a debit to one asset and a credit to another asset.

   _____

   _____

4. Describe a transaction that will require a debit to a liability and a credit to an asset.

   _____

   _____

True-False

Circle T if the statement is true, F if it is false. Please provide explanations for the false answers, using the blank lines at the end of the section.

T F 1. A sale should be recorded only on the date of payment.

T F 2. Historical cost is another term for original cost.

T F 3. There must be a separate account for each asset, liability, owners' equity component, revenue, and expense.

T F 4. The credit side of an account implies something favorable.

T F 5. For a given account, total debits must always equal total credits.

T F 6. Management can quickly determine cash on hand by referring to the journal.

T F 7. The number and titles of accounts will vary among businesses.

T F 8. Promissory Note is an example of an account title.

T F 9. Prepaid expenses are classified as assets.

T F 10. Increases in liabilities require credits.

T F 11. In all journal entries, at least one account must be increased, and another decreased.

T F 12. Journal entries are made after transactions have been entered into the ledger accounts.

T F 13. In the journal, all liabilities and owners' equity accounts must be indented.

T F 14. A debit is never indented in the journal.

T F 15. Posting refers to transferring data from the journal to the ledger.

T F 16. The Post. Ref. column of a journal or ledger should be empty until posting is done.

T F 17. In practice, the ledger account form is used, but the T account form is not.

T F 18. The chart of accounts is a table of contents to the general journal.

T F 19. Unearned Revenues has a normal debit balance.

T F 20. Retained Earnings is a cash account placed in the asset section of the balance sheet.

T F 21. The Common Stock account represents owners' investments, but not corporate profits and losses.

_____

_____

_____

_____

_____

_____

_____

_____

_____

_____

_____

_____

_____

_____

_____

_____

_____

_____

_____

_____

_____

_____

_____

_____

Circle the letter of the best answer.

1. Which of the following is *not* considered in initially recording a business transaction?
   a. Classification
   b. Recognition
   c. Summarization
   d. Valuation

2. When a liability is paid, which of the following is true?
   a. Total assets and total liabilities remain the same.
   b. Total assets and total owners' equity decrease.
   c. Total assets decrease by the same amount that total liabilities increase.
   d. Total assets and total liabilities decrease.

3. Which of the following is *not* true about a proper journal entry?
   a. All credits are indented.
   b. All debits are listed before the first credit.
   c. An explanation is needed for each debit and each credit.
   d. A debit is never indented, even if a liability or owners' equity account is involved.

4. When an entry is posted, what is the last step to be taken?
   a. The explanation must be transferred.
   b. The account number is placed in the reference column of the ledger.
   c. The journal page number is placed in the reference column of the journal.
   d. The account number is placed in the reference column of the journal.

5. Which of the following errors will probably be disclosed by the preparation of a trial balance (i.e., would cause it to be out of balance)?
   a. Failure to post an entire journal entry (i.e., nothing is posted).
   b. Failure to record an entry in the journal (i.e., nothing is entered).
   c. Failure to post part of a journal entry.
   d. Posting the debit of a journal entry as a credit, and the credit as a debit.

6. When cash is received in payment of an account receivable, which of the following is true?
   a. Total assets increase.
   b. Total assets remain the same.
   c. Total assets decrease.
   d. Total assets and total owners' equity increase.

7. Which of the following is increased by debits?
   a. Dividends
   b. Unearned Revenue
   c. Bonds Payable
   d. Retained Earnings

8. Which of the following accounts is an asset?
   a. Unearned Revenue
   b. Prepaid Rent
   c. Retained Earnings
   d. Fees Earned

9. Which of the following accounts is a liability?
   a. Interest Payable
   b. Interest Expense
   c. Interest Receivable
   d. Interest Income

10. A company that rents an office (i.e., a lessee or tenant) would never record which account for that particular lease?
    a. Prepaid Rent
    b. Unearned Rent
    c. Rent Payable
    d. Rent Expense

11. Which of the following accounts has a normal credit balance?
    a. Prepaid Insurance
    b. Dividends
    c. Sales
    d. Advertising Expense

Applying Your Knowledge

Exercises

1. Following are all the transactions of Pinnacle Printing Company for the month of May. For each transaction, provide *in good form* the journal entries required. Use the journal provided on the following page.

May 2 Pinnacle Printing, Inc., was granted a charter by the state, and investors contributed $28,000 in exchange for 2,800 shares of $10 par value common stock.

      3 Rented part of a building for $300 per month. Paid three months' rent in advance.

      5 Purchased a small printing press for $10,000 and photographic equipment for $3,000 from Irvin Press, Inc. Paid $2,000 and agreed to pay the remainder as soon as possible.

      8 Hired a pressman, agreeing to pay him $200 per week.

      9 Received $1,200 from Doherty's Department Store as an advance for brochures to be printed.

   11 Purchased paper for $800 from Pulp Supply Company. Issued Pulp a promissory note for the entire amount.

   14 Completed a $500 printing job for Sullivan Shoes. Sullivan paid for half, agreeing to pay the remainder next week.

   14 Paid the pressman his weekly salary.

   15 Paid Irvin Press, Inc., $1,000 of the amount owed for the May 5 transaction.

   18 Received remainder due from Sullivan Shoes for the May 14 transaction.

   20 A $700 cash dividend was declared and paid by the corporation.

   24 Received an electric bill of $45. Payment will be made in a few days.

   30 Paid the electric bill.

2. Following are three balance sheet accounts, selected at random from Holding Company's ledger. For each, determine the account balance.

Accounts Receivable		Accounts Payable	
2,000	1,000	1,200	4,200
750		2,000	

Cash	
15,000	1,000
4,000	1,200
	2,200

a. Accounts Receivable has a (debit or credit) balance of $_____.

b. Accounts Payable has a (debit or credit) balance of $_____.

c. Cash has a (debit or credit) balance of $_____.

(Continued on page 35)

General Journal				
Date		**Description**	**Debit**	**Credit**
May	2	Cash	28,000	
		Common Stock		28,000
		To record the stockholders' original investment		

3. Two journal entries are presented below. Post both entries to the ledger accounts provided. Only those accounts needed have been provided, and previous postings have been omitted to simplify the exercise.

		General Journal				Page 7
Date		Description	Post. Ref.	Debit	Credit
Apr.	3	Cash		1,000	
		Revenue from Services			1,000
		Received payment from Malden Company for services			
	5	Accounts Payable		300	
		Cash			300
		Paid Douglas Supply Company for supplies purchased on March 31 on credit			

Cash   Account No. 11

Date		Item	Post. Ref.	Debit	Credit	Balance Debit	Balance Credit

Accounts Payable   Account No. 21

Date		Item	Post. Ref.	Debit	Credit	Balance Debit	Balance Credit

Revenue from Services   Account No. 41

Date		Item	Post. Ref.	Debit	Credit	Balance Debit	Balance Credit

Reading

Some Computer Software Makers' Earnings Likely to Slide; Blame It on the Accountants

NEW YORK—Wall Street is bracing for a lot more earnings "surprises" from computer-software makers in the year ahead. But this time the problem isn't bad input or fuzzy logic. It's accountants.

Until recently, thanks to a quirk of accounting, makers of software for large mainframe computers were allowed to report sales—and to book the resulting profits—before they actually delivered software, technology upgrades or maintenance services. Now they'll have to stop, under a recent proposal from a task force on the American Institute of Certified Public Accountants.

The proposed rule change could reduce dozens of companies' sales next year by 3% to 30%, analysts say. Profits will undoubtedly be hit, too, by 7% to 15%, according to one analyst. Stock prices of mainframe-software companies could bounce around as a result, say analysts who have been working hard to assess the change. (The rule, to take effect with fiscal years starting after Dec. 15, doesn't apply to makers of software for personal computers and microcomputers.)

The bright spot for investors, analysts say, is that a few years from now, the rule could produce more realistic, reliable and comparable earnings in a stock group that has been highly volatile.

"The rule has been a long time in coming," says software analyst Louis Giglio, at Bear Stearns. "Some software makers were throwing everything into revenues including the kitchen sink —even if they hadn't yet delivered it."

Under the rule, sales must be booked not when a contract is signed—the current practice— but when the software is delivered. Dozens of software makers would have to record sales on their maintenance contracts over a longer period, rather than up front when the contract is signed.

Martin Hurwitz, a software analyst for American Express's IDS Financial Services unit, says the rule may have the biggest effect starting next year on results of Goal Systems International, Computer Associates International and BMC Software.

"Big portions of these companies' revenues derive from long-term maintenance contracts with customers, and so they'll be hit the hardest by the accounting rule," says Mr. Hurwitz. He estimates that the rule could reduce Goal's reported profit by as much as 30%, Computer Associates' by as much as 10% and BMC's by 10% to 15%.

Beset by collections problems and pressure from analysts for more conservative accounting practices, two major software makers, Oracle Systems and Informix, already have adopted the rule. Both booked charges against recently reported results; Oracle took sizable write-downs on accounts receivable—bills owed by customers.

Charles Phillips, software analyst for Sound-View Financial Group, says that under the rule, stricter scrutiny by outside auditors will force many mainframe software makers to write off more doubtful accounts receivable. He estimates that profits of most makers of software for mainframe computers will be cut 7% to 15% by the new rule.

At Goal, based in Columbus, Ohio, Wade Monroe, vice president, finance, concedes that the accounting rule will reduce Goal's sales in the year starting Feb. 1, 1992, by somewhere between 3% and 11%, probably "in the middle of this range."

As to the effect on Goal's future profit, Mr. Monroe said, "it's going to be significant, but we haven't yet determined the exact reduction." He says about 20% of Goal's sales of $117 million in the year ended Jan. 31 resulted from "separately priced maintenance contracts with customers."

At Computer Associates in Garden City, N.Y., Peter Schwartz, vice president, finance, says the company hasn't yet evaluated how the accounting rule will reduce its sales and profit. But, he says, "there's no question it will bite into the approximate $400 million in our annual maintenance-fee contract revenues starting in the fiscal year beginning April 1, 1992."

Problems at a few other software makers persuaded accounting rule-makers to force all software companies to spread out maintenance revenue over the life of the contract rather than book it when the contract is signed, Mr. Schwartz says.

Source: From "Some Computer Software Makers' Earnings Likely to Slide; Blame It on the Accountants" by Lee Berton, *The Wall Street Journal*, May 8, 1991. Reprinted by permission of *The Wall Street Journal*, © 1991 Dow Jones & Company, Inc. All Rights Reserved Worldwide.

"As a conservative company, we find that only 1% of our contracts aren't eventually delivered," he says.

In Sugar Land, Texas, David Farley, chief financial officer of BMC Software, says that in the year starting next April 1, 1992, the rule will reduce BMC's revenue by about 10% and have "a bigger impact on our bottom line." For the year ended March 31, BMC reported a profit of $31.4 million, or $1.25 a share, on sales of $139.5 million.

About a third of BMC's revenue derives from maintenance contracts, Mr. Farley says. "But 97% of our customers renew their maintenance con-tracts after a 30-day free trial period, and we only book revenues when the contract is signed after the trial," he says.

Other companies that could be affected by the rule, analysts say, are Continuum, Knowl-edgeware, Legent, Pansophic Systems, Sterling Software and System Software.

Financial executives at many software com-panies deny that their own companies book reve-nue and profits too early. But some concede that excessively aggressive sales bookings haven't been uncommon in the industry. "There's no question some hanky-panky has been going on," one execu-tive says. "Don't quote me."

Reading

Setting the Date

When does a sale become a sale? There are lots of answers to this question, and folks who manage earnings know them all.

When savvy investors scrutinize a company's financial results, they tend to search for hidden footnotes and misleading language. All too frequently, however, the real monkey business involves something much more obvious: total revenues. Accountants triple-check depreciation schedules and hand-count inventories, but managers have a good bit of freedom to determine when and how a sale gets put on the books.

Sure, the more unusual methods of revenue recognition are disclosed in annual reports. But sometimes a greedy firm's methods can get completely out of hand. Just weeks ago, for example, the SEC charged Datapoint, a onetime high-flier, with materially overstating its revenues. One modus operandi, says the SEC: shipping computers without customer authorizations in order to book sales and profits early.

But you don't have to break the law to bend the rules. Old-fashioned companies don't book business until they deposit the customer's check, an approach that minimizes chicanery. But modern practice is chock-full of temptation.

Consider the computer world, where the pressure to boost quarterly results is intense. A 1982 survey of 200 software companies reveals that only 13% wait until they receive payment before ringing up a sale. Instead, many book business at far fuzzier times, such as at delivery or installation. A full 15% of the firms recognize a sale as soon as they get an order. Not surprisingly, the American Institute of Certified Public Accountants has set up a task force to make sense out of this confusion.

But problems aren't limited to the realm of high tech. "When you're talking about a can opener manufacturer, there should be no real opportunity for selecting a more aggressive or more conservative way of booking sales," says Howard Levy, Laventhol & Horwath's national director

Source: Article by Jill Andresky; edited by Richard Greene. Reprinted by permission of *Forbes* magazine, July 16, 1984. © Forbes, Inc., 1984.

for quality control. "Still, a little cheat happens every now and then."

Not that there aren't standards. Old-time accountants remember the days when payments had to be received before business went on the books. But now the basic rule is that sales are recorded as soon as goods are shipped. This approach goes back decades, on the logic that revenue should be recognized when the earnings process is complete and an exchange has taken place.

General Electric, for example, recognizes its revenue when title passes to customers, which almost always means at the time of shipment. The only exceptions, according to a company spokesman, are cases where orders are so large or complicated that customers have agreed, by contract, that title has been transferred earlier.

From here on, things get more complicated. Publishers, for example, work differently because customers can return their products 60 days or more after a sale. Although it might be more conservative not to book income until the return period ends, no one operates this way. "It's generally accepted that if firms can estimate the rate of return, there's no need to wait," says Levy. "All they're required to do is subtract the estimated returns from the total sales and then readjust discrepancies in the next quarter." Some firms, such as Harper & Row, actually record estimated returns separately from sales on their financial statements.

Service businesses follow other practices, ranging from recording sales immediately, to prorating income over the length of contracts, to anything in between. "The most conservative method is to prorate," says Levy, "but plenty of companies do otherwise."

The practice of booking sales as soon as orders are placed is especially common among mail-order businesses and sellers of custom products or services. A case in point: SNA, which provides satellite transmissions of video conferences. "Ours is a planned purchase, not an impulse buy," says Rob Drasin, SNA's president. "By the time a customer places an order and pays us our one-third deposit, his purchase has already received the blessing of management."

Booking early may make sense with high-ticket custom sales. But even mass-market retailers have started to book business more aggressively, a practice that's tougher to defend. Harper & Row, for example, records sales as soon as it invoices customers—anywhere from a week to a month before it ships orders. "There are very few differences for us between billing and shipping," says Robert Evanson, the publisher's assistant comptroller, "and it's easier to do it that way."

Easier and, perhaps, seemingly more profitable. But investors should pay attention to how corporations recognize income, The more liberal the policy, the greater the risk that reported earnings aren't real. And the easier it is to create a little extra business when times get tough.

CHAPTER 3 BUSINESS INCOME AND ADJUSTING ENTRIES

Reviewing the Chapter

OBJECTIVE 1: Define *net income* and its two major components, *revenues* and *expenses* (pp. 114–116).

1. Earning a **profit** is an important goal of most businesses. A major function of accounting is to measure and report a company's success or failure in achieving this goal. This is done by means of an income statement.

2. **Net income** is the net increase in owners' equity resulting from the operations of the company. Net income results when revenues exceed expenses, and a **net loss** results when expenses exceed revenues.

3. **Revenues** are the price of goods sold and services rendered during a specific period of time. Examples of revenues are Sales (the account used when merchandise is sold), Commissions Earned, and Advertising Fees Earned.

4. **Expenses** are the costs of goods and services used in the process of earning revenues. Examples of expenses are Telephone Expense, Wages Expense, and Advertising Expense.

5. Revenue and expense accounts are sometimes referred to as **temporary** or **nominal accounts** because they are temporary in nature. Their purpose is to record revenues and expenses during a particular accounting period. At the end of that period, their totals are transferred to the Retained Earnings account, leaving zero balances to begin the next accounting period.

6. Balance sheet accounts are sometimes referred to as **permanent** or **real accounts** because their balances can extend past the end of an accounting period. They are *not* set back to zero.

OBJECTIVE 2a: Explain the difficulties of income measurement caused by the accounting period issue (pp. 116–117).

7. The **periodicity** assumption (the solution to the **accounting period issue**) states that although measurements of net income for short periods of time are approximate, they are nevertheless useful to statement users. Income statement comparison is made possible through accounting periods of equal length. A **fiscal year** covers any twelve-month accounting period used by a company. Many companies use a fiscal year that corresponds to a calendar year, which is a twelve-month period that ends on December 31.

OBJECTIVE 2b: Explain the difficulties of income measurement caused by the continuity issue (p. 117).

8. Under the **going concern** assumption (the solution to the **continuity issue**), the accountant assumes that the business will continue to operate indefinitely, unless there is evidence to the contrary.

OBJECTIVE 2c: Explain the difficulties of income measurement caused by the matching issue (pp. 117–118).

9. When the **cash basis of accounting** is used, revenues are recorded when cash is received, and expenses are recorded when cash is paid. This method, however, can lead to distortion of net income for the period.

10. According to the **matching rule,** revenues should be recorded in the period(s) in which they are actually earned, and expenses should be recorded in the period(s) in which the expenses are incurred; the timing of cash payments or receipts is irrelevant.

OBJECTIVE 3: Define *accrual accounting* and explain two broad ways of accomplishing it (pp. 118–119).

11. **Accrual accounting** consists of all techniques used to apply the matching rule. Specifically, it involves (1) recognizing revenues when earned (**revenue recognition**) and expenses when incurred, and (2) adjusting the accounts at the end of the period.

OBJECTIVE 4: State the four principal situations that require adjusting entries (pp. 119–120).

12. A problem arises when revenues or expenses apply to more than one accounting period. The problem is solved by making **adjusting entries** at the end of the accounting period. Adjusting entries allocate to the current period the revenues and expenses that apply to that period, deferring the remainder to future periods. A **deferral** is the postponement of the recognition of an expense already paid or of a revenue already received [see 13(a) and (b) below]. An **accrual** is the recognition of an expense or revenue that has arisen but has not yet been recorded [see 13(c) and (d) below].

13. Adjusting entries are required to accomplish several things:
    a. To divide recorded costs (such as the cost of machinery or prepaid rent) among two or more accounting periods.
    b. To divide recorded revenues (such as commissions collected in advance) among two or more accounting periods.
    c. To record unrecorded revenues (such as commissions earned but not yet billed to customers).

d. To record unrecorded expenses (such as wages earned by employees after the last payday in an accounting period).

OBJECTIVE 5: Prepare typical adjusting entries (pp. 121–128).

14. When an expenditure is made that will benefit more than just the current period, the initial debit is usually made to an asset account instead of to an expense account. Then, at the end of the accounting period, the amount that has been used up is transferred from the asset account to an expense account.
    a. **Prepaid expenses,** like Prepaid Rent and Prepaid Insurance, are debited when they are paid for in advance.
    b. An account for supplies, such as Office Supplies, is debited when supplies are purchased. At the end of the accounting period, an inventory of supplies is taken. The difference between supplies available for use during the period and ending inventory is the amount used up during the period.
    c. A long-lived asset such as a building, trucks, or office furniture is debited to an asset account when purchased. At the end of each accounting period, an adjusting entry must be made to transfer a part of the original cost of each long-lived asset to an expense account. The amount transferred or allocated is called **depreciation** or **depreciation expense.**
    d. The **Accumulated Depreciation** account is called a **contra account** because on the balance sheet it is subtracted from its associated asset account. Thus proper balance sheet presentation will show the original cost, the accumulated depreciation as of the balance sheet date, and the undepreciated balance (called **carrying value** or book value).

15. In making the adjusting entry to record depreciation, Depreciation Expense is debited and Accumulated Depreciation is credited.

16. Sometimes payment is received for goods before they are delivered or for services before they are rendered. In such cases, a liability account such as **Unearned Revenues** or Unearned Fees would appear on the balance sheet. This account is a liability because it represents revenues that still must be earned.

17. Often at the end of an accounting period, revenues have been earned but not recorded because no payment has been received. An adjusting entry must be made to record these **accrued (unrecorded) revenues.** For example, interest that has been earned might not be received until the next period. A debit must be made to Interest Receivable and a credit to Interest Income to record the current period's interest for the income statement. This entry will also record the asset for the balance sheet.

18. Similarly, expenses have often been incurred but not recorded in the accounts because cash has not yet been paid. An adjusting entry must be made to record these **accrued expenses.** For example, interest on a loan may have accrued that does not have to be paid until the next period. A debit to Interest Expense and a credit to Interest Payable will record the current period's interest for the income statement.

OBJECTIVE 6: Prepare financial statements from an adjusted trial balance (pp. 129–130).

19. After all the adjusting entries have been posted to the ledger accounts and new account balances have been computed, an **adjusted trial balance** should be prepared. If it is in balance, the adjusted trial balance is then used to prepare the financial statements.

OBJECTIVE 7: State all the steps in the accounting cycle (pp. 130–133).

20. The steps in the **accounting system** (also called the **accounting cycle**) are as follows:
    a. The transactions are analyzed from the source documents.
    b. The transactions are recorded in the journal.
    c. The journal entries are posted to the ledger.
    d. The accounts are adjusted at the end of the period to achieve the adjusted trial balance.
    e. Financial statements are prepared from the adjusted trial balance.
    f. The nominal accounts are closed to conclude the current accounting period and to prepare for the new accounting period.

Summary of Journal Entries Introduced in Chapter 3

A. (L.O. 5) Rent Expense   XX (amount expired)
           Prepaid Rent   XX (amount expired)
                Expiration of prepaid rent

B. (L.O. 5) Insurance Expense   XX (amount expired)
           Prepaid Insurance   XX (amount expired)
                Expiration of prepaid insurance

C. (L.O. 5) Supplies Expense   XX (amount consumed)
           Supplies   XX (amount consumed)
                Consumption of supplies

D. (L.O. 5) Depreciation Expense, Equipment   XX (amount allocated to period)
           Accumulated Depreciation, Equipment   XX (amount allocated to period)
                Depreciation recorded

E. (L.O. 5) Unearned Art Fees   XX (amount earned)
           Art Fees Earned   XX (amount earned)
                Performance of service paid for in advance

F. (L.O. 5) Fees Receivable   XX (amount to be received)
           Advertising Fees Earned   XX (amount earned)
                Accrual of unrecorded revenue

G. (L.O. 5) Office Wages Expense   XX (amount incurred)
           Wages Payable   XX (amount to be paid)
                Accrual of unrecorded wages

H. (L.O. 5) Income Taxes Expense   XX (amount estimated)
           Income Taxes Payable   XX (amount estimated)
                Accrual of estimated income taxes

Testing Your Knowledge

Matching

Match each term with its definition by writing the appropriate letter in the blank.

_____ 1. Net income

_____ 2. Revenues

_____ 3. Expenses

_____ 4. Expired cost

_____ 5. Unexpired cost

_____ 6. Nominal (temporary) accounts

_____ 7. Real (permanent) accounts

_____ 8. Fiscal year

_____ 9. Going concern assumption

_____ 10. Cash basis of accounting

_____ 11. Accrual accounting

_____ 12. Matching rule

_____ 13. Adjusting entry

_____ 14. Depreciation expense

_____ 15. Accumulated depreciation

_____ 16. Contra account

_____ 17. Unearned revenue

_____ 18. Adjusted trial balance

_____ 19. Deferral

_____ 20. Accrual

a. All techniques used to apply the matching rule

b. A liability that represents an obligation to deliver goods or render services

c. That portion of an asset that has not yet been charged as an expense

d. A general term for the price of goods sold or services rendered

e. The assumption that a business will continue indefinitely (solution to the continuity issue)

f. Accounts whose balances extend beyond the end of a period

g. A method of determining whether accounts are still in balance

h. The idea that revenues are recorded (recognized) when earned and that expenses are recorded when incurred

i. The amount by which revenues exceed expenses (opposite of net loss)

j. An account that is subtracted from an associated account

k. Any twelve-month accounting period used by a company

l. An example of a contra account to plant assets

m. An end-of-period allocation of revenues and expenses relevant to that period

n. The cost of doing business

o. Recording revenues and expenses when payment is received or made

p. The expired cost of a plant asset for a particular accounting period

q. Accounts that begin each period with zero balances

r. A descriptive term for expense

s. Recognition of an expense or revenue that has arisen but has not yet been recorded

t. Postponement of the recognition of an expense already paid or of a revenue already received

Use the lines provided to answer each item.

1. Briefly summarize the four situations requiring adjusting entries.

    _____

    _____

    _____

    _____

2. Briefly explain the matching rule.

    _____

    _____

    _____

    _____

3. Define depreciation as the term is used in accounting.

    _____

    _____

    _____

4. Distinguish between prepaid expenses and unearned revenues.

    _____

    _____

    _____

    _____

5. The six steps in the accounting cycle are presented here in the wrong order. Place the numbers 1 through 6 in the spaces provided to indicate the correct order.

    _____ The journal entries are posted to the ledger.

    _____ The income statement and dividends accounts are closed.

    _____ The transactions are analyzed from the source documents.

    _____ The accounts are adjusted, and an adjusted trial balance is produced.

    _____ The transactions are recorded in the journal.

    _____ Financial statements are prepared from the adjusted trial balance.

True-False

Circle T if the statement is true, F if it is false. Please provide explanations for the false answers, using the blank lines at the end of the section.

T F **1.** Accumulated Depreciation is a real account, whereas Depreciation Expense is a nominal account.

T F **2.** Expired costs can be found in the income statement.

T F **3.** A calendar year refers to any twelve-month period.

T F **4.** The cash basis of accounting often violates the matching rule.

T F **5.** Under the accrual basis of accounting, the timing of cash payments is vital for recording revenues and expenses.

T F **6.** Adjusting entries must be made immediately after the financial statements are prepared.

T F **7.** Prepaid Insurance represents an unexpired cost.

T F **8.** Office Supplies Expense must be debited for the amount in ending inventory of office supplies.

T F **9.** Since Accumulated Depreciation appears on the asset side of the balance sheet, it will have a debit balance.

T F **10.** As a machine is depreciated, its accumulated depreciation increases and its unexpired cost decreases.

T F **11.** Unearned Revenues is a contra account to Earned Revenues in the income statement.

T F **12.** When an expense has accrued but payment has not yet been made, a debit is needed for the expense and a credit for Prepaid Expenses.

T F **13.** The adjusted trial balance is the same as the trial balance, except that it has been modified by adjusting entries.

T F **14.** If one has made a sale for which the money has not yet been received, one would debit Unearned Revenues and credit Earned Revenues.

T F **15.** The original cost of a long-lived asset should appear on the balance sheet even after depreciation has been recorded.

_____

_____

_____

_____

_____

_____

_____

_____

_____

_____

_____

_____

_____

Multiple Choice

Circle the letter of the best answer.

1. Which of the following is an example of a nominal account?
   a. Prepaid Rent
   b. Unearned Revenues
   c. Wages Expense
   d. Accumulated Depreciation, Building

2. Depreciation does *not* apply to
   a. trucks.
   b. office supplies.
   c. machinery.
   d. office equipment.

3. An account called Unearned Fees is used when there are
   a. recorded costs that must be divided among periods.
   b. recorded revenues that must be divided among periods.
   c. unrecorded (accrued) expenses that must be recorded.
   d. unrecorded (accrued) revenues that must be recorded.

4. Depreciation best applies to
   a. recorded costs that must be divided among periods.
   b. recorded revenues that must be divided among periods.
   c. unrecorded expenses that must be recorded.
   d. unrecorded revenues that must be recorded.

5. Which of the following will *not* appear in the adjusted trial balance?
   a. Prepaid Insurance
   b. Unearned Management Fees
   c. Net Income
   d. Depreciation Expense

6. An adjusting entry made to record accrued interest on a note receivable due next year would consist of
   a. a debit to Cash and a credit to Interest Income.
   b. a debit to Cash and a credit to Interest Receivable.
   c. a debit to Interest Expense and a credit to Interest Payable.
   d. a debit to Interest Receivable and a credit to Interest Income.

7. The periodicity assumption solves the accounting period issue by recognizing that
   a. net income for a short period of time is an estimate.
   b. a business is assumed to continue indefinitely.
   c. revenues should be recorded in the period earned.
   d. a twelve-month accounting period must be used.

8. Prepaid Rent is
   a. an expense.
   b. a contra account.
   c. a liability.
   d. an asset.

9. An adjusting entry would *never* include which of the following accounts?
   a. Unearned Revenue
   b. Cash
   c. Prepaid Advertising
   d. Wages Expense

10. Which of the following accounting-cycle steps is accomplished after all the others listed?
    a. Adjusting entries
    b. Financial statements
    c. Closing entries
    d. Adjusted trial balance

Applying Your Knowledge

Exercises

1. On January 1, 19x1, Gotham Bus Company began its business by buying a new bus for $24,000. One-eighth of the cost of the bus is depreciated each year. Complete *in good form* the balance sheet as of December 31, 19x3.

Gotham Bus Company
Partial Balance Sheet
December 31, 19x3

Assets

Cash	$5,000
Accounts Receivable	3,000
Company Vehicles	
	$____
Total Assets	$____

---

2. For each set of facts, provide the dollar amount that would be recorded.

a. The cost of supplies at the beginning of the period was $510. During the period, supplies that cost $800 were purchased. At the end of the period, supplies that cost $340 remained. Supplies Expense should be recorded for $_____ .

b. The company signed a lease for $14,000 on July 1, 19x1, to cover the four-year period beginning July 1, 19x1. How much Rent Expense should the company record on December 31, 19x1? $_____

c. The company was paid $600 in advance for services to be performed. By the end of the period, only one-fourth of it had been earned. How much of the $600 will appear as Unearned Revenues on the balance sheet? $_____

3. Following is the trial balance for Darby Company.

Darby Company
Trial Balance
December 31, 19x1

	Debit	Credit
Cash	$ 77,300	
Notes Receivable	5,000	
Prepaid Advertising	8,000	
Prepaid Insurance	1,000	
Supplies	500	
Office Equipment	9,000	
Buildings	90,000	
Accumulated Depreciation		$ 6,000
Notes Payable		1,500
Unearned Revenues		2,800
Common Stock		100,000
Dividends	13,000	
Revenues from Services		212,000
Wages Expense	118,500	
	$322,300	$322,300

The facts that follow are based on this trial balance. For each item, make the adjusting entry in the journal provided on the next page. Keep in mind that Darby Company operates on a calendar year.

a. Cost of supplies on hand, based on physical count, is $375.

b. Wages of $2,500 for the five-day work week ($500 per day) are paid and recorded every Friday. December 31 falls on a Thursday.

c. Services amounting to $600 were rendered during 19x1 for customers who had paid in advance.

d. Five percent of the cost of the building is taken as depreciation for 19x1.

e. One-quarter of the prepaid advertising expired during 19x1.

f. All of the insurance shown on the trial balance was paid for on July 1, 19x1, and covers the two-year period beginning July 1, 19x1.

g. Work performed for customers which has not been billed or recorded amounts to $2,200.

h. Accured interest on the notes payable amounts to $52. This interest will be paid when the note matures.

i. Accrued income tax expense for the year amounts to $21,700. This amount will be paid early next year.

Date		Description	Debit	Credit
		General Journal		

Crossword Puzzle
For Chapters 2 and 3

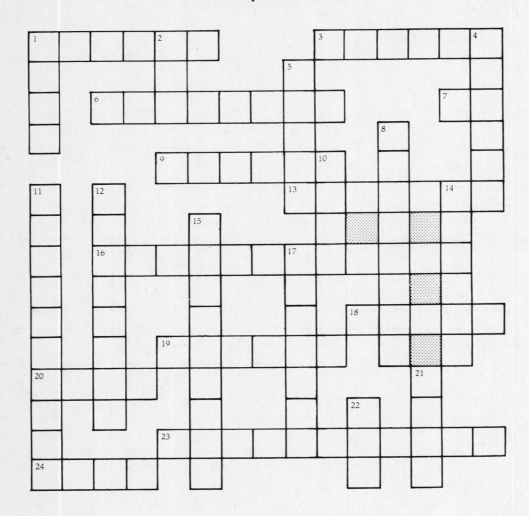

ACROSS

1. An account subtracted from another
3. See 22-Down
6. Postponement of a revenue or expense
7. Journal column title (same as 2-Down)
9. Where the accounts are kept
13. A source of revenues
16. Test of debit and credit equality (2 words)
18. Left side of journal or ledger
19. Monthly- or yearly-rate compensation
20. One asset not subject to depreciation
23. _____ bookkeeping (hyphenated)
24. Realize (revenues)

DOWN

1. Historical _____ principle
2. Post. _____ column
4. Become an expense
5. Hourly- or piecework-rate compensation
8. Income statement item
10. Opposite of nominal
11. Record transactions
12. Rule applied through accrual accounting
14. Right side of journal or ledger
15. Assignment of a dollar amount to
17. Recognition of unrecorded revenues or expenses
21. Written promise to pay
22. With 3-Across, the term accountants use in referring to *profit*

Reading

Soft Numbers

Can market pressures bring more uniformity to software industry accounting than accountants' rule have?

"Comparability is everything in financial statements," grumbles Lawrence Schoenberg, chairman of AGS Computers, which designs software, "and there isn't any comparability among software company disclosures."

That's a pretty strong statement, but Schoenberg isn't exaggerating. Look at the ever thorny issue of how much of their research and development costs the software companies should capitalize and how much they should expense against earnings. Last year the Financial Accounting Standards Board, prodded by the Securities & Exchange Commission, issued Statement No. 86. It says software companies may capitalize a portion of development costs—but only after a new software program has become a working model or specific design (*Forbes,* June 16, 1986).

Does that sound a little too vague to provide a uniform disclosure standard? It is. Under Statement 86, Cullinet Software, a $175 million (sales) software producer from Westwood, Mass., capitalizes no development costs and expenses all of them. Under the same rule, competitor Management Science America expenses only about two-thirds of its development and capitalizes the balance. MSA reported net income last year of $18.7 million. But if it accounted for its development expenses the way Cullinet does, MSA would have reported earnings of just $11 million. So much for comparability.

Now the American Institute of Certified Public Accountants wants the Financial Accounting Standards Board to write a new rule dealing with software program maintenance contracts. Many of these highly profitable, yearlong contracts are sold in the fourth quarter, with the entire purchase price paid up front.

The software companies argue that they should be able to book the income as revenues when they get the cash. But the accountants say that violates accrual accounting. The AICPA wants the FASB to order the companies to stretch out recognition of their maintenance contract revenues over the life of the contract. Thus, if a one-year contract were sold for $12,000 in December 1986, only $1,000 of the revenue received could be booked in 1986. The balance would be amortized over the rest of the contract period—even though the cash was safe in the till.

This would result in some nasty surprises. Even earnings at Cullinet, which is known for its conservative accounting practices, would be adversely affected. Stretching out revenues "would have made a bad year significantly worse," says Cullinet Executive Vice President for Finance and Administration James Pitts, of fiscal 1987 (ended April), when Cullinet reported a $27.6 million loss.

Yet Pitts says Cullinet would support new rules. "There would be more comparability, and that would be a good thing—especially after the tragedy of Statement 86."

In any event, the industry may have little choice, no matter what the accountants say.

The financial markets have a way of rewarding companies with high standards of financial disclosure and penalizing those with lower standards.

Example: Cash-hungry software companies used to sell a lot of multiyear maintenance contracts, good for up to five years, and book the revenues in advance to give an extra kick to earnings. "You can imagine how profitable that was," recalls Stephen McClellan, a software industry analyst with Merrill Lynch, "since they had few direct up-front costs." But analysts like McClellan began questioning the quality of some companies' reported earnings, leaving the companies little choice but to change their ways. Management Science America used to get 14% of its maintenance revenue from multiyear contracts. Last year multiyear contracts were down to 4% of revenue.

"The financial community—the analysts—didn't like the multiyear contracts," says William Laney, MSA's chief financial officer. "That's one reason we de-emphasized the [multiyear] program."

Analysts, Laney adds, are now "pressuring" the software companies to book one-year maintenance contract revenues over the life of the contracts. Such pressure could well do more to bring uniform financial reporting to the $15 billion software industry than books full of accounting rules and regulations.

Source: Article by Laura Jereski. Reprinted by permission of *Forbes* magazine, August 10, 1987. © Forbes, Inc., 1987.

CHAPTER 4 COMPLETING THE ACCOUNTING CYCLE

Reviewing the Chapter

OBJECTIVE 1: Prepare a work sheet (pp. 165–173).

1. Accountants use **working papers** to help organize their work and to provide evidence in support of the financial statements. The **work sheet** is one such working paper. It lessens the chance of overlooking an adjustment, acts as a check on the arithmetical accuracy of the accounts, and aids in preparing financial statements. The work sheet is never published but is a useful tool for the accountant.

2. The five steps in the preparation of the work sheet are as follows:
   a. Enter the account balances (debit or credit) into the Trial Balance columns, and total the columns.
   b. Enter the adjustments into the Adjustments columns, and total the columns. A letter identifies the debit and credit for each adjustment and may act as a key to a brief explanation at the bottom of the work sheet.
   c. Enter the account balances, as adjusted, into the Adjusted Trial Balance columns (by means of **crossfooting**), and total the columns.
   d. Extend (transfer) the account balances from the Adjusted Trial Balance columns to either the Income Statement columns or the Balance Sheet columns, depending on which type of account is involved.
   e. Total the Income Statement and Balance Sheet columns. Then enter the net income or loss into the Income Statement and Balance Sheet columns (one will be a debit, the other a credit) as a balancing figure. Finally, recompute the column totals.

OBJECTIVE 2: Identify the three principal uses of a work sheet (p. 173).

3. Once the work sheet is completed, it can be used to (a) prepare the financial statements, (b) record the adjusting entries in the journal, and (c) record the closing entries in the journal, thus preparing the records for the new period.

OBJECTIVE 3: Prepare financial statements from a work sheet (pp. 173–175).

4. The income statement may be prepared from the information found in the work sheet's Income Statement columns. Calculations of the change in retained earnings for the period are shown in the statement of retained earnings. Information for this calculation may be found in the Balance Sheet columns of the work sheet (beginning retained earnings, net income, and dividends). The balance sheet may be prepared from information found in the work sheet's Balance Sheet columns and in the statement of retained earnings.

OBJECTIVE 4: Record the adjusting entries from a work sheet (pp. 175–176).

5. Formal adjusting entries must be recorded in the journal and posted to the ledger so that

the account balances on the books will agree with those on the financial statements. This is easily accomplished by referring to the Adjustments columns (and footnoted explanations) of the work sheet.

OBJECTIVE 5: Explain the purposes of closing entries (pp. 176–177).

6. **Closing entries** serve two purposes. First, they transfer net income or loss to the Retained Earnings account. Second, they reduce revenue and expense accounts to zero so that these accounts may begin accumulating net income for the next accounting period. So that the Retained Earnings account may be fully updated, the Dividends account is also closed in the process.

OBJECTIVE 6: Prepare the required closing entries (pp. 178–182).

7. There are four closing entries, as follows:
   a. Revenue accounts are closed. This is accomplished with a compound entry that debits each revenue account for the amount required to give it a zero balance and credits its **Income Summary** for the revenue total. The Income Summary account exists only during the closing process and does not appear in the work sheet or in the financial statements.
   b. Expense accounts are closed. This is accomplished with a compound entry that credits each expense for the amount required to give it a zero balance, and debits Income Summary for the expense total.
   c. The Income Summary account is closed. After revenue and expense accounts have been closed, the Income Summary account will have either a debit balance or a credit balance. If a credit balance exists, then Income Summary must be debited for the amount required to give it a zero

balance, and Retained Earnings is credited for the same amount. The reverse is done when Income Summary has a debit balance.
   d. The Dividends account is closed. This is accomplished by crediting Dividends for the amount required to give it a zero balance, and debiting Retained Earnings for the same amount. Note that the Income Summary account is not involved in this closing entry.

OBJECTIVE 7: Prepare the post-closing trial balance (p. 182).

8. After the closing entries are posted to the ledger, a **post-closing trial balance** must be prepared to verify again the equality of the debits and credits in the accounts. Only balance sheet accounts appear because all income statement accounts have zero balances at this point.

OBJECTIVE 8: Prepare reversing entries as appropriate (pp. 182–187).

9. At the end of each accounting period, the accountant makes adjusting entries to record accrued revenues and expenses. Many of the adjusting entries are followed in the next period by the receipt or payment of cash. Thus it would become necessary in the next period to make a special entry dividing amounts between the two periods. To avoid this inconvenience, the accountant can make **reversing entries** (dated the beginning of the new period). Reversing entries, though not required, allow the bookkeeper to simply make the routine bookkeeping entry when cash finally changes hands. Not all adjusting entries may be reversed. In the system we will use, only adjustments for accruals may be reversed. Deferrals may not.

Summary of Journal Entries Introduced in Chapter 4

A. (L.O. 6) Advertising Fees Earned   XX (current credit balance)
        Art Fees Earned   XX (current credit balance)
           Income Summary   XX (sum of revenue amounts)
             To close revenue accounts

B. (L.O. 6) Income Summary   XX (sum of expense amounts)
           Office Wages Expense   XX (current debit balance)
           Utility Expense   XX (current debit balance)
             To close expense accounts

C. (L.O. 6) Income Summary   XX (current credit balance)
           Retained Earnings   XX (net income amount)
             To close Income Summary account,
             profit situation

D. (L.O. 6) Retained Earnings   XX (net loss amount)
           Income Summary   XX (current debit balance)
             To close Income Summary account,
             loss situation

E. (L.O. 6) Retained Earnings   XX (dividends for period)
           Dividends   XX (dividends for period)
             To close Dividends account

F. (L.O. 8) Office Wages Expense   XX (amount incurred)
           Wages Payable   XX (amount to be paid)
             To accrue unrecorded wages

G. (L.O. 8) Wages Payable   XX (amount previously accrued)
           Office Wages Expense   XX (amount accrued this period)
           Cash   XX (amount paid)
             Paid wages; entry F above was *not* reversed

H. (L.O. 8) Wages Payable   XX (amount to be paid)
           Office Wages Expense   XX (amount incurred)
             Reversing entry for F above (assume Office
             Wages Expense had been closed at end
             of period)

I. (L.O. 8) Office Wages Expense   XX (amount paid)
           Cash   XX (amount paid)
             Paid wages; entry F above *was* reversed

J. (L.O. 8) Income Taxes Payable   XX (amount estimated)
           Income Taxes Expense   XX (amount estimated)
             Reversing entry for income taxes adjustment

K. (L.O. 8) Advertising Fees Earned   XX (amount accrued)
           Fees Receivable   XX (amount accrued)
             Reversing entry for accrued fees adjustment

Testing Your Knowledge

Matching

Match each term with its definition by writing the appropriate letter in the blank.

—— 1. Accounting cycle

—— 2. Working papers

—— 3. Work sheet

—— 4. Foot

—— 5. Crossfooting

—— 6. Reversing entry

—— 7. Closing entries

—— 8. Income Summary

—— 9. Post-closing trial balance

a. An account used only during closing entries
b. Add a column
c. The means of transferring net income or loss to the Retained Earnings account
d. The sequence from transaction analysis to closing entries
e. A final proof that the accounts are in balance
f. The opposite of an adjusting entry, journalized to facilitate routine bookkeeping entries
g. Documents that help accountants organize their work
h. Adding from left to right
i. A working paper that facilitates the preparation of financial statements

Short Answer

Use the lines provided to answer each item.

1. What four accounts or kinds of accounts are closed out each accounting period?

_____

_____

_____

_____

2. List the five columnar headings of a work sheet in their proper order.

_____

_____

_____

_____

3. In general, what accounts will appear in the post-closing trial balance? What accounts will *not* appear?

_____

_____

_____

_____

4. Briefly, explain the *purpose* of reversing entries.

_____

_____

_____

_____

Completing the Accounting Cycle.

True-False

Circle T if the statement is true, F if it is false. Please provide explanations for the false answers, using the blank lines at the end of the section.

T F **1.** The work sheet is prepared before the formal adjusting entries have been made in the journal.

T F **2.** Preparation of a work sheet helps reduce the possibility of overlooking an adjustment.

T F **3.** Total debits will differ from total credits in the Balance Sheet columns of a work sheet by the amount of the net income or loss.

T F **4.** The statement of retained earnings is prepared after the formal income statement, but before the formal balance sheet.

T F **5.** The Income Summary account can be found in the statement of retained earnings.

T F **6.** Closing entries convert real and nominal accounts to zero balances.

T F **7.** When revenue accounts are closed, the Income Summary account will be credited.

T F **8.** The Dividends account is closed to the Income Summary account.

T F **9.** When the Income Summary account is closed, it always requires a debit.

T F **10.** Reversing entries are never required.

T F **11.** The work sheet is published with the balance sheet and income statement, as a supplementary statement.

T F **12.** A key letter is needed in the Adjusted Trial Balance columns of a work sheet to show whether the entry is extended to the Balance Sheet columns or the Income Statement columns.

T F **13.** If total debits exceed total credits (before balancing) in the Income Statement columns of a work sheet, that means that a net loss has occurred.

T F **14.** The post-closing trial balance will include the Dividends account.

Multiple Choice

Circle the letter of the best answer.

1. Which account will appear in the post-closing trial balance?
   a. Interest Income
   b. Income Summary
   c. Retained Earnings
   d. Dividends

2. Which of the following statements is true?
   a. Closing entries are prepared before formal adjusting entries.
   b. The work sheet is prepared after the post-closing trial balance.
   c. Formal adjusting entries are prepared before the work sheet.
   d. The financial statements are prepared before closing entries.

3. Reversing entries
   a. are dated as of the end of the period.
   b. are the opposite of adjusting entries.
   c. may be made for depreciation previously recorded.
   d. are the opposite of closing entries.

4. If total debits exceed total credits (before balancing) in the Balance Sheet columns of a work sheet,
   a. a net income has occurred.
   b. a net loss has occurred.
   c. a mistake has definitely been made.
   d. no conclusions can be drawn until the closing entries have been made.

5. Which of the following accounts would *not* be involved in closing entries?
   a. Unearned Commissions
   b. Retained Earnings
   c. Telephone Expense
   d. Dividends

6. When a net loss has occurred,
   a. all expense accounts are closed with debits.
   b. the Income Summary account is closed with a credit.
   c. the Dividends account is closed with a debit.
   d. all revenue accounts are closed with credits.

7. Which of the following is *not* an objective of closing entries?
   a. To transfer net income or loss into Retained Earnings
   b. To produce zero balances in all nominal accounts
   c. To update the revenue and expense accounts
   d. To be able to measure net income for the following period

8. A corporation began the accounting period with $50,000 in retained earnings, ended with $75,000 in retained earnings, and declared $30,000 in dividends. What was the corporation's net income or loss for the period?
   a. $55,000 net income
   b. $30,000 net loss
   c. $5,000 net loss
   d. $5,000 net income

Applying Your Knowledge

Exercises

1. Following are the accounts of a work sheet's Adjusted Trial Balance for the month of July. In the journal provided, make the necessary closing entries. All accounts have normal balances.

Accounts Payable	$ 1,000
Accounts Receivable	2,000

Cash	$13,500
Common Stock	10,000
Dividends	2,500
Rent Expense	500
Retained Earnings	3,000
Revenue from Services	4,700
Telephone Expense	50
Utility Expense	150

General Journal				
Date		Description	Debit	Credit

2. Using the information from Exercise 1, complete the following statement of retained earnings.

Barrett's Fix-It Services, Inc.
Statement of Retained Earnings
For the Month Ended July 31, 19xx

3. The following items *a* through *g* provide the information needed to make adjustments for Steve's Maintenance, Inc., as of December 31, 19xx. Complete the entire work sheet on the next page using this information. Remember to use key letters for each adjustment.

a. On December 31, there is $200 of unexpired rent on the storage garage.

b. Depreciation taken on the lawn equipment during the period amounts to $1,500.

c. An inventory of lawn supplies shows $100 remaining on December 31.

d. Accrued wages on December 31 amount to $280.

e. Grass-cutting fees earned but as yet uncollected amount to $50.

f. Of the $300 landscaping fees paid for in advance, $120 had been earned by December 31.

g. Accrued income tax expense for the year amounts to $1,570. This amount will be paid early next year.

4. On December 1, Bowman Company borrowed $20,000 from a bank on a note for 90 days at 12 percent (annual) interest. Assuming that interest is not included in the face amount, prepare the following journal entries:

a. December 1 entry to record the note

b. December 31 entry to record accrued interest

c. December 31 entry to close interest

d. January 1 reversing entry

e. March 1 entry to record payment of note plus interest.

General Journal				
Date		Description	Debit	Credit

Steve's Maintenance, Inc.
Work Sheet
For the Year Ended December 31, 19xx

Account Name	Trial Balance		Adjustments		Adjusted Trial Balance		Income Statement		Balance Sheet	
	Debit	Credit	Debit	Credit	Debit	Credit	Debit	Credit	Debit	Credit
Cash	2,560									
Accounts Receivable	880									
Prepaid Rent	750									
Lawn Supplies	250									
Lawn Equipment	10,000									
Accum. Deprec., Lawn Equip.		2,000								
Accounts Payable		630								
Unearned Landscaping Fees		300								
Common Stock		5,000								
Retained Earnings		1,000								
Dividends	6,050									
Grass-Cutting Fees		15,000								
Wages Expense	3,300									
Gasoline Expense	140									
	23,930	23,930								
Rent Expense										
Depreciation Expense										
Lawn Supplies Expense										
Landscaping Fees Earned										
Wages Payable										
Income Taxes Expense										
Income Taxes Payable										
Net Income										

Reading

Accounting for Baseball

In May 1985 I received a call from Lee MacPhail, chairman of the Player Relations Committee. The committee represented the baseball club owners in the then ongoing contract negotiations with the Players' Association. MacPhail asked me if I'd be willing to analyze the financial statements of the major league clubs and express an opinion (professorial, not auditorial) on whether these clubs, in the aggregate, were "making or losing" money on baseball operations. This issue was one of the bones of contention between the owners and the players in the negotiations.

Would I be willing? What a question to ask a lifelong, avid baseball fan. (Actually, I'm a fan of the Chicago Cubs, a club that hasn't always been synonymous with baseball.) When I was at the University of Chicago, I instructed my students to yell "Debit!" instead of "Charge!" whenever the bugle blew at Wrigley Field. Of course I was willing; indeed, I suggested to MacPhail that I'd waive compensation if he assured me that the Cubs would continue to play all post-season games in the daytime at Wrigley Field. He opted for monetary compensation.

What would be so difficult about determining whether the clubs were profitable? I soon found out that the adage, "If all economists were laid end to end they still wouldn't reach a conclusion about what 'income' meant," arguably—and with even greater force—applied to those concerned with discovering baseball's profit or loss.

The alleged loss or profit from baseball operations varied from an announced $65 million loss to a reported $43 million loss to a profit of $9 million. It depended on whom you listened to. It will come as no great surprise that my analysis convinced me that the correct answer was "D. None of the above." As a result, I united owners and players in being mad at me, thereby convincing me that I must have done a good job.

In conducting the analysis, I soon found that baseball accounting was plagued by almost all of today's hotly debated theoretical accounting issues—present value, the accounting unit, executory contracts, intangibles, related-party transactions and more. Even more important, I was reinforced in my belief that we—academic and public accountants alike—have been deficient in explaining what accounting is—and is not—to vitally concerned and interested audiences.

This article briefly describes the data available, the basis for my findings and a discussion of the implications of the accounting and communications issues I encountered.

The Data

Most baseball clubs are either limited partnerships or divisions of other entities and thus ordinarily wouldn't be required to issue audited financial statements. The baseball commissioner, however, has for a number of years required each club to provide audited financial statements. Since there is no uniform baseball accounting—even when a consensus about the bottom-line figures exists (which is not always the case)—there is dazzling geographical variety in terms of where the numbers are reported and how they are aggregated in the various clubs' financial statements. This situation makes comparison and compilation difficult.

To cure this diversity, the commissioner requires each club to respond annually to a questionnaire on its reporting system that utilizes a standard format and is conducted by the CPA firm Ernst and Whinney. The resulting data are then summarized and communicated in what is popularly called the "8–10–8 report," which aggregates the data in terms of the highest, middle and lowest clubs.

According to the audited financial statements, the clubs, in the aggregate, had a bottom-line loss of $65 million in 1984. The E&W report reduced this loss of $65 million to $43 million by excluding nonbaseball operations and interest expense. Interest expense was excluded because it is a function of the capital structure of a club rather than of its baseball operations.

Parenthetically, one of the early concerns of the expert hired by the players was that owners were taking out concealed profits in the form of interest on loans they provided to the clubs, thus inflating losses. In the event, this concern proved to be unfounded because the E&W data (the data

Source: Article by George H. Sorter. Reprinted with permission from the *Journal of Accountancy*, Copyright © 1986 by American Institute of Certified Public Accountants, Inc. Opinions of the authors are their own and do not necessarily reflect policies of the AICPA.

communicated to the players' union in the contract negotiations) always reported losses before any interest charge. It was the $43 million loss figure that the owners consistently maintained was baseball's operating loss for 1984, and it was this figure that I was asked to comment on.

The Findings

Before I could reach any conclusions, I first did what had to be done: I traced the E&W figures to the audited financial statements and examined the reasonableness of the nonbaseball-item adjustments made by E&W. As I'd expected, there were no surprises. The monotony of doing this work was relieved when I realized that (1) a few minor adjustments needed to be made in addition to E&W's and (2) three major areas required further consideration and analysis.

The minor adjustments, which were readily agreed to by E&W and the owners, concerned some nonbaseball losses that one club had included as a baseball item and some reserves that two clubs had set up to provide for possible pension plan increases arising from the negotiations then being conducted. I thought this somewhat premature. These noncontroversial adjustments reduced the reported loss by about $1.5 million.

The three major areas that required further analysis were initial-roster depreciation, accounting for deferred compensation and related-party transactions.

Initial-roster depreciation. This represented the major and most controversial item that I believed had to be adjusted. When a club changes ownership, up to 50 percent of the purchase price is allocated to an asset that normally isn't considered an accounting asset—the players. This treatment is required by and consistent with both generally accepted accounting principles and rulings of the Internal Revenue Service. Once this asset is set up, it clearly must be amortized because baseball players don't play forever.

It is this amortization that is termed "initial-roster depreciation." This is a proper and required charge under GAAP, but should it be included under baseball operations? I think not.

The simplest explanation of why it should not, and the one I used in public, is that this charge arises *only* when ownership changes. Therefore two clubs with identical baseball operations would report different GAAP results if one was sold and the other wasn't. I concluded that this expense properly should be associated with ownership changes and therefore be excluded from the operating results. (While this explanation is valid as far as it goes, a more comprehensive analysis of initial-roster depreciation and its implications is provided later.)

Tracing the amount of initial-roster depreciation was somewhat difficult. It was included in various line items for different clubs and under different circumstances—if, for instance, the player on the initial roster was subsequently sold or released. After a diligent search I concluded that the proper initial-roster depreciation amount in 1984 was approximately $12 million, and I reduced the loss accordingly.

Deferred compensation. As everyone who reads the sports pages knows, baseball contracts today are complex, and most players have compensation that is deferred for extensive periods well beyond the players' contractual obligations. There is no real question, despite widespread misunderstanding, that deferred compensation (under GAAP and common sense) must be considered an expense of the period in which the player plays and not of the period in which he gets paid. There is also no question—or should be none—that the proper amount to be expensed is the present value of such compensation.

"Should," however, is the operative word here. Inquiry soon disclosed that those keeping the clubs' books shared the usual confusion about present value and that a diversity of practice existed, depending on how the contract was worded.

Basically, three types of deferred compensation contracts exist. One states that a player, in addition to his current compensation, will receive $100,000 in the year 2000. In a sense this represents a defined-benefit plan and, invariably and appropriately, it was discounted and the present value reported as the expense.

A second type of contract states that a player will receive $500,000 a year, of which $100,000 is deferred at an interest rate of, say, 10 percent to the year 2000. In this contract the $100,000 accretes and compounds by the stated interest rate each year. As long as the stated interest rate approximates market, which it generally did, no discounting is required because the plan is essentially both a defined-contribution and a defined-benefit plan.

It was the third type of contract that posed the major problem. This type, now rare, states that a player will receive $500,000 a year, of which $100,000 is deferred to the year 2000. No interest rate is stated or implied by the contract and, thus, only $100,000 will be received in the year 2000.

In essence, this plan is a defined-benefit plan ($100,000) masquerading as a defined-contribution plan. Most, if not all, clubs in this circumstance didn't present-value the $100,000 in figuring player compensation expense and thus overstated the reported losses.

To determine which contract types existed and how much they amounted to, I queried each club about contract type and accounting method. This wasn't an easy task because, as noted earlier, there was a great deal of confusion about what discounting and present value represented and how it should be accounted for. I also had to determine whether the yearly interest accretions under the first and third types of contracts were appropriately reported as interest rather than as operating expense and thus excluded from baseball operating losses. The final adjustment I made wasn't significant amounting to approximately $700,000.

Related-party transactions. I found one related-party transaction that was easy to adjust. Until recently the parking and concession revenue of one baseball club was realized by a municipal corporation and thus didn't affect the operating results of the club. A year or so ago, however, the club's parent company purchased the municipal corporation's parking and concession rights, but the income of this now-related entity continued not to be reflected in the club's operations. For the purpose of my analysis, I consolidated the two entities and made an adjustment that further reduced the loss by $1.8 million.

A more important type of related-party transaction proved much more intractable. Two of the clubs, the Atlanta Braves and the Chicago Cubs, had television contracts with related "superstations." The Tribune Company owns both WGN-TV and the Cubs, and Ted Turner owns WTBS-TV and the Braves. What were the appropriate arm's-length fees that the Cubs and the Braves would receive from television contracts if they weren't with related parties?

In each case we have one buyer and one seller in a unique national market. I found no way to determine what an independently bargained price might be, especially in the case of the Braves, since there was no contract before the club and the station were related. There is no doubt that, as national stations, WTBS-TV and WGN-TV derive benefits from having exclusive and enduring rights to the two clubs as stable, salable programming items. And the Braves and the Cubs benefit from the increased home and road attendance by virtue of the national exposure they receive. This is especially true for the Braves, who are labeled "America's team."

An extensive economic and marketing analysis would be required to determine what the appropriate fee arrangement might be and, I would hazard to guess, it would be open to question and challenge even then. I believed that, given these circumstances, no reasonable adjustment could be made, and I contented myself with noting and disclosing the relationship and the problem in my report.

After all these adjustments were made, I expressed my view that baseball's operating loss for 1984 was $27 million—or approximately $1 million a club on the average. This appeared a hard loss, but would there be any favorable tax consequences?

The tax consequences, it turned out, couldn't be determined because they depended on the tax status of the person or corporation that owned the club. In any case, I didn't consider the tax consequences relevant in assessing the operating results. It is clear that baseball clubs did not and do not possess the characteristics of an attractive tax shelter. There may be many reasons for owning a baseball club, but making money—before or after taxes—doesn't appear to be one of them. (This finding wasn't greeted with tumultuous applause—but more about that later.)

Implications of the Accounting Issues

The initial-roster depreciation problem, on reflection, isn't confined to the esoteric, isolated situation prevailing in professional sports. It arises whenever an economic asset that generally isn't treated as an accounting asset is recognized as one. In these cases a type of double counting inevitably results.

Perhaps the clearest example is provided when a company conducting research is acquired by another company. The patents of the acquiring company result from past research expenditures and, under GAAP, weren't recorded as assets of the original company. They are, however, shown as assets for the parent. In future periods, when the parent continues to conduct research, it will recognize as an expense both past research expenditures (through amortization of the acquired patents) and current research expenditures (which cannot be capitalized). Though a case may be made for treating both as expenses, I think only one can properly be treated as an operating expense. The depreciation of the acquired asset is caused by the sale of a company, not by its operations.

This example is analogous to the matter at hand—initial-roster depreciation. Player development expenditures aren't capitalized unless a club is sold, at which time it is capitalized in the initial roster. Thus the club that has been sold recognizes both past and current player development expenditures as an expense, and the operating income of a club that has been sold will be less over its lifetime than the operating income of one that hasn't been.

It seems clear that operating expenditures should include either past or current player development expenditures—but not both.

The initial-roster asset may not be due to past player development expenditures but, rather, to "appreciation of player value." In this case the past value appreciation, which was never part of operating income, is expensed while the current appreciation isn't recorded as operating income. Thus, over the lifetime of the club, operating income for a club that is sold is again, less than the operating income for a club that has never been sold.

Even more general is the implication that the allocation of excess of cost over book value required under Accounting Principles Board Opinion no. 16, *Business Combinations,* is faulty to the extent that this allocation is allowed to affect the operating income of an entity whose operations continue relatively unchanged. Perhaps the approach of the good old days—when the excess of cost over book value was allocated to goodwill rather than to individual assets—wasn't so unrealistic and produces more reasonable results if goodwill amortization is excluded from operating income.

As for the questions that arose about present value, it is clear that accounting doesn't adequately solve the problem of how to report the impact of the timing of cash flows. The diverse accounting treatments of deferred compensation, as well as some balance sheet items found in baseball's financial statements that aren't discussed here, provide only minor evidence of this deficiency. More important is the prevailing impression that baseball's operating losses are irrelevant because an immense profit can always be reaped by selling a club.

This impression indicates a widespread lack of understanding of the impact of compound interest and is best illustrated by a question I always ask beginning students: "When the Indians sold Manhattan Island for $24, who got the better deal?" Rarely will a student give the correct answer: "It depends—on the interest rate."

We see a similar confusion about what the profits realized by the sale of a baseball club really are. If a club is sold every 15 years in order to compensate for the average $1 million operating loss a year, a "profit" on sale of almost $32 million would have to be realized if the interest rate is 10 percent (the future value of an annuity of $1 million for 15 years at an assumed 10 percent interest rate is $31.8 million). This gain doesn't include any interest or return on the original purchase price. If we include interest on an assumed purchase price of $15 million at 10 percent, the "profit" on sale would have to increase by an additional $47.7 million.

Thus, to recoup the original purchase price plus the operating losses (after adjusting for the time value of money) would require that a club purchased for $15 million would have to be sold 15 years later for $94.5 million. Even though the seller would then just break even, a profit on sale of $79.5 million would be reported. So much for the "obscene profits" achieved by selling a club.

The diversity of practice and the misunderstanding of results raise another question: How good a job is the accounting profession doing in reporting the impact of differences in timing when cash flows of different time periods are "matched" in financial reports?

Accountants have spent a great deal of time in debating the proper accounting treatment in periods of changing prices, but they've spent much less time worrying about the more basic problem of reporting the impact of differential timing of cash flows. In the American Institute of CPAs 1973 Trueblood report on the objectives of financial statements, which I helped draft, it was concluded for the first time that "the amount, timing, and uncertainty of cash flows" are basic to the objectives of accounting. (This conclusion was later affirmed in Financial Accounting Standards Board Concepts Statement no. 1, *Objectives of Financial Reporting by Business Enterprises.*)

I must admit I'd thought that, more than a decade after the report, this problem would have been addressed and resolved. But the FASB still occasionally issues standards that can only be interpreted as ignoring their stated objective of reflecting differences in timing. The standard on restructured debt recognizes a loss only when the arithmetic but not the present value of a receivable is impaired, thus ignoring timing differences.

The board's proposed treatment of deferred taxes suggests that the liability method for deferred taxes should be adopted. But that liability isn't discounted to present value. I find it difficult to believe that sanctioning a nondiscounted liability will greatly advance an understanding of the importance of the timing dimension.

Implications of the Communication Issues

I've already observed that everyone was unhappy with my findings. The owners couldn't understand why proper GAAP accounting doesn't serve every purpose and had to be adjusted in their circumstances. The players couldn't understand why and how there could be a loss when there was a $9 million excess of cash receipts over disbursements for the clubs as a whole. It is that excess which the players' union insisted on calling income.

Thus, in some sense, GAAP accounting was simultaneously being challenged for doing too much—it went beyond the actual "cash flow"—and too little—it wasn't always appropriate and didn't serve every need and purpose.

This confusion strongly suggests that the profession hasn't done all that it might in communicating what accounting is and does, what it is not and does not, what its strengths and limitations are.

The players' misunderstanding was somewhat easier to clear up than the owners'. I was able to demonstrate to the players that the accounting data did indeed deal with hard cash flows rather than paper flows but that these cash flows included not only present cash flows but also past and highly probable future cash flows; that the accounting data had to include not only the cash paid to players but also the payments required to be made under deferred compensation contracts and the payments that had been made to acquire a stadium.

I was also able to explain that there are necessary differences between revenues and receipts and between expenses and expenditures. I told them that, basically, revenues represent past, present and future cash receipts that require no future outflows, whereas expenses are past, present or future expenditures that occasion no future inflows. Thus I was somewhat successful in indicating that deferred compensation didn't decrease cash because it really could be thought of as payment to a player who then loaned the money to the club. That implied loan clearly shouldn't be considered a revenue item that offsets the salary expense.

What's disturbing is that this explanation was necessary. If we had done our job, a vitally concerned and well-educated audience would have understood more readily.

It is more difficult to convince owners, among others, that accounting is *not* the final word or the ultimate answer and, indeed, isn't an answer at all. Accounting data don't provide answers—they're helpful in trying to arrive at some. Accounting data are basically an archival, interpretive history of actual and highly probable cash flows. Clearly such an archival history is useful in disclosing important relationships among past events that, in turn, are helpful in illuminating the present and in making decisions about the future. Equally obviously, however, such a data base of cash-significant events doesn't say everything about the past or present and says nothing, in and of itself, about the future.

The fact that the nature—the substance—of accounting is so little understood, even by intelligent, interested parties, is reflected not only in the response to a basically trivial report about baseball but also, and of more importance, in today's litigious environment. Clearly we have to do a better job explaining what we do and why we do it.

In retrospect, accounting for baseball was easy—accounting for accounting may be more difficult.

CHAPTER 5 ACCOUNTING FOR MERCHANDISING OPERATIONS

Reviewing the Chapter

OBJECTIVE 1: Compare the income statements for service and merchandising concerns (pp. 210–212).

1. A merchandising firm is a wholesaler or retailer that buys and sells goods (merchandise) in finished form. Such a firm uses the same basic accounting methods as a service company. However, merchandising requires some additional accounts and concepts and results in a more complicated income statement.

2. Service companies calculate net income by simply deducting expenses from revenues. However, the income of a merchandising firm is computed as follows:

   Revenues from sales
   − Cost of goods sold
   = Gross margin from sales
   − Operating expenses
   = Income before income taxes
   − Income taxes
   = **Net income**

   a. **Revenues from sales** (net sales) consist of gross proceeds from the sale of merchandise (gross sales) less sales returns and allowances and sales discounts.

   b. **Cost of goods sold** is the amount that the merchandising company originally paid for the goods that it sold during a given period. If; for example, a merchandising firm sells for $100 a radio that cost the company $70, then revenues from sales

are $100, cost of goods sold is $70, and **gross margin from sales** (also called **gross margin**) is $30. This $30 gross margin helps pay for **operating expenses** (all expenses other than cost of goods sold and income taxes). What is left after subtracting operating expenses represents **income before income taxes** (also called **operating income** or **income from operations**). Preparing an income statement in this way provides useful information to management, which is continually trying to improve net income.

OBJECTIVE 2: Record transactions involving revenues for merchandising concerns (pp. 212–215).

3. When a cash sale is made, Cash is debited and Sales is credited for the amount of the sale. When a credit sale is made, Accounts Receivable is debited and Sales is credited. (At the point of sale, it is not known whether the customer will pay within the discount period or will return some goods.) Generally, a sale is recorded when the goods are delivered and title passes to the customer, regardless of when payment is made.

4. As a matter of convenience, manufacturers and wholesalers frequently quote prices of merchandise based on a discount from the list or catalog price (called a **trade discount**).

5. When a cash customer returns goods for a refund, **Sales Returns and Allowances** is debited and Cash is credited. For a credit

customer, Sales Returns and Allowances is debited and Accounts Receivable is credited. The Sales Returns and Allowances account is debited instead of the Sales account to provide management with data about dissatisfied customers. In the income statement it is a contra account to **Gross Sales.**

6. When goods are sold on credit, terms will vary as to when payment must be made. For instance, n/30 means that full payment is due within 30 days after the invoice date, and n/10 eom means that full payment is due 10 days after the end of the month.

7. Often a customer is given a discount for early payment, and the merchandiser records a sales discount. Terms of **2/10, n/30,** for example, mean that a 2 percent discount will be given if payment is made within 10 days of the invoice date. Otherwise, the net amount is due within 30 days.

8. **Sales discounts** are recorded when payment is received within the discount period. Cash and Sales Discounts are debited; Accounts Receivable is credited. Sales Discounts is a contra account to Gross Sales in the income statement. When Sales Discounts and Sales Returns and Allowances are deducted from gross sales in the income statement, the difference is labeled **net sales.**

OBJECTIVE 3: Calculate cost of goods sold (pp. 215–216).

9. A merchandiser's amount of goods on hand at any one time is called **merchandise inventory.** The accountant uses merchandise inventory figures to calculate cost of goods sold as follows:

    Beginning inventory (at cost)
 + Net purchases (see paragraph 10)
 = **Goods available for sale**
 − Ending inventory (at cost)
 = Cost of goods sold

10. Net purchases is calculated as follows:

    (Gross) purchases
 − Purchases returns and allowances
 − Purchases discounts
 = Subtotal
 + Freight in
 = Net purchases

OBJECTIVE 4: Record transactions involving purchases of merchandise (pp. 216–220).

11. Under the periodic inventory system, all purchases of merchandise are debited to the **Purchases** account and credited to Cash or Accounts Payable. The purpose of the Purchases account is to accumulate the cost of merchandise purchased for resale during the period. **Net purchases** equals gross purchases minus purchases returns and allowances and purchases discounts, plus freight in.

12. If goods are returned to a supplier, the merchandiser debits Cash or Accounts Payable and credits **Purchases Returns and Allowances.** Purchases Returns and Allowances is a contra account to Purchases in the income statement.

13. Often a merchandising company is offered a discount if it pays within a given number of days. It may select either the gross method or the net method of recording the transaction.
  a. Under the **gross method,** the purchase is initially recorded at the gross purchase price. If the company makes payment within the discount period, it debits Accounts Payable, credits **Purchases Discounts,** and credits Cash.
  b. Under the **net method,** the purchase is recorded at first at the net purchase price (that is, the gross purchase price less the purchase discount offered). If the company does *not* make payment within the discount period, it debits Accounts Payable, debits Purchases Discounts Lost, and credits Cash. However, if payment *is* made within the discount period, no discount account is recorded.

14. When a merchandising firm pays for transportation costs on goods purchased, it debits **Freight In** (or **Transportation In**) and credits Cash. A merchandiser in Chicago, for instance, must pay the freight in from Boston if the terms specify FOB Boston or **FOB shipping point.** However, the supplier in Boston pays if the terms are FOB Chicago or **FOB destination.** Freight out is a cost of selling (not buying) merchandise, and should not be confused with freight in.

OBJECTIVE 5: Differentiate the perpetual inventory system from the periodic inventory system (pp. 220–223).

15. There are two ways of determining inventory.
    a. The **perpetual inventory system** is used when it is necessary to keep a record of the cost of each inventory item when it is purchased and when it is sold.
    b. The **periodic inventory system** is used when it is unnecessary or impractical to keep track of the cost of each item. Under this method, the company instead waits until the end of the accounting period to **take a physical inventory.** This physical count figure is then multiplied by a derived cost-per-unit figure (explained in Chapter 8) to arrive at the cost of ending inventory.

16. The **ending inventory** of one period automatically becomes the **beginning inventory** of the next period. The beginning inventory is removed from the inventory account and the ending inventory is entered into the inventory account by means of closing entries.

17. Merchandise inventory appears as an asset in the balance sheet and includes all salable goods owned by the company, no matter where the goods are located. Goods in transit to which a company has acquired title are included in ending inventory. However, goods that the company has formally sold are not included, even if the company has not yet delivered them. To simplify inventory taking, which usually takes place on the last day of the fiscal year, many companies end their fiscal year during the slow season.

18. Inventory losses result from theft and spoilage, and are automatically included in the cost of goods sold under the periodic inventory system.

19. Operating expenses consist of selling expenses and general and administrative expenses. Selling expenses are advertising expenses, salespeople's salaries, sales office expenses, freight out, and all other expenses directly related to the sales effort. General and administrative expenses are all expenses not directly related to the manufacturing or sales effort. Examples are general office expenses and executive salaries.

OBJECTIVE 6: Prepare an income statement for a merchandising concern (pp. 224–225).

20. The income statement of a merchandising company consists of a revenues from sales section, a cost of goods sold section, a gross margin from sales figure, and an operating expenses section consisting of selling expenses and general and administrative expenses. In addition, income taxes will be shown directly above net income.

OBJECTIVE 7: Explain the objectives of handling merchandise inventory at the end of the accounting period and how they are achieved (pp. 224–227).

21. Under a periodic inventory system, the objectives of dealing with inventory at the end of the period are to (a) remove the beginning balance from the Merchandise Inventory account, (b) enter the ending balance into the Merchandise Inventory account, and (c) enter these two amounts into the Income Summary account. These objectives are met by applying either the adjusting entry method or the closing entry method. Though different in form, both methods credit Merchandise Inventory and debit Income Summary for the beginning balance and debit Merchandise Inventory and credit Income Summary for the ending balance.

OBJECTIVE 8: Prepare a work sheet and adjusting and closing entries for a merchandising concern (pp. 227–231).

22. Preparation of a merchandiser's work sheet depends on whether the adjusting entry method or the closing entry method is being used. (However, only the closing entry method is illustrated in the textbook.) Under either method, the Adjusted Trial Balance column may be eliminated if only a few adjustments are necessary. In addition, many income statement accounts that appear in the merchandiser's work sheet do not appear in the service company's work sheet. Merchandise Inventory, however, must receive special treatment. Under the closing entry method, Merchandise Inventory bypasses the Adjustments column. Instead, beginning inventory appears as a debit in the Income Statement column. Ending inventory appears as a credit in the Income Statement column and as a debit in the Balance Sheet column.

23. The formal adjusting and closing entries for a merchandiser are similar to those for a service company, with the following exceptions. Under the closing entry method, Beginning Inventory, Sales Returns and Allowances, Sales Discounts, Purchases, Freight In, and Freight Out are closed in the same entry that closes expenses. Purchases Returns and Allowances and Purchases Discounts are closed, and Ending Inventory is debited (to record the new balance), in the same entry that closes revenues.

OBJECTIVE 9: Define *internal control* and identify the three elements of the internal control structure, including seven examples of control procedures (pp. 232–233).

24. A business establishes a system of **internal control** to (a) safeguard its assets, (b) check the accuracy and reliability of its accounting data, (c) promote operational efficiency, and (d) encourage adherence to prescribed managerial policies. To achieve these objectives, management must establish an **internal control structure** consisting of three elements: the control environment, the accounting system, and the control procedures.

    a. The **control environment** reflects such things as management's philosophy and operating style, the company's organizational structure, methods of assigning authority and responsibility, and personnel policies and practices.

    b. The **accounting system** consists of methods and records established by management to provide assurance that the objectives of internal control are achieved.

    c. Management must establish **control procedures** to ensure the safeguarding of assets and the reliability of the accounting records. Examples of control procedures are (1) required authorization for certain transactions, (2) recording of all transactions, (3) design and use of adequate documents, (4) limited access to assets, (5) periodic independent verification of records, (6) separation of duties, and (7) sound personnel procedures. **Bonding** an employee (an example of a good control procedure) means insuring the company against theft by that individual.

OBJECTIVE 10: Describe the inherent limitations of internal control (pp. 233–234).

25. To be effective, a system of internal control must rely on the people who perform the du-

ties assigned. Thus, the effectiveness of internal control is limited by the people involved. For example, human error, collusion, and changing conditions can all contribute to the weakening of a system of internal control.

OBJECTIVE 11: Apply control procedures to certain merchandising transactions (pp. 234–241).

26. Accounting controls over merchandising transactions help prevent losses from theft or fraud, and help assure accurate accounting records. Administrative controls over merchandising transactions should help to keep inventory levels balanced, to keep enough cash on hand to make early payments for purchases discounts, and to avoid credit losses.

27. Several procedures should be followed to achieve effective internal control over sales and the exchange of cash.

28. Cash received by mail should be handled by two or more employees. Cash received from sales over the counter should be controlled through the use of cash registers and prenumbered sales tickets. At the end of each day, Cash is debited for cash receipts, and Sales is credited for the amount on the cash register tape.

29. All cash payments for purchases should be made by check. However, before employees pay cash, they should get authorization in the form of certain signed documents. The system of authorization and the documents used will differ among companies, but the most common documents are described below.

    a. A **purchase requisition** is completed by a department requesting that the company purchase something for the department.

    b. A **purchase order** is completed by the department responsible for the company's purchasing activities; it is sent to the vendor.

    c. An **invoice** is the bill sent to the buyer from the vendor.

    d. A **receiving report** is completed by the receiving department; it contains information about the quantity and condition of goods received.

    e. A **check authorization** is a document showing that the purchase order, purchase requisition, receiving report, and invoice are in agreement, and that payment is therefore approved.

f. When payment is approved, a **check** is issued to the vendor for the amount of the invoice, less the appropriate discount. Remittance advice should be attached to the check, describing the articles being paid for.

Summary of Journal Entries Introduced in Chapter 5

A. (L.O. 2) Cash   XX (amount received)
     Sales   XX (sales price)
       Sale of merchandise for cash

B. (L.O. 2) Accounts Receivable   XX (amount to be received)
     Sales   XX (sales price)
       Sale of merchandise on credit

C. (L.O. 2) Sales Returns and Allowances   XX (price of goods returned)
     Accounts Receivable   XX (amount credited to account)
       Customer returned merchandise, account
       credited

D. (L.O. 2) Sales Returns and Allowances   XX (price of goods returned)
     Cash   XX (amount refunded)
       Customer returned merchandise for cash
       refund

E. (L.O. 2) Cash   XX (net amount received)
     Sales Discounts   XX (discount taken)
     Accounts Receivable   XX (gross amount settled)
       Customer paid within discount period

F. (L.O. 2) Cash   XX (gross amount received)
     Accounts Receivable   XX (gross amount settled)
       Customer paid after discount period

G. (L.O. 4) Purchases   XX (purchase price)
     Accounts Payable   XX (amount to be paid)
       Purchased merchandise on credit

H. (L.O. 4) Accounts Payable   XX (amount returned)
     Purchases Returns and Allowances   XX (amount returned)
       Returned merchandise to supplier, for credit

I. (L.O. 4) Accounts Payable   XX (gross amount settled)
     Purchases Discounts   XX (discount taken)
     Cash   XX (net amount paid)
       Paid supplier within discount period

J. (L.O. 4) Accounts Payable   XX (gross amount settled)
     Cash   XX (gross amount paid)
       Paid supplier after discount period

K. (L.O. 4) Freight In   XX (price charged)
     Accounts Payable (or Cash)   XX (amount due or paid)
       Incurred freight charges

L. (L.O. 4) Accounts Payable   XX (net of discount)
     Purchases Discounts Lost   XX (late payment penalty)
     Cash   XX (amount paid)
       Paid supplier after discount period; net
       method used

*Adjusting Entry Method**

M. (L.O. 7) Income Summary   XX (beginning inventory amount)
        Merchandise Inventory   XX (beginning inventory amount)
           Adjusting entry #1

N. (L.O. 7) Merchandise Inventory   XX (ending inventory amount)
        Income Summary   XX (ending inventory amount)
           Adjusting entry #2

*Closing Entry Method***

O. (L.O. 8) Income Summary   XX (sum of credits)
        Merchandise Inventory   XX (beginning amount)
        Sales Returns and Allowances   XX (current debit balance)
        Sales Discounts   XX (current debit balance)
        Purchases   XX (current debit balance)
        Freight In   XX (current debit balance)
        All other expenses   XX (current debit balance)
           Closing entry #1

P. (L.O. 8) Merchandise Inventory   XX (ending amount)
        Sales   XX (current credit balance)
        Purchases Returns and Allowances   XX (current credit balance)
        Purchases Discounts   XX (current credit balance)
        Income Summary   XX (sum of debits)
           Closing entry #2

Q. (L.O. 8) Income Summary   XX (current credit balance)
        Retained Earnings   XX (net income amount)
           Closing entry #3

R. (L.O. 8) Retained Earnings   XX (amount declared)
        Dividends   XX (amount declared)
          Closing entry #4

---

*Subsequent closing entries for adjusting entry method not illustrated in text.

**Inventory-related adjusting entries not needed for closing entry method.

Testing Your Knowledge

Matching

Match each term with its definition by writing the appropriate letter in the blank.

_____ 1. Merchandiser

_____ 2. Cost of goods sold

_____ 3. Gross margin from sales

_____ 4. Operating expenses

_____ 5. Sales returns and allowances

_____ 6. Sales discounts

_____ 7. Purchases discounts lost

_____ 8. Purchases

_____ 9. Goods available for sale

_____ 10. Perpetual inventory system

_____ 11. Periodic inventory system

_____ 12. Freight in

_____ 13. FOB (free on board)

_____ 14. Purchases returns and allowances

_____ 15. Purchases discounts

_____ 16. Internal control

_____ 17. Purchase requisition

_____ 18. Purchase order

_____ 19. Receiving report

_____ 20. Check authorization

a. Transportation cost for goods purchased

b. A document that authorizes payment

c. A buyer and seller of goods that are in finished form

d. A system whereby continuous cost records are maintained for merchandise

e. All expenses except for cost of goods sold

f. The point after which the buyer must bear the transportation cost

g. The account used to accumulate the cost of goods bought during the period

h. What a merchandising firm paid for the goods that it sold during the period

i. Beginning inventory plus net purchases

j. Revenue from sales minus cost of goods sold

k. Under the gross method of handling discounts, the account used by the seller when the buyer pays for goods early

l. The account used by the seller when the buyer returns goods

m. A system whereby continuous cost records are _not_ maintained for merchandise

n. Under the gross method of handling discounts, the account used by the buyer when it pays for goods early

o. An order for goods that is sent to the vendor

p. The account used by the buyer when it returns goods

q. A description of goods received by a company

r. A system designed to safeguard assets, promote operational efficiency, encourage adherence to managerial policies, and help achieve accounting accuracy

s. Under the net method of handling discounts, the account used by the buyer when it does not pay for goods early

t. A document requesting the purchasing department to order certain items

Short Answer

Use the lines provided to answer each item.

1. List the seven parts of a merchandiser's condensed income statement in their proper order. Use mathematical signs to indicate their relationship.

_____

_____

_____

_____

_____

_____

2. List the items in the condensed cost of goods sold section of an income statement. Use mathematical signs to indicate their relationship.

_____

_____

_____

_____

_____

3. Using mathematical signs, write the sequence of items involved in computing net purchases.

_____

_____

_____

_____

_____

4. Using mathematical signs, write the sequence of items involved in computing revenues from sales (net sales).

_____

_____

_____

_____

_____

5. Explain briefly how merchandise inventory is handled in the accounts at the end of the period under the adjusting entry method.

_____

_____

_____

_____

_____

_____

6. List and briefly describe the three elements of an internal control structure.

a. _____

_____

b. _____

_____

c. _____

_____

7. List seven control procedures that help make a system of internal control effective.

_____

_____

_____

_____

_____

_____

8. List any six procedures that may be employed to control and safeguard cash.

_____

_____

_____

_____

_____

_____

True-False

Circle T if the statement is true, F if it is false. Please provide explanations for the False answers, using the blank lines at the end of the section.

T F 1. Failure to include a warehouse's merchandise in ending inventory will result in an overstated net income.

T F 2. Terms of n/10 eom mean that payment must be made 10 days before the end of the month.

T F 3. An overstated beginning inventory will result in an overstated cost of goods sold.

T F 4. A low-volume car dealer is more likely to use the periodic inventory system than the perpetual inventory system.

T F 5. FOB destination means that the seller is bearing the transportation cost.

T F 6. The difference between the adjusting entry method and the closing entry method mainly concerns the treatment of merchandise inventory.

T F 7. Sales Discounts is a contra account to Net Sales.

T F 8. Ending inventory is needed for both the balance sheet and the income statement.

T F 9. Goods available for sale minus cost of goods sold equals ending inventory.

T F 10. The perpetual inventory system requires more detailed record keeping than does the periodic system.

T F 11. The beginning inventory of a period is the same as the ending inventory of the previous period.

T F 12. Purchases Returns and Allowances is closed with a credit.

T F 13. Sales Returns and Allowances normally has a credit balance.

T F 14. A cash purchase of office supplies that are meant to be used in the day-to-day operation of a business requires a debit to Purchases and a credit to Cash.

T F 15. Cost of goods sold will not appear in the income statement of a company that provides services only.

T F 16. If gross margin from sales is not enough to cover operating expenses, then a net loss has been suffered.

T F 17. Under a periodic inventory system, as soon as a sale is made, the cost of the goods sold must be recorded and the inventory account must be decreased.

T F 18. One example of a trade discount is 2/10, n/30.

T F 19. When goods are shipped FOB shipping point, title passes when the goods are received by the buyer.

T F 20. A good system of internal control will guarantee that the accounting records are accurate.

T F 21. Collusion refers to a secret agreement between two or more persons to defraud a company.

T F 22. The mail should be opened in the accounting department so that transactions may be recorded immediately.

T F 23. A company orders goods by sending the supplier a purchase requisition.

T F 24. Rotating employees in job assignments is poor internal control because employees would continually be forced to learn a new job skill.

_____

_____

_____

_____

_____

_____

_____

_____

_____

_____

Accounting for Merchandising Operations

Multiple Choice

Circle the letter of the best answer.

1. Burns buys $600 of merchandise from Allen, with terms of 2/10, n/30. Burns immediately returns $100 of goods, and pays for the remainder eight days after purchase. Assuming the gross method of handling discounts, Burns's entry on the date of payment would include a
   a. debit to Accounts Payable for $600.
   b. debit to Sales Discounts for $12.
   c. credit to Purchases Returns and Allowances for $100.
   d. credit to Purchases Discounts for $10.

2. Which of the following normally has a credit balance?
   a. Sales Discounts
   b. Merchandise Inventory
   c. Purchases Returns and Allowances
   d. Freight In

3. If an item of ending inventory is counted twice, then
   a. net income will be understated.
   b. beginning inventory for the next period will be understated.
   c. goods available for sale will be overstated.
   d. cost of goods sold will be understated.

4. Which of the following is irrelevant in computing cost of goods sold?
   a. Freight In
   b. Freight Out
   c. Merchandise Inventory, beginning
   d. Merchandise Inventory, ending

5. A company purchases $100 of goods on credit with terms of 2/10, n/30. If it initially records the purchase net of the discount available and subsequently pays within the discount period, its journal entry would include a
   a. debit to Purchases Discounts for $2.
   b. credit to Purchases Discounts for $2.
   c. credit to Cash for $100.
   d. debit to Accounts Payable for $98.

6. Which of the following is always credited when closed?
   a. Purchases Returns and Allowances
   b. Sales
   c. Beginning inventory
   d. Income Summary

7. Which of the following documents is prepared (by a buyer of goods) before all of the others?
   a. Purchase order
   b. Receiving report
   c. Check authorization (or voucher)
   d. Purchase requisition

8. Which of the following is an example of poor internal control?
   a. The receiving department comparing goods received with the related purchase order
   b. Forcing employees to take earned vacations
   c. Requiring someone other than the petty cash custodian to enter petty cash transactions into the accounting records
   d. Bonding employees

9. Which of the following accounts would appear as an operating expense in a merchandiser's income statement?
   a. Freight Out
   b. Sales Discounts
   c. Freight In
   d. Purchases

10. On the work sheet, assuming the closing entry method, ending inventory will appear on the
    a. debit side of the Income Statement columns.
    b. credit side of the Income Statement columns.
    c. debit side of the Balance Sheet columns.
    d. credit side of the Balance Sheet columns.

Applying Your Knowledge

Exercises

1. Following are the May transactions of Apex Merchandising Corporation. For each transaction, prepare the journal entry in the journal provided on the next page. Assume that the periodic inventory system is being used, as well as the gross method of handling purchases discounts.

May 1 Purchased merchandise for $500 on credit, terms 2/10, n/60.

3 Sold merchandise for $500 on credit, terms 2/10, 1/20, n/30.

4 Paid $42 for freight charges relating to a merchandise purchase of April.

5 Purchased office supplies for $100, on credit.

6 Returned $20 of the May 5 office supplies, for credit.

7 Returned $50 of merchandise purchased on May 1, for credit.

9 Sold merchandise for $225, on credit, terms 2/10, 1/15, n/30.

10 Paid for the merchandise purchased on May 1, less the return and any discount.

14 The customer of May 9 returned $25 of merchandise, for credit.

22 The customer of May 9 paid for the merchandise, less the return and any discount.

26 The customer of May 3 paid for the merchandise.

General Journal				
Date		Description	Debit	Credit

2. Following are the accounts and data needed to prepare the 19xx closing entries for Jefferson Merchandising Company. In the journal provided, prepare Jefferson's closing entries. Assume the closing entry method of handling merchandise inventory.

Advertising Expense	$ 5,000	Purchases	$ 50,000
Dividends	12,000	Purchases Discounts	500
Freight In	2,000	Purchases Returns and Allowances	500
Freight Out	4,000	Rent Expense	3,000
Income Taxes Expense	4,780	Retained Earnings	15,000
Income Taxes Payable	4,780	Sales	100,000
Interest Income	150	Sales Discounts	300
Merchandise Inventory (Jan. 1)	10,000	Sales Returns and Allowances	200
Merchandise Inventory (Dec. 31)	8,000	Wages Expense	7,000

General Journal				
Date		**Description**	**Debit**	**Credit**

3. Using the information from Exercise 2, prepare a partial income statement showing just the computation of gross margin from sales.

Jefferson Merchandising Company Partial Income Statement For the Year 19xx			

4. Using the information from Exercise 2, prepare Jefferson's *adjusting* entries to deal with merchandise inventory, if instead the adjusting entry method were used. Use the journal provided below.

General Journal				
Date		Description	Debit	Credit

5. The work sheet for Mammoth Mart, Inc., has
   been started, as shown on the next page. Use
   the following information to complete the
   work sheet (remember to key the adjustments).
   Assume the closing entry method of handling
   merchandise inventory. You will notice that
   the Adjusted Trial Balance column has been
   provided, even though it is not absolutely
   necessary.
   a. Expired rent, $250
   b. Accrued salaries, $500
   c. Depreciation on equipment, $375
   d. Ending merchandise inventory, $620
   e. Accrued Income Taxes Expense, $180

Mammoth Mart, Inc.
Work Sheet
For the Month Ended March 31, 19xx

Account Name	Trial Balance		Adjustments		Adjusted Trial Balance		Income Statement		Balance Sheet	
	Debit	Credit	Debit	Credit	Debit	Credit	Debit	Credit	Debit	Credit
Cash	1,000									
Accounts Receivable	700									
Merchandise Inventory	400									
Prepaid Rent	750									
Equipment	4,200									
Accounts Payable		900								
Common Stock		3,000								
Retained Earnings		1,200								
Sales		9,800								
Sales Discounts	300									
Purchases	3,700									
Purchases Returns and Allowances		150								
Freight In	400									
Salaries Expense	3,000									
Advertising Expense	600									
	15,050	15,050								

Crossword Puzzle
For Chapters 4 and 5

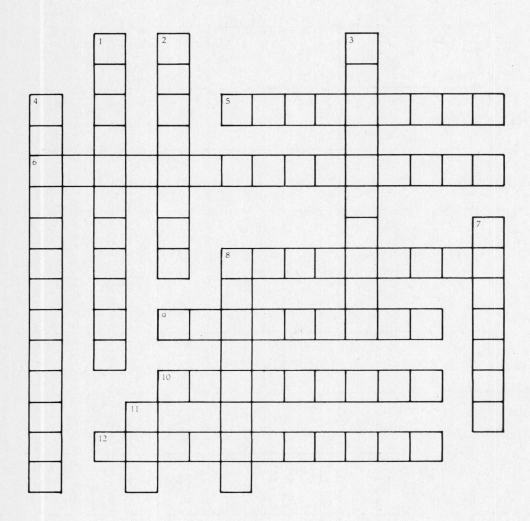

ACROSS

5. Entry opposite of adjusting
6. Inventory-related expense (4 words)
8. Method of accounting for inventory
9. Inventory-acquisition account
10. Add horizontally
12. FOB _____

DOWN

1. Income statement subtotal (2 words)
2. Reward for paying early
3. Aids to financial statement preparation (2 words)
4. Account used when clearing the accounts (2 words)
7. Clearing the accounts
8. Method of accounting for inventory
11. Method of accounting for discounts

Reading

Many Colleges Learn the Hard Way That They Are Vulnerable to Embezzlement by Employees and Need Strict Procedures

For eight years the Rev. John J. Steinberger worked diligently to help make the lives of poor students at Marquette University easier. As a manager of Marquette's Educational Opportunity Program, Father Steinberger administered a budget of about $1-million and oversaw grants and tutoring for 350 students.

People who knew the priest said he had dedicated himself to the destitute. While working toward his doctorate at Marquette, he drove 180 miles on weekends to work with poor Roman Catholic parishes in Chicago. When a job opened at the Educational Opportunity Program, Father Steinberger was hired with high recommendations from faculty members.

But there was another side to the man described as trustworthy and hardworking. While Father Steinberger was paying the program's bills, he was also pocketing thousands of dollars himself—about $100,000 in all—to support his cocaine habit.

John G. Hill, Jr., general counsel for Marquette, describes the reaction of many at the university: "We were shocked."

More Than 2 Dozen Colleges Stung

Shock is the response of most colleges and universities that have fallen victim to embezzlement. Although it is not known how many cases of embezzlement occur each year on campuses, more than two dozen colleges have been stung in the past few years—a sign, some observers say, that the wave of greed and fraud that swept through Wall Street in the 1980's has washed into academe.

Many financial officials say colleges and universities are acutally more vulnerable to embezzlement schemes than private businesses, because financial control on most campuses is decentralized. Too many people, they say, are managing too much money. The risk has increased somewhat because more campuses are consolidating jobs in an effort to cut costs, some officials add.

Employee theft has hit all kinds of institutions all across the country. The School of Theology at Claremont, for example, was taking steps to

Source: "Many Colleges Learn the Hard Way" by Julie L. Nicklin, *The Chronicle of Higher Education,* April 10, 1991. Reprinted by permission.

deal with the case of an employee who had stolen $15,000 in 1985 only to discover two years later that the business officer it had hired to correct the problem had pocketed about $270,000 himself.

The Kokomo campus of Indiana University learned in 1988 that it had lost about $430,000—mostly in petty-cash accounts—to a business manager who had forged and changed post-office receipts, among other practices.

Abuses at the Top

Sometimes, the abuse occurs at the very top. In 1988 the chancellor of the University of California at Santa Barbara was convicted of illegally using $174,000 of university money to renovate a house he had purchased. He is now appealing the conviction, arguing that the spending was appropriate because his home was often used for university events and fund raising.

Frederick J. Turk, national director for services to higher education with the accounting firm KPMG Peat Marwick, says the increasing number of employee thefts on campuses over the past few years has become "a disturbing trend."

Colleges are not immune to "the deterioration of our societal values which has led to an increase in fraud and abuse and misuse of power," says Mr. Turk. "The risk is greater today than it was."

Although some financial experts do not agree that embezzlement at universities is on the upswing, many warn that colleges are setting themselves up for problems if they do not establish a tone on their campuses that discourages employees from stealing. Many have learned that lesson the hard way and have since strengthened or adopted procedures to guard against theft.

Says Kurt R. Sjoberg, acting Auditor General for the State of California: "You shouldn't have to wait to create a bad apple. If someone thinks they have an opportunity to abuse the system, they're more likely to." Mr. Sjoberg has investigated many cases of embezzlement, including several at college campuses in the state.

Long-Time Employees

Like Marquette, most colleges say employees who stole from them appeared responsible and trustworthy—a situation that, according to auditors, lawyers, and investigators, explains how they often concealed their schemes. Most embezzlers, they say, were not seasoned thieves, but rather long-time employees—pressed for money—who discovered a way to get around a control.

That was the case at the Stanford University School of Medicine. Two years ago the university accused Rose L. Meller, an assistant to the head of neurology, of stealing more than $285,000. The university charged that Ms. Meller had obtained the money from 1976 to 1988 through petty cash, overtime payments, and other accounts, says Sarah Scholer Andersen, an agent for the fraud division of the Palo Alto police department, who investigated the case.

"They were trusting people too much," Ms. Andersen says of the university. Ms. Meller, who had worked at Stanford for about 16 years, "knew how to beat the system." Under terms of a settlement with Ms. Meller, university officials cannot discuss the case. The university was able to prove only that Ms. Meller had taken several thousand dollars, according to an official in the Santa Clara County District Attorney's office.

After discovering an embezzlement, many business officers say, a campus should immediately fire the employee and press charges to let other workers know the institution won't tolerate theft.

The University of New Orleans wasted no time deciding whether to file charges when officials discovered that George S. Wurz, director of financial aid, had cheated the university out of about $62,300 from 1986 to 1989. Mr. Wurz, an employee for 15 years, deposited checks into an account for a phony corporation he had set up. Mr. Wurz, who pleaded guilty, was sentenced to one year in prison.

"Naturally an institution doesn't like bad publicity," says Patrick M. Gibbs, vice-chancellor for business affairs at the University of New Orleans. But he adds: "It's important to prosecute people for crimes—particularly in an environment where the person is trusted."

Some Don't Press Charges

The sensitive nature of the allegations, however, has kept some colleges from pressing charges—especially private institutions, which, unlike their public counterparts, are not held accountable by state governments.

The Board of Trustees at Elon College, for example, voted unanimously last fall not to press charges when Robert E. Poindexter, vice-president for administrative services, resigned amid allegations that he had embezzled nearly $100,000 by billing construction work on his home to the private college.

Royall Spence, Jr., chairman of Elon's Board of Trustees, says there was "nothing more to be gained" through legal action. Controls caught the problem, he says, and Elon recovered its money.

Whether they try to put embezzlers behind bars, many campuses don't like to talk about the issue because it sometimes creates an aura of mistrust, officials say.

"Once you have an embezzlement, it gives the whole community credence to think, 'Gee, we didn't know about this. I wonder what else we don't know about,'" says Mark Lee, chairman of the finance committee of the Board of Trustees at the School of Theology at Claremont.

In the last several years, two financial managers embezzled a total of $285,000 from the theology school. The first theft, of $15,000, was discovered in 1985. The school then asked its treasurer, John W. Kirkman, to take over as business manager. He admitted in 1987 to taking $270,000, and was sentenced three years later to five years' probation.

Any campus office that handles money is at risk, financial experts say—especially financial aid, campus stores, and private fund-raising foundations. Positions of special concern are those in which one person has control over several financial processes—such as writing checks and balancing the checkbook—or access to several accounts within the university, a foundation, or both. Separate foundations present extreme risks, many financial officials say, because they are independent organizations that often don't follow controls set by the university.

3 Positions on Single Campus

Take the case of the University of Illinois. In 1981, officials at the Urbana-Champaign campus discovered that a foundation account they considered inactive had actually been quite active. Robert Parker, an employee, had over six years transferred $630,000 from several foundation accounts into the long-forgotten account. Mr. Parker then withdrew $608,000 from it to pay credit-card bills and other expenses and to hire strippers and prostitutes.

The fact that Mr. Parker held three positions on the campus allowed him access to the accounts, says Richard Margison, the university's associate vice-president for business and finance. At the foundation, Mr. Parker was assistant treasurer; at the university, he was both senior associate vice-president for business and financial affairs and assistant comptroller.

"The problem was in the lack of segregation of duties," says Mr. Margison. Mr. Parker, who had worked on the campus since 1952, "had too much control."

Other procedures broke down, Mr. Margison adds. Bank employees allowed Mr. Parker to cash checks with one signature instead of the required two. And because Mr. Parker was their boss, staff members didn't question his transactions, Mr. Margison says. Mr. Parker was convicted of theft and sentenced to five years in prison.

Financial experts say top managers and administrators must set examples for their employees by adhering to strict policies themselves. "If management doesn't cultivate vigilance and caution, they invite the crime," says Mr. Turk of Peat Marwick.

Such a situation arose in the California Community Colleges system. During the 1980's, certain financial practices used by colleges in the system created an opportunity for a nearly $1-million embezzlement, says Mr. Sjoberg, California's Acting Auditor General.

Mr. Sjoberg investigated the case, which led to the 1988 arrest of Robert F. Howard, an official with the system, for allegedly taking about $950,000 from a disabled-students program. Mr. Howard was said to have written checks to a phony consulting company that he had set up. Mr. Howard's case has not yet gone to trial. Mr. Howard had access to the money because of the way the chancellor's office was distributing money, a method that skirted state procedures, Mr. Sjoberg says. The method was not illegal, he adds, but it sent a bad message to employees. System officials say funds are no longer channeled that way. "If your bosses are circumventing the system," Mr. Sjoberg says, it's more difficult to keep others from trying.

Financial experts and investigators warn that campuses must conduct audits, both scheduled and unscheduled, to protect themselves against fraud.

They add, however, that the best system of audits and the toughest set of procedures will do nothing if universities do not enforce them. Policies must be looked at regularly to be sure that employees not only understand what they need to do, but also why they must do it.

Marquette officials say they have learned the importance of that—twice. About the same time Father Steinberger's theft was being investigated, the university's bursar, C. Michael Murphy, pleaded guilty to taking about $16,000.

In both cases, the university pressed charges and tightened its existing controls. Father Steinberger was released in January after serving 15 months in prison and 15 months on parole; Mr. Murphy received a suspended sentence. As a result of both cases, Marquette conducts more surprise audits.

Like most of the other campuses, Marquette wants to erase the incidents from memory, but not the lessons learned. Says Sande Robinson, director of Marquette's Educational Opportunity Program: "We just want to put it behind us and go on."

CHAPTER 6 ACCOUNTING CONCEPTS AND CLASSIFIED FINANCIAL STATEMENTS

Reviewing the Chapter

OBJECTIVE 1: State the objectives of financial reporting (pp. 273–274).

1. Financial reporting should fulfill three objectives. It should (a) provide information that is useful in making investment and credit decisions; (b) provide information that is useful in assessing cash flow prospects; and (c) provide information about business resources, claims to those resources, and changes in them. **General-purpose external financial statements** are the main way of presenting financial information to interested parties. They consist of the balance sheet, income statement, statement of retained earnings, and statement of cash flows.

OBJECTIVE 2: State the qualitative characteristics of accounting information, and describe their interrelationships (pp. 274–276).

2. Accounting attempts to provide decision makers with useful and understandable information that displays the **qualitative characteristics** or standards of relevance and reliability.
   a. **Relevance** means that the information is capable of influencing the decision maker. To be relevant, information must provide feedback, aid in making predictions, and be timely.
   b. **Reliability·** means that accounting information should accurately reflect what it is meant to represent. To be reliable, infor-

mation must be verifiable, neutral, and objective.

OBJECTIVE 3: Define and describe the use of the conventions of comparability and consistency, materiality, conservatism, full disclosure, and cost-benefit (pp. 276–279).

3. To aid in the interpretation of financial information, accountants depend on the following conventions: comparability, consistency, materiality, conservatism, full disclosure, and cost-benefit.
   a. **Comparability** means that the information allows the decision maker to compare the same company over two or more accounting periods, or different companies for the same accounting period.
   b. **Consistency** means that a particular accounting procedure, once adopted, should not normally be changed from period to period. However, if a company does change a procedure, it must justify the change and disclose the dollar effect on the statements.
   c. The **materiality** convention states that strict accounting practice need not be applied to items of insignificant dollar amount.
   d. The **conservatism** convention states that an accountant who has a choice of acceptable accounting procedures should choose the one that would be least likely to over-

state assets and income. Applying the lower-of-cost-or-market rule to inventory valuation is an example of conservatism.

e. The **full disclosure** convention states that financial statements and their accompanying footnotes should contain all relevant information.

f. The **cost-benefit** convention states that the cost of providing additional accounting information should not exceed the benefits to be gained from it.

OBJECTIVE 4: Summarize the concepts underlying financing accounting and their relationship to ethical financial reporting (pp. 279–282).

4. The accounting information system is a circular, continuous process whereby decision makers make decisions and take actions that affect economic activities. These economic activities, in turn, are measured, processed, and communicated back to the decision makers in the form of financial statements that are in accordance with the information needs or objectives of those decision makers.

5. The decision makers consist of internal users (management) and direct and indirect external users of accounting information. Accounting information must be in accordance with GAAP; authoritative bodies such as the FASB currently dictate GAAP.

6. When measuring a business transaction, the problems of recognition, valuation, and classification must be solved (covered in Chapter 2). When processing business transactions, stored data should be quickly retrievable, internal accounting controls should be established, and the matching rule should be applied (covered in Chapters 3 and 5). When communicating financial data, the qualitative characteristics presented in this chapter should be followed, aided by the accounting conventions also presented.

7. Users depend on the accountant to act ethically and with good judgment in the preparation of financial statements. However, when misleading financial statements are intentionally prepared, **fraudulent financial reporting** is said to have occurred.

OBJECTIVE 5: Identify and describe the basic components of a classified balance sheet (pp. 282–287).

8. **Classified financial statements** divide assets, liabilities, owners' equity, revenues, and expenses into subcategories to offer the reader more useful information.

9. On a classified balance sheet, assets are usually divided into four categories: (a) current assets; (b) investments; (c) property, plant, and equipment; and (d) intangible assets. (Sometimes another category called other assets is added for miscellaneous items.)

10. These categories are usually listed in order of liquidity (the ease with which an asset can be turned into cash).

11. **Current assets** are cash and assets that are expected to be turned into cash or used up within the normal operating cycle of the company or one year, whichever is longer. (From here on we will call this time period the current period.)

a. A company's normal operating cycle is the average time between the purchase of inventory and the collection of cash from the sale of that inventory.

b. Cash, short-term investments, accounts receivable, notes receivable, prepaid expenses, supplies, and inventory are current assets.

12. Examples of **investments** are stock and bonds held for long-term investment, land held for future use, plant or equipment not used in the business, special funds, and a controlling interest in another company.

13. **Property, plant, and equipment** include things like land, buildings, delivery equipment, machinery, and office equipment. All except land are subject to depreciation.

14. **Intangible assets** have no physical substance. More importantly, they represent certain long-lived rights or privileges. Examples are patents, copyrights, goodwill, franchises, and trademarks.

15. The liabilities of a classified balance sheet are usually divided into current and long-term liabilities.

a. **Current liabilities** are obligations for which payment (or performance) is due in the current period. They are paid from current assets or by incurring new short-term liabilities. Examples are notes payable, accounts payable, taxes payable, and unearned revenues.

b. **Long-term liabilities** are debts that are due after the current period or that will be paid from noncurrent assets. Examples are mortgages payable, long-term notes payable, bonds payable, employee pension obligations, and long-term leases.

16. The owners' equity section of a classified balance sheet is usually called owner's equity, partners' equity, or stockholders' equity. The exact name depends on whether the business is a sole proprietorship, a partnership, or a corporation.

17. In a corporation, the stockholders' equity sections consists of contributed capital (also called paid-in capital) and retained earnings.

18. In a sole proprietorship or partnership, the owner's or partners' equity section shows the name of the owner or owners. Each is followed by the word *capital* and the dollar amount of investment as of the balance sheet date.

OBJECTIVE 6: Prepare the multistep and single-step types of classified income statements (pp. 287–291).

19. A **condensed financial statement,** which contains the statement's major categories with little or no detail, may be presented in either multistep or single-step form.
    a. The **multistep form** is the more detailed of the two, containing several subtractions and subtotals. It has separate sections for cost of goods sold, operating expenses, and **other** (nonoperating) **revenues and expenses.** One important subtotal is **income from operations,** which equals gross margin from sales minus operating expenses.
    b. In the **single-step form,** the revenues section lists all revenues, including other revenues, and the operating costs section lists all expenses, including other expenses. The difference is labeled net income or net loss.

20. A corporation's income statement should disclose **provision for income taxes** or **income taxes expense** separately from the other expenses. Sole proprietorships and partnerships are not taxable units.

21. **Earnings per share,** also called **net income per share,** equals net income divided by the number of shares of common stock. It usually appears below net income in the income statement and is a measure of the company's profitability.

22. Two other statements that are necessary to an understanding of a company's financial operations are the statement of retained earnings and the statement of cash flows.

OBJECTIVE 7: Use classified financial statements for the simple evaluation of liquidity and profitability (pp. 292–299).

23. Classified financial statements help the reader evaluate liquidity and profitability.

24. **Liquidity** refers to a company's ability to pay its bills when they are due and to meet unexpected needs for cash. Two measures of liquidity are working capital and the current ratio.
    a. **Working capital** equals current assets minus current liabilities. It is the amount of current assets that would remain if all the current debts were paid.
    b. The **current ratio** equals current assets divided by current liabilities. A current ratio of 1:1, for example, shows that current assets are barely enough to pay current liabilities. A 2:1 current ratio would be considered more satisfactory.

25. **Profitability** means more than just a company's net income. And to draw conclusions, one must compare profitability measures with industry averages and past performance. Five common measures of profitability are profit margin, asset turnover, return on assets, debt to equity ratio, and return on equity.
    a. The **profit margin** equals net income divided by net sales. A 12.5 percent profit margin, for example, means that 12½¢ has been earned on each dollar of sales.
    b. **Asset turnover** equals net sales divided by average total assets. This measures how efficiently assets are used to produce sales.
    c. **Return on assets** equals net income divided by average total assets. This measure shows how efficiently the company is using its assets.
    d. The **debt to equity ratio** measures the proportion of a business financed by creditors relative to the proportion financed by owners. It equals total liabilities divided by stockholders' equity. A debt to equity ratio of 1.0, for instance, indicates equal financing by creditors and owners.

e. **Return on equity** shows what percentage was earned on the owners' investment. It equals net income divided by average stockholders' equity.

OBJECTIVE 8: Identify the major components of a corporate annual report (pp. 299–311).

26. Financial statements of corporations are usually complicated and have a number of features not found in a sole proprietorship's or partnership's statements. Published statements appear in the company's **annual report,** a publication distributed to stockholders each year. The annual report usually also gives nonfinancial information.

27. **Consolidated** financial statements are the combined statements of a company and its controlled subsidiaries (Chapter 16 explains them in more detail). A company's financial statements may show data from consecutive periods side by side for comparison. Such statements are called **comparative financial statements.**

28. The statement of consolidated earnings should contain information regarding earnings per share. A measure of a company's profitability, it equals net income divided by the average number of shares of common stock outstanding.

29. A section called **notes to the financial statements** usually accompanies, and is considered an integral part of, the financial statements. Its purpose is to help the reader interpret some of the complex financial statement items.

30. A **summary of significant accounting policies** discloses the generally accepted accounting principles used in preparing the statements. It usually follows the last financial statement, perhaps as the first note to the financial statements.

31. Corporations are often required to issue **interim financial statements.** These statements give financial information covering less than a year (for example, quarterly data).

32. An annual report usually also includes a report of management's responsibilities and management's discussion and analysis of operating performance.

33. The **accountants' report** (or **auditors' report**) is issued by an independent auditor. It conveys to third parties that the financial statements were examined in accordance with generally accepted auditing standards (**scope section**), and expresses the auditor's opinion on how fairly the financial statements reflect the company's financial condition (**opinion section**). The language of the accountants' report has recently been reworded to emphasize management's responsibility for the financial statements and to clarify the nature and purpose of an audit.

Testing Your Knowledge

Matching

Match each term with its definition by writing the appropriate letter in the blank.

_____ 1. Qualitative characteristics

_____ 2. Relevance

_____ 3. Reliability

_____ 4. Fraudulent financial reporting

_____ 5. Classified financial statements

_____ 6. Liquidity

_____ 7. Current assets

_____ 8. Property, plant, and equipment

_____ 9. Intangible assets

_____ 10. Current liabilities

_____ 11. Long-term liabilities

_____ 12. Other revenues and expenses

_____ 13. Consolidated financial statements

_____ 14. Interim financial statements

_____ 15. General-purpose external financial statements

_____ 16. Comparative financial statements

_____ 17. Earnings per share (net income per share or net earnings per share)

_____ 18. Summary of significant accounting policies

_____ 19. Notes to the financial statements

_____ 20. Accountants' report

a. Statements that cover less than a year

b. Financial statements with data from consecutive periods placed side by side for analysis

c. The auditor's opinion concerning the financial statements

d. Long-lived tangible assets

e. The balance sheet, income statement, statement of owners' equity, and statement of cash flows

f. A listing of the accounting principles used in preparing the financial statements

g. Guidelines for evaluating the quality of accounting reports

h. Short-term obligations

i. Financial reports broken down into subcategories

j. Combined financial statements of a parent company and its subsidiaries

k. Net income divided by outstanding shares of common stock

l. The income statement section that contains nonoperating items

m. The subcategory of assets that are expected to be turned into cash or used up within one year or the normal operating cycle, whichever is longer

n. The standard that accounting information should be related to the user's needs

o. Assets that lack physical substance and that grant rights or privileges to their owner

p. A section that interprets or supplements financial statement information

q. Obligations due after the current period

r. The standard that accounting information should accurately reflect what it is meant to represent

s. The ability to pay bills when due and to meet unexpected needs for cash

t. The intentional preparation of misleading financial statements

Short Answer

Use the lines provided to answer each item.

1. List the three forms of business organization, with each one's name for the owners' equity section in the balance sheet.

Business Organization

a. _____

b. _____

c. _____

Name for Owners' Equity Section

a. _____

b. _____

c. _____

2. What does each of the following ratios have to do with a company's profitability?

Profit margin

_____

_____

_____

Asset turnover

_____

_____

_____

Return on assets

_____

_____

_____

Return on equity

_____

_____

_____

Debt to equity ratio

_____

_____

_____

3. Define each of the following liquidity ratios.

Working capital

_____

_____

Current ratio

_____

_____

4. Explain the basic point of each of the following conventions:

Consistency and comparability

_____

_____

Materiality

_____

_____

Cost-benefit

_____

_____

Conservatism

_____

_____

Full disclosure

_____

_____

Circle T if the statement is true, F if it is false. Please provide explanations for the false answers, using the blank lines at the end of the section.

T F 1. Receivables are not current assets if collection requires more than one year.

T F 2. Accounting is best described as an information system with a series of starting points and ending points.

T F 3. Gross margin from sales minus operating expenses equals income from operations.

T F 4. Operating expenses are made up of selling expenses and cost of goods sold.

T F 5. Accounting information is relevant if it could make a difference to the outcome of a decision.

T F 6. The net income figure is needed to compute the profit margin, the return on assets, and the return on equity.

T F 7. The investments section of a balance sheet would include both short- and long-term investments in stock.

T F 8. One meaning of the term *profitability* is the ease with which an asset can be converted into cash.

T F 9. A company's normal operating cycle cannot be less than one year.

T F 10. Net worth refers to the current value of a company's assets.

T F 11. Other revenues and expenses is a separate classification in a multistep income statement.

T F 12. The net income figures for a multistep and a single-step income statement will differ, given the same accounting period for the same company.

T F 13. The notes to the financial statements are divided into a scope section and an opinion section.

T F 14. Working capital equals current assets divided by current liabilities.

T F 15. The proportion of a company financed by the owners is shown by the debt to equity ratio.

T F 16. The qualitative characteristic of relevance means that accounting information can be confirmed or duplicated by independent parties.

T F 17. A corporate annual report usually includes much nonfinancial information, in addition to financial information.

T F 18. Condensed financial statements and consolidated financial statements are essentially the same thing.

_____

_____

_____

_____

_____

_____

_____

_____

_____

_____

_____

_____

_____

_____

_____

_____

_____

_____

Multiple Choice

Circle the letter of the best answer.

1. The basis for classifying assets as current or noncurrent is the period of time normally required by the business to turn cash invested in
   a. noncurrent assets back into current assets.
   b. receivables back into cash, or 12 months, whichever is shorter.
   c. inventories back into cash, or 12 months, whichever is longer.
   d. inventories back into cash, or 12 months, whichever is shorter.

2. Which of the following will not be found anywhere in a single-step income statement?
   a. Cost of goods sold
   b. Other expenses
   c. Gross margin from sales
   d. Operating expenses

3. The current ratio would probably be of *most* interest to
   a. stockholders.
   b. creditors.
   c. management.
   d. customers.

4. Which item below will *not* appear in the stockholders' equity section of a corporation's balance sheet?
   a. Retained earnings
   b. Common stock
   c. Paid-in capital in excess of par value
   d. James Esmay, Capital

5. The accountants' report
   a. expresses an opinion as to the fairness of the financial statements audited.
   b. states whether or not a company is a sound investment.
   c. is prepared by a company's own internal auditors.
   d. should include forecasts to help the reader assess future profitability.

6. Net income divided by net sales equals
   a. the profit margin.
   b. return on assets.
   c. working capital.
   d. income from operations.

7. Operating expenses consist of
   a. other expenses and cost of goods sold.
   b. selling expenses and cost of goods sold.
   c. selling expenses and general and administrative expenses.
   d. selling expenses, general and administrative expenses, and other expenses.

8. Applying the lower-of-cost-or-market rule to inventory valuation and short-term investments follows the convention of
   a. consistency.
   b. materiality.
   c. conservatism.
   d. full disclosure.

9. A corporation began the accounting period with retained earnings of $5,000, ended with retained earnings of $12,000, and earned a $20,000 net income during the period. Apparently, how much did it declare in dividends during the period?
   a. $3,000
   b. $12,000
   c. $13,000
   d. $27,000

10. Which of the following is *not* an objective of financial reporting, according to FASB *Statement of Financial Accounting Concepts No. 1?*
    a. To provide information about the timing of cash flows
    b. To provide information to investors, creditors, and others
    c. To provide information about business resources
    d. To provide information not found in the accountant's report

Applying Your Knowledge

Exercises

1. Assume that Springfield Company uses the following group headings on its classified balance sheet:
   a. Current assets
   b. Investments
   c. Property, plant, and equipment
   d. Intangible assets
   e. Current liabilities
   f. Long-term liabilities
   g. Owner's equity

   Indicate by letter where each of the following should be placed. Write an "X" next to items that do not belong on the balance sheet.

   _____ 1. Franchises
   _____ 2. Short-term advances from customers
   _____ 3. Accumulated depreciation
   _____ 4. Mark Mathews, Capital
   _____ 5. Prepaid rent
   _____ 6. Delivery truck
   _____ 7. Office supplies
   _____ 8. Fund for the purchase of land
   _____ 9. Notes payable due in ten years
   _____ 10. Bonds payable currently due (payable out of current assets)
   _____ 11. Goodwill
   _____ 12. Short-term investments
   _____ 13. Provision for income taxes
   _____ 14. Inventory
   _____ 15. Accounts payable

2. The following information relates to Spiffy Appliances, Inc., for 19xx.

Current assets	$ 60,000
Average total assets	200,000
Current liabilities	20,000
Long-term liabilities	30,000
Average stockholders' equity	150,000
Net sales	250,000
Net income	25,000

   In the spaces provided, indicate each measure of liquidity and profitability.
   a. Working capital = $ _____
   b. Current ratio = _____ to _____
   c. Profit margin = _____ %
   d. Return on assets = _____ %
   e. Return on equity = _____ %
   f. Asset turnover = _____ times

3. The following data relate to the Confrey Corporation for 19xx.

Cost of goods sold	$150,000
Interest revenues	2,000
Income tax expense	5,000
Net sales	200,000
Common stock outstanding	3,500 shares
Operating expenses	30,000

a. In the space provided, complete the condensed multistep income statement in good form. Include earnings per share information in the proper place.

Confrey Corporation Income Statement (Multistep) For the Year Ended December 31, 19xx		

b. In the space provided, complete the condensed single-step income statement in good form. Include earnings per share information in the proper place.

Confrey Corporation Income Statement (Single-Step) For the Year Ended December 31, 19xx		

Reading

Who's Responsible for the Content of Financial Statements?

In publicly held companies, management produces the financial statements showing the results of operations and the financial position of the company. The auditor's role is to consult with management if any deficiencies have been identified through an audit. Assuming that all discovered material deficiencies are accounted for, the external auditor certifies that, based on his examination of the financial statements and their underlying documentation, the statements do fairly represent the financial position of a firm at that time.

The depth of the audit can vary; it depends on the cost of more audit time versus the potential benefit of a greater level of assurance. Thus, if external auditors are assigned the task of assuring that there is no fraud in financial statements, the cost of audits inevitably will rise—probably dramatically.

Only management has the resources (internal auditors) and the authority to institute internal controls and the leadership to establish and maintain the standards of ethics. Such leadership is necessary to provide even a reasonable level of assurance that the financial statements are fair representations of the company's financial condition.

In an effort to increase management's awareness of and responsiveness to its responsibility for the financial statements, the Commission on Fraudulent Financial Reporting, in its April 1987 report, made many significant recommendations, among which the following two would be most far reaching:

"The Auditing Standards Board should revise the auditor's standard report to state that the audit provides reasonable but not absolute assurance that the audited financial statements are free from material misstatements as a result of fraud or error."

"All public companies should be required by SEC rule to include in their annual reports to stockholders management reports signed by the

Source: "Who's Responsible for the Content of Financial Statements?" by M. Frank Barton and L. Mason Rockwell, *Management Accounting.* Reprinted from January 1991 issue of *Management Accounting.* Copyright 1991 by Institute of Management Accountants (formerly National Association of Accountants).

chief executive officer and chief accounting officer. The management report should acknowledge management's responsibilities for the financial statements and internal control, discuss how these responsibilities were fulfilled, and provide management's assessment of the effectiveness of the company's internal controls."[1]

Together, these two recommendations not only would make the public aware of the inherent limitations of cost/benefit-driven external audits and management's ultimate responsibility for the financial statements, but they would also force management to assume its responsibility for assuring that the statements are fair.

The Survey

As part of a larger ongoing research project to discover the views of management as to the relative responsibilities of management and of external auditors, we sent survey questionnaires to 250 presidents and CEOs of the top 1,000 businesses according to sales, selected from *Ward's Business Directory*. We received 77 responses (31%) to our mailing. The survey identified areas of responsibility likely to be presented in financial statements and the functions involved in gathering the information for the statements. Items were selected to determine the presidents' and CEOs' perceptions of who is responsible for completeness and accuracy of information presented in financial statements, specifically how much responsibility the external auditor has for:

- Detection of fraud,
- Reasonableness of estimates,
- Inadequacy of internal control.

The questions were asked and answered as follows: Assuming management's responsibility for the financial statements is 100, what is the external auditor's responsibility (so that an answer of 50 versus 120 would indicate the auditor had 50% or 120% of the responsibility of management respectively)?

1. Exposure Draft, Report of the National Commission on Fraudulent Financial Reporting, April 1987.

Detection of Fraud

We expected the answers to share two characteristics: consistency and the opinion that the auditor's responsibility should be minimal. This expectation was consistent with the cost/benefit-constrained audit and with the wording of the opinions given by the external auditor, specifically, that the financial statements are representations of management.

As it turned out, however, the coefficient of variation, which measures the degree of dispersion in the responses, was 77% for fraud and indicated that the CEOs have no consistent view of the external auditor's responsibility for fraud detection. CEOs' views on estimates and internal control were somewhat more consistent.

[T]he presidents and CEOs are split into two groups, one indicating that the external auditor's relative responsibility is significantly less than management's responsibility (61% answered 50 or less) and the other responding that the external auditor's responsibility is equal or even greater than that of management.

Specifically, 39% of these corporate leaders perceive the external auditor as having a factor of 75 to management's 100 of the responsibility, or higher, which gives the external auditor essentially equal responsibility for detecting fraud. Also, 27% of managers perceive the external auditors as shouldering equal or more responsibility.

Considering that external auditors spend as little as a month pulling samples of transactions based on judgment and/or a statistical method, it would seem obvious that there is little guarantee of their uncovering any fraud. Granted, the external auditor also analyzes internal control, but this analysis in no way assures that internal controls are adhered to throughout the year. Maintaining compliance with internal controls is the domain of management. Again, the external auditor uses samples to assess the level of compliance, based on judgment and/or statistical methods.

To be more emphatic, management must have a clear and consistent understanding of its primary role as guardian of the firm's assets. Only management has:

- The *resources* in the form of internal auditors,
- The *authority* to institute and enforce internal control procedures, and
- The *leadership position* to establish and maintain the standards of ethics necessary to provide even a reasonable level of assurance that the financial statements are fair representations of the company's financial condition.

Reasonableness of Estimates

As to the responsibility for assuring reasonableness of estimates, again we expected the CEO's responses to show a consensus and an understanding of the extent of management's responsibility. Who else but management would know or should know whether estimates are reasonable or deceptive? Consider, for example, the case of the division controller of a consumer products corporation who decreased the amount of reserves set aside for inventory obsolescence, bad debts, and coupon redemption by a total of $2 million (as compared to sales of $98 million) at the end of a quarter because the corporation needed the profit.[2]

It is true that, out of necessity and in an effort to meet their professional responsibilities, public accounting firms have developed or have hired experts to assess the reasonableness of various estimates. Nevertheless, how, in fact, can the external auditor be expected to know more about a business than the ones who manage it day in and day out, year after year?

[T]he results were not only inconsistent, but a large percentage of presidents and CEOs consider the external auditor to have a significant responsibility for assuring that estimates are reasonable. More than one-fifth of the managers believe that external auditors have equal responsibility. Note, however, that the mode for this question is 50 with 35% and that 65% indicated 50 or below.

Inadequacy of Internal Control

Judging the adequacy of internal control usually is considered the domain of accountants, so it was anticipated that some CEOs would assign more responsibility to the external auditor than other CEOs. Specifically, some companies have established professionally competent internal auditors and management accountants whom they rely on to audit and manage internal control, respectively. Other CEOs would rely more extensively on the internal control evaluations. Thus, it would be more likely that this question would generate a wide range of responses. The anticipated results were verified with a coefficient of variation of 52%. . . .

Again, many CEOs do not fully appreciate management's critical role as guardian of the firm's assets. Almost 36% of the CEOs give the

2. Merchant, Kenneth A., *Fraudulent and Questionable Financial Reporting: A Corporate Perspective,* Financial Executives Research Foundation, 1987.

external auditor equal or greater responsibility. Yet is it not management that establishes and oversees the procedures that constitute internal control?

Solutions

As pointed out earlier the revision of the auditor's standard report and a decision by the SEC to mandate a management letter would bring about two important changes:

- Management would be required to understand and accept its ultimate responsibility, and
- Management would have to document and assess its own efforts at preventing fraudulent financial statements.

To reduce the discrepancies in management's view of its role, managers must be educated at all levels as to their responsibility for the integrity of financial statements. Along the same lines, managers must learn which factors can lead to fraudulently misstated financial statements and how to institute the internal control measures necessary.

Finally, any president or CEO who may view the external auditor as an adversary to be swayed to management's interest would now have an incentive to change this outlook. In particular, because management would be acknowledging its responsibility by way of the signed statements of the CEO and the chief financial officer, it then should look on the external auditor as an advisor and consultant and not just as a necessary step to satisfy a regulatory requirement.

In spite of the disparity in the presidents' and CEOs' responses, a significant number of CEOs appear to understand the extent of management responsibility. For example, 15% of the respondents indicated that external auditors had a factor of less than 15 of the responsibility as compared with management's 100. Although some other presidents and CEOs apparently perceive the auditor as having essentially equal or even more responsibility than management, the previous suggestions will do much to increase the consciousness of management as to its ultimate responsibility for detecting and preventing fraud.

Reading

How Do CFOs Evaluate the Annual Report?

Annual reports are expected to be all things to all people. Originally conceived as a timely and thorough presentation of financial results to shareholders, today's reports serve a substantially broader range of purposes. Of 134 financial executives who answered a recent *FE*/Lefkowith Inc. survey, the majority agreed that this increase in secondary purposes constitutes a continuing trend. While shareholders remain the primary audience, many respondents indicated that future annual reports will provide more financial data. This information will be geared to analysts and investors, as well as to shareholders (see Table 1). At the same time, however, additional emphasis will be placed on editorial content, and on making annual reports more effective in getting marketing and public relations messages communicated to various audiences (see Table 2).

The printed annual report's central role in financial communications has, if anything, been bolstered by the increase in purposes and audiences. It does not seem threatened by emerging technologies, such as advanced software programs or the video annual report. More notably, the SEC's EDGAR (Electronic Data Gathering Analysis and Retrieval) system, which will shortly become a required form of filing annual statements, will not affect the annual report's role as the centerpiece of most financial communications programs.

Although EDGAR has been heralded as the first on-line data access system, those surveyed tended to approach its benefits cautiously. As one financial executive who had participated in its pilot program said, the system "still has too many bugs and causes more headaches than it's worth." It may be too early to judge EDGAR fairly, since it is still in a formative stage. But given a choice of how the development of EDGAR would affect the role of annual reports, well over half of the respondents indicated that the printed annual report will maintain its current level of importance, regardless of the availability of the same financial information by computer.

A large majority of respondents (70 percent) showed no interest in using video annual reports. A small number of financial executives intend to experiment with video supplements, highlighting financial information or focusing on editorial content. At this point, we can assume that this medium offers little competition to the printed report.

Questions about the 10-K and its relationship to the annual report prompted a variety of responses concerning the diverse audiences, and needs, that the report must meet. Some respondents stressed the entirely separate objectives of the two documents, with the 10-K meeting regulatory requirements and the annual report telling the company story. The survey substantiates this, with over 40 percent considering both the 10-K and the annual report important for key audiences. Another 30 percent stressed the usefulness of the 10-K to a more limited audience. While the 10-K is a required document, only 15 percent of the survey's respondents agreed that it could be combined with a summary report as a replacement for the printed annual. Several financial chiefs added that their annual and their 10-Ks "were essentially the same thing," or at least, that "the annual now incorporated essentially all of the information provided in the 10-K."

"Key audiences." "Limited audiences." Who reads a company's annual report? It comes as no surprise that 60 percent of financial executives questioned perceive existing shareholders as the annual's most important audience. Ranked second is the securities analyst. And prospective institutional investors and funds managers are ranked third and fourth in importance, ahead of prospective individual investors and employees.

Source: Used by permission from *Financial Executive,* December 1986, copyright 1986, by Financial Executives Institute.

FE sought to track current and probable future trends for the annual report, and worked with Lefkowith Inc. (a New York–based communications consulting firm) on a survey of financial executives. A six-page questionnaire was mailed to 500 CFOs of the Financial Executive Institute, and 134 returned completed questionnaires, for a response rate of over 25 percent. The survey's respondents represent a broad range of company sizes and industry groups.

TABLE 1
Who is the Most Important Audience for the Annual Report?

	Degree of Importance				
	Most	**Very**	**Little**	**None**	**No Answer**
Existing shareholders	59.0%	32.8%	2.2%	2.2%	3.7%
Securities analysts	42.5	35.8	5.2	14.9	1.5
Prospective institutional investors	28.4	42.5	11.9	14.9	2.2
Funds managers	22.4	42.5	16.4	14.9	3.7
Prospective individual investors	21.6	43.3	21.6	11.2	2.2
Employees	18.7	49.3	27.6	3.7	.7
Customers	15.7	46.3	27.6	9.0	1.5
Suppliers	7.5	38.1	41.8	10.4	2.2
Stockbrokers	12.7	34.3	32.8	14.9	5.2
Prospective acquisitions	5.2	31.3	45.5	16.4	1.5
Prospective recruits	5.2	34.3	44.8	12.7	3.0
Governments/Agencies	6.7	15.7	44.0	31.3	2.2

TABLE 2
How Will the Annual Report Change in the Next Three Years?

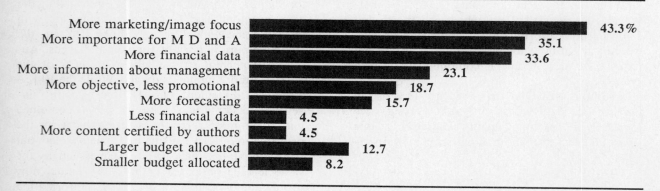

More marketing/image focus	43.3%
More importance for M D and A	35.1
More financial data	33.6
More information about management	23.1
More objective, less promotional	18.7
More forecasting	15.7
Less financial data	4.5
More content certified by authors	4.5
Larger budget allocated	12.7
Smaller budget allocated	8.2

Audiences and purposes of the annual report are closely interrelated, with each audience segment requiring different degrees of detail and different styles of presentation. Three-quarters of the sample cited presentation of financial and operating results as a major purpose of the annual report. Another 50 percent indicated that reporting on management's stewardship is a major purpose (see Table 3).

When asked to rate the relative importance of both the editorial and financial sections of their annual reports, almost 60 percent gave them equal weight. One respondent commented that while he views the financial segment as most important, "the chief executive officer would consider the editorial segment to be of greater importance."

In projecting changes over the next three years, nearly half of the respondents saw the an-

TABLE 3
What is the Purpose of the Annual Report?

	Most Important	Important	Negligible	No Answer
Report on companies' financial position and operating results	72.4%	26.9%	0.0%	0.7%
Report to shareholders on management's stewardship	50.0	44.0	6.0	0.0
Provide information for an informed investment decision	36.6	50.0	11.9	1.5
General public relations tool/ recruiting	25.4	46.3	26.1	2.2
Provide information for an informed shareholder voting decision	8.2	47.0	41.0	3.7
Promote a higher PE ratio	3.7	38.1	55.2	3.0

nual report as having greater focus on marketing and image development. Financial executives appear to accept more fully than in the past that annual reports provide an important opportunity, on a yearly basis, to communicate the full scope of a company's activities, strategies for growth, and corporate image. By developing annuals with these objectives, they not only do a better job of reaching the investment community, but also produce an effective document for marketing, recruiting, and public relations purposes.

More than a third of those surveyed predicted that, in the future, their reports will provide more financial data (see Table 2). In addition, a similar percentage of the sample expects their report will place more importance on the Management's Discussion and Analysis section of their annuals.

The annual report is one of the most crucial corporate communications projects, and potentially, one of the most complex. Asked whether the CEO or the CFO is more directly involved, about one-third of the respondents indicated that the CFO usually takes primary responsibility for producing the annual report. Another 20 percent reported that their annual is managed directly by the CEO, who is assisted by both the financial and the communications staffs. In order to augment their internal resources, over 80 percent of those surveyed indicated that outside consultants and suppliers are used to develop key aspects of the report. Those most cited for external support were basically graphics-related. And the larger the company, the more likely it is to use these external suppliers.

Timing as well as coordination is fundamental to the efficient, cost-effective development of reports. Over 85 percent of the survey participants begin planning their annual reports at least 60 days before the end of the fiscal year.

In examining the size of the annual, the quantity printed, and the cost involved, the survey supported other available data. As expected, the larger the company, the more pages there are in the annual report, and the larger the press run. Consequently, these larger companies obtained lower cost per copy for their annuals. To illustrate:

About 50 percent of the largest companies (over $2 billion in sales) printed more than 100,000 copies of their annuals. Therefore, while their annuals are larger (from 33 to 50 pages), their per copy cost is under $2.00.

Inversely, close to 70 percent of the smaller companies (with sales under $100 million) produced fewer than 10,000 copies. And even with fewer pages (generally running under 24 pages), almost 40 percent of the smaller companies indicated that their per copy costs exceed $5.00.

The financial executives who participated in this survey play a key role in their company's annual. They provided valuable data on how the annual report is and will be used. The annual is clearly viewed as a major financial communications tool, and one whose audiences and purposes will continue to grow.

Reading

Wiping Away Cosmetics in Corporate Earnings Reports

What's in an earnings number?

That's the crucial question for investors—especially in today's jumpy market, where shifts in a company's profit picture translate quickly into windfall or disaster for its stockholders.

But finding out what a company's earnings really are made of may be more difficult than ever. This is because in a faltering economy, companies come under greater pressure to spruce up reported earnings with cosmetic fixes; for example, understating costs or overstating revenue at the expense of future performance.

And individuals probably can't expect much help from brokers in fathoming the earnings murk. Wall Street's cost-cutting frenzy has thinned the ranks of stock analysts who study such things, so a lot less guidance is to be had nowadays from professionals. The situation is especially dire among smaller stocks, the main stomping ground for individual stock-pickers, where scores of companies have been left without any research coverage at all.

But far from being bad news, "That's like waving a green flag for individual investors," Michael Murphy, editor of the Overpriced Stock Service, a San Francisco-based newsletter, says. "There's an incredible opportunity to discover companies whose fortunes are improving, but Wall Street hasn't caught on."

Spotting Potential Disasters

Moreover, with the bear market still on the prowl, investors who do their homework have a better chance to spot disasters in the making, and to keep their portfolios from getting mauled.

"It's a dangerous environment out there" for stock investors, David Tice, editor of Behind the Numbers, an institutional stock research service, says. "You don't want to be blind-sided.

So what should an investor look for?

Baruch Lev, an accounting professor at the

University of California at Berkeley, has tested several gauges that analysts typically use, to see which of them are best in measuring a company's earnings potential, and in predicting its stock performance, too.

The most important items on financial statements, he says, are trends in inventory, accounts receivable and order backlogs. "These are the strongest indicators, and are much more closely related to stock returns than reported earnings," he says.

Tracking Inventories

In particular, investors should look at how companies' inventories of finished goods track their sales. If inventories are rising faster than sales, "It's a bad signal, because it shows the company is having difficulty selling its product, and suggests a hit to future earnings as a result of management's efforts to get rid of those inventories," he says.

For similar reasons, he says, it pays to watch accounts receivable, or IOUs from customers that have received goods but not yet paid for them. If these are rising faster than sales, not only can this signal trouble with sales but may show vulnerability to customer defaults.

Mr. Lev also advises comparing the percentage change in a company's order backlog to the percentage change in its sales. This "turns out to be a *very* important indicator for future stock returns," he says. If the order backlog is growing faster than sales, this is a good sign for investors, but if it is lagging, this spells trouble.

Companies aren't required to report their order backlogs, however. If a particular company doesn't do this, Mr. Lev says, check the trend in its gross operating margins compared with its sales trend. If margin growth lags behind sales growth, this can mean future earnings are on shaky footing; if margin growth is outpacing sales growth, this can be a sign of strength.

Poised for a Fall?

The prospect of slowing margin growth is one reason why Mr. Tice of Behind the Numbers is negative on General Electric Co.'s stock these days. "This is a case where operating margins are

Source: From "Wiping Away Cosmetics in Corporate Earnings Reports" by Barbara Donnelly, *The Wall Street Journal,* December 17, 1990. Reprinted by permission of *The Wall Street Journal,* © 1990 Dow Jones & Company, Inc. All Rights Reserved Worldwide.

at an all-time high, but sales growth is anemic," he says. "How long can that continue," he wonders, before margin growth lags. The market, meanwhile, still prices GE's stock as though the company's growth prospects were much rosier, indicating the stock may be poised for a fall, he says.

Conversely, Mr. Murphy of the Ovepriced Stock Service likes Network Equipment Technologies Inc. and Vitalink Communications Corp. as "turnaround situations," based on their low stock prices and improving fundamentals. He also favors MacNeal-Schwendler Corp. and Archive Corp. as strong earners that have been overlooked by institutional investors.

Aside from balance-sheet data, accounting signals can tell a lot about the integrity of a company's earnings, Mr. Lev says. For example, last-in, first-out accounting produces much more reliable earnings figures than first-in, first-out methods, because LIFO more accurately captures the real cost of sales, he says. And when auditors qualify a company's results, or don't give an opinion, he says this is "obviously a strong negative."

In general, lax accounting policies mean a company's reported earnings aren't as good as they look. For example, companies that use 40-year depreciation schedules, or that suddenly shift to a longer depreciation schedule from a shorter one, are probably overstating earnings.

"Strong Balance Sheet"

High debt is another red flag, particularly in these days of scarce credit and economic uncertainty, professional investors say. "You really want a strong balance sheet, just in case after doing all this work, your assessment is wrong," Boniface Zaino, managing director at Trust Co. of the West, says.

If long-term debt as a percentage of a company's equity is high, relative to other companies in the same industry or the market as a whole, this means the company doesn't have much of a buffer against lean times. "Until we're past the eye of the economic storm, you really don't want any part of leverage," Richard Bernstein, senior quantitative analyst at Merrill Lynch & Co., says.

By contrast, a large cash position is a big plus, not only for safety but also because it indicates the company is in a position to take advantage of competitors' problems.

Merrill Corp., a financial printing firm, is a favorite with Mr. Zaino for this reason. The company recently bought the assets of two failed competitors at bargain-basement prices, and continues to produce good earnings, even though business is lean. "The stock is still reasonably priced, and when times get good, their ability to increase profit margins and earnings will be dramatic," he says.

CHAPTER 7 SHORT-TERM LIQUID ASSETS

Reviewing the Chapter

OBJECTIVE 1: Account for cash and short-term investments (pp. 337–340).

1. **Short-term liquid assets** consist of cash and cash equivalents, short-term investments, accounts receivable, and notes receivable.

2. **Cash** and **cash equivalents** consist of coin and currency on hand, checks and money orders, investments of less than ninety days, and bank deposits. A company's Cash account may include a **compensating balance.** This balance is a minimum amount that a bank requires a company to keep in its bank account.

3. Companies frequently have excess cash on hand for short periods of time. To put this idle cash to good use, most companies purchase **short-term investments** (also called **marketable securities**). Short-term investments consist of time deposits, certificates of deposit, and government and other securities (stocks and bonds) that the company intends to hold for ninety days to one year.
   a. When cash is first invested, Short-Term Investments is debited and Cash credited. When income from the investment is received, Cash is debited and Dividend Income or Interest Income is credited. The account used depends on whether the investment is in equity securities (such as stocks) or debt securities (such as bonds).
   b. When a short-term investment is sold, Cash is debited, Short-Term Investments is credited, and a loss is debited or a gain

is credited for any difference between the original purchase price and the sale price.
   c. On the balance sheet, short-term investments in equity securities are presented at the lower of cost or market. This presentation is justified by the conservatism convention. It shows immediate recognition of a potential loss but puts off recognition of a potential gain until it is realized. Short-term investments in debt securities are presented on the balance sheet at cost, unless the value of the securities has been permanently impaired.

OBJECTIVE 2: Define *accounts receivable,* and explain the relationships among credit policies, sales, and uncollectible accounts (pp. 340–344).

4. **Accounts receivable** are short-term liquid assets that represent payment due from credit customers.

5. Wholesalers and retailers usually allow customers to pay for merchandise over a period of time (that is, they extend credit). They do so because the customer might decide against a purchase that required full payment immediately. This type of credit is often called **trade credit.** It makes expensive items affordable and increases sales for the merchant. Most companies that sell on credit have credit departments, whose responsibility it is to approve or refuse credit to individuals or companies. **Uncollectible accounts** (also called **bad debts**), the accounting term for

credit accounts that are not paid, are an expense of selling on credit.

6. The matching rule requires that uncollectible accounts expense appear on the same income statement as the corresponding sale, even if the customer defaults in a future period. At the time of a credit sale, however, the company does not know which customers will or will not pay. Therefore, an estimate of uncollectible accounts must be made at the end of the accounting period. An adjusting entry is then made debiting Uncollectible Accounts Expense and crediting Allowance for Uncollectible Accounts for the estimated amount. Uncollectible Accounts Expense is closed out much as other expenses are and appears on the income statement. **Allowance for Uncollectible Accounts** is a contra account to Accounts Receivable, reducing Accounts Receivable to the amount estimated to be collectible.

OBJECTIVE 3: Apply the allowance method of accounting for uncollectible accounts, including using the percentage of net sales method and the accounts receivable aging method to estimate uncollectible accounts (pp. 344–350).

7. The two most common methods for estimating uncollectible accounts are the percentage of net sales method and the accounts receivable aging method.

8. Under the **percentage of net sales method,** the estimated percentage for uncollectible accounts is multiplied by net sales for the period. The resulting figure is then used in the adjusting entry for uncollectible accounts. Any previous balance in Allowance for Uncollectible Accounts represents estimates from previous years that have not yet been written off. It has no bearing on the adjusting entry under this method.

9. Under the **accounts receivable aging method,** customer accounts are placed into a "not yet due" category or into one of several "past due" categories (called the **aging of accounts receivable**). The amounts in each category are totaled. Each total is then multiplied by a different percentage for estimated bad debts. The sum of these products represents estimated bad debts on ending Accounts Receivable. Again, the debit is to Uncollectible Accounts Expense and the credit is to Allowance for Uncollectible Accounts. However, the entry is for the amount that will bring Allowance for

Uncollectible Accounts to the figure arrived at under the aging calculation.

10. When it becomes clear that a specific account will not be collected, it should be written off by a debit to Allowance for Uncollectible Accounts and a credit to Accounts Receivable. The debit is *not* made to Uncollectible Accounts Expense. After a specific account is written off, Accounts Receivable and Allowance for Uncollectible Accounts decrease by the same amount, but the net figure for expected receivables stays the same.

11. When a customer whose account has been written off pays in full or in part, two entries must be made. First, the customer's receivable is reinstated by a debit to Accounts Receivable and a credit to Allowance for Uncollectible Accounts for the amount now thought to be collectible. Second, Cash is debited and Accounts Receivable is credited for each collection.

OBJECTIVE 4: Identify methods of financing accounts receivable and other issues related to accounts receivable (pp. 350–352).

12. Occasionally, companies cannot afford to wait until their receivables are collected. Accordingly, there are ways to obtain cash *before* collection from customers occurs. A business may borrow funds by pledging its accounts receivable as collateral. Also, a business may sell its receivables to a **factor** (e.g., a bank or finance company) through a process called **factoring**. Receivables may be factored without recourse (as with major credit cards) or with recourse; the factoring fee is much greater when receivables are factored without recourse, because of the greater risk involved.

13. **Installment accounts receivable** are receivables that will be collected in a series of payments; they are usually classified on the balance sheet as current assets.

14. Companies that allow customers to use national credit cards (such as MasterCard) must follow special accounting procedures. The credit card company reimburses the company for the sale, less a service charge. The credit card company levies this service charge because it is responsible for establishing credit and collecting the money from the customer. One of two procedures is used in accounting for credit card sales, depending upon whether

the merchant must wait for collection from the credit card company or may deposit the sales invoices into a checking account immediately. In either case, the *goal* is to record debits to Cash and Credit Card Discount Expense and a credit to Sales.

15. The **direct charge-off method** charges uncollectible accounts to an expense in the period of default, which may or may not coincide with the period of the related sale. There is no estimate for bad debts at the end of the period. When an account is deemed uncollectible, a debit to Uncollectible Accounts Expense and a credit to Accounts Receivable are made. The direct charge-off method often violates the matching rule because accounts may be written off in periods after the sale.

16. When a customer overpays, his or her account will have a credit balance. When a balance sheet is prepared, Accounts Receivable should be the sum of all accounts with debit balances. An account called Credit Balances in Customer Accounts should appear under current liabilities for the sum of all accounts with credit balances.

17. When loans and sales are made to the company's officers, employees, or stockholders, they should be shown separately on the balance sheet with a title such as Receivables from Employees and Officers.

OBJECTIVE 5: Define and describe a promissory note, and make calculations involving promissory notes (pp. 353–357).

18. A **promissory note** is a written promise to pay a definite sum of money on demand or at a future date. The person who signs the note and thereby promises to pay is called the maker of the note. The person to whom money is owed is called the payee. The payee records long- or short-term **notes receivable,** and the maker records long- or short-term **notes payable.**

19. Either the **maturity date** and the **duration of note** must be stated on the promissory note or it must be possible to figure them out from the information on the note.

20. To the borrower, **interest** is the cost of borrowing money. To the lender, it is the reward for lending money. The principal is the amount of money borrowed or loaned. The interest rate is the annual charge for borrowing money, and is expressed as a percentage. A note may be either interest-bearing or non-interest-bearing.

21. Interest (not interest rate) is a dollar figure, which is figured as follows:

$$\text{Interest} = \text{principal} \times \text{interest rate} \times \text{time (length of loan)}$$

For example, interest on $800 at 5 percent for 90 days is $10, calculated as ($800/1) × (5/100) × (90/360). A 360-day year is commonly used to simplify the computation. If the length of the note were expressed in months, then the third fraction would be the number of months divided by 12.

22. The **maturity value** (of an interest-bearing note) is the face value of the note (principal) plus interest.

23. It is common for banks to deduct the interest in advance when lending money on promissory notes. This practice is called discounting a note. The **discount** is the amount of interest deducted, and it is computed as follows:

$$\text{Discount} = \text{maturity value} \times \text{discount rate} \times \text{discount period}$$

The **proceeds from discounting** is the amount received by the borrower and equals the maturity value minus the discount.

OBJECTIVE 6: Journalize entries involving notes receivable (pp. 357–360).

24. There are five situations that result in journal entries for notes receivable: (a) receipt of a note, (b) collection on a note, (c) recording a dishonored note, (d) selling or discounting a note, and (e) recording adjusting entries.

25. When a promissory note is received, as in settlement (extension) of an existing account receivable, Notes Receivable is debited and Accounts Receivable is credited.

26. When collection is made on a note, Cash is debited for the maturity value, Notes Receivable is credited for the face value, and Interest Income is credited for the difference.

27. A **dishonored note** is one that is not paid at the maturity date. The payee would debit Accounts Receivable for the principal plus in-

terest, credit Notes Receivable, and credit Interest Income.

28. To raise immediate cash, companies often sell notes receivable to banks or financing companies before maturity. This practice is called discounting because the bank deducts the interest from the maturity value of the note to determine the proceeds. The company then debits Cash for the proceeds, credits Notes Receivable for the principal, and credits Interest Income for the difference.

29. On the maturity date, the maker of a note that has been discounted must pay the bank or financing company directly. The original payee (endorser) must make good on the note if the maker does not, and is therefore said to have a **contingent liability.** When such an event occurs, the bank or financing company first issues a **notice of protest** to the endorser. The endorser then debits Accounts Receivable and credits Cash for the principal plus interest plus **protest fee.**

30. End-of-period adjustments must be made for notes that apply to both the current and future periods. In this way interest may be properly divided among the periods.

OBJECTIVE 7: Demonstrate control of cash by preparing a bank reconciliation (pp. 360–365).

31. Once a month, the bank will return a company's canceled checks with the **bank statement.** The bank statement shows the bank balance at the beginning of the month, all additions and deductions during the month, and the balance at the end of the month.

32. A bank statement's end-of-month balance will rarely agree with the balance in the company's books for that date. Thus the accountant must prepare a **bank reconciliation** to account for this difference and to locate any errors made by the bank or the company. The bank reconciliation begins with the "balance per books" and "balance per statement" figures as of the bank statement date. Each figure is adjusted by certain additions and deductions resulting in two adjusted cash balance figures, which should agree. The balance per books figure is adjusted by information that the bank knew at the bank statement date but the company did not. The balance per bank statement figure is adjusted by information that the company knew at the bank statement date but the bank did not. Examples of adjustments follow.
   a. Outstanding checks are a deduction from the balance per bank statement.
   b. Deposits in transit are an addition to the balance per bank statement.
   c. Service charges by the bank appear on the bank statement, and are a deduction from the balance per books.
   d. A customer's NSF (nonsufficient funds) check is deducted from the balance per books.
   e. Interest earned on a checking account is added to the balance per books.
   f. Miscellaneous charges are deducted from the balance per books. Miscellaneous credits are added to the balance per books.

33. After the bank reconciliation has been prepared, adjusting entries must be made so that the accounting records will reflect the new information supplied by the bank statement. Each adjustment will include either a debit or a credit to Cash.

OBJECTIVE 8: Demonstrate the use of a simple imprest system (pp. 366–367).

34. Though it is good practice for a company to pay by check, this is often not practical for items of small value. For items like postage, a few inexpensive supplies, and taxi fare, many firms use a **petty cash fund.** One of the best ways to operate a petty cash fund is by the **imprest system.** Under this system, when the fund is started, Petty Cash is debited, and Cash is credited. When payment is made from the fund, the fund's custodian should prepare a **petty cash voucher** showing the date, amount, and purpose of the expenditure. The petty cash fund is replenished periodically and at the end of the accounting period. In each case, all of the expenditures since the fund was last replenished are debited, and Cash is credited. Discrepancies are recorded as Cash Short or Over.

Summary of Journal Entries Introduced in Chapter 7

A. (L.O. 1) Short-Term Investments   XX (purchase price)
          Cash   XX (amount paid)
             Purchased U.S. Treasury bills

B. (L.O. 1) Cash   XX (maturity amount)
          Interest Income   XX (amount earned)
          Short-Term Investments   XX (purchase price)
             U.S. Treasury bills matured

C. (L.O. 1) Short-Term Investments   XX (purchase price)
          Cash   XX (amount paid)
             Purchased investment in stock

D. (L.O. 1) Cash   XX (amount received)
          Dividend Income   XX (amount received)
             Dividends received on stock

E. (L.O. 1) Cash   XX (proceeds on sale)
          Loss on Sale of Investments   XX (the difference)
          Short-Term Investments   XX (purchase price)
             Sale of stock at a loss

F. (L.O. 1) Cash   XX (proceeds on sale)
          Gain on Sale of Investments   XX (the difference)
          Short-Term Investments   XX (purchase price)
             Sale of stock at a gain

G. (L.O. 1) Loss on Decline in Short-Term Investments   XX (market decline amount)
          Allowance to Reduce Short-Term Investments to   XX (market decline amount)
          Market
             Year-end adjustment for decline in value of
             stock

H. (L.O. 2) Uncollectible Accounts Expense   XX (amount estimated)
          Allowance for Uncollectible Accounts   XX (amount estimated)
             Year-end adjustment for estimated bad debts

I. (L.O. 3) Allowance for Uncollectible Accounts   XX (defaulted amount)
          Accounts Receivable   XX (defaulted amount)
             Wrote off account of specific customer who
             defaulted on debt

J. (L.O. 3) Accounts Receivable   XX (amount reinstated)
          Allowance for Uncollectible Accounts   XX (amount reinstated)
             Reinstated account that had been written off

K. (L.O. 3) Cash   XX (amount received)
          Accounts Receivable   XX (amount received)
             Collected from customer in J above

L. (L.O. 4) Uncollectible Accounts Expense   XX (defaulted amount)
          Accounts Receivable   XX (defaulted amount)
             Wrote off account of specific customer, direct
             charge-off method used

M. (L.O. 4) Accounts Receivable, Credit Card Company   XX (net amount receivable)
             Credit Card Discount Expense   XX (fee charged)
                 Sales   XX (gross amount sold)
                     To record credit card sales; vendor must wait
                     for collection

N. (L.O. 4) Cash   XX (amount received)
                 Accounts Receivable, Credit Card Company   XX (amount received)
                     Received credit card company payment (see M
                     above)

O. (L.O. 4) Cash   XX (amount net of fee)
             Credit Card Discount Expense   XX (fee charged)
                 Sales   XX (gross amount sold)
                     To record credit card sales; invoices deposited
                     in special credit card bank account

P. (L.O. 6) Notes Receivable   XX (establishing amount)
                 Accounts Receivable   XX (eliminating amount)
                     Received note in settlement of existing account
                     receivable

Q. (L.O. 6) Cash   XX (maturity amount)
                 Notes Receivable   XX (face amount)
                 Interest Income   XX (amount earned)
                     Made collection on note

R. (L.O. 6) Accounts Receivable   XX (maturity amount)
                 Notes Receivable   XX (face amount)
                 Interest Income   XX (amount earned)
                     To record dishonored note

S. (L.O. 6) Cash   XX (proceeds)
                 Notes Receivable   XX (face amount)
                 Interest Income   XX (amount earned)
                     Discounted note at bank prior to maturity date
                     (note: Interest Expense would have been in-
                     cluded as a debit if face amount had exceeded
                     proceeds)

T. (L.O. 6) Accounts Receivable   XX (see explanation)
                 Cash   XX (see explanation)
                     Paid bank maturity amount plus protest fee on
                     dishonored note

U. (L.O. 6) Interest Receivable   XX (amount accrued)
                 Interest Income   XX (amount earned)
                     To accrue interest on note at end of period

V. (L.O. 6) Cash   XX (maturity amount)
                 Notes Receivable   XX (face amount)
                 Interest Receivable   XX (interest previously accrued)
                 Interest Income   XX (interest this period)
                     To record collection on note (see U above)

W. (L.O. 7) After a bank reconciliation is prepared, journal entries must be made to record the items on the bank statement that the company has not yet recorded (service charges, NSF checks, etc.). The sample entries presented in your textbook will not be duplicated here, but please note that all entries contain either a debit or a credit to Cash.

X. (L.O. 8) Petty Cash   XX (amount established for)
        Cash   XX (amount established for)
            To establish petty cash fund

Y. (L.O. 8) Postage Expense   XX (amount incurred)
        Supplies   XX (amount purchased)
        Freight In   XX (amount incurred)
        Cash Short or Over   XX (amount short)
            Cash   XX (amount replenished)
                To replenish petty cash fund

Testing Your Knowledge

Matching

Match each term with its definition by writing the appropriate letter in the blank.

_____ 1. Compensating balance

_____ 2. Bank reconciliation

_____ 3. Outstanding check

_____ 4. NSF check

_____ 5. Petty cash fund

_____ 6. Credit

_____ 7. Uncollectible accounts expense

_____ 8. Allowance for uncollectible accounts

_____ 9. Installment accounts receivable

_____ 10. Promissory note

_____ 11. Maker

_____ 12. Payee

_____ 13. Maturity date

_____ 14. Maturity value

_____ 15. Interest rate

_____ 16. Interest

_____ 17. Principal

_____ 18. Discount

_____ 19. Dishonored note

_____ 20. Discounting a note

_____ 21. Notice of protest

a. The debtor named in a promissory note

b. The amount of money borrowed or loaned

c. An accounting for the difference between balance per books and balance per bank statement at a particular date

d. A note that is not paid at the maturity date

e. A written promise to pay

f. Estimated bad debts as represented on the income statement

g. A check that has been issued, but has not yet been presented to the bank for payment

h. The amount of interest deducted from the maturity value of a note

i. The time at which payment is due on a note

j. A policy of allowing customers to pay for merchandise over a period of time

k. A statement indicating that a discounted note has been dishonored

l. The creditor named in a promissory note

m. Cash set aside to pay for items of small value

n. Selling a note prior to maturity

o. The annual charge for borrowing money, expressed in dollars

p. Receivables that will be collected in a series of payments

q. A bad check

r. The annual charge for borrowing money, expressed as a percentage

s. A minimum amount that a bank requires a company to keep in its account

t. Bad debts as represented in the balance sheet

u. A note's principal plus interest

Use the lines provided to answer each item.

1. List three methods used in computing uncollectible accounts.

   _____

   _____

   _____

2. Explain the concept of *contingent liability* as it relates to discounted notes receivable.

   _____

   _____

   _____

3. Under what circumstance would there be a debit balance in Allowance for Uncollectible Accounts?

   _____

   _____

   _____

4. Using mathematical signs, list the sequence of items involved in computing proceeds from discounting a note receivable.

   _____

   _____

   _____

   _____

   _____

5. List three items that would be deducted from balance per books in a bank reconciliation.

   _____

   _____

   _____

True-False

Circle T if the statement is true, F if it is false. Please provide explanations for the false answers, using the blank lines at the end of the section.

T F   1. Under the direct charge-off method, Allowance for Uncollectible Accounts does not exist.

T F   2. The percentage of net sales method violates the matching principle.

T F   3. Under the accounts receivable aging method, the balance in Allowance for Uncollectible Accounts is ignored in making the adjusting entry.

T F   4. Allowance for Uncollectible Accounts is a contra account to Accounts Receivable.

T F   5. Loans to officers of the company should *not* be included in Accounts Receivable on the balance sheet.

T F   6. When a customer overpays, his or her account on the company's books will have a credit balance.

T F   7. Interest of 5 percent on $700 for 90 days would be computed as follows: .05 x 700 x 90.

T F   8. Trade credit refers to credit sales made to wholesale or retail customers.

T F   9. When a note is discounted at the bank, the maker must make good on the note if the payee defaults.

T F   10. A note dated December 14 and due February 14 has a duration of 60 days.

T F   11. It is possible for the proceeds of a discounted note receivable to be less than its face value.

T F   12. Under the allowance method, the entry to write off a specific account as uncollectible will decrease total assets.

T F **13.** The maturity value of a note equals interest plus principal.

T F **14.** Under the allowance method, a specific account is written off with a debit to Uncollectible Accounts Expense and a credit to Accounts Receivable.

T F **15.** When a note is dishonored, the payee should nevertheless record interest income.

T F **16.** Uncollectible accounts may be viewed as an expense of selling on credit.

T F **17.** When a petty cash fund is established, Cash is debited and Petty Cash is credited.

T F **18.** A check that is outstanding for two consecutive months should be included in both months' bank reconciliations.

T F **19.** After a bank reconciliation has been completed, the company must make journal entries to adjust for all outstanding checks.

T F **20.** A bank reconciliation for the month of September will begin with balance per books and balance per bank statement at September 1.

T F **21.** A credit memorandum on a bank statement indicates an addition to the bank balance.

T F **22.** Accounts receivable is an example of a cash equivalent.

T F **23.** The use of a major credit card (e.g., MasterCard) is an example of factoring with recourse.

Multiple Choice

Circle the letter of the best answer.

1. A company has credit card sales for the day of $1,000. If there is a 5 percent charge by credit card companies, then the company's entries to record sales and the eventual receipt of cash would include a
   a. credit to Sales for $950.
   b. debit to Accounts Receivable, Credit Card Companies for $1,050.
   c. credit to Credit Card Revenue for $50.
   d. debit to Cash for $950.

2. Which of the following does not equal the others?
   a. $600 for 60 days at 6 percent
   b. $1,200 for 120 days at 3 percent
   c. $300 for 120 days at 6 percent
   d. $600 for 30 days at 12 percent

3. At the balance sheet date, a company estimates that $1,500 of net sales for the year will not be collected. There is a debit balance of $600 in Allowance for Uncollectible Accounts. Under the percentage of net sales method, Uncollectible Accounts Expense and Allowance for Uncollectible Accounts would be debited and credited for
   a. $600.
   b. $1,100.
   c. $1,500.
   d. $2,100.

4. A contingent liability exists when
   a. a note is discounted.
   b. a note is dishonored.
   c. interest accrues on a note.
   d. a note reaches maturity.

5. Under the direct charge-off method, a specific customer's account is written off by
   a. debiting Uncollectible Accounts Expense and crediting Allowance for Uncollectible Accounts.
   b. debiting Accounts Receivable and crediting Allowance for Uncollectible Accounts.
   c. debiting Allowance for Uncollectible Accounts and crediting Accounts Receivable.
   d. debiting Uncollectible Accounts Expense and crediting Accounts Receivable.

6. Under the aging of accounts receivable method, a specific customer's account is written off by

   a. debiting Uncollectible Accounts Expense and crediting Allowance for Uncollectible Accounts.
   b. debiting Accounts Receivable and crediting Allowance for Uncollectible Accounts.
   c. debiting Allowance for Uncollectible Accounts and crediting Accounts Receivable.
   d. debiting Uncollectible Accounts Expense and crediting Accounts Receivable.

7. Which of the following cannot be determined from the information on a note?
   a. Discount rate
   b. Interest rate
   c. Interest
   d. Maturity date

8. Which method for handling bad debts often violates the matching principle?
   a. Percentage of net sales method
   b. Direct charge-off method
   c. Accounts receivable aging method
   d. Both *a* and *c*

9. Which of the following is *not* considered a short-term liquid asset?
   a. Notes receivable
   b. Short-term investments
   c. Inventory
   d. Cash

10. On the balance sheet, short-term investments in stock (marketable securities) are presented at
    a. cost, in accordance with the historical cost principle.
    b. market only if the assets are permanently impaired.
    c. lower of cost or market.
    d. market, regardless of original cost.

11. When a petty cash fund is replenished,
    a. Petty Cash is credited.
    b. Petty Cash is debited.
    c. Cash is credited.
    d. Cash is debited.

12. Deposits in transit should be included in a bank reconciliation as
    a. an addition to the bank statement balance.
    b. a deduction from the bank statement balance.
    c. an addition to the company's book balance.
    d. a deduction from the company's book balance.

Short-Term Liquid Assets

Applying Your Knowledge

Exercises

1. Calculate interest on the following amounts:
   a. $7,200 at 4% for 20 days = $_____
   b. $52,000 at 7% for 3 months = $_____
   c. $4,317 at 6% for 60 days = $_____
   d. $18,000 at 8% for 1 day = $_____

2. The facts that follow are needed to prepare a bank reconciliation for the Nelson Company as of March 31, 19xx. For each, provide the proper symbol (a, b, c, or d) to indicate where it should appear.

   a = Addition to the bank statement balance

   b = Deduction from the bank statement balance

   c = Addition to the company's book balance

   d = Deduction from the company's book balance

   _____ 1. The service charge by the bank was $8.

   _____ 2. A $1,700 note receivable was collected for the company by the bank. No collection fee was charged.

   _____ 3. There were two outstanding checks, totaling $3,200.

   _____ 4. A $355 NSF check drawn by a customer was deducted from the company's bank account and returned to the company.

   _____ 5. A deposit of $725 was made after banking hours on March 31.

   _____ 6. Check no. 185 was drawn for $342 but was erroneously recorded in the company's books as $324.

3. A petty cash fund of $100 was set up. Petty cash vouchers for the month totaled $86, and cash in the petty cash box totaled $12.50. The fund should be reimbursed in the amount of $_____.

4. For the following set of facts, make the necessary entries for Green's Department Store in the journal provided on the next page.

   Dec. 31 Interest of $75 has accrued on notes receivable.

   31 Net sales for the year were $600,000. It is estimated that 4 percent will not be collected. Make the entry for uncollectible accounts.

   Jan. 3 Anna Kohn purchased $10,000 worth of goods on credit in November. She now issues Green's her $10,000, 30-day, 6 percent note, thus extending her credit period.

   8 Tom O'Brien goes bankrupt and notifies Green's that he cannot pay for the $1,000 worth of goods he had purchased last year on account.

   14 The only credit card that Green's accepts is MasterCard. The store now records its credit card sales of $4,000 for the first two weeks in January. MasterCard will send payment to Green's upon receipt of invoices, and charges 5 percent for this service.

   18 Green's discounts Anna Kohn's note at the bank, receiving $10,020.

   24 A check is received from MasterCard for the first two weeks' credit sales, less the service charge.

   25 Tom O'Brien notifies Green's that he will in fact be able to pay $600 of the $1,000 that he owes.

   28 A check for $200 is received from Tom O'Brien.

   Feb. 2 Anna Kohn dishonors her note, and Green's must pay the bank the maturity value of the note plus a $10 protest fee.

		General Journal		
Date		Description	Debit	Credit

Crossword Puzzle
For Chapters 6 and 7

ACROSS

4. Interest deducted on a note
6. Section of accountant's report
8. Measure of profitability (3 words)
9. Promissory _____
10. Charge for default on note (2 words)
14. Length of note
16. Property
17. Income statement form (hyphenated)
18. Petty _____

DOWN

1. Source of information about a company (2 words)
2. Normal operating _____
3. Measure of liquidity (2 words)
4. _____ to equity ratio
5. See 11-Down
7. Combined, as financial statements
11. With 15-Down and 5-Down, income statement measure
12. Financial statements of less than a year
13. Method for estimating bad debts
15. See 11-Down

Reading

Investing Excess Corporate Cash

In the corporate treasury environment, treasury staff managers have responsibility for a number of activities, including; among other things, collections, disbursements, bank relationships, borrowing, and—of course—the investment of excess cash. With the pressure of all of the managers' other responsibilities, the investment of cash often falls to the bottom of the list of priorities, and managers come to rely on securities salespeople or on the investment departments of the banks with which their companies do business.

But by abdicating responsibility for the investment of excess cash to others, and by not attempting to improve their own knowledge of the techniques and financial instruments that are best suited to such investments, they may expose their companies to loss and their superiors—and themselves—to embarrassment.

The Cash Cushion

Excess cash typically refers to a surplus of cash resulting from company operations or the proceeds of the sale of a major asset—in other words, cash that is the product of normal business activity that is being held until it is used to pay down debt or reinvested in a long-term investment. In addition, there are circumstances in which companies find it advisable to maintain a certain amount of excess cash to meet unusual needs, even if they borrow funds regularly through lines of credit at banks or commercial paper or other forms of debt.

A cash cushion is often advisable because a company may not always have access to capital when it needs it. For example, if the company has an opportunity to purchase a large quantity of raw material, a capital asset, or other business opportunity with short notice, it may be difficult to arrange for the additional credit. There are also situations in which revenue falls suddenly as a result of a breakdown in the delivery of the company's product, for example, or problems with a billing system, or a labor dispute. And, if the company's earnings are down or its industry is in disfavor, the treasury manager may not be able to

Source: Used by permission from *Financial Executive,* January/February 1991, copyright 1991, by Financial Executives Institute.

renew or expand credit lines or go into the commercial paper or corporate debt market. Finally, the company that has gone to the top of its borrowing lines or is negotiating to expand them will need a cushion of cash to meet liquidity requirements until the credit is secured.

So excess cash is, in effect, an insurance policy to cover the risk of a liquidity crisis. The cost of this insurance is the lower yield the company earns on the investment of its portfolio in reasonably secure, liquid investments.

Setting Investment Guidelines

Each company needs to define the degree of risk it is willing to take in investing excess cash. Some companies invest with the objective of contributing to the company's bottom line, and they are willing to take a reasonable amount of risk to do so. If this is a company's objective, management needs to define exactly what percentage of its principal—5 percent, 10 percent, or more—it is willing to risk. It is often the case, however, that companies that say they want to maximize return are not willing to risk principal. Other companies want to take no risk whatsoever, and prefer to invest in U.S. Treasury securities. And others, which may not appreciate the fact that they can improve yield without sacrificing liquidity, simply leave their excess money in bank accounts.

A practical approach for investing company cash lies between these extremes. The appropriate objective in investing excess cash is to achieve a competitive rate of return with minimum risk and to have the money available when it is needed. The company should define its investment objectives, and the approach it will take to achieve them, in a written investment policy and set of guidelines. . . .

The major concern in investing excess cash is the maturity of the investments. The maturity date of any investment should be determined by the date on which the cash will be needed. In deciding on the appropriate maturities, the investor must bear in mind that the longer the maturity, the greater the exposure to a loss of principal should the instrument have to be sold at a time interest rates are higher than they were when the instrument was purchased. Obviously, the longer the maturity and the higher the move in interest rates, the greater the loss.

The company's need for liquidity determines the choice of both the maturity and the instrument; yield is a lesser concern. So the investor needs to know what instruments are available at what yield and with what liquidity.

Selecting Investment Maturities

Depending upon the size of the company, the amount of excess cash it has, and the need it anticipates for the cash in the future, the manager will want to invest in instruments that mature at different times. The manager may choose to invest a small portion of the total investment pool in a short maturity to meet an immediate need for funds. The treasury department will need to determine the amount to be invested in short maturities. Some large investment portfolios have longer-term investments to achieve a higher rate of return, and maintain only a small portion of their total investments for immediate, unforeseen cash needs.

Once the treasury department has established the company's need for liquidity, the investor should begin with an analysis of the yield curves of the various instruments available (the yield curve is the rate of return for various maturities). Longer maturities should carry a higher rate of return because, as mentioned above, they will decline faster in price than those with shorter maturities if interest rates move higher. It is often difficult to separate analysis of yield curves from speculation on interest rates, but to the extent possible, the investor should avoid making investment decisions based on interest rate forecasts. The purpose of maintaining liquidity is to have funds readily available when they are needed, not to support speculation in interest rates. Having to liquidate a portfolio at a loss of capital is hard to defend.

The objective of active portfolio management is to obtain the best relative value. Let us say, for example, the investor has invested in certificates of deposit, which yielded a higher return at the time they were purchased than did commercial paper. But if commercial paper has since become "cheap," and has begun to produce a higher yield than the CDs, the investor will sell the CDs and buy commercial paper. By so doing, the investor uses yield spreads to enhance yield without increasing risk.

The investor can also move on the yield curve to look for higher yielding maturities. Let's say

you have an investment with a 90-day maturity, but the yield curve has changed so that yields have become sharply higher at six months than was the case when you bought the investment. You can sell your 90-day maturity and buy the six-month maturity in what is called an extension swap—extending the maturity—and pick up an additional margin of yield. Of course, when you extend maturities you should bear in mind when the funds will be needed.

Interest-bearing securities are the mainstay of the corporate excess cash portfolio. The prices of equities in general are too volatile to be reliable investments for short-term cash needs. The one exception is preferred stocks, which generally pay high dividends. Because dividends are entitled to a substantial exclusion from federal income taxes, these investments have a relatively high net after-tax return to the corporate investor. Further, variations in certain types of preferred stocks provide some immunity to fluctuations in market price and therefore put them in the category of interest-bearing securities, even though they do not have a specific maturity.

Money market mutual funds may be attractive to the investor who has a small pool of invested funds. These funds typically are invested in short maturities—less than 60 days—so their asset values remain constant and their yields are acceptable. But because management charges for money market funds range up to 0.7 percent, they are likely to be too expensive for the large investor. Companies with portfolios of $15 million or more may find it more efficient to manage their investments internally or to hire a money manager, from whom they will get personalized service, tailored reports, and a specific investment approach.

In assessing the different instruments, the investor must be well aware of the risk of default for each obligation. The most common way to protect against default or credit risk is to retain the services of credit review organizations that, for a fee, will provide you with credit ratings on the organizations that issue debt instruments to help you assess the default risk on the instruments you purchase.

Buying Investment Expertise

Several options are available to the company that wants to improve its investment expertise. The least expensive option, of course, is to encourage those responsible for investing in corporate cash to enroll in one of the many education programs provided by a number of different organizations.

Although this option is inexpensive, sending the investment staff to such courses is time-consuming, and the company may not get the results it wants. Management may choose instead to bring in a consultant to train the staff, establish investment guidelines, tell them what credit services to use, what software, and so on.

Finally, the company may decide to hire a full-time investment manager, who would take responsibility for investing excess cash in coordination with the company's needs and guidelines. The investment management firm should give management periodic reports that provide a complete description of the instruments purchased, credit ratings, yield calculations, and perhaps accounting information, such as interest accruals, amortization, and accretion.

Outside money managers can be expensive. They typically charge from 0.15 percent to 0.40 percent of the dollars managed, depending on the amount of money involved and the type of portfolio. But credit review services, analytical databases, reporting software, training, and other necessary investment services are not inexpensive, and management should be certain to include the costs of these services in deciding how to improve investment capabilities.

Investment Services

A number of excellent investment services are available. But because these services can be costly —and because they require considerable skill to be used effectively—they typically are appropriate only for the larger portfolios—those with $50 million or more.

Subscription financial data services give the corporate investor access to market prices and other data essential to the analysis of the relative values of the different instruments and yield curves. These services may cost between $600 and $1,500 a month. But with such a service, an experienced investor can fine-tune an investment decision and get a very competitive execution price.

Experienced corporate investors also need systems that give them the capability to compute yields quickly and accurately and to put into a single yield formula a number of different instruments—treasuries, government agencies, corporates, bank obligations, taxable equivalent yields for tax-exempt securities—in such a way that they are truly comparable.

Other data bases and software packages are also available that give the corporate investor the capability of doing "what-if" calculations: "What will happen to the portfolio if I buy such-and-such an instrument and interest rates go up—or down— by certain amounts?" Because systems are available to meet the needs of investors with varying skills, the system selected should match the level of sophistication of those who use it.

Nothing Is Easy

As is the case in any program, time and effort must be spent in finding the approach that best meets your company's needs and objectives. But in a time of increasing complexity of financial instruments and deteriorating profit margins, companies cannot afford to overlook opportunities for enhancing investment yield and minimizing risk of loss through well-informed, effective investment of excess cash.

CHAPTER 8 INVENTORIES

Reviewing the Chapter

OBJECTIVE 1: Define *merchandise inventory,* **and show how inventory measurement affects income determination (pp. 396–401).**

1. To measure income properly and observe the matching rule, the following two questions must be answered for each nonfinancial asset:
   a. How much of the asset has been used up (expired) during the current period and should be transferred to expense?
   b. How much of the asset is unused (unexpired) and should remain on the balance sheet as an asset?

2. **Merchandise inventory** consists of all goods owned and held for sale in the regular course of business. It appears in the current asset section of the balance sheet below receivables.

3. Beginning inventory plus purchases equals cost of goods available for sale. Cost of goods sold is determined indirectly by deducting ending inventory from the cost of goods available for sale.

4. Because the cost of ending inventory is needed to compute cost of goods sold, it affects net income dollar for dollar. It is important to match cost of goods sold with sales so that net income will be reasonably accurate.

5. This year's ending inventory automatically becomes next year's beginning inventory. Because beginning inventory also affects net income dollar for dollar, an error in this year's ending inventory will result in misstated net income for both this year and next year.
   a. When ending inventory is understated, net income for the period will be understated.
   b. When ending inventory is overstated, net income for the period will be overstated.
   c. When beginning inventory is understated, net income for the period will be overstated.
   d. When beginning inventory is overstated, net income for the period will be understated.

6. Ending inventory is computed by (a) counting the items on hand, (b) finding the cost of each item, and (c) multiplying unit cost by quantity. Inventory includes all items to which a company has title, even if they have not yet been delivered.

7. Goods in transit should be included in inventory only if the company has title to the goods. When goods are sent FOB shipping point, title passes to the buyer when the goods reach the common carrier. When goods are shipped FOB destination, title passes when the goods reach the buyer. Goods that have been sold but are still on hand should not be included in the seller's inventory count.

8. When goods are held on **consignment,** the consignee (who earns a commission upon making the sale) has possession of the goods, but the consignor retains title and thus includes the goods on its balance sheet.

OBJECTIVE 2: Define *inventory cost,* and relate it to goods flow and cost flow (pp. 401–402).

9. **Inventory cost** is defined as the purchase price plus any charges incurred in bringing the inventory to its existing condition and location.

10. When identical items of merchandise are purchased at different prices during the year, it is usually impractical to monitor the actual **goods flow** and record the corresponding costs. Instead, the accountant will make an assumption of the **cost flow,** and will use one of the following methods: (a) specific identification, (b) average-cost, (c) first-in, first-out (FIFO), or (d) last-in, first-out (LIFO).

OBJECTIVE 3a: Calculate the pricing of inventory, using the cost basis according to the specific identification method (p. 403).

11. Under the **specific identification method,** the units of ending inventory can be identified as having come from specific purchases. The flow of costs reflects the actual flow of goods in this case. However, the specific identification method is not practical in most cases.

OBJECTIVE 3b: Calculate the pricing of inventory, using the cost basis according to the average-cost method (pp. 403–404).

12. Under the **average-cost method,** the average cost per unit is first figured for the goods available for sale during the period. That is, the cost of goods available for sale is divided by the units available for sale. Then the average cost per unit is multiplied by the number of units in ending inventory to get the cost of ending inventory.

OBJECTIVE 3c: Calculate the pricing of inventory, using the cost basis according to the first-in, first-out (FIFO) method (p. 404).

13. Under the **first-in, first-out (FIFO) method,** the cost of the first items purchased is assigned to the first items sold. Therefore, ending inventory cost is determined from the prices of the most recent purchases. During periods of rising prices, FIFO yields the highest net income of the four methods.

OBJECTIVE 3d: Calculate the pricing of inventory, using the cost basis according to the last-in, first-out (LIFO) method (pp. 404–405).

14. Under the **last-in, first-out (LIFO) method,** the last items purchased are assumed to be the first items sold. Therefore, the ending inventory cost is determined from the prices of the earliest purchases. During periods of rising prices, LIFO yields the lowest net income of the four methods. However, it best matches current merchandise costs with current sales prices.

OBJECTIVE 4: State the effects of each method on income determination and income taxes in periods of changing prices (pp. 405–408).

15. During periods of rising prices, FIFO will produce a higher net income than LIFO. During periods of falling prices, the reverse is true. The average-cost and specific identification methods will produce net income figures that are somewhere between those of FIFO and LIFO. Even though LIFO best follows the matching rule, FIFO provides a more up-to-date ending inventory figure for balance sheet purposes.

16. There are several rules for the valuation of inventory for federal income tax purposes. For example, even though a business has a wide choice of methods, once a method has been chosen, it must be applied consistently. In addition, several regulations apply to LIFO, such as the requirement that LIFO be used for reporting purposes when it is being used for tax purposes.

17. A **LIFO liquidation** occurs when sales have reduced inventories below the levels established in prior years. When prices have been rising steadily, a LIFO liquidation will produce unusually high profits.

OBJECTIVE 5: Apply the perpetual inventory system to accounting for inventories and cost of goods sold (pp. 409–412).

18. When the **periodic inventory system** is used, a physical inventory is taken at the end of the period, and cost of goods sold is derived by subtracting ending inventory from cost of goods available for sale.

19. The **perpetual inventory system** is used by companies that want more control over their inventories. A continuous record is kept of the balance of each inventory item. Thus a physical count is not needed (although one should be taken periodically to confirm the perpetual records). Specifically, Merchandise Inventory is maintained as a controlling account supported by a subsidiary file of indi-

vidual inventory records (such as inventory cards or computer files).

20. The journal entries for the cost of merchandise purchased and sold differ for the periodic and perpetual systems. The periodic system records all purchases of goods in a Purchases account, closes out Purchases and beginning inventory at the end of the period, and records ending inventory. The perpetual system records all purchases of goods with a debit to Merchandise Inventory, and records Cost of Goods Sold and a reduction in Merchandise Inventory after each sale. No Purchases account is needed, and the only merchandise-related entry made at the end of the period is to close out Cost of Goods Sold.

OBJECTIVE 6: Apply the lower-of-cost-or-market rule to inventory valuation (pp. 412–414).

21. The **market** value of inventory (current replacement cost) may fall below its cost as a result of physical deterioration, obsolescence, or decline in price level. Accordingly, it should be valued at the **lower of cost or market (LCM)**. The three basic methods of valuing inventory at lower of cost or market are the **item-by-item method,** the **major category method,** and the **total inventory method.** However, the total inventory method is not acceptable for federal income tax purposes.

OBJECTIVE 7a: Estimate the cost of ending inventory using the retail inventory method (pp. 414–415).

22. The **retail method** of inventory estimation may be used when the difference between the cost and sales prices of goods is a constant percentage over a period of time. It may be used whether or not the business makes a physical count of goods. To apply the retail method, goods available for sale are first figured both at cost and at retail. Next, a cost-to-retail ratio is computed. Sales for the period are then subtracted from goods available for sale at retail to produce ending inventory at retail. Finally, ending inventory at retail is multiplied by the cost-to-retail ratio to produce an estimate of ending inventory at cost.

OBJECTIVE 7b: Estimate the cost of ending inventory using the gross profit method (pp. 415–416).

23. The **gross profit method** of inventory estimation assumes that the gross margin for a business remains relatively stable from year to year. This method is used when inventory records are lost or destroyed, and when records of beginning inventory and purchases are not kept at retail. To apply the gross profit method, cost of goods available for sale is first determined by adding purchases to beginning inventory. Then cost of goods sold is estimated as follows:

Sales × (1 − gross margin %)

The resulting estimated cost of goods sold is subtracted from the cost of goods available for sale to arrive at estimated ending inventory.

Summary of Journal Entries Introduced in Chapter 8

A. (L.O. 5) The journal entries for the periodic inventory system presented in your textbook will not be duplicated here, as they were introduced in Chapter 5. Accordingly, all entries presented below assume the use of a *perpetual inventory system.* Neither the gross nor the net method of handling discounts is assumed here.

B. (L.O. 5) Merchandise Inventory   XX (purchase price)
                 Accounts Payable   XX (purchase price)
                       Purchased inventory on credit

C. (L.O. 5) Accounts Receivable   XX (sales price)
                 Sales   XX (sales price)
                       To record credit sales (see accompanying entry D below)

D. (L.O. 5) Cost of Goods Sold   XX (merchandise cost)
                 Merchandise Inventory   XX (merchandise cost)
                       To record cost of goods sold relative to entry C above

E. (L.O. 5) Accounts Payable   XX (amount returned)
                 Merchandise Inventory   XX (amount returned)
                       To record return of goods

F. (L.O. 5) Accounts Payable   XX (amount paid)
                 Cash   XX (amount paid)
                       To record payment to supplier

Testing Your Knowledge

Matching

Match each term with its definition by writing the appropriate letter in the blank.

_____ 1. LIFO liquidation

_____ 2. Merchandise inventory

_____ 3. Specific identification method

_____ 4. FIFO method

_____ 5. LIFO method

_____ 6. Average-cost method

_____ 7. Lower of cost or market

_____ 8. Retail method

_____ 9. Gross profit method

_____ 10. Periodic inventory system

_____ 11. Perpetual inventory system

_____ 12. Market

_____ 13. Consignment

a. The inventory method that utilizes an average-cost-per-unit figure

b. Current replacement cost of inventory

c. The inventory estimation method used when inventory is lost or destroyed

d. The inventory method in which the assumed flow of costs matches the actual flow of goods

e. The inventory system that maintains continuous records

f. The rule that governs how inventory should be valued on the financial statements

g. The inventory method that yields the highest ending inventory during periods of rising prices

h. Goods held for sale in the regular course of business

i. The inventory estimation method that uses a cost-to-retail ratio

j. The inventory method that best follows the matching principle

k. An arrangement whereby one company sells goods for another company, for a commission

l. The inventory system that does not maintain continuous records

m. An occurrence that produces unusually high profits under steadily rising prices

Short Answer

Use the lines provided to answer each item.

1. List the four basic cost-flow assumptions used to determine the cost of merchandise inventory.

   _____

   _____

   _____

   _____

2. List the three basic methods of valuing inventory at lower of cost or market.

   _____

   _____

   _____

3. List two methods of estimating ending inventory.

   _____

   _____

4. Briefly distinguish between the periodic and perpetual inventory systems in terms of record keeping and inventory taking.

   _____

   _____

   _____

   _____

True-False

Circle T if the statement is true, F if it is false. Please provide explanations for the false answers, using the blank lines at the end of the section.

T F **1.** The unexpired portion of a nonfinancial asset will appear on the balance sheet.

T F **2.** When beginning inventory is understated, cost of goods sold for the period will also be understated.

T F **3.** When ending inventory is overstated, net income for the period will also be overstated.

T F **4.** An error in 19x1's ending inventory will cause net income to be misstated in both 19x1 and 19x2.

T F **5.** Goods in transit belong in the buyer's ending inventory only if the buyer has paid for them.

T F **6.** If prices were never to change, then all four methods of inventory valuation would result in identical net income figures.

T F **7.** Under FIFO, goods are sold in exactly the same order as they are purchased.

T F **8.** Of the four inventory methods, LIFO will result in the lowest income during periods of falling prices.

T F **9.** Under the retail method, each item sold must be recorded at both cost and retail.

T F **10.** Under the gross profit method, cost of goods sold is estimated by multiplying the gross profit percentage by sales.

T F **11.** A perpetual inventory system does not close out beginning inventory at the end of the period.

T F **12.** Under rising prices, the average-cost method will result in a lower net income than LIFO will.

T F **13.** When a periodic inventory system is used, a subsidiary file of inventory accounts must be kept.

T F **14.** If FIFO is being used for tax purposes, it must be used for reporting purposes as well.

T F **15.** When goods are held on consignment, the consignee has both possession and title until the goods are sold.

_____

_____

_____

_____

_____

_____

_____

_____

_____

_____

_____

_____

_____

_____

_____

_____

_____

_____

_____

_____

_____

_____

_____

_____

_____

_____

Multiple Choice

Circle the letter of the best answer.

1. Which of the following is *least* likely to be included in the cost of inventory?
   a. Freight in
   b. Cost to store goods
   c. Purchase cost of goods
   d. Excise tax on goods purchased

2. Under rising prices, which inventory method will probably result in the highest tax liability?
   a. FIFO
   b. LIFO
   c. Both LIFO and average-cost
   d. Average-cost

3. Forgetting to inventory the merchandise in a warehouse will result in
   a. overstated net income.
   b. overstated total assets.
   c. understated owners' equity.
   d. understated cost of goods sold.

4. Which inventory method is best suited for low-volume, high-priced goods?
   a. FIFO
   b. LIFO
   c. Specific identification
   d. Average-cost

5. Which of the following is not used or computed in applying the retail inventory method?
   a. Ending inventory at retail
   b. Freight at retail
   c. Beginning inventory at cost
   d. Sales during the period

6. The cost of inventory becomes an expense in the period in which
   a. the inventory is sold.
   b. the merchandiser obtains title to the inventory.
   c. the merchandiser pays for the inventory.
   d. the merchandiser is paid for inventory that it has sold.

7. Goods in transit should be included in the inventory of
   a. neither the buyer nor the seller.
   b. the buyer when the goods have been shipped FOB destination.
   c. the seller when the goods have been shipped FOB shipping point.
   d. the company that has title to the goods.

8. Under the perpetual inventory system, two journal entries are made when goods are
   a. purchased.
   b. paid for.
   c. sold.
   d. returned.

Applying Your Knowledge

Exercises

1. Swanson Company had a beginning inventory of 100 units at $20. The firm made successive purchases as follows:

   Feb. 20 Purchased 200 units at $22
   May   8 Purchased 150 units at $20
   Oct. 17 Purchased 250 units at $24

   Calculate the cost that would be assigned to the ending inventory of 310 units and cost of goods sold under the following methods:

		Cost of Ending Inventory	Cost of Goods Sold
a.	LIFO	$ _____	$ _____
b.	FIFO	$ _____	$ _____
c.	Average-cost	$ _____	$ _____

2. The records of Morgan Company show the following data for the month of May:

Sales	$ 156,000
Beginning inventory (at cost)	70,000
Beginning inventory (at retail)	125,000
Net purchases (at cost)	48,000
Net purchases (at retail)	75,000
Freight in	2,000

   Compute the estimated cost of ending inventory, using the retail inventory method.

3. At the beginning of the accounting period, the cost of merchandise inventory was $150,000. Net sales during the period were $300,000, net purchases totaled $120,000, and the historical gross margin has been 20 percent. Compute the estimated cost of ending inventory, using the gross profit method.

4. Rudena Enterprises uses the perpetual LIFO method for valuing its inventory. On May 1, its inventory consisted of 100 units that cost $10 each. Successive purchases and sales for May were as follows:

May   4   Purchased 60 units at $12.00 each
May   8   Sold 50 units
May 17   Purchased 70 units at $11.00 each
May 25   Sold 100 units

In the perpetual inventory record card provided here, enter all inventory data for the month of May.

5. Assume the same facts as in Exercise 4 and that the goods retail for $20 each. In the journal at the bottom of this page, prepare the journal entries to record the May 17 purchase (assume a credit purchase) and the May 25 sale (assume a cash sale). You will need to refer to the completed perpetual inventory record card in Exercise 4 to answer this question.

Date		Purchased			Sold			Balance		
		Units	Cost	Total	Units	Cost	Total	Units	Cost	Total

	General Journal			
Date		Description	Debit	Credit

Reading

"How Inventories Could Bury 1985 Computer Profits"

In the creative world of computers, high-tech managers are reluctant to admit that their innovations have either become obsolete or been outclassed by the competition. That has made computer companies notorious for "watery," or overvalued inventory. But in the past few months, managers and their accountants are coming under urgent pressure to make more realistic judgments.

The problem was festering at yearend, as companies displayed high levels of inventory in relation to profits (table). But since sales turned ice-cold in January, the quantity of inventories has been rising sharply. As more of those computers or parts used to make them languish in warehouses, the greater the chance that technological advances or foreign competition will chop the market value of those products or even make them worthless. If that happens, inventory must be written off against pretax profits. The concern is that managers or their auditors will shrink from making some tough decisions. Investors will find out shortly when first-quarter reports are issued.

Lower Projections

The inventory problem is underscored by International Business Machines Corp.'s late-March decision to give up on its PCjr home computer and Apple Computer Inc.'s plans to shut down production entirely for a week in April. IBM's decision to stop making the PCjr will knock its earnings down only about 10 cents per share, says Jonathan M. Fram, a technology analyst with PaineWebber Inc. But "their mainframe business is sluggish," he says, noting that Big Blue's inventory swelled $2.2 billion during 1984. Like many on Wall Street, Fram has cut IBM's 1985 earning projections by nearly $1 a share, to $11.65. IBM's stock has faltered, pulling other technology stocks down with it.

Apple's inventory, unencumbered by mainframes, normally turns over faster than its older competitors'. But "there's no question that they have excess inventory," says Ulric Weil, a com-

Source: Article by Stuart Weiss. Reprinted from April 8, 1985 issue of *Business Week* by special permission, copyright © 1985 by McGraw-Hill, Inc.

puter analyst with Morgan Stanley & Co. Just since February, Wall Street has cut Apple's 1985 earnings prospects by 20%.

During the same week that Apple and IBM announced their rollbacks, the Securities & Exchange Commission fired off a stark reminder of how vulnerable computer company earnings can be to misjudgment of inventory values. In publicly chastising Burroughs Corp. for being too slow to partially write down $154 million of inventory as obsolete, the SEC forced Burroughs to pare back pretax earnings by $61 million over a five-quarter period. "A company has to step up to the bad news when they know it," says Robert J. Sack, chief accountant with the enforcement division of the SEC, "and they have to be prepared to share it with shareholders."

"Worst-Hit"

The SEC action, coming four years after the affected period, didn't budge Burroughs stock. The company won't comment on the action, but its annual report clearly shows the potential for further write-downs. Burroughs' total inventories have an average life of 230 days, nearly double the time that units normally stay on the shelf at other big-ticket computer companies.

Other analysts see far worse problems at Control Data Corp. "It is probably one of the worst-hit companies," says Fram, "because it is a supplier of disk drives to the computer industry." He notes that the company has been forced to slash its prices by 50% in the past 12 months to compete with the Japanese. The company also sells floppy disks, which "were selling for $150 a unit nine months ago." Now, he says, the company would be lucky to get $60.

Excess inventory is also plaguing the high-tech upstarts that fueled 1983's record-breaking market for initial public offerings. And it is at these companies that inventory accounting practices are most questionable. "I'm sure that IBM has a process whereby someone outside the group that built the product asks whether the valuation is correct," says the SEC's Sack. At little companies, he adds, it's less likely.

WHY COMPUTER COMPANY EARNINGS ARE VULNERABLE

Having lots of inventory on the shelf can be a sign of slow sales—which could lead to price cuts and inventory write-downs. When inventories are relatively large, even a small write-down can clobber profits.

	INVENTORY ON HAND*	INVENTORY VALUE*	PRETAX PROFITS**
	DAYS	MILLIONS OF DOLLARS	
Apple	71	$261	$231
Honeywell	106	1,090	431
IBM	162	6,598	11,623
Control Data	190	865	58
Data General	202	353	132
Sperry	205	1,586	286
Datapoint	218	106	13
Burroughs	230	1,368	363
Wang	232	649	291
Digital Equipment	260	2,069	496

*Most recent quarter   DATA:BW   **Latest four quarters

Pushed Around

Moreover, accountants say the little companies are often the toughest to audit. "The whole guts of a high-tech company is its inventory," notes Phillip Goodman, partner in charge of Laventhol & Horwath's Mountain View (Calif.) office. "If you can't agree" with the company's management about the worth of its products, "then you have to resign the account." The SEC requires companies to report any change in outside auditors, and it asks accountants why they resigned. "I sense that management is trying to push [the accountants] around more," says Sack.

As the computer industry's sluggish sales and falling prices become more evident, investors can only wonder how many more write-downs might be lurking in the warehouses.

CHAPTER 9 LONG-TERM ASSETS: ACQUISITION AND DEPRECIATION

Reviewing the Chapter

OBJECTIVE 1: Describe the nature, types, and issues of accounting for long-term assets (pp. 438–439).

1. **Long-term assets** (also called **fixed assets**) are assets that (a) have a useful life of more than one year, (b) are acquired for use in the operation of the business, and (c) are not intended for resale to customers. Assets such as land and buildings that are not being used in the normal course of business should be classified as long-term investments. Property, plant, and equipment is the balance sheet classification for **tangible assets,** which have physical substance, such as land, buildings, equipment, and **natural resources. Intangible assets** is the balance sheet classification for assets that do not have physical substance, such as patents, trademarks, goodwill, copyrights, leaseholds, franchises, and organization costs.

2. In dealing with long-term assets, the major accounting problem is to figure out how much of the asset has benefited the current period, and how much should be carried forward as an asset to benefit future periods. This allocation of costs to different accounting periods is called **depreciation** in the case of plant and equipment (plant assets), **depletion** in the case of natural resources, and **amortization** in the case of intangible assets. Because land has an unlimited useful life, its cost is never converted into an expense.

3. To account for long-term assets, one must determine (a) the cost of the asset, (b) the method of matching the cost with revenues, (c) the treatment of subsequent expenditures such as repairs and maintenance, and (d) the treatment of asset disposal.

OBJECTIVE 2: Account for the cost of property, plant, and equipment (pp. 439–442).

4. The cost of a long-term asset includes the purchase cost, freight charges, insurance while in transit, installation, and other costs involved in acquiring the asset and getting it ready for use. Interest incurred during the construction of a plant asset is included in the cost of the asset. However, interest incurred for the purchase of a plant asset is expensed when incurred.

5. When land is purchased, the Land account should be debited for the price paid for the land, real estate commissions, lawyers' fees, and such expenses as back taxes assumed; draining, clearing, and grading costs; assessments for local improvements; and the cost (less salvage value) of tearing down a building on the property.

6. Land improvements, such as driveways, parking lots, and fences, are subject to depreciation and require a separate Land Improvements account.

7. When long-term assets are purchased for a lump sum, the cost should be divided among the assets acquired in proportion to their appraisal values.

OBJECTIVE 3: Define *depreciation,* **state the factors that affect its computation, and show how to record it (pp. 442–443).**

8. Depreciation, as used in accounting, refers to the allocation of the cost (less the residual value) of a plant asset to the periods benefited by the asset. It does not refer to the physical deterioration or the decrease in market value of the asset. That is, it is a process of allocation, not of valuation.

9. A plant asset should be depreciated over its estimated useful life in a systematic and rational manner. Plant assets have limited useful lives because of **physical deterioration** and **obsolescence** (the process of becoming out of date).

10. Depreciation may be computed after determining the asset's cost, residual value, depreciable cost, and estimated useful life. **Residual value** is the estimated value at the disposal date and is often referred to as **salvage value** or **disposal value. Depreciable cost** equals the asset's cost less its residual value. **Estimated useful life** may be measured in time or in units, and requires careful consideration by the accountant.

OBJECTIVE 4: Compute periodic depreciation under each of four methods (pp. 444–448).

11. The most common depreciation methods are (a) straight-line, (b) production, (c) sum-of-the-years'-digits, and (d) declining-balance. The last two are examples of accelerated methods.

OBJECTIVE 4a: Compute periodic depreciation under the straight-line method (p. 444).

12. Under the **straight-line method,** the depreciable cost is spread evenly over the life of the asset. Under this method, depreciation for each year is computed as follows:

$$\frac{\text{Cost} - \text{residual value}}{\text{Estimated useful life in years}}$$

OBJECTIVE 4b: Compute periodic depreciation under the production method (pp. 444–445).

13. Under the **production method,** depreciation is based not on time but on use of the asset in units. Under this method, depreciation for each year is computed as follows:

$$\frac{\text{Cost} - \text{residual value}}{\text{Estimated useful life in units}} \times \begin{array}{c}\text{actual units}\\\text{of output}\end{array}$$

OBJECTIVE 4c(1): Compute periodic depreciation under the sum-of-the-years'-digits method (pp. 445–446).

14. Sum-of-the-years'-digits and declining-balance are described as **accelerated methods** because depreciation is greatest in the first year and declines each year thereafter. These methods are justified by the matching rule (high depreciation charges in the most productive years) and by the smoothing effect that results when annual depreciation and repair expense are combined (that is, over the years, depreciation charges decrease and repair costs increase).

15. Under the **sum-of-the-years'-digits method,** depreciation is computed by multiplying depreciable cost by a fraction that changes every year. Under this method, depreciation for the first year (where n = estimated useful life) is computed as follows:

$$(\text{Cost} - \text{residual value}) \times \frac{n}{1 + 2 + \ldots + n}$$

In each succeeding year, the numerator decreases by one, but the denominator remains the same.

OBJECTIVE 4c(2): Compute periodic depreciation under the declining-balance method (pp. 447–448).

16. Under the **declining-balance method,** depreciation is computed by multiplying the existing carrying value of the asset by a fixed percentage. The **double-declining-balance method** is a form of the declining-balance method that uses a fixed percentage that is twice the straight-line percentage. Under the double-declining-balance method, depreciation for each year is computed as follows:

$$2 \times \frac{100\%}{\text{useful life in years}} \times \begin{array}{c}\text{existing}\\\text{carrying}\\\text{value}\end{array}$$

Under the declining-balance or double-declining-balance method, the asset may not be depreciated below its residual value.

OBJECTIVE 5: Apply depreciation methods to problems of partial years, revised rates, items of low unit cost, groups of similar items, and accelerated cost recovery (pp. 448–454).

17. When an asset is purchased after the beginning of the year or discarded before the end of the year, depreciation should be recorded for only part of the year. The accountant figures the year's depreciation and multiplies this figure by the fraction of the year that the asset was in use.

18. Often, the estimated useful life or residual value is found to be over- or understated after some depreciation has been taken. The accountant must then produce a revised figure for the remaining useful life or remaining depreciable cost. Future depreciation is then calculated by spreading the remaining depreciable cost over the remaining useful life, leaving previous depreciation unchanged.

19. Assets of low unit cost, such as small tools, generally are not depreciated on an individual basis. Instead, they are either charged as expenses or recorded in an inventory account when purchased. In the latter case, an inventory of small tools must be taken at the end of each period to determine the amount consumed in that period.

20. When a company has several plant assets that are similar, it will probably use **group depreciation** rather than individual depreciation. Under group depreciation, the original costs of all similar assets are lumped together in one summary account. Then depreciation is figured for the assets as a whole.

21. Under the **Accelerated Cost Recovery System (ACRS)**, each depreciable asset is placed in a category for tax purposes only, and depreciated according to percentages established by Congress; estimated useful life and salvage value are ignored. ACRS depreciation allows the rapid write-off of tangible assets to reduce current taxes, but is not acceptable for financial reporting purposes.

22. In 1986, Congress passed the **Tax Reform Act of 1986.** This law retains the ACRS concept described above, but incorporates a new **Modified Accelerated Cost Recovery System (MACRS).** Under MACRS, the write-off of assets for tax purposes is generally more rapid than under ACRS. For example, property

other than real estate is depreciated by a 200 percent declining-balance method. In addition, light tools are depreciated over three-year lifetimes, and automobiles and light trucks are depreciated over five-year lifetimes. Recovery of the cost of property placed in service after December 31, 1986, is calculated according to this law.

OBJECTIVE 6: Apply the matching rule to the allocation of expired costs for capital expenditures and revenue expenditures (pp. 454–457).

23. Before recording an expenditure in connection with a long-term asset, one must determine whether it was a capital expenditure or a revenue expenditure. **Capital expenditures** are **expenditures** (payments or incurrence of liabilities) for plant and equipment, **additions** (such as a building wing), **betterments** (such as the installation of an air-conditioning system), and intangible assets. A capital expenditure is recorded as an asset because it will benefit several accounting periods. **Revenue expenditures** are expenditures for repairs, maintenance, fuel, and anything else necessary to maintain and operate the plant and equipment. A revenue expenditure is charged as expense in the period incurred, under the theory that it benefits only the current accounting period.

24. **Ordinary repairs** are expenditures that are necessary to maintain an asset in good operating condition, and are charged as expense in the period incurred. **Extraordinary repairs** are expenditures (as for a major overhaul) that either increase the asset's residual value or lengthen its useful life. They are recorded by debiting Accumulated Depreciation and crediting Cash.

OBJECTIVE 7: Account for disposal of depreciable assets not involving exchanges (pp. 457–459).

25. When an asset is still in use after it has been fully depreciated, no more depreciation should be taken, and the asset should not be written off until its disposal. Disposal occurs when the asset is discarded, sold, or traded in.

26. When a business disposes of an asset, depreciation should be recorded for the period preceding disposal. This will bring the asset's Accumulated Depreciation account up to the date of disposal.

27. When a machine, for example, is discarded (thrown out), Accumulated Depreciation, Machinery is debited and Machinery is credited for their present balances. If the machine has not been fully depreciated, then Loss on Disposal of Machinery must be debited for the carrying value to balance the entry.

28. When a machine is sold for cash, Accumulated Depreciation, Machinery is debited, Cash is debited, and Machinery is credited. If the cash received is less than the carrying value of the machine, then Loss on Sale of Machinery would also be debited. On the other hand, if the cash received is greater than the carrying value, then Gain on Sale of Machinery would be credited to balance the entry.

OBJECTIVE 8: Account for disposal of depreciable assets involving exchanges (pp. 459–463).

29. When an asset is traded in (exchanged) for a similar one, the gain or loss should first be computed, as follows:

Trade-in allowance
− Carrying value of asset traded in
= Gain (loss) on trade-in

a. For financial reporting purposes, both gains and losses should be recognized (recorded) on the exchange of dissimilar assets, and losses should be recognized on the exchange of similar assets. However, gains should *not* be recognized on the exchange of similar assets.
b. For income tax purposes, neither gains nor losses should be recognized on the exchange of similar assets, but both *should* be recognized on the exchange of dissimilar assets.
c. When a gain or loss is to be recognized, the asset acquired should be debited for its list price (cash paid plus trade-in allowance); a realistic trade-in value is assumed. The old asset is removed from the books, as explained in paragraph 28 above.
d. When a gain or loss is *not* to be recognized, the asset acquired should be debited for the carrying value of the asset traded in plus cash paid (this will result in nonrecognition of the gain or loss).

OBJECTIVE 9: Identify natural resource accounting issues and compute depletion (pp. 463–465).

30. Natural resources are tangible assets in the form of valuable substances that may be extracted and sold. They are sometimes referred to as **wasting assets,** and include standing timber, oil and gas fields, and mineral deposits.

31. **Depletion** refers to the allocation of a natural resource's cost to accounting periods based on the amount extracted in each period. Depletion for each year is computed as follows:

$$\frac{\text{Cost} - \text{residual value}}{\text{Estimated units to be extracted}} \times \begin{array}{c} \text{units extracted} \\ \text{during period} \end{array}$$

Units extracted but not sold in that year are recorded as inventory, to be charged as expense in the year sold.

32. Assets that are acquired in conjunction with the natural resource, and that cannot be used after the natural resource is depleted, should be depreciated on the same basis as depletion is computed.

33. In accounting for the exploration and development of oil and gas resources, two methods have been used. Under **successful efforts accounting,** the cost of a dry well is written off immediately as a loss. The **full-costing method,** on the other hand, capitalizes and depletes the costs of both successful and dry wells. Both methods are in accordance with GAAP.

OBJECTIVE 10: Apply the matching rule to intangible asset accounting issues (pp. 465–469).

34. Intangible assets are long-term assets that have no physical substance. They represent certain rights and advantages to their owner. Examples of intangible assets are **patents, copyrights, trademarks, goodwill, leaseholds, leasehold improvements, franchises, licenses,** brand names, formulas, and processes. An intangible asset should be written off over its useful life (not to exceed 40 years) through amortization.

35. Research and development involves developing new products, testing existing ones, and doing pure research. According to GAAP, the costs associated with these activities should normally be charged to expense in the period incurred.

36. The cost to develop computer software should be treated as research and development up to the point that a product is deemed technologically feasible (i.e., when a detailed working program has been designed). At that point, software production costs should be capitalized and amortized over the useful life of the software, using the straight-line method.

37. Goodwill, as the term is used in accounting, refers to a company's ability to earn more than is normal for its particular industry. Goodwill should be recorded only when a company is purchased; it equals the excess of the purchase cost over the fair market value of the net assets. Once it is recorded, goodwill should be amortized over its estimated useful life, not to exceed 40 years.

Summary of Journal Entries Introduced in Chapter 9

A. (L.O. 3) Depreciation Expense, Equipment   XX (amount allocated)
      Accumulated Depreciation, Equipment   XX (amount allocated)
        To record depreciation (reminder of entry introduced in Chapter 3)

B. (L.O. 5) Spare Parts Expense   XX (amount consumed)
      Spare Parts   XX (amount consumed)
        To record spare parts used or lost during the period

C. (L.O. 6) Your textbook introduces the topic of capital versus revenue expenditures by stating the following in the opening paragraphs: capital expenditures are typically debited to an asset account (such as Buildings or Equipment), and revenue expenditures are typically debited to an expense account (such as Repair Expense). An exception to the above rules is for extraordinary repairs, as shown below.

D. (L.O. 6) Accumulated Depreciation, Machinery   XX (amount of repair)
      Cash   XX (amount of repair)
        To record extraordinary repair

E. (L.O. 7) Accumulated Depreciation, Machinery   XX (existing balance)
      Loss on Disposal of Machinery   XX (carrying value)
      Machinery   XX (purchase price)
        Discarded machinery written off books

F. (L.O. 7) Cash   XX (proceeds on sale)
      Accumulated Depreciation, Machinery   XX (existing balance)
      Machinery   XX (purchase price)
        Machinery sold for amount of carrying value

G. (L.O. 7) Cash   XX (proceeds on sale)
      Accumulated Depreciation, Machinery   XX (existing balance)
      Loss on Sale of Machinery   XX (C.V. minus cash)
      Machinery   XX (purchase price)
        Machinery sold for amount less than carrying value (C.V.)

H. (L.O. 7) Cash   XX (proceeds on sale)
      Accumulated Depreciation, Machinery   XX (existing balance)
      Gain on Sale of Machinery   XX (cash minus C.V.)
      Machinery   XX (purchase price)
        Machinery sold for amount in excess of carrying value (C.V.)

I. (L.O. 8) Regarding the topic of exchanges of plant assets, the journal entries are all very similar (see entry J below). The amounts, however, depend upon a variety of factors, such as the similarity of assets exchanged and the purpose of the entry (financial accounting or income tax). In addition, gains and losses are sometimes recognized, sometimes not. Please see your textbook for a thorough explanation.

J.   (L.O. 8) Machinery (new)   XX (see text)
              Accumulated Depreciation (old)   XX (existing balance)
                  Machinery (old)   XX (purchase price)
                  Cash   XX (payment required)
                      Old machinery traded in for new machinery. If gain or
                      loss must be recognized, it would be credited or deb-
                      ited, respectively.

K.   (L.O. 9) Depletion Expense, Coal Mine   XX (amount allocated)
                  Accumulated Depletion, Coal Mine   XX (amount allocated)
                      To record depletion of coal mine

L.   (L.O. 10) Patent   XX (purchase price)
                  Cash   XX (purchase price)
                      Purchased patent. Note: debit could have been to
                      trademarks, copyrights, etc.

M. (L.O. 10) Amortization of Patent   XX (amount allocated)
                  Patent   XX (amount allocated)
                      Annual amortization of patent

N.   (L.O. 10) Loss on Patent   XX (carrying value)
                  Patent   XX (carrying value)
                      Patent written off as worthless

Testing Your Knowledge

Matching

Match each term with its definition by writing the appropriate letter in the blank.

_____ 1. Long-term assets (fixed assets)

_____ 2. Depreciation

_____ 3. Obsolescence

_____ 4. Franchise

_____ 5. Residual value (salvage or disposal value)

_____ 6. Accelerated method

_____ 7. Straight-line method

_____ 8. Production method

_____ 9. Sum-of-the-years'-digits method

_____ 10. Double-declining-balance method

_____ 11. Group depreciation

_____ 12. Natural resources

_____ 13. Depletion

_____ 14. Amortization

_____ 15. Accelerated Cost Recovery System (ACRS)

_____ 16. Capital expenditure

_____ 17. Revenue expenditure

_____ 18. Patent

_____ 19. Copyright

_____ 20. Leasehold

_____ 21. Trademark

_____ 22. Successful efforts accounting

_____ 23. Full-costing method

a. The exclusive right to sell a particular product or use a specific process for 17 years

b. The method of accounting for oil and gas that capitalizes the cost of dry wells

c. The allocation of an intangible asset's cost to the periods benefited by the asset

d. Payment for the right to use property

e. Assets to be used in the business for more than one year

f. The method of accounting for oil and gas that immediately writes off the cost of dry wells

g. An item charged as an expense in the period incurred

h. The depreciation method whose cost allocation is based on units, not time

i. The exclusive right to publish literary, musical, or artistic materials or computer programs for the author's life plus 50 years

j. The accelerated depreciation method based on twice the straight-line rate

k. The depreciation method used for tax purposes only

l. The estimated value of an asset at the disposal date

m. An item recorded as an asset because it will benefit future periods

n. One reason for an asset's limited useful life

o. Assets in the form of valuable substances that may be extracted and sold

p. An identifying symbol or name for a product or service that may be used only by its owner

q. The accelerated depreciation method that involves a changing fraction

r. The depreciation method that charges equal depreciation each year

s. The exclusive right to sell a product within a certain territory

t. The practice of charging the highest depreciation in the first year, and decreasing depreciation each year thereafter

u. The allocation of a natural resource's cost to the periods over which the resource is extracted and sold

v. Using one depreciation rate for several similar items

w. The allocation of the cost of a plant asset to the periods benefited by the asset

Use the lines provided to complete each item.

1. Distinguish between an addition and a betterment.

_____

_____

_____

_____

2. When a plant asset is sold for cash, under what unique circumstance would no gain or loss be recorded?

_____

_____

3. List four pieces of information necessary to compute the depletion expense of an oil well for a given year.

_____

_____

_____

_____

4. Distinguish between an ordinary and an extraordinary repair.

_____

_____

_____

_____

5. For each asset category, provide the accounting term for the allocation of its cost to the periods benefited.

Category	Term for Cost Allocation
Intangible assets	_____
Plant and equipment	_____
Natural resources	_____

6. Plant assets have *limited* useful lives for two reasons. What are they?

_____

_____

_____

True-False

Circle T if the statement is true, F if it is false. Please provide explanations for the false answers, using the blank lines at the end of the section.

T F   1. Land is not subject to depreciation.

T F   2. The loss recorded on a discarded asset is equal to the carrying value of the asset at the time it is discarded.

T F   3. Land held for speculative reasons is not classified as property, plant, and equipment.

T F   4. Depreciation is a process of valuation, not of allocation.

T F   5. Depreciation for a machine may be calculated by having an appraiser determine to what extent the machine has worn out.

T F   6. When land is purchased for use as a plant site, its cost should include the cost of tearing down a building and clearing and draining the land.

T F   7. Each type of depreciable asset should have its own accumulated depreciation account.

T F   8. Estimated useful life in years is irrelevant when applying the production method of depreciation.

T F   9. Under the straight-line method, if depreciation expense is $1,000 in the first year, it will be $2,000 in the second year.

T F   10. When the estimated useful life of an asset is revised after some depreciation has been taken, the accountant should not go back to previous years to make corrections.

T F **11.** For financial accounting purposes, both gains and losses on the exchange of dissimilar assets are recognized in the accounting records.

T F **12.** Accelerated depreciation will result in less net income than will straight-line depreciation in the asset's last year of depreciation.

T F **13.** Depreciable cost equals cost minus accumulated depreciation.

T F **14.** Under the double-declining-balance method, the carrying value of an asset will equal zero at the end of its estimated useful life if no residual value has been assumed.

T F **15.** Estimated useful life and residual value are ignored when applying ACRS depreciation.

T F **16.** A copyright is a name or symbol that may be used only by its owner.

T F **17.** If ordinary maintenance were erroneously capitalized instead of being charged as expense, then net income for the period would be overstated.

T F **18.** A betterment is an example of a revenue expenditure.

T F **19.** Recording an extraordinary repair will leave the carrying value of the asset unchanged.

T F **20.** When a machine is sold for less than its carrying value, one of the debits is to Loss on Sale of Machinery and one of the credits is to Accumulated Depreciation, Machinery.

T F **21.** Expenditure is another term for expense.

T F **22.** For income tax purposes, neither gains nor losses are recognized on the exchange of similar plant assets.

T F **23.** When a plant asset is sold in mid-year, depreciation expense need not be brought up to date and recorded.

T F **24.** In determining the number of years over which to amortize intangible assets, useful life is far more important than legal life.

T F **25.** As accumulated depreciation increases, carrying value will decrease.

T F **26.** Goodwill should not be recorded unless it has been purchased.

T F **27.** Research and development costs chould be capitalized when they can be associated with a specific new product.

T F **28.** The full-costing method capitalizes the cost of both successful and dry wells.

_____

_____

_____

_____

_____

_____

_____

_____

_____

_____

_____

_____

Multiple Choice

Circle the letter of the best answer.

1. If a building and land are purchased for a lump-sum payment of $66,000, how much would be allocated to land if the land is appraised at $20,000 and the building at $60,000?
   a. $22,000
   b. $20,000
   c. $16,500
   d. $13,750

2. The expired cost of a plant asset is referred to as its
   a. accumulated depreciation.
   b. carrying value.
   c. depreciable cost.
   d. residual value.

3. Which depreciation method, when applied to an asset in its first year of use, will result in the greatest depreciation charge?
   a. Declining-balance
   b. Production
   c. Sum-of-the-years'-digits
   d. Impossible to determine without more information

4. When a certain machine was purchased, its estimated useful life was 20 years. However, after it had been depreciated for 5 years, the company decided that it had originally overestimated the machine's useful life by 3 years. What should be done?
   a. Go back and adjust depreciation for the first 5 years.
   b. Depreciate the remainder of the depreciable cost over the next 15 years.
   c. Depreciate the remainder of the depreciable cost over the next 12 years.
   d. Both *a* and *b*

5. According to GAAP, intangible assets should never be amortized over more than
   a. 5 years.
   b. 17 years.
   c. 40 years.
   d. 50 years.

6. Land improvements
   a. should be included in the cost of land.
   b. are subject to depreciation.
   c. should be deducted from the cost of land.
   d. should be charged as expense in the year purchased.

7. A company began the accounting period with $200 in spare parts, purchased $400 in spare parts during the period, and ended the period with $100 in spare parts. What adjusting entry should the company make, assuming that it uses the inventory basis to account for spare parts?
   a. Debit Spare Parts Expense and credit Spare Parts for $500.
   b. Debit Spare Parts Expense and credit Spare Parts for $100.
   c. Debit Spare Parts and credit Spare Parts Expense for $100.
   d. Debit Spare Parts and credit Spare Parts Expense for $500.

8. A machine that cost $9,000 with a carrying value of $2,000 is sold for $1,700, and an entry is made. Which of the following is true about the entry?
   a. Accumulated Depreciation is debited for $2,000.
   b. Machinery is credited for $2,000.
   c. Loss on Sale of Machinery is credited for $300.
   d. Accumulated Depreciation is debited for $7,000.

9. Which of the following is not a revenue expenditure?
   a. Ordinary maintenance of a machine
   b. Replacing the old roof with a new one
   c. The installation of new light bulbs
   d. A tire repair on the company truck

10. Charging a depreciable item as expense when it should have been capitalized will result in
    a. overstated total assets.
    b. understated net income for the succeeding period.
    c. overstated depreciation expense for the succeeding period.
    d. understated net income for the period.

11. Overestimating the number of barrels that can be pumped from an oil well over its lifetime will result in
    a. understating net income each year.
    b. understating depletion cost per unit each year.
    c. overstating depletion expense each year.
    d. understating total assets each year.

12. The cost of developing computer software should be
    a. expensed, up to the point that the product is technologically feasible.
    b. capitalized in its entirety and amortized over 40 years.
    c. expensed, once the product is deemed to be technologically feasible.
    d. expensed in its entirety when incurred.

13. Which of the following should normally be charged as expense in the period of expenditure?
    a. Goodwill
    b. Leaseholds
    c. Leasehold improvements
    d. Research and development costs

Applying Your Knowledge

Exercises

1. A machine that cost $26,000 had an estimated useful life of five years and a residual value of $2,000 when purchased on January 1, 19x1. Fill in the amount of depreciation expense for 19x2 and the accumulated depreciation and carrying value of the machine as of December 31, 19x2, under each of the listed methods.

	Depreciation Expense for 19x2	Accumulation Depreciation as of 12/31/x2	Carrying Value as of 12/31/x2
a. Straight-line	$_____	$_____	$_____
b. Sum-of-the-years'-digits	$_____	$_____	$_____
c. Double-declining balance	$_____	$_____	$_____

2. A machine that was to produce a certain type of toy was purchased for $35,000 on April 30, 19xx. The machine was expected to produce 100,000 toys during the ten years that the company expected to keep the machine. The company estimated that it could then sell the machine for $5,000. Calculate depreciation expense in 19xx, when it produced 7,500 toys.

3. Classify each of the following expenditures as a capital or revenue expenditure by placing a C or an R next to each item.
   _____ a. Replacement of the roof on a building
   _____ b. Replacement of the battery in a company vehicle
   _____ c. The cost of painting the executive offices
   _____ d. Installation of aluminum siding on a building
   _____ e. Replacement of the motor in a machine
   _____ f. The cost to repair an air-conditioning unit
   _____ g. The cost to install a piece of machinery
   _____ h. Addition of a building wing
   _____ i. Tune-up of a company vehicle

4. On January 1, 19xx, Sharon Enterprises traded in, along with $15,500 in cash, a machine that cost $25,000 and had a carrying value of $8,000, for a new machine with a retail price of $23,000. The machines are similar in nature. Prepare the journal entry that Sharon would make to conform to GAAP, *as well as* the entry that would conform to income tax rulings. Prepare the entry in the journal provided on the next page.

Long-Term Assets: Acquisition and Depreciation

General Journal				
Date		Description	Debit	Credit

5. In 19xx the Porter Coal Company purchased a coal mine for $800,000. It is estimated that 2 million tons of coal can be extracted from the mine. In the space provided, prepare Porter's adjusting entry for December 31, 19xx, to reflect the extraction and sale of 100,000 tons during the year.

General Journal				
Date		Description	Debit	Credit

Crossword Puzzle
For Chapters 8 and 9

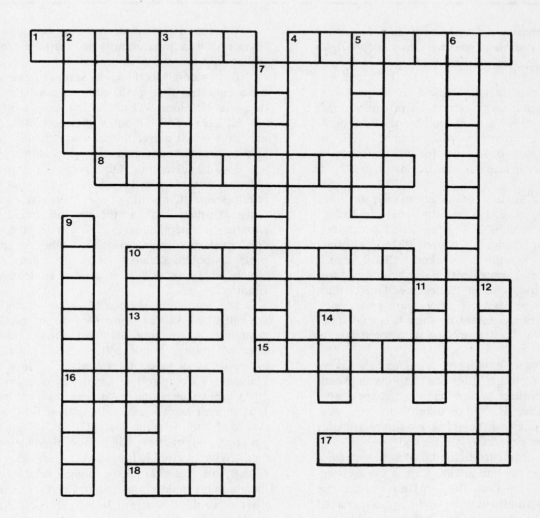

ACROSS

1. Residual (value)
4. Allocate the cost of a natural resource
8. Improvement to plant assets
10. _____-balance method
13. _____-of-the-years'-digits method
15. Trade in
16. _____ profit method
17. Inventory estimation technique
18. Inventory method

DOWN

2. Tax depreciation method
3. Allocate the cost of an intangible asset
5. Intangible with a 17-year life
6. Possessing physical substance
7. Allocate the cost of plant assets
9. (Goods) sold by one for another
10. Sale, trade-in, or abandonment
11. Asset not subject to allocation process
12. _____ life
14. Inventory valuation rule (abbr.)

Long-Term Assets: Acquisition and Depreciation

Reading

High Dudgeon in the Ivory Tower

Aren't depreciation charges on fixed assets at the core of responsible accounting? Not according to many college administrators.

Accounting rulemakers kicked a sleeping dog when they took on the country's private colleges and universities. Last fall the Financial Accounting Standards Board issued Statement 93. Effective May 15, it orders not-for-profit groups to depreciate their fixed assets, just as private businessmen do.

"The FASB has completely missed the mark on this one," says Dartmouth Treasurer Robert Field, of Statement 93. Agrees David Alexander, president of Pomona College: "The traditional [accounting] system has worked well for years." Richard Rosser, president of the National Association of Independent Colleges & Universities, reports that at least 80 schools are considering taking qualified opinions on their financial statements, rather than complying with the depreciation rule.

What's wrong with something as basic as recording depreciation? Like tire factories and headquarters buildings, lecture halls and chapels wear out over time. If college administrators ignore depreciation, aren't they cheating future students by undercharging today's?

Not according to Richard Bauer. Bauer is vice president for finance at tiny Centre College (enrollment, 860) in Danville, Ky. He notes that the Old Centre administration building, constructed in 1819 and later renovated, has been carried on the college books at $45,000 for years. Following the FASB's depreciation rule, says Bauer, would require him to write down nearly the entire book value of the building. Statement 93 "makes no sense to us," complains Bauer.

What of a new building? Robert Anthony, chairman of the audit committee at Colby College, replies that most academic buildings are bought or built with contributions. This, he says, makes a college different from a business. "The only reason to depreciate is to figure out whether you broke even," says Anthony. "Who needs to know the depreciation expense of a cathedral?"

What does matter, in this view, is good relations with wealthy alumni, who will take care of the assets when the need arises.

Bond-raters Moody's and Standard & Poor's have indicated that qualified opinions based on depreciation alone will not affect ratings on the $40 billion to $50 billion of private college and university bonds outstanding. So why, really, is the administration crowd so upset over Statement 93?

Two basic reasons. One, because complying will be a costly hassle. Two, because many administrators fear that writing down their fixed assets will make them look, in the eyes of alumni and trustees, like inept managers. They seem especially concerned about comparisons with their counterparts at public colleges and universities, with which private schools compete for students and funding.

The accounting policies of public institutions are ruled by FASB's sister organization, the Governmental Accounting Standards Board. GASB does not require public colleges and universities under its sway to depreciate assets. Notes Yale University Comptroller Leonard Wesolowski: "[Private] colleges that have been investing regularly in their assets—maintaining their facilities—will be able to offset the depreciation. But one that isn't investing in assets will be at a disadvantage."

"With this turf battle between the FASB and GASB, we feel that all of higher education is caught in the middle," says John Frazer, executive director of the Council of Independent Kentucky Colleges & Universities. "Reporting practices should be the same for the whole industry."

That's a fair point. But a better one is made by Ronald Bossio, the FASB project manager for Statement 93. Bossio says many school administrators have deferred maintenance costs and now lack adequate capital to repair and replace assets. "Some college administrators have simply not been managing their assets," says Bossio, "and don't know what they have or how much has walked out the door."

The solution lies not in holding fast to inferior accounting standards, but in bringing all institutions—public and private—up to the same higher standards. If doing so embarrasses some members of the ivory tower crowd, the benefits are worth it.

Source: Article by Penelope Wang. Reprinted by permission of *Forbes* magazine, April 4, 1988. © Forbes Inc., 1988.

Reading

When Does Life Begin?

Accountants, like theologians, have trouble defining when life begins. Consider the FASB's controversial new ruling for software development costs.

Three theologians debate the issue of when life begins. "Three months after conception," posits the first. "At the moment of conception," counters the second. "You're both wrong," says the third. "Life begins when the dog dies and the kids leave home."

Accountants, too, argue about when life begins—not human life, but product life. The debate reached a new level of ambiguity last year, when the Financial Accounting Standards Board's mandarins issued Financial Accounting Standard 86.

FAS 86 addresses the issue of how to account for the $7 billion spent last year by the computer software industry, according to Hambrecht & Quist's Osman Eralp, to develop new products. Should software producers expense the development costs as they are incurred? Or capitalize them on the theory that the expense is creating a productive asset? In short, when does product life begin?

The answer matters. Had IBM been forced to expense its $785 million "investment in program products" in 1985, its earnings would have been cut by $443 million, or 72 cents a share. With IBM selling at 14 times earnings, expensing software development might have knocked over $10 off IBM's share price. Meanwhile, Management Science America has already used FAS 86 to reduce its first-quarter 1986 loss from 12 cents a share to 2 cents.

If FAS 86 is a victory for IBM, it is a setback for uniform accounting. "What's different about software that makes capitalization dangerous is that you're constantly redesigning it," worries Eralp. "There is no such thing as a real, specific, baseline design. But you could make it look like you have one as early or as late as you like."

The accountants have been going in circles on this one for years. IBM and a few other software producers had been capitalizing a large part of their development costs, while 90% of publicly

held softwaremakers were expensing. Still, by 1983 software companies' financials were virtually impossible to compare, and the Securities & Exchange Commission ordered a moratorium on new software accounting methods until the FASB unmuddied the waters. Hence FAS 86.

In FAS 86 the FASB has ruled that softwaremakers must expense development costs when the product is still in the R&D phase. But as soon as the product is deemed to be an asset, companies must capitalize any further development costs and amortize them over the life of the product.

When does life begin?

This is where the theology comes in. Life begins, says FAS 86, as soon as the product is "technologically feasible." And when is that? Basically, whenever management says so. It could be three months after initial research. Or 18 months. Or after the dog dies, as it were.

Joseph Smith, IBM's director of financial reporting, argues: "It's unreasonable to expense all software costs, and it's unreasonable to capitalize all software costs. If you subscribe to those two statements, then it follows that there is somewhere in between where development ends and capitalization begins. Now you have to define that point."

But who is to define the right moment? That's the gaping loophole in FAS 86. Company A's managers want to capitalize? Fine. They quickly write up what FAS 86 calls a "detailed program design" of the product. That allows management to call the product an asset and to capitalize future development expenses.

Company B's managers want to expense? Also fine. They simply hold off writing a detailed program design. No asset, no capitalization.

Once an asset is capitalized, companies can even decide over how long a period to amortize a product by specifying the useful life they believe it has. More management discretion. "Most of the discussions I have with my clients," says Arthur Young & Co. senior partner and software specialist Steven Burrill, "start from the standpoint of 'How do you want to be portrayed' and then back into how they should develop their software."

Notice something odd: Of the 116 software companies that responded to the FASB exposure draft leading up to FAS 86, a sizable majority (63%) supported expensing over capitalizing, even

Source: Article by Subrata N. Chakravarty and Rita Koselka. Reprinted by permission of *Forbes* magazine, June 16, 1986. © Forbes Inc., 1986.

though doing so risks penalizing reported earnings.

So why are they against capitalizing? Harvard Business School Professor David Hawkins has a good answer: "Remember, the IRS has been lurking in the back of all this," says he. "The new rule strengthens its hand." Meaning that the IRS likes capitalizing because it increases taxable income in the current year.

Will shareholders be better informed with FAS 86? Up to a point, yes. The products that software companies—in fact, all service companies—create may have real economic value. Softwaremaker Applied Data Research recently sold out for $215 million. "We were sold for the value of our software," says ADR President Martin Goetz, "yet none of it showed in book value." Seems sensible that real values should be shown.

Of course, the values can be nonexistent should a software product flop. Then all those capitalized costs will have to be written off.

FAS 86's real problem, however, is that it renders comparability of competing software-makers' financial statements nearly impossible. James Pitts, Cullinet Software's executive vice president, says he has heard of companies capitalizing 3% to 25% of total software development costs this year. IBM capitalized 67% of its $1.2 billion investment in software products in 1984. Quite a range, that. And capitalization becomes increasingly important as the industry grows. Some analysts predict, for example, that software will be IBM's fastest-growing business, accounting for some $50 billion of estimated 1995 sales of $200 billion. That means even heavier development expenditures.

"In theory, the FASB drew the line in the right place," says Harvard Business School Professor Krishna Palepu. "In practice, it will be a problem for outsiders to read the financial statements of these companies and see if this asset is worth anything."

Question: If each company's definition of when a product's asset life begins is as good as the next company's, what's the point of having accounting standards?

Reading

Earnings Helper

With a simple bookkeeping change, companies can turn profits into losses—and vice versa. In many cases, the changes are perfectly justified, but the practice creates big opportunities for abuse.

No one ever said accounting was an exact science. How inexact it can be has been illustrated in two recent cases: Cineplex Odeon (*Forbes,* May 29) and Blockbuster Entertainment. Both companies minimized the amortization of assets to the benefit of reported earnings.

In the case of Cineplex Odeon, the movie theater circuit amortizes its leasehold improvements—seats, carpet, equipment and the like—over an average of 27 years, despite the fact that many of these assets will almost certainly be on the scrap heap long before 27 years have elapsed.

In Blockbuster's case, the aggressive videotape rental store chain recently spread the amortization period for its tapes from a fast writeoff over 9 months to a slow one over 36 months. That bookkeeping gimmick added $3 million, or nearly 20%, to Blockbuster's reported 1988 income. Last month a Bear, Stearns report critical of Blockbuster's accounting policies sliced over $226 million off the company's market value within two days.

Questions about proper amortization and depreciation schedules even involve companies that have never been accused of dubious accounting practices, as Cineplex and Blockbuster have. Consider General Motors. Until 1987 GM wrote off tools and dies at by far the fastest rate in the car business. But in that year the company slowed amortization of its tools and dies down to a level comparable with those of Ford and Chrysler. GM was in no wise cooking the books, but the move did increase GM's reported earnings by $2.55 per share; total earnings came to $10.06 per share that year.

In 1984 IBM shifted from accelerated depreciation to the straight-line method for its rental machines, plant and other property. According to Thornton O'Glove, author of the *Quality of Earn-* ings Report, the change increased IBM's reported earnings by $375 million, or 37 cents a share.

What's going on here? When it comes to amortization and depreciation, Generally Accepted Accounting Principles provide only the vaguest of guidelines. Management is supposed to write off assets over their estimated useful lives. But asset life expectancy is highly subjective, and is influenced by a myriad of factors. A state-of-the-art computer that will function mechanically for 50 years could become technologically obsolete in 5. Is its estimated useful life 5 years, 50 years or somewhere in between?

Another tough question: If something happens that will reduce (or lengthen) an asset's useful life, should management be required to change the depreciation schedule, to better reflect economic reality?

In a situation like this, where there can be honest differences of opinion, there is clearly room for the kind of abuse that prevailed in the Cineplex case. Many depreciation abuses are probably going undetected. Howard Hodges, chief accountant for the SEC's corporation finance division, cites lump sum writeoffs. "All of the restructuring charges—with big, lump sum writeoffs—are recognition that companies haven't been depreciating fast enough," says Hodges.

Why doesn't the SEC insist upon more conformity in companies' depreciation and amortization policies? Hodges replies: "We try to be observant, but when a company says it's depreciating its plant over 3 to 40 years, we don't know the intimate details. And there's no practical way we could. I'd like the accountants to take more responsibility for it."

For their part, the accountants retort that they're doing the best they can—that when reviewing depreciation, they look at engineering reports, industry practices and the company's historical use of its assets. Even so, they say, it is difficult to pass judgment on how much value can be squeezed from the assets. As Robert Fenimore, a partner at the accounting firm KPMG Peat Marwick, puts it: "You can count fixed assets and make sure they're there, but what are they worth? It's hard to say. There could be numerous studies done, all of which could give you reasonable answers with different conclusions."

Source: Article by Dana Wechsler. Reprinted by permission of *Forbes* magazine, June 12, 1989. © Forbes Inc., 1989.

As a result, the corporation's auditors will probably go along with management's judgment as long as the writeoff period doesn't diverge too much from general industry practice. Yet the permissible variations are so great as to make it difficult to compare two companies' earnings without intimate knowledge of their accounting practices.

Take the case of the airlines, which write off the same kinds of equipment over very different periods, with significant consequences for their bottom lines. Delta Air Lines depreciates its planes over 15 years and figures on a 10% residual value. Pan Am estimates a life of 25 years for the same 727s that Delta writes off in 15—and assumes a 15% residual value. Texas Air also writes off its planes over up to 25 years.

Are Pan Am and Texas Air being too aggressive? Is Delta too conservative? "There is justification for lives well beyond 20 years, if the planes are properly maintained," says KPMG Peat Marwick's Fenimore, an airline specialist. "But in reality, it's obvious that the airlines with less financial strength are the ones with longer depreciation lives."

What can an investor do? Under Generally Accepted Accounting Principles, whenever a company stretches out the lives of its assets, management must note (but not justify) any material change in the reported earnings in the footnotes to the annual report. And an accounting shift from accelerated to straight-line depreciation must be both footnoted and justified—although the justification can be vague. When IBM changed its depreciation schedule on its rental machines five years ago, for example, it cited only "evolving changes in our operations, maintenance costs and technology."

In December 1987 the SEC asked the American Institute of Certified Public Accountants to consider having any change in the length of depreciation highlighted in the auditor's report accompanying financial statements. Presumably this would draw attention to the change and put investors on the alert.

But the accountants retort that disclosure in the footnotes is enough. Says Daniel Guy, vice president for auditing for the American Institute of Certified Public Accountants: "Footnotes are very important. Why is it necessary to highlight them? I can't imagine anyone being hoodwinked by changes in depreciation anyway." Maybe so, but some pretty smart investors were taken in by the Cineplex Odeon and Blockbuster Entertainment amortization schedules.

CHAPTER 10   CURRENT LIABILITIES AND THE TIME VALUE OF MONEY

Reviewing the Chapter

OBJECTIVE 1: Explain how the issues of recognition, valuation, and classification apply to liabilities (pp. 497–498).

1. **Liabilities** are present obligations for either the future payment of assets or the future performance of services. A liability generally should be recorded when an obligation arises, but it is also necessary to make end-of-period adjustments for accrued and estimated liabilities. On the other hand, contracts representing future obligations are not recorded as liabilities until they become current obligations.

2. Liabilities are valued at the actual or estimated amount due, or at the fair market value of goods or services that must be delivered.

3. **Current liabilities** are present obligations that are expected to be satisfied within one year or the normal operating cycle, whichever is longer. Payment is expected to be out of current assets or by taking on another current liability. **Long-term liabilities** are obligations that are not expected to be satisfied in the current period.

4. The FASB now requires significant increases in the disclosure of a corporation's **financial instruments** (i.e., any contracts that result in an asset in one entity's records and a liability in another's). Financial assets include cash, short-term investments, accounts receivable, and notes receivable. Financial liabilities, on the other hand, include loans, mortgages, bonds, and leases. **Off-balance-sheet liabilities,** such as the guarantee of another's loan, do not appear as liabilities on the balance sheet, but must nevertheless be disclosed.

OBJECTIVE 2: Identify, compute, and record definitely determinable and estimated current liabilities (pp. 498–506).

5. Current liabilities consist of definitely determinable liabilities and estimated liabilities.

6. **Definitely determinable liabilities** are obligations that can be measured exactly. They include trade accounts payable, short-term notes payable, dividends payable, sales and excise taxes payable, current portions of long-term debt, accrued liabilities, payroll liabilities, and unearned or deferred revenues.
   a. Trade accounts payable are current obligations due to suppliers of goods and services.
   b. Companies often obtain a **line of credit** from a bank in order to finance operations. In addition, a company may borrow short-term funds by issuing **commercial paper** (unsecured loans sold to the public).
   c. Short-term notes payable are current obligations evidenced by promissory notes. Interest may be either stated separately or

included in the face amount. In the latter case, the actual amount borrowed is less than the face amount.

d. Accrued liabilities are actual or estimated liabilities that exist at the balance sheet date but are unrecorded. An end-of-period adjustment is needed to record both the expenses and the accrued liabilities.

e. Dividends payable is an obligation to distribute the earnings of a corporation to its stockholders. It arises only when the board of directors declares a dividend.

f. Most states and many cities levy a sales tax on retail transactions. The federal government also charges an excise tax on some products. The merchant must collect the taxes at the time of the sale and would record both the receipt of cash and the proper tax liabilities.

g. If a portion of long-term debt is due within the next year and is to be paid from current assets, then this amount should be classified as a current liability; the remaining debt should be classified as a long-term liability.

h. **Unearned** or **deferred revenues** represent obligations to deliver goods or services in return for advance payment. When delivery takes place, Deferred Revenues is debited and a revenue account is credited.

7. **Estimated liabilities** are definite obligations. However, the amount of the obligation must be estimated at the balance sheet date because the exact figure will not be known until a future date. Examples of estimated liabilities are income taxes, property taxes, product warranties, and vacation pay.

a. A corporation's income tax depends on its net income, a figure that often is not determined until well after the balance sheet date.

b. Property taxes are taxes levied on real and personal property. Very often a company's accounting period ends before property taxes have been assessed. Therefore, the company must make an estimate. The debit is to Property Tax Expense, and the credit is to Estimated Property Tax Payable.

c. When a company sells its products, many of the warranties will still be in effect during the next accounting period. However, the warranty expense and liability must be recorded in the period of the sale no matter when the company makes good on the warranty. Therefore, at the end of each accounting period, the company should make an estimate of future warranty expense that will apply to the present period's sales.

d. In most companies, employees earn vacation pay for working a certain length of time. Therefore, the company must estimate the vacation pay that applies to each payroll period. The debit is to Vacation Pay Expense, and the credit is to Estimated Liability for Vacation Pay.

OBJECTIVE 3: Define a contingent liability (pp. 507–508).

8. A **contingent liability** is a potential liability that may or may not become an actual liability. The uncertainty about its outcome is settled when a future event does or does not occur. Contingent liabilities arise from things like pending lawsuits, tax disputes, discounted notes receivable, the guarantee of another company's debt, and failure to follow government regulations.

OBJECTIVE 4: Distinguish simple from compound interest (pp. 508–509).

9. The timing of the receipt and payment of cash (measured in interest) should be a consideration in making business decisions. **Interest** is the cost of using money for a specific period of time, and may be calculated on a simple or compounded basis.

a. When **simple interest** is computed for two or more periods, the amount on which interest is computed does not increase each period (that is, interest is not computed on accrued interest).

b. However, when **compound interest** is computed for two or more periods, the amount on which interest is computed *does* increase each period (that is, interest is computed on accrued interest).

OBJECTIVE 5: Use compound interest tables to compute the future value of a single invested sum at compound interest and of an ordinary annuity (pp. 509–511).

10. **Future value** is the amount that an investment will be worth at a future date if invested at compound interest.

a. Future value may be computed on a single sum invested at compound interest. Table F-1 of your text facilitates this computation.

b. Future value may also be computed on an **ordinary annuity** (that is, a series of equal payments made at the end of equal intervals of time) at compound interest. Table F-2 of your text facilitates this computation.

OBJECTIVE 6: Use compound interest tables to compute the present value of a single sum due in the future and of an ordinary annuity (pp. 511–515).

11. **Present value** is the amount that must be invested now at a given rate of interest to produce a given future value or values.

a. Present value may be computed on a single sum due in the future. Table F-3 of your text facilitates this computation.

b. Present value may also be computed on an ordinary annuity. Table F-4 of your text facilitates this computation.

12. All four tables may facilitate both annual compounding and compounding for less than a year. For example, when computing 12 percent annual interest that is compounded quarterly, one would refer to the 3 percent column for four periods per year.

OBJECTIVE 7: Apply the concept of present value to accounting situations (pp. 517–522).

13. Present value may be used in accounting to (a) impute interest on noninterest-bearing notes, (b) determine the value of an asset being considered for purchase, (c) determine the value of a bond, (d) calculate the lease obligation on a capital lease, (e) account for assets purchased on deferred payment plans, (f) assist in the investment of idle cash, (g) calculate amounts that will accumulate in a fund, and (h) determine numerous other accounting quantities, such as pension obligations and depreciation.

Summary of Journal Entries Introduced in Chapter 10

A. (L.O. 2) Cash   XX (amount received)
       Notes Payable   XX (face amount)
       Borrowed cash, issued note with interest stated
       separately

B. (L.O. 2) Notes Payable   XX (face amount)
       Interest Expense   XX (amount incurred)
       Cash   XX (maturity amount)
       Payment of note with interest stated separately

C. (L.O. 2) Cash   XX (face amount minus interest)
       Discount on Notes Payable   XX (interest in face amount)
       Notes Payable   XX (face amount)
       Borrowed cash, issued note with interest included
       in face amount

D. (L.O. 2) Notes Payable   XX (face amount)
       Cash   XX (face amount)
       Payment of note with interest included in face
       amount (see also E below)

E. (L.O. 2) Interest Expense   XX (amount incurred)
       Discount on Notes Payable   XX (amount incurred)
       Interest expense recorded on note with interest in-
       cluded in face amount

F. (L.O. 2) Interest Expense   XX (amount accrued)
       Interest Payable   XX (amount accrued)
       Adjustment for note with interest stated separately

G. (L.O. 2) Interest Expense   XX (amount accrued)
       Discount on Notes Payable   XX (amount accrued)
       Adjustment for note with interest included in face
       amount

H. (L.O. 2) Cash   XX (amount collected)
       Sales   XX (price charged)
       Sales Tax Payable   XX (amount to remit)
       Excise Tax Payable   XX (amount to remit)
       To record sales and collection of taxes

I. (L.O. 2) Cash   XX (amount prepaid)
       Unearned Subscriptions   XX (amount to earn)
       Advance payment received on subscriptions

J. (L.O. 2) Unearned Subscriptions   XX (amount earned)
       Subscription Revenues   XX (amount earned)
       Earned previously unearned revenues

K. (L.O. 2) Federal Income Tax Expense   XX (amount incurred)
      Federal Income Tax Payable   XX (amount to be paid)
        To record estimated income taxes

L. (L.O. 2) Property Taxes Expense   XX (amount incurred)
      Estimated Property Taxes Payable   XX (amount to be paid)
        To record accrued property taxes

M. (L.O. 2) Estimated Property Taxes Payable   XX (amount incurred)
      Prepaid Property Taxes   XX (amount to incur)
      Cash   XX (amount paid)
        Paid property tax bill

N. (L.O. 2) Property Taxes Expense   XX (amount incurred)
      Prepaid Property Taxes   XX (amount prepaid)
        To record property taxes, prepayment included

O. (L.O. 2) Product Warranty Expense   XX (estimated amount)
      Estimated Product Warranty Liability   XX (estimated amount)
        To record product warranty expense

P. (L.O. 2) Cash   XX (fee charged)
      Estimated Product Warranty Liability   XX (cost of part)
      Service Revenue   XX (fee charged)
      Merchandise Inventory   XX (cost of part)
        To record replacement of part under warranty

Q. (L.O. 2) Vacation Pay Expense   XX (amount earned)
      Estimated Liability for Vacation Pay   XX (amount earned)
        To accrue vacation pay expense

R. (L.O. 2) Estimated Liability for Vacation Pay   XX (amount taken)
      Cash (or Wages Payable)   XX (amount paid or to pay)
        Vacation taken by employee

S. (L.O. 7) Purchases   XX (present value of note)
      Discount on Notes Payable   XX (imputed interest)
      Notes Payable   XX (face amount)
        Issued noninterest-bearing note in exchange for
        merchandise purchased

T. (L.O. 7) Interest Expense   XX (amount accrued)
      Discount on Notes Payable   XX (amount accrued)
        Adjustment for noninterest-bearing note (see S
        above)

U. (L.O. 7) Interest Expense   XX (interest for period)
      Notes Payable   XX (face amount)
      Discount on Notes Payable   XX (interest for period)
      Cash   XX (face amount)
        To record payment of note (see S above)

V. (L.O. 7) Notes Receivable   XX (face amount)
   Discount on Notes Receivable   XX (imputed interest)
   Sales   XX (present value of note)
    Received noninterest-bearing note in exchange for
    merchandise sold

W. (L.O. 7) Discount on Notes Receivable   XX (amount accrued)
   Interest Income   XX (amount accrued)
    Adjustment for noninterest-bearing note (see V
    above)

X. (L.O. 7) Discount on Notes Receivable   XX (interest for period)
   Cash   XX (face amount of note)
   Interest Income   XX (interest for period)
   Notes Receivable   XX (face amount)
    Received payment on note (see V above)

Y. (L.O. 7) Tractor   XX (present value of payment)
   Accounts Payable   XX (present value of payment)
    Purchased tractor on deferred payment plan

Z. (L.O. 7) Accounts Payable   XX (present value of payment)
   Interest Expense   XX (imputed amount)
   Cash   XX (amount paid)
    To record eventual payment for tractor (see Y
    above)

AA. (L.O. 7) Accounts Receivable   XX (present value of payment)
   Sales   XX (present value of payment)
    Sold tractor on deferred payment plan

BB. (L.O. 7) Cash   XX (amount received)
   Accounts Receivable   XX (present value of payment)

   Interest Income   XX (imputed amount)
    To record eventual receipt of cash for tractor
    (see AA above)

CC. (L.O. 7) Short-Term Investments   XX (amount invested)
   Cash   XX (amount invested)
    To record investment of idle cash

DD. (L.O. 7) Short-Term Investments   XX (interest for month)
   Interest Income   XX (interest for month)
    To record one month's interest

EE. (L.O. 7) Loan Repayment Fund   XX (amount contributed)
   Cash   XX (amount contributed)
    To record annual contribution to loan repayment
    fund

Testing Your Knowledge

Matching

Match each term with its definition by writing the appropriate letter in the blank.

_____ 1. Current liabilities

_____ 2. Long-term liabilities

_____ 3. Definitely determinable liabilities

_____ 4. Estimated liabilities

_____ 5. Contingent liabilities

_____ 6. Unearned (deferred) revenues

_____ 7. Vacation pay

_____ 8. Interest

_____ 9. Simple interest

_____ 10. Compound interest

_____ 11. Future value

_____ 12. Present value

_____ 13. Ordinary annuity

_____ 14. Line of credit

_____ 15. Commercial paper

a. The amount that must be invested now to produce a given future value

b. Unsecured loans sold to the public

c. The computation whereby interest is computed without considering accrued interest

d. Obligations that exist but cannot be precisely measured at the balance sheet date

e. A series of equal payments made at the end of each period

f. Obligations that can be precisely measured

g. The cost of using money for a specific period of time

h. The amount an investment will be worth at a future date

i. An arrangement with the bank that allows a company to borrow funds when needed

j. The computation whereby interest is computed on the original amount plus accrued interest

k. Obligations that are not expected to be satisfied in the current period

l. Potential liabilities that may or may not become actual liabilities

m. Obligations to deliver goods or services in return for advance payment

n. Obligations that are expected to be satisfied within one year or the normal operating cycle, whichever is longer

o. Compensation received during one's earned time off

Short Answer

Use the lines provided to answer each item.

1. Current liabilities fall into two principal categories. What are they?

_____

_____

2. Give three examples of contingent liabilities.

_____

_____

_____

3. Give three examples of estimated liabilities.

_____

_____

_____

4. Give three examples of definitely determinable liabilities.

_____

_____

_____

5. What is a financial instrument?

_____

_____

_____

True-False

Circle T if the statement is true, F if it is false. Please provide explanations for the false answers, using the blank lines at the end of the section.

T F   1. Deferred revenues can be found on the income statement.

T F   2. A contract to purchase goods in the future does not require the recording of a current liability.

T F   3. Failure to record an accrued liability will result in an overstatement of net income.

T F   4. The current portion of a long-term debt is a current liability (assume that it is to be satisfied with cash).

T F   5. Sales Tax Payable is an example of an estimated liability.

T F   6. Warranties fall into the category of definitely determinable liabilities.

T F   7. The multipliers incorporated into the "present value of a single sum to be received in the future" table are all less than 1.000.

T F   8. An ordinary annuity is a series of equal payments made at the beginning of equal intervals of time.

T F   9. The higher the interest rate applied, the higher the present value of an amount or annuity to be received in the future.

T F   10. Every contingent liability must eventually become an actual liability or no liability at all.

T F   11. The account Disount on Notes Payable is associated with notes whose interest is stated separately on the face of the note.

T F   12. If a refrigerator is sold in year 1 and repairs are made in year 2, Product Warranty Expense should be recorded in year 2.

Multiple Choice

Circle the letter of the best answer.

1. Which of the following is not a definitely determinable liability?
   a. Dividends payable
   b. Deferred revenues
   c. Property taxes payable
   d. Excise tax payable

2. Estimated liabilities would not apply to
   a. warranties.
   b. vacation pay.
   c. a corporation's income tax.
   d. pending lawsuits.

3. When an employee receives vacation pay, the company should
   a. debit Vacation Pay Expense and credit Cash.
   b. debit Vacation Pay Receivable and credit Cash.
   c. debit Estimated Liability for Vacation Pay and credit Cash.
   d. debit Vacation Pay Expense and credit Estimated Liability for Vacation Pay.

4. A company that uses a calendar year receives a property tax bill each March (for that particular calendar year), to be paid by April 10. If entries are made at the end of each month to record property tax expense, the April 10 entry to record payment would include a
   a. debit to Cash.
   b. credit to Estimated Property Taxes Payable.
   c. debit to Property Taxes Expense.
   d. debit to Prepaid Property Taxes.

5. Compound interest is computed semiannually on $100 in the bank for five years at 10 percent annual interest. The future value table is used by multiplying the $100 by which multiplier?
   a. 5 periods at 10 percent
   b. 10 periods at 5 percent
   c. 10 periods at 10 percent
   d. 5 periods at 5 percent

Use the following present value information to answer Questions 6 and 7.

Period	Present Value of $1 Discounted at 12% Per Period
1	0.893
2	0.797

6. What amount should be deposited in a bank today at 12 percent interest (compounded annually) to grow to $100 two years from today?
   a. $100/0.797
   b. $100 × 0.893 × 2
   c. ($100 × 0.893) + ($100 × 0.797)
   d. $100 × 0.797

7. If $200 were placed in the bank today at 12 percent interest (compounded annually), what amount would be available two years from today?
   a. $200 × 0.797
   b. $200 × 0.797 × 2
   c. $200/0.797
   d. ($200/0.893) × 2

8. Marina Pools, Inc., purchased some equipment by executing a $10,000 noninterest-bearing note due in three years. The equipment should be recorded by Marina at
   a. $10,000 minus the discounted interest on the note.
   b. $10,000 plus the discounted interest on the note.
   c. the amount of the discounted interest on the note.
   d. $10,000.

9. When accounting for a note whose interest is included in its face amount, the account Discount on Notes Payable is eventually converted into
   a. Interest Receivable.
   b. Interest Expense.
   c. Interest Payable.
   d. Interest Income.

Applying Your Knowledge

Exercises

1. During 19x1, White's Appliance Store sold 300 washing machines, each with a one-year guarantee. It was estimated that 5 percent will eventually require some type of repair, with an average cost of $35. Prepare the adjusting entry that White's would make concerning the warranty. Also, prepare the entry that the store would make on April 9, 19x2, for one such repair that cost $48.

General Journal				
Date		Description	Debit	Credit

2. Use Appendix F of your text to answer the following questions.

   a. What amount received today is equivalent to $1,000 receivable at the end of five years, assuming a 6 percent annual interest rate compounded annually? $_____

   b. If payments of $1,000 are invested at 8 percent annual interest at the end of each quarter for one year, compute the amount that will accumulate by the time the last payment is made. $_____

   c. If $1,000 is invested on June 30, 19x1, at 6 percent annual interest compounded semi-annually, how much will be in the account on June 30, 19x3? $_____

   d. Compute the equal annual deposits required to accumulate a fund of $100,000 at the end of twenty years, assuming a 10 percent interest rate compounded annually. $_____

3. The manager of Foxfield Lanes is considering replacing the existing automatic pinsetters with improved ones that cost $10,000 each. It is estimated that each new pinsetter will save $2,000 annually and will last for 10 years. Using an interest rate of 18 percent and Appendix F of your text, what is the present value of each new pinsetter to Foxfield Lanes? $_____
Should the purchase be made? _____

4. On January 1, 19x1, McKenzie Corporation purchased equipment from Courtright Sales by signing a two-year, noninterest-bearing note for $10,000. McKenzie currently pays 10 percent interest on money borrowed. In the journal provided on page 166, prepare McKenzie's journal entries (a) to record the purchase and the note, (b) to adjust the accounts after one year, and (c) to record payment of the note after two years. Use Appendix F of your text for time value of money information. Omit explanations.

General Journal				
Date		Description	Debit	Credit

CHAPTER 11 LONG-TERM LIABILITIES

Reviewing the Chapter

OBJECTIVE 1: Identify and contrast the major characteristics of bonds (pp. 546–547).

1. Corporations frequently issue long-term **bonds** or notes to raise funds. The holders of these bonds or notes are creditors of the corporation. They are entitled to periodic interest, plus the principal of the debt on some specified date. As is true for all creditors, their claims for interest and principal take priority over stockholders' claims.

2. Bonds are normally due ten to fifty years after issue, and interest is usually paid semiannually. When bonds are issued, the corporation executes a contract with the bondholders called a **bond indenture**. In addition, the company issues **bond certificates** as evidence of its debt to the bondholders. A **bond issue** is made up of the total number of bonds available at the same time. Bonds are usually issued with a face value that is some multiple of $1,000, and carry a variety of features.
   a. **Secured bonds** give the bondholders a claim to certain assets of the company upon default. **Unsecured bonds** (called **debentures**) do not.
   b. When all the bonds of an issue mature on the same date, they are called **term bonds**. When the bonds mature over several maturity dates, they are called **serial bonds**.
   c. When **registered bonds** are issued, the corporation maintains a record of all bondholders and pays interest by check to the bondholders of record. **Coupon bonds**, on the other hand, entitle the bearer to interest when the detachable coupons are deposited with the bank.

3. Bond prices are expressed as a percentage of face value. For example, when bonds with a face value of $100,000 are issued at 97, the company will receive $97,000.

OBJECTIVE 2: Record the issuance of bonds at face value and at a discount or premium (pp. 547–550).

4. Bonds payable due in the current period can be classified as a current liability only if they will be paid with current assets. In addition, the characteristics of all bonds should be disclosed in the notes to the financial statements.

5. When the **face interest rate** equals the **market interest rate** for similar bonds on the issue date, the company will probably receive face value for the bonds.

6. Regardless of the issue price, bondholders are entitled to interest, which is based on the face amount. Interest for a period of time is computed by the formula:

$$\text{Interest} = \text{principal} \times \text{rate} \times \text{time}$$

7. When the face interest rate is less than the market interest rate for similar bonds on the issue date, the bonds will probably sell at a **discount** (less than face value).

8. Unamortized Bond Discount is a contra account to Bonds Payable on the balance sheet. The difference between the two amounts is called the carrying value. The carrying value increases as the discount is amortized and equals the face value of the bonds at maturity.

9. When the face interest rate is greater than the market interest rate for similar bonds on the issue date, the bonds usually sell at a **premium** (greater than face value). Unamortized Bond Premium is added to Bonds Payable in the balance sheet to produce the carrying value.

10. A separate account should be established for bond issue costs. These costs are amortized over the life of the bonds.

OBJECTIVE 3: Determine the value of bonds using present values (pp. 550–551).

11. Theoretically, the value of a bond is equal to the sum of the present values of (a) the periodic interest payments and (b) the single payment of principal at maturity. The discount rate used is based on the current market rate of interest.

OBJECTIVE 4a: Amortize bond discounts by using the straight-line and effective interest methods (pp. 551–556).

12. When bonds are issued at a discount or premium, the interest payments will *not* equal the (true) total interest cost. Instead, total interest cost equals (a) interest payments over the life of the bond, plus (b) the original discount amount, or minus (c) the original premium amount.

13. A **zero coupon bond** is a promise to pay a fixed amount at maturity, with no periodic interest payments. Investor earnings consist of the large discount upon issue, which in turn is amortized by the issuing corporation over the life of the bond.

14. A discount on bonds payable is considered an interest charge that must be amortized (spread out) over the life of the bond. Amortization is generally recorded on the interest payment dates, using either the straight-line method or the effective interest method.

15. Under the **straight-line method** of amortization, the amount to be amortized each interest period equals the bond discount divided by the number of interest payments during the life of the bond.

16. The effective interest method of amortization is more difficult to apply than the straight-line method but should be used instead when the amounts differ significantly.

17. To apply the **effective interest method** when a discount is involved, the market rate of interest for similar securities when the bonds were issued (called the **effective rate** of interest) must first be determined. This interest rate (halved for semiannual interest) is multiplied by the existing carrying value of the bonds for each interest period to obtain Bond Interest Expense to be recorded. The actual interest paid is then subtracted from the bond interest expense recorded to obtain the discount amortization for the period. Because the unamortized discount is now less, the carrying value is now greater. This new carrying value is applied to the next period, and the same amortization procedure is applied.

OBJECTIVE 4b: Amortize bond premiums by using the straight-line and effective interest methods (pp. 556–560).

18. Amortization of a premium acts as an offset against interest paid in determining Interest Expense to be recorded. Under the straight-line method, the premium to be amortized in each period equals the bond premium divided by the number of interest payments during the life of the bond.

19. The effective interest method is applied to bond premiums in the same way that it is applied to bond discounts. The only difference is that the amortization for the period is computed by subtracting the Bond Interest Expense recorded from actual interest paid (the reverse is done for amortizing a discount).

OBJECTIVE 5: Account for bonds issued between interest dates and make year-end adjustments (pp. 561–563).

20. When bonds are issued between interest dates, the interest that has accrued since the last interest date is collected from the investor upon issue. It is then returned to the investor (along with the interest earned) on the next interest date.

21. When the accounting period ends between interest dates, the accrued interest and the proportionate discount or premium amortization must be recorded.

OBJECTIVE 6: Account for the retirement of bonds and the conversion of bonds into stock (pp. 563–565).

22. **Callable bonds** are bonds that may be retired by the corporation before the maturity date (called **early extinguishment of debt**). When the market rate for bond interest drops, a company may wish to call its bonds and substitute debt with a lower interest rate. When bonds are called (for whatever reason), an entry is needed to eliminate Bonds Payable and any unamortized premium or discount, and to record the payment of cash at the call price. In addition, an extraordinary gain or loss on the retirement of the bonds would be recorded. (Extraordinary items are explained fully in Chapter 13.)

23. **Convertible bonds** are bonds that may be exchanged for other securities (usually common stock) at the option of the bondholder. When a bondholder converts his or her bonds into common stock, the common stock is recorded by the company at the carrying value of the bonds. Specifically, the entry will eliminate Bonds Payable and any unamortized discount or premium, and will record common stock and paid-in capital in excess of par value. No gain or loss is recorded.

OBJECTIVE 7: Explain the basic features of mortgages payable, installment notes payable, long-term leases, pensions, and postretirement benefits as long-term liabilities (pp. 566–573).

24. A **mortgage** is a long-term debt secured by real property, usually payable in equal monthly installments. Upon payment of the mortgage, both Mortgage Payable and Mortgage Interest Expense are debited, and Cash is credited. Each month, the interest portion of the payment decreases, while the principal portion of the payment increases.

25. The principal and interest on long-term notes are either payable on one maturity date or due in periodic payments. The latter notes are known as **installment notes payable,** and are commonly used by businesses to finance equipment. The installment payments may be structured to include either (a) accrued interest plus equal amounts of principal or (b) accrued interest plus increasing amounts of principal. The former method results in decreasing payments, whereas the latter method produces equal payments. The effective interest calculation would be applied in either case.

26. A lease is a contract that allows a business or individual to use an asset for a specific length of time in return for periodic payments. A **capital lease** is so much like a sale (as determined by certain criteria) that it should be recorded by the lessee as an asset (to be depreciated) and a related liability. An **operating lease** is a lease that does not meet the criteria for capital leases; it should be recorded only as Rent Expense for each period that the asset is leased.

27. A **pension plan** is a program whereby a company agrees to pay benefits to its employees after they retire. Benefits to retirees are usually paid out of a **pension fund.** Pension plans are classified as defined contribution plans or defined benefit plans. **Other postretirement benefits,** such as for health care, should be estimated and accrued while the employee is still working (in accordance with the matching rule).

Summary of Journal Entries Introduced in Chapter 11

A. (L.O. 2) Cash   XX (amount received)
    Bonds Payable   XX (face value)
    Issued bonds at face value

B. (L.O. 2) Bond Interest Expense   XX (amount incurred)
    Cash   XX (amount paid)
    Paid interest to bondholders

C. (L.O. 2) Cash   XX (amount received)
    Unamortized Bond Discount   XX (amount of discount)
    Bonds Payable   XX (face value)
    Issued bonds at a discount

D. (L.O. 2) Cash   XX (amount received)
    Unamortized Bond Premium   XX (amount of premium)
    Bonds Payable   XX (face value)
    Issued bonds at a premium

E. (L.O. 4a) Bond Interest Expense   XX (amount incurred)
    Unamortized Bond Discount   XX (amount amortized)
    Cash   XX (amount paid)
    Paid interest and amortized discount

F. (L.O. 4b) Bond Interest Expense   XX (amount incurred)
    Unamortized Bond Premium   XX (amount amortized)
    Cash   XX (amount paid)
    Paid interest and amortized premium

G. (L.O. 5) Cash   XX (amount received)
    Bond Interest Expense   XX (accrued amount)
    Bonds Payable   XX (face value)
    Issued bonds between interest dates (see entry H below)

H. (L.O. 5) Bond Interest Expense   XX (six months' amount)
    Cash   XX (amount paid)
    Paid semiannual interest on bonds issued in G above

I. (L.O. 5) The year-end accrual for bond interest expense is identical to entry E above for discounts and entry F above for premiums, except that in both cases Interest Payable is credited instead of Cash.

J. (L.O. 6) Bonds Payable   XX (face value)
    Unamortized Bond Premium   XX (current credit balance)
    Loss on Retirement of Bonds   XX (see explanation)
    Cash   XX (amount paid)
    To record retirement of bonds; loss equals excess of call price over carrying value (note: an unamortized bond discount or a gain on retirement would have been credited in the above entry)

K. (L.O. 6) The early extinguishment of debt is journalized as in J above. However, any gain or loss would be treated as extraordinary.

L. (L.O. 6) Bonds Payable   XX (face value)
Unamortized Bond Premium   XX (current credit balance)
  Common Stock   XX (par value)
  Paid-in Capital in Excess of Par Value, Common   XX (excess of par)
   Converted bonds into common stock (note: no gain or loss recorded; also, an unamortized bond discount would have been credited in the above entry)

M. (L.O. 7) Mortgage Payable   XX (principal)
Mortgage Interest Expense   XX (interest)
  Cash   XX (monthly payment)
   To record monthly payment of mortgage

N. (L.O. 7) Cash   XX (amount borrowed)
  Notes Payable   XX (amount borrowed)
   To record long-term installment note

O. (L.O. 7) Notes Payable   XX (principal)
Interest Expense   XX (interest)
  Cash   XX (installment payment)
   To record installment payment

P. (L.O. 7) Rent Expense   XX (amount incurred)
  Cash   XX (amount paid)
   Made payment on operating lease

Q. (L.O. 7) Equipment Under Capital Lease   XX (present value)
  Obligations Under Capital Lease   XX (present value)
   Capital lease contract recorded

R. (L.O. 7) Depreciation Expense   XX (amount allocated)
  Accumulated Depreciation, Leased Equipment Under Capital Lease   XX (amount allocated)
   Recorded depreciation under capital lease

S. (L.O. 7) Interest Expense   XX (amount incurred)
Obligations Under Capital Lease   XX (amount reduced)
  Cash   XX (amount paid)
   To record lease payment under capital lease

Testing Your Knowledge

Matching

Match each term with its definition by writing the appropriate letter in the blank.

_____ 1. Bonds

_____ 2. Bond indenture

_____ 3. Secured bonds

_____ 4. Debentures

_____ 5. Term bonds

_____ 6. Serial bonds

_____ 7. Registered bonds

_____ 8. Coupon bonds

_____ 9. Callable bonds

_____ 10. Bond discount

_____ 11. Bond premium

_____ 12. Effective interest method

_____ 13. Capital lease

_____ 14. Operating lease

_____ 15. Convertible bonds

_____ 16. Pension plan

_____ 17. Pension fund

_____ 18. Bond certificate

_____ 19. Early extinguishment of debt

_____ 20. Zero coupon bonds

a. Unsecured bonds
b. A lease that amounts to a sale
c. Bonds that may be retired by the company before maturity
d. The contract between the bondholder and the corporation
e. The difference between par and a lower amount paid for bonds
f. Bonds with detachable forms that are redeemed for interest
g. A true lease, recorded with debits to Rent Expense
h. Proof of a company's debt to a bondholder
i. Long-term debt instruments
j. Bonds whose owners receive interest by check directly from the company
k. The retirement of bonds prior to maturity
l. The amortization method based on carrying value
m. The difference between par and a greater amount paid for bonds
n. A program whereby a company agrees to pay benefits to its employees when they retire
o. Bonds that mature on one specific date
p. The source of benefits that are paid to retirees
q. Bonds that are backed by certain assets
r. Bonds that may be exchanged for common stock
s. Bonds that mature in installments
t. Bonds whose holders receive no periodic interest, but that are issued at a large discount

Short Answer

Use the lines provided to answer each item.

1. Distinguish between the terms _debenture_ and _indenture_.

_____

_____

2. Under what circumstances would a premium probably be received on a bond issue?

_____

_____

3. What is the formula for computing interest for a period of time?

_____

_____

4. When valuing a bond, what two components are added together to determine the present value of the bond?

_____

_____

Circle T if the statement is true, F if it is false. Please provide explanations for the false answers, using the blank lines at the end of the section.

T F 1. Bondholders are creditors of a corporation.

T F 2. A term bond matures on one particular date.

T F 3. Bond interest can be paid only when declared by the board of directors.

T F 4. Bonds with a lower interest rate than the market rate (for similar bonds) will probably sell at a discount.

T F 5. When a bond premium is amortized, the bond interest expense recorded will be greater than the cash paid.

T F 6. When the effective interest method is used to amortize a bond discount, the amount amortized will increase each year.

T F 7. When bonds are issued between interest dates, Bond Interest Expense is debited for accrued interest since the last interest date.

T F 8. As a bond premium is amortized, the carrying value of bonds payable will decrease.

T F 9. When bonds are issued at a discount, the total interest cost to the issuing corporation equals the interest payments minus the bond discount.

T F 10. When bonds are retired, all of the premium or discount associated with the bonds must be canceled.

T F 11. When the effective interest method is used to amortize a premium on bonds payable, the premium amortized will decrease in amount each year.

T F 12. When bonds are issued at a premium, the total interest cost to the issuing corporation equals the interest payments minus the bond premium.

T F 13. Under capital leases, assets should be recorded at the present value of future lease payments.

T F 14. Pension Expense is usually difficult to measure because it is based on many estimates, such as employee life expectancy and employee turnover.

T F 15. When bonds are converted into stock, no gain or loss should be recorded.

T F 16. Bond issue costs should be amortized over the life of the bonds.

T F 17. Postretirement health care benefits should be expensed while the employee is still working.

_____

_____

_____

_____

_____

_____

_____

_____

_____

_____

_____

Multiple Choice

Circle the letter of the best answer.

1. Assume that $900,000 of 5 percent bonds are issued (at face value) two months before the next semiannual interest date. Which of the following statements correctly describes the journal entry?
   a. Cash is debited for $800,000.
   b. Cash is debited for $807,500.
   c. Bond Interest Expense is credited for $7,500.
   d. Bond Interest Expense is credited for $15,000.

2. As a mortgage is paid off,
   a. the principal portion of the fixed payment increases.
   b. the interest portion of the fixed payment increases.
   c. the principal and interest portions do not change each interest period.
   d. the monthly payments increase.

3. Unamortized Bond Premium is presented on the balance sheet as
   a. a long-term asset.
   b. a stockholders' equity account.
   c. a deduction from Bonds Payable.
   d. an addition to Bonds Payable.

4. When the interest dates on a bond issue are May 1 and November 1, the adjusting entry to record Bond Interest Expense on December 31 might include a
   a. debit to Bond Interest Payable.
   b. credit to Cash.
   c. credit to Unamortized Bond Discount.
   d. credit to Bond Interest Expense.

5. Under the effective interest method, as a discount is amortized,
   a. the amount amortized will decrease each period.
   b. the Interest Expense recorded will increase each period.
   c. interest paid to bondholders will increase each period.
   d. the bonds' carrying value will decrease each period.

6. Which of the following would probably be considered an operating lease?
   a. A 6-year lease on equipment with an option to renew for another 6 years
   b. A 5-year lease on machinery, cancelable at the end of the lease period by the lessor
   c. A 40-year lease on a building, equal to its useful life
   d. A 7-year lease on a company vehicle with an option to buy the vehicle for $1 at the end of the lease period

7. A $200,000 bond issue with a carrying value of $195,000 is called at 102 and retired. Which of the following statements is true about the journal entry prepared?
   a. An extraordinary gain of $5,000 is recorded.
   b. An extraordinary loss of $4,000 is recorded.
   c. An extraordinary loss of $9,000 is recorded.
   d. No gain or loss is recorded.

8. A company has $600,000 in bonds payable with an unamortized premium of $12,000. If one-third of the bonds are converted to common stock, the carrying value of the bonds payable will decrease by
   a. $196,000.
   b. $200,000.
   c. $204,000.
   d. $208,000.

Applying Your Knowledge

Exercises

1. A corporation issues $600,000 of 7 percent, 10-year bonds at 98½ on one of its semiannual interest dates. Assuming straight-line amortization, answer each of the following questions.
    a. What is the amount of the bond discount?
        $ _____
    b. How much interest is paid on the next interest date? $ _____
    c. How much bond interest expense is recorded on the next interest date? $ _____
    d. After 3 years, what is the carrying value of the bonds? $ _____

2. A corporation issues $500,000 of 7 percent, 20-year bonds at 110. Interest is paid semiannually, and the effective interest method is used for amortization. Assume that the market rate for similar investments is 6 percent, and the bonds are issued on an interest date.
    a. What amount was received for the bonds? $ _____
    b. How much interest is paid each interest period? $ _____
    c. How much bond interest expense is recorded on the first interest date? $ _____
    d. How much of the premium is amortized on the first interest date? $ _____
    e. What is the carrying value of the bonds after the first interest date? $ _____

3. Pennco issued $600,000 of 8 percent, 10-year bonds at 106. In the space provided, calculate the total interest cost.

4. On December 31, 19x1, Oakdale Company borrows $50,000 on a 10 percent installment note, to be paid annually over 5 years. In the journal provided, prepare the entry to record the note, as well as the December 31, 19x2, and December 31, 19x3, entries to record the first two annual payments. Assume that the principal is paid in equal installments and that the interest on the unpaid balance accrues annually.

	General Journal			
Date		Description	Debit	Credit

5. Assume the same facts and requirements as in Exercise 4 above, except that payments are made in equal installments of $13,190.

	General Journal			
Date		Description	Debit	Credit

Crossword Puzzle
For Chapters 10 and 11

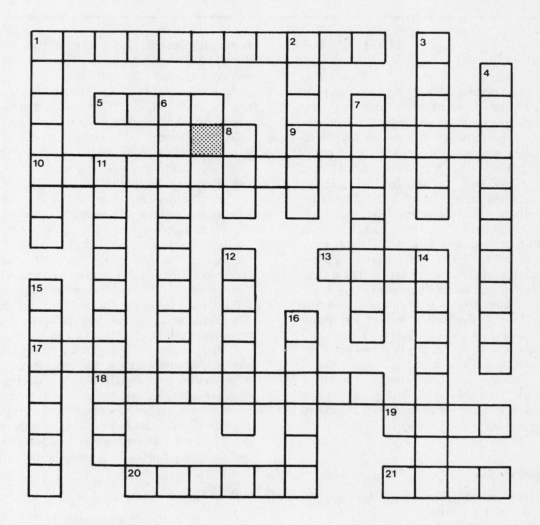

ACROSS

1. Arrangement for retirement income (2 words)
5. Principal amount
9. Fund to retire bonds
10. Bond contract
13. Bonds with one maturity date
17. Remaining after deductions
18. Liability type
19. Buy back, as bonds
20. With 7-Down, time value of money amount
21. _____ coupon bonds

DOWN

1. Opposite of bond discount
2. Uses another's property for a fee
3. Bonds that mature in installments
4. Bond whose owner is recorded by the company
6. Potential liability
7. See 20-Across
8. Payable
11. _____ determinable liability
12. _____ tax liability
14. Debt secured by property
15. Series of equal payments
16. _____ value tables

Reading

Bondholders Are Mad as Hell—and They're Not Going to Take It Anymore

Not so long ago, blue-chip corporate bonds were considered ideal investments for widows and orphans. These days, bonds are so volatile that even sophisticated pros can lose billions on them—overnight. It can happen whenever a company gets caught up in a takeover or management-led buyout. The prospect that the company will have to take on more debt sends its bond prices plummeting. Look what happened last fall to the investment-grade bonds issued by RJR Nabisco Inc. Their prices dropped a dizzying 20% after management proposed the largest LBO in history.

Now, bondholders are fighting back. Metropolitan Life Insurance Co. and Jefferson Pilot Life Insurance Co., for example, have filed a potentially far-reaching suit arguing that RJR's management violated its fiduciary responsibility to existing bondholders by initiating an LBO. Says Met Life CEO John J. Creedon: "We had a relationship of mutual trust and fair dealing, and it's not right to take action that destroyed the value of the bonds." Met Life faces an uphill battle. Traditionally, managers are fiduciaries only for their stockholders. With bondholders, they must honor only the specific terms, or covenants, that are laid out in a bond contract.

Sharing the Wealth

Still, bondholders are getting tough about enforcing those terms. Levi Strauss Associates Inc. recently ran smack into the new militancy. It went private in a $1.6 billion LBO in 1985. Late last year management wanted to change the terms of its bond covenants to let the company buy back 7% of the stock held by members of the founding family. The managers also wanted the freedom to pay out cash dividends to stockholders—the sort of stuff that investors routinely approved in the past.

Not this time. Bondholders worried that shareholders would siphon off precious cash today, leaving them at greater risk tomorrow. Putnam Management Co., a huge mutual fund operator, lobbied other investors to unite against the

Source: Reprinted from February 6, 1989 issue of *Business Week* by special permission, copyright © 1989 by McGraw-Hill, Inc.

covenant changes. Levi Strauss eventually abandoned its dividend proposal. Then, to win bondholders' consent for the proposed stock repurchase, it paid them $17.50 per $1,000 unit—a total of $4.8 million. "If your borrower says he wants a new relationship, we want to be reasonable, but we want to be compensated," says Edward D'Alelio, a senior portfolio manager at Putnam. Call it the new quid pro quo: We share the risk, we share the wealth.

Bondholders are also pushing companies to issue new bonds with covenants that limit losses in any future restructuring. Already, some blue-chip companies have offered protection against a debt meltdown. Harris Corp., Northwest Pipeline, and Grumman Corp. all recently issued bonds with "poison puts." The put gives investors the right to sell their bonds back to the company at face value if a restructuring lowers their rating to less-than-investment grade.

The influence of bondholders on U.S. companies is bound to grow for one simple reason: Money talks. Increasingly, debt is replacing equity as America's risk capital. And as companies leverage themselves more, bondholders are groping for ways to control the risks of living with the new debt. "Bondholders are going to want a say, just like an equity holder," says a Grumman official.

Riskier World

Being taken seriously in executive suites will take time, though. After all, the bondholder backlash is partly a belated realization that it was a mistake to let companies get rid of most covenants in the 1970s. With strong demand from mutual funds, pension funds, and overseas investors, companies could buy management freedom with slightly higher coupon rates. Investors were eager to boost short-term returns anyway, and covenants are more of a long-term concern. The trade-off made sense since managers and creditors share a similar worldview. Both "liked low debt, good credit ratings, and low insolvency risk," says John C. Coffee, Jr., a law professor at Columbia University.

They agreed, that is, until deal mania swept the country and broke the bond between borrower and lender. Managers realized they could lose their jobs to a raider if they didn't work their balance sheets harder. A new philosophy of debt took hold: Untapped borrowing power, no less than an idle factory, is wasteful. That view is partly behind the growth in the junk-bond market and a decline in corporate creditworthiness. . . .

In this riskier world, however, tougher covenants aren't a panacea. A good lawyer and a determined management can almost always get around contract-language barriers. And many companies won't willingly limit their freedom of action. "How can you say we will agree to pay at par when there might be an opportunity to make a brilliant acquisition and suffer a temporary downgrade?" asks Richard K. Goeltz, Seagram Co.'s chief financial officer. "It ties too severely the hands of management."

Hence the outburst of litigation. Bondholders are asking the courts to make it clear that any shareholder gain in a restructuring can't come at bondholder expense. But some lawyers are skeptical that the Met Life suit, for one, will succeed. After all, the giant insurers' professional money managers are hardly neophytes. They were well aware of the risks that LBOs posed for bonds —including RJR's—and bought them anyway. Yet creditors are getting some support among corporate borrowers. Consider ITT Corp., which has about $6 billion in stock and about $2.2 billion in bonds outstanding. "For me to say that I have no obligation for that $2.2 billion I think is sick," says Chairman Rand V. Araskog.

New Yardsticks

Few institutional investors would disagree, but they can't afford to step fully into the bondholder camp. For every dollar that corporate restructurings lopped off its investment-grade bond portfolio last year, Prudential Insurance Co. enjoyed $1.75 in gains on those companies' shares. Even Met Life, which lost $40 million on its RJR bonds, made more than $20 million on its RJR stock. Institutional investors are still grappling with the investment implications of deal mania.

Some fixed-income investors just say no. Pacific Investment Management Co., with $18 billion in bonds of all sorts, hasn't bought an industrial-company debt issue in almost three years. Others, such as T. Rowe Price Associates Inc., are changing their modus operandi. When the mutual fund's managers consider buying investment-grade bonds, they no longer just look at a company's credit rating and traditional financial strength yardsticks. The fund now uses the expertise of its junk-bond analysts and equity analysts to study whether the company is a potential restructuring candidate.

Understanding these risks is helpful. So is flexing some economic muscle. Campeau Corp., for instance, needed to raise $1.15 billion to help pay for its acquisition of Federated Department Stores Inc. last year. When Campeau offered junk bonds yielding an average of 14%, investors turned up their noses. Campeau ended up slashing the amount to $750 million and sweetened the rate on some of the bonds to 17¾.

Collision Course?

One consequence of such high-risk bonds is that the distinction between debt and equity is eroding. Many junk bonds are really "quasi equity," says a money manager. This becomes clear when a company gets into trouble. Storage Technology Corp. filed for Chapter 11 bankruptcy protection on Halloween, 1984. When it came out of Chapter 11 in 1987, bondholders were paid off not only with cash and new bonds, but also with enough equity to make them one-third owners.

These days, more than ever, bondholders' fortunes are tied to a company's performance. That can put creditors on a collision course with stockholders and managers—especially when managers go for quick, short-term gains. So far, when these powerful interests clash, debt owners have often been the losers. But don't count them out. They are only beginning to flex their economic muscle.

CHAPTER 12 CONTRIBUTED CAPITAL

Reviewing the Chapter

OBJECTIVE 1: Define a corporation, and state the advantages and disadvantages of the corporate form of business (pp. 595–598).

1. A **corporation** is a business organization authorized by the state to conduct business that is a separate legal entity from its owners. It is the dominant form of American business because it makes it possible to gather together large amounts of capital.

2. The corporate form of business has several advantages over the sole proprietorship and the partnership. It is a separate legal entity and offers limited liability to the owners. It also offers ease of capital generation and ease of transfer of ownership. Other advantages are the lack of mutual agency in a corporation and its continuous existence. In addition, a corporate form of business allows centralized authority and responsibility and professional management.

3. The corporate form of business also has several disadvantages compared with the sole proprietorship and the partnership. It is subject to greater government regulation and **double taxation.** Limited liability of the owners may limit how much a small corporation can borrow. In addition, separation of ownership and control may allow management to make harmful decisions.

OBJECTIVE 2: Account for organization costs (p. 598).

4. The costs of forming a corporation (such as attorneys' fees and incorporation fees) are debited to an intangible asset account called **Organization Costs.** These costs are amortized over the early period of the corporation's life, usually five years.

OBJECTIVE 3: Identify the components of stockholders' equity (pp. 599–601).

5. A corporation's balance sheet contains assets, liabilities, and a stockholders' equity section. Stockholders' equity is made up of **contributed capital,** representing the stockholders' investment, and retained earnings, representing earnings that have remained in the business.

6. Ownership in a corporation is evidenced by a document called a **stock certificate.** A stockholder sells stock by endorsing the stock certificate and sending it to the corporation's secretary or its transfer agent. The secretary or transfer agent is responsible for transferring the corporation's stock, maintaining stockholders' records, and preparing a list of stockholders for stockholders' meetings and for the payment of dividends. In addition, corporations often engage an underwriter to assist in the initial issue of stock.

7. The articles of incorporation will indicate the number of shares of stock that a corporation is **authorized** to issue. Stock that has been **issued** to stockholders and has not been bought back by the corporation is called **outstanding stock. Par value** is the **legal capital** contributed by a share of stock.

8. When only one type of stock is issued, it is called **common stock.** A second type of stock, called preferred stock, may also be issued. Because common stockholders' claim to assets upon liquidation ranks behind that of creditors and preferred stockholders, common stock is considered the **residual equity** of a company.

OBJECTIVE 4: Account for cash dividends (pp. 601–602).

9. A **dividend** is a distribution of assets, usually in cash, by a corporation to its stockholders. Dividends are usually stated as a specified dollar amount per share of stock and are declared by the board of directors. Dividends are declared on the date of declaration, specifying that the owners of the stock on the date of record will receive the dividends on the date of payment. After the date of record, stock is said to be **ex-dividend** (without dividend rights). A **liquidating dividend** is the return of contributed capital to the stockholders and is normally paid when a company is going out of business or reducing its operations.

10. When cash dividends are declared, the Dividends Declared account is debited and Dividends Payable is credited; when they are paid, Dividends Payable is debited and Cash is credited. The Dividends Declared account is closed to Retained Earnings at the end of the year. No journal entry is made on the date of record.

OBJECTIVE 5: Calculate the division of dividends between common and preferred stockholders (pp. 602–605).

11. Holders of **preferred stock** are given preference over common shareholders upon dividend declaration and liquidation. Each share of preferred stock entitles its owner to a dollar amount or percentage of par value each year before common stockholders receive anything. Once the preferred stockholders have received the annual dividends to which they are entitled, however, the common stockholders generally receive the remainder.

12. In addition, preferred stock (a) is cumulative or noncumulative, (b) is convertible or nonconvertible, and (c) may be callable. It usually has no voting rights.
    a. When the preferred stockholders do not receive the full amount of their annual dividend, the unpaid amount is carried over to the next year when the preferred stock is **cumulative.** Unpaid back dividends are called **dividends in arrears** and should be disclosed either in the balance sheet or as a footnote. When the preferred stock is **noncumulative,** unpaid dividends are not carried over to the next period.
    b. An owner of **convertible preferred stock** has the option to exchange each share of preferred stock for a set number of shares of common stock.
    c. Most preferred stocks are **callable preferred stocks,** meaning that the corporation has the right to buy the stock back at a specified call or redemption price. Convertible preferred stock can be converted to common stock instead if its holder so desires.

OBJECTIVE 6: Account for the issuance of common and preferred stock for cash and other assets (pp. 606–610).

13. Capital stock (common or preferred) may or may not have a par value, depending on the specifications in the charter. When par value stock is issued, the Capital Stock account is credited for the legal capital (par value), and any excess is recorded as Paid-in Capital in Excess of Par Value. In the stockholders' equity section of the balance sheet, the entire amount is labeled Total Contributed Capital. On rare occasions, stock is issued at a discount (less than par value), requiring a debit to Discount on Capital Stock.

14. **No-par stock** is stock for which par value has not been established. It may be issued with or without a stated value. **Stated value** (when established by the board of directors) is the legal capital for a share of no-par stock. The total stated value is recorded in the Capital Stock account. Any amount received in excess of stated value is recorded as Paid-in Capital in Excess of Stated Value. If no stated value is

set, however, the entire amount received is legal capital and is credited to Capital Stock.

15. Sometimes stock is issued in exchange for assets or for services rendered. Such a transaction should be recorded at the fair market value of the stock. However, if the stock's fair market value cannot be determined, the fair market value of the assets or services should be used.

OBJECTIVE 7: Account for stock subscriptions (pp. 610–612).

16. An investor who signs a **stock subscription** agrees to pay a set price for a certain amount of stock at some later date or in installments. When subscriptions are received, Subscriptions Receivable is debited, and Common Stock Subscribed (a contributed capital account) and Paid-in Capital in Excess of Par Value are credited. Upon collection, Cash is debited and Subscriptions Receivable is credited. When the stock is issued upon full payment, Common Stock Subscribed is debited and Common Stock is credited.

OBJECTIVE 8: Account for the exercise of stock options (pp. 612–613).

17. A **stock option plan** is an agreement whereby certain corporate employees may purchase a certain quantity of the company's stock at a certain price for a certain period of time. If the plan allows virtually all employees to purchase stock at the existing market price, then the journal entry upon issue would resemble the entry made when stock is sold to outsiders. However, if only certain employees (usually management) are allowed to purchase the corporation's stock in the future at a fixed price, the plan is said to be compensatory. The amount of compensation per share equals the market price on the date the option is granted minus the option price. Journal entries are made to record compensation expense (covered in a more advanced course) and the issuance of the stock upon exercise of the option.

Summary of Journal Entries Introduced in Chapter 12

A. (L.O. 2) Organization Costs   XX (amount incurred)
         Cash   XX (amount paid)
                To record costs of forming corporation

B. (L.O. 2) Amortization Expense, Organization Costs   XX (amount allocated)
         Organization Costs   XX (amount allocated)
                To amortize organization costs

C. (L.O. 4) Dividends Declared   XX (amount declared)
         Dividends Payable   XX (amount declared)
                To record declaration of cash dividend

D. (L.O. 4) Dividends Payable   XX (amount paid)
         Cash   XX (amount paid)
                To record payment of cash dividend

E. (L.O. 6) Cash   XX (amount invested)
         Common Stock   XX (legal capital amount)
         Paid-in Capital in Excess of Par (Stated) Value, Common   XX (excess amount)
                Stock issued for amount in excess of par (stated)
                value

F. (L.O. 6) Cash   XX (amount invested)
         Common Stock   XX (legal capital amount)
                No-par stock issued, no stated value established

G. (L.O. 6) Organization Costs   XX (fair market value)
         Common Stock   XX (par value)
         Paid-in Capital in Excess of Par Value, Common   XX (excess of par)
                Issued stock in exchange for incorporation services
                performed

H. (L.O. 7) Subscriptions Receivable, Common   XX (subscribed amount)
         Common Stock Subscribed   XX (par value)
         Paid-in Capital in Excess of Par Value, Common   XX (excess of par)
                Received subscription for common stock

I. (L.O. 7) Cash   XX (amount received)
         Subscriptions Receivable, Common   XX (amount received)
                Made collection on subscriptions

J. (L.O. 7) Common Stock Subscribed   XX (par value)
         Common Stock   XX (par value)
                Issued stock now paid for

K. (L.O. 8) Cash   XX (amount invested)
         Common Stock   XX (par value)
         Paid-in Capital in Excess of Par Value, Common   XX (excess of par)
                Issued stock to employees under stock option plan

Testing Your Knowledge

Matching

Match each term with its definition by writing the appropriate letter in the blank.

_____ 1. Corporation

_____ 2. Organization costs

_____ 3. Issued stock

_____ 4. Authorized stock

_____ 5. Outstanding stock

_____ 6. Common stock

_____ 7. Preferred stock

_____ 8. Dividends in arrears

_____ 9. Par value

_____ 10. No-par stock

_____ 11. Stated value

_____ 12. Stock subscription

_____ 13. Ex-dividend

_____ 14. Liquidating dividend

_____ 15. Convertible preferred stock

_____ 16. Callable preferred stock

_____ 17. Cumulative preferred stock

_____ 18. Stock option plan

_____ 19. Stock certificate

_____ 20. Residual equity

a. Unpaid back dividends

b. Descriptive of common stockholders' ownership in a corporation

c. Without dividend rights

d. The amount of legal capital of a share of no-par stock

e. Stock that is presently held by stockholders

f. The dominant form of business in the United States

g. The type of stock whose holders have prior claim over common stockholders to dividends

h. An agreement by an investor to pay for stock at some later date or in installments

i. Stock whose unpaid dividends "carry over" to future years until paid

j. Proof of ownership in a corporation

k. Expenditures necessary to form a corporation

l. The maximum amount of stock that a corporation may issue

m. The name of the stock when only one type of stock has been issued

n. Stock that may or may not have a stated value

o. The legal value for stock that is stated in the charter

p. Stock that has been sold to stockholders, and may or may not have been bought back by the corporation

q. Stock that may be bought back at the option of the issuing corporation

r. An agreement whereby certain employees may purchase stock at a fixed price

s. The return of contributed capital to a corporation's stockholders

t. Preferred stock that an investor may exchange for common stock

Short Answer

Use the lines provided to answer each item.

1. List eight advantages of the corporate form of business.

   _____
   _____
   _____
   _____
   _____
   _____
   _____
   _____

2. List four disadvantages of the corporate form of business.

   _____
   _____
   _____
   _____

3. Name the two major portions of the stockholders' equity section of a balance sheet.

   _____
   _____

4. Preferred shareholders are given preference over common shareholders under what two circumstances?

   _____
   _____

True-False

Circle T if the statement is true, F if it is false. Please provide explanations for the false answers, using the blank lines at the end of the section.

T F   1. Corporate income is taxed at the corporate level and at the individual level when it is distributed as dividends.

T F   2. The concept of legal capital was established to protect the corporation's creditors.

T F   3. Ordinarily, creditors cannot attach the personal assets of the corporation's stockholders.

T F   4. Organization costs must be charged to expense in the year of the corporation's formation.

T F   5. Contributed capital consists of capital stock plus paid-in capital in excess of par (stated) value.

T F   6. A transfer agent keeps records of stock transactions.

T F   7. Preferred stock may not be both convertible and cumulative.

T F   8. Dividends in arrears do not exist when all preferred stock is noncumulative.

T F   9. The worth of a share of stock can be measured by its par value.

T F   10. As cash is received on stock subscriptions, the stockholders' equity section of the balance sheet will increase in amount.

T F   11. Preferred stockholders are guaranteed annual dividends, whereas common stockholders are not.

T F   12. Preferred stock is considered the residual equity of a corporation.

T F   13. The amount of compensation in connection with a stock option plan is measured on the date the option is exercised.

T F   14. On the date of payment of a dividend, total assets and total stockholders' equity decrease.

T F   15. Dividends in arrears should appear as a liability on the balance sheet.

_____

_____

_____

_____

_____

_____

_____

_____

_____

_____

_____

_____

_____

_____

_____

Multiple Choice

Circle the letter of the best answer.

1. Which of the following should not appear in the stockholders' equity section of a balance sheet?
   a. Paid-in Capital in Excess of Par Value
   b. Common Stock Subscribed
   c. Discount on Capital Stock
   d. Subscriptions Receivable

2. With a stock subscription, what account is credited when the stock is actually issued?
   a. Common Stock
   b. Common Stock Subscribed
   c. Subscriptions Receivable
   d. Paid-in Capital in Excess of Par (Stated) Value

3. Which of the following statements is true?
   a. Outstanding shares plus issued shares equals authorized shares.
   b. Unissued shares plus outstanding shares equals authorized shares.
   c. Authorized shares minus unissued shares equals issued shares.
   d. Unissued shares minus issued shares equals outstanding shares.

4. McFarland Corporation has outstanding 1,000 shares of $100 par value, 7 percent noncumulative preferred stock, and 20,000 shares of $10 par value common stock. Last year, the company paid no dividends, but this year it distributed $40,000 in dividends. What portion of this $40,000 will common stockholders receive?
   a. $0
   b. $2,800
   c. $26,000
   d. $33,000

5. Which of the following is not a characteristic of corporations in general?
   a. Separation of ownership and management
   b. Ease of transfer of ownership
   c. Double taxation
   d. Unlimited liability of stockholders

6. On which date associated with a cash dividend would a journal entry be made?
   a. Date of record
   b. Date of payment
   c. Date of declaration
   d. Both b and c are correct.

7. Stock is said to be "ex-dividend" after
   a. it has been sold to another party.
   b. the date of record.
   c. the date of payment.
   d. the date of declaration.

8. When callable preferred stock is called and surrendered, the stockholder is *not* entitled to
   a. a call premium.
   b. the par value of the stock.
   c. any dividends in arrears.
   d. the market value of the stock.

Applying Your Knowledge

Exercises

1. Hamilton Corporation paid no dividends in its first two years of operations. In its third year, it paid $51,000 in dividends. For all three years there have been 1,000 shares of 6 percent, $100 par value cumulative preferred stock, and 5,000 shares of $10 par value common stock outstanding. How much of the $51,000 in dividends goes to preferred stockholders? to common stockholders?

Preferred stockholders receive $_____.

Common stockholders receive $_____.

2. On May 1, Burr Corporation accepted subscriptions to 1,000 shares of $50 par value common stock at $70 per share. A 20 percent down payment was also received on that date. On June 3, an additional 40 percent was received. On June 18, the remaining 40 percent was received, and the stock was issued. Prepare all necessary entries in the journal provided.

	General Journal			
Date		Description	Debit	Credit

Reading

It Can Pay Off Big to Turn Common into Preferred

When Teledyne Inc. bought back some 18% of its common shares in 1980, the company's executives got more or less what they had hoped for: a 28% higher price in a year's time. But when Advanced Systems Inc. swapped a new issue of preferred shares for 24% of its common in 1982, Chief Financial Officer Norman Walack got a lot more than he expected: a 100% jump in the common stock's price, from 11 a share to 22 a year later.

Shelling out cash to repurchase common shares has become an increasingly popular way for corporations to obtain, among other things, a more favorable balance between the market supply of their stock and the demand for it. But, according to a study by Mitchell & Co., a Boston management-consulting firm, creating new preferred shares and swapping them for common stock is often more rewarding.

"Reacquiring common shares through an exchange of preferred stock generally does not hurt the company in any way, and avoids all the negatives that have thrown the entire stock-buyback idea into a deep well of controversy," says Carol Bruckner Coles, Mitchell's president and chief operating officer. While analysts increasingly criticize the costs of stock repurchases (BW—June 25), companies keep on doing them, for a variety of reasons: to reduce dividend payments, to gain an almost automatic assurance of higher earnings per share, to make feared takeover plots or proxy fights more difficult, and to reinvest excess cash in the companies' own "undervalued assets."

Thinking Big

The still relatively undiscovered method of swapping preferred serves the same purposes but skirts most of the pitfalls; about the only drawback to a company is that it may have to jack up its preferred dividend to compete with any rise in interest rates. The swappers, notes Coles, do not have to divert cash from more productive purposes, nor do they have to take on extra debt. "For a company that borrows funds to reacquire shares, interest charges may offset any earnings benefits

Source: Reprinted from the July 2, 1984 issue of *Business Week* by special permission, copyright © 1984 by McGraw-Hill, Inc.

and increase as well its debt-to-equity ratio," notes a Standard & Poor's Corp. analyst.

The stocks of companies that have resorted to straight buybacks, according to Mitchell analysts' calculations, increased, on average, over the past five years by about 30% above where the stock would have been without the repurchase. But the stocks of companies that have swapped preferred shares or, in some cases, even convertible debentures, for their common stock have, on the same basis, jumped an average of 199%. Thinking big helps, strategists contend: For maximum impact, the conversion should involve no fewer than 20% of outstanding shares.

Thus, not all stocks involved in swaps enjoy a surge in price. Manufacturers Hanover Trust Co., for example, pulled in only 11.8% of its common for new preferred shares in May, 1982. Result: Its common stock rose a meager 2% after a year. And Ashland Oil Inc. reacquired 14% of its common in January, 1980, with a $2.50-a-share dividend, in return for preferred shares that will pay a dividend almost twice that on its common stock. Dividends on preferred stock typically run up to 60% above the yield on common stocks. Even so, the Ashland common rose a disappointing 5%.

Snowball?

A large-scale preferred swap, however, may have preserved Development Corp. of America as a public company. Officers of the Hollywood (Fla.) real estate company had considered taking the company private, recalls Pedro Diaz, its chief financial officer. Then they had thought of economizing by cutting the dividend on the common stock. "But on second thought, we just decided to issue subordinated 12% debentures in exchange for about 27% of our common stock," he says. The stock, trading at about 5 1/2 before the swap, rose to about 16 a year later.

That may, in part, explain why Advanced Systems' exchange of preferred shares was so well received. "Investors would do well to scout for companies that are in the process of, or about to offer, such a preferred-for-common stock swap," says Coles. Such offers have yet to snowball on Wall Street, "but we expect to see many more companies in the latter half of the 1980s use this kind of stock swap," says Coles.

Companies whose stocks are trading below their year-earlier prices, and which have authorized-but-unissued preferred stock, are likely to resort to such swaps. A number of steel companies, suggests Coles, could find the swaps rewarding. Among other logical candidates, she adds, are Johnson & Johnson, Gulf & Western Industries, Bristol-Meyers, and Revlon.

CHAPTER 13 RETAINED EARNINGS AND CORPORATE INCOME STATEMENTS

Reviewing the Chapter

OBJECTIVE 1: Define *retained earnings,* **and prepare a statement of retained earnings (pp. 634–635).**

1. The stockholders' equity section of a corporation's balance sheet is composed of contributed capital and retained earnings. Contributed capital represents the owners' capital investment. **Retained earnings** are the profits that a corporation has earned since its beginning, minus any losses, dividends declared, or other transfers out of retained earnings.

2. The statement of retained earnings is a labeled summary of the changes in retained earnings during the accounting period.

3. Ordinarily, Retained Earnings will have a credit balance. However, when a debit balance exists, the corporation is said to have a **deficit**.

4. **Prior period adjustments** are entries made in the current period for certain transactions that relate to, but were not determinable in, prior accounting periods. A prior period adjustment can be made only for one of two reasons. First, it may be done to correct an error in the financial statements of a prior period. Second, it may be done to record a tax gain from carrying forward a preacquisition operating loss of a purchased subsidiary. Prior period adjustments appear on the current period's retained earnings statement as an adjustment to the beginning balance, but not on the income statement. All other items of income and loss during the period that do not qualify as prior period adjustments must appear on the income statement. Prior period adjustments are rare.

OBJECTIVE 2: Account for stock dividends and stock splits (pp. 635–640).

5. A **stock dividend** is a proportional distribution of shares of stock to a corporation's stockholders. Stock dividends are declared to (a) give evidence of the company's success without paying a cash dividend, (b) reduce a stock's market price, and (c) allow a nontaxable distribution. The result of a stock dividend is the transfer of a part of retained earnings to contributed capital. For a small stock dividend (less than 20–25 percent), the market value of the shares distributed is transferred from retained earnings. For a large stock dividend (greater than 20–25 percent), the par or stated value is transferred. A stock dividend does not change total stockholders' equity or any individual's proportionate equity in the company.

6. A **stock split** is an increase in the number of shares of stock outstanding, with a corresponding decrease in the par or stated value of the stock. For example, a 3 for 1 split on 40,000 shares of $30 par value would result in the distribution of 80,000 additional shares.

(That is, a former owner of one share would now own two more shares.) The par value would be reduced to $10. The balances in stockholders' equity would not be affected.

7. The purpose of a stock split is to improve the stock's marketability by causing the stock's market price to go down. In the above example, if the stock were selling for $180 per share, a 3 for 1 split would probably cause the market price to fall to about $60 per share. A memorandum entry should be made for a stock split, disclosing the decrease in par or stated value as well as the increase in number of shares of stock outstanding.

OBJECTIVE 3: Account for treasury stock transactions (pp. 640–642).

8. **Treasury stock** is common or preferred stock that has been issued and reacquired by the issuing company. That is, it is issued but no longer outstanding stock. Treasury stock is purchased (a) to distribute to employees through stock option plans, (b) to maintain a favorable market for the company's stock, (c) to increase earnings per share, (d) to use in purchasing other companies, and (e) to prevent a hostile takeover of the company.

9. Treasury stock may be held indefinitely, reissued, or canceled, and has no rights until it is reissued. Treasury stock, the last item in the stockholders' equity section of the balance sheet, appears as a deduction.

10. When treasury stock is purchased, its account is debited for the purchase cost. It may be reissued at cost, above cost, or below cost. When cash received from reissue exceeds the cost, the difference is credited to Paid-in Capital, Treasury Stock Transactions. When cash received is less than cost, the difference is debited to Paid-in Capital, Treasury Stock Transactions (and Retained Earnings if needed). In no case should a gain or loss be recorded.

11. When treasury stock is retired, all the contributed capital associated with the retired shares must be removed from the accounts. When less is paid than was originally contributed, the difference is credited to Paid-in Capital, Retirement of Stock. When more is paid, the difference is debited to Retained Earnings.

OBJECTIVE 4: Describe the disclosure of restrictions on retained earnings (pp. 643–644).

12. Retained earnings consist of unrestricted and restricted retained earnings. Unrestricted retained earnings dictate the asset amount (if available) that can be distributed to stockholders as dividends. A **restriction on retained earnings** dictates the asset amount that is to be retained in the business for other purposes. Retained earnings are restricted for contractual, legal, or voluntary reasons—by the board of directors only. Retained Earnings is not a cash account; it is simply a guide to asset distribution. Restrictions on retained earnings are disclosed in the retained earnings portion of the balance sheet or as notes to the financial statements.

OBJECTIVE 5: Prepare a statement of stockholders' equity (pp. 644–645).

13. The **statement of stockholders' equity** may be used in place of the statement of retained earnings. It is basically a labeled computation of the changes in stockholders' equity accounts during the accounting period. It contains all the components of the statement of retained earnings, as well as a summary of the period's stock transactions.

OBJECTIVE 6: Calculate book value per share, and distinguish it from market value (pp. 645–647).

14. The **book value** of a share of stock equals the net assets represented by one share of a company's stock. If the company has common stock only, the book value per share is arrived at by dividing stockholders' equity by the number of outstanding and subscribed shares. When the company also has preferred stock, the liquidating value of the preferred stock plus any dividends in arrears are deducted from stockholders' equity in computing book value per share of common stock.

15. **Market value** is the price that investors are willing to pay for a share of stock on the open market.

OBJECTIVE 7: Prepare a corporate income statement (p. 648).

16. Corporate income statements should present **comprehensive income,** or all revenues, expenses, gains, and losses except for prior period adjustments. This approach to the measurement of income has resulted in several items being added to the income state-

ment—discontinued operations, extraordinary items, and accounting changes. In addition, earnings per share figures should be disclosed.

OBJECTIVE 8: Show the relationships among income taxes expense, deferred income taxes, and net of taxes (pp. 648–653).

17. Corporate taxable income is determined by subtracting allowable business deductions from includable gross income. Tax rates currently range from a 15 percent to a 39 percent marginal rate.

18. Computing income taxes for financial reporting differs from computing income taxes due the government for the same accounting period. This difference is caused by the fact that financial reporting income is governed by generally accepted accounting principles, whereas taxable income is governed by the Internal Revenue Code. Accordingly, when income for financial reporting differs materially from taxable income, the **income tax allocation** technique should be used. Under this method, the difference between the current tax liability and income tax expense is debited or credited to an account called **Deferred Income Taxes.** Adjustments to this amount must be made when changes in tax rates are legislated.

19. Certain income statement items must be reported **net of taxes** to avoid a distorted net operating income figure. These items are discontinued operations, extraordinary gains and losses, and accounting changes.

OBJECTIVE 9: Describe the disclosure on the income statement of discontinued operations, extraordinary items, and accounting changes (pp. 653–655).

20. The results of operations for the period and any gains or losses from the **discontinued operations** of a segment of a business should be disclosed (net of taxes) after Income from Continuing Operations. A segment is defined as a separate major line of business or class of customer.

21. An **extraordinary item** is an event that is unusual and occurs infrequently. Extraordinary items should be disclosed separately in the income statement (net of taxes) after Discontinued Operations.

22. A company may change from one accounting principle to another (as from FIFO to LIFO) only if it can justify the new method as better accounting practice. The **cumulative effect of an accounting change** on prior years (net of taxes) should appear on the income statement after extraordinary items.

OBJECTIVE 10: Compute earnings per share (pp. 655–657).

23. Investors use the earnings per share figure to judge a company's performance, to estimate its future earnings, and to compare it with other companies. Earnings per share figures should be disclosed for (1) income from continuing operations, (2) income before extraordinary items, (3) cumulative effect of accounting changes, and (4) net income. These figures should appear on the face of the income statement.

24. A company that has issued no securities that are convertible into common stock has a **simple capital structure.** In this case, earnings per share is computed by dividing net income applicable to common stock by the weighted-average shares outstanding.

25. A company that has issued securities that may be converted into common stock has a **complex capital structure.** For example, **common stock equivalents** such as stock options and certain convertible securities might exist, producing a **potential dilution** (decrease) in earnings per share. In this case, a dual presentation of **primary** and **fully diluted earnings per share** is required.

Summary of Journal Entries Introduced in Chapter 13

A. (L.O. 2) Retained Earnings   XX (amount transferred)
    Common Stock Distributable   XX (par value amount)
    Paid-in Capital in Excess of Par Value, Common   XX (excess of par)
        To record declaration of stock dividend

B. (L.O. 2) Common Stock Distributable   XX (par value amount)
    Common Stock   XX (par value amount)
        To record distribution of stock dividend

C. (L.O. 3) Treasury Stock, Common   XX (cost)
    Cash   XX (cost)
        To record purchase of treasury stock

D. (L.O. 3) Cash   XX (resale price)
    Treasury Stock, Common   XX (cost)
        Reissuance of treasury stock at cost

E. (L.O. 3) Cash   XX (resale price)
    Treasury Stock, Common   XX (cost)
    Paid-in Capital, Treasury Stock   XX ("gain")
        Reissuance of treasury stock at above cost

F. (L.O. 3) Cash   XX (resale price)
    Paid-in Capital, Treasury Stock   XX ("loss")
    Retained Earnings (only if needed)   XX ("loss")
    Treasury Stock, Common   XX (cost)
        Reissuance of treasury stock at below cost

G. (L.O. 3) Common Stock   XX (par value)
    Paid-in Capital in Excess of Par Value   XX (excess of par)
    Retained Earnings (only if needed)   XX (premium paid)
    Treasury Stock   XX (cost)
        To record retirement of treasury stock; cost exceeded
        original investment amount

H. (L.O. 3) If the above treasury stock had been retired for an amount less than the original investment amount, then instead of Retained Earnings being debited for the excess paid, Paid-in Capital, Retirement of Stock would be credited for the difference retained.

I. (L.O. 8) Income Taxes Expense   XX (amount per GAAP)
    Income Taxes Payable   XX (currently payable)
    Deferred Income Taxes   XX (eventually payable)
        To record current and deferred income taxes

Testing Your Knowledge

Matching

Match each term with its definition by writing the appropriate letter in the blank.

_____ 1. Retained earnings

_____ 2. Deficit

_____ 3. Prior period adjustment

_____ 4. Income tax allocation

_____ 5. Simple capital structure

_____ 6. Complex capital structure

_____ 7. Discontinued operations

_____ 8. Comprehensive income

_____ 9. Stock dividend

_____ 10. Stock split

_____ 11. Restricted retained earnings

_____ 12. Treasury stock

_____ 13. Statement of retained earnings

_____ 14. Extraordinary item

_____ 15. Earnings per share

_____ 16. Accounting change

_____ 17. Book value per share

_____ 18. Market value

_____ 19. Statement of stockholders' equity

_____ 20. Potentially dilutive securities

a. An unusual and infrequent gain or loss

b. The make-up of a corporation when convertible securities have been issued

c. A negative figure for retained earnings

d. Issued stock that has been reacquired by the corporation

e. A summary of the changes in stockholders' equity accounts during the period

f. The net assets represented by one share of a company's stock

g. All revenues, expenses, gains, and losses, except for prior period adjustments

h. Use of a different but more appropriate accounting method

i. A proportional distribution of stock to a corporation's stockholders

j. The profits that a corporation has earned since its inception, minus any losses, dividends declared, or transfers to contributed capital

k. A measure of net income earned for each share of stock

l. A corporate stock maneuver in which par or stated value is changed

m. The make-up of a corporation when no convertible securities have been issued

n. The income statement section immediately before extraordinary items

o. A summary of the changes in retained earnings during the period

p. The quantity of assets that are unavailable for dividends

q. The price that investors will pay for a share of stock

r. An entry made in the current period that relates to an earlier period

s. The technique to reconcile accounting income and taxable income

t. Stocks, etc., that lower the earnings per share figure

Short Answer

Use the lines provided to answer each item.

1. List five ways in which the Retained Earnings account may be reduced.

   _____

   _____

   _____

   _____

   _____

2. What are the two major distinctions between a stock dividend and a stock split?

   _____

   _____

   _____

   _____

3. What two conditions must be met for an item to qualify as extraordinary?

   _____

   _____

4. What is the difference between treasury stock and unissued stock?

   _____

   _____

   _____

Circle T if the statement is true, F if it is false. Please provide explanations for the false answers, using the blank lines at the end of the section.

T F **1.** If an extraordinary gain of $20,000 has occurred, it should be reported net of taxes at more than $20,000.

T F **2.** A restriction on retained earnings represents cash set aside for a special purpose.

T F **3.** The book value of a share of common stock will decrease when dividends are declared.

T F **4.** After a stock dividend is distributed, each stockholder owns a greater percentage of the corporation.

T F **5.** When a 30 percent stock dividend is declared, the market value of the stock on that date is irrelevant in making the journal entry.

T F **6.** The main purpose of a stock split is to reduce the stock's par value.

T F **7.** The purchase of treasury stock will reduce total assets and total stockholders' equity.

T F **8.** When treasury stock is issued at more than its cost, Gain on Sale of Treasury Stock should be recorded by the corporation.

T F **9.** Treasury stock is listed in the balance sheet as an asset.

T F **10.** A gain on the sale of a plant asset qualifies as an extraordinary item.

T F **11.** Extraordinary items should appear on the statement of retained earnings.

T F **12.** The effect of the change from straight-line depreciation to sum-of-the-years'-digits should be reported in the income statement immediately after extraordinary items.

T F **13.** Common Stock Distributable is a current liability in the balance sheet.

T F **14.** Both primary and fully diluted earnings per share data should be provided for a corporation with a complex capital structure.

T F **15.** If taxable income were always equal to accounting income, there would be no need for income tax allocation.

T F **16.** A prior period adjustment should never appear in the current period's income statement.

T F **17.** Common stock equivalents are never included in the earnings per share calculation.

_____

_____

_____

_____

_____

_____

_____

_____

_____

_____

_____

Retained Earnings and Corporate Income Statements

Multiple Choice

Circle the letter of the best answer.

1. Which of the following has no effect on retained earnings?
   a. Stock split
   b. Stock dividend
   c. Cash dividend
   d. Prior period adjustment

2. A company with 10,000 shares of common stock outstanding distributed a 10 percent stock dividend and then split its stock 4 for 1. How many shares are now outstanding?
   a. 2,750
   b. 41,000
   c. 44,000
   d. 55,000

3. When retained earnings are restricted, which of the following statements is true?
   a. Total retained earnings are increased.
   b. The company is no longer limited in the amount of dividends it can pay.
   c. Total retained earnings are reduced.
   d. Total stockholders' equity remains the same.

4. On the date that a stock dividend is distributed,
   a. Common Stock Distributable is credited.
   b. Cash is credited.
   c. Retained Earnings remains the same.
   d. no entry is made.

5. When treasury stock is reissued below cost, which of the following will never be true?
   a. Retained Earnings is debited.
   b. Treasury Stock is credited.
   c. Contributed Capital, Treasury Stock Transactions is debited.
   d. Loss on Reissue of Treasury Stock is debited.

6. The purchase of treasury stock will not affect
   a. the amount of stock outstanding.
   b. the amount of stock issued.
   c. total assets.
   d. total stockholders' equity.

7. An extraordinary item should appear
   a. on the income statement.
   b. on the balance sheet.
   c. on the statement of retained earnings.
   d. as a footnote.

8. The BNJ Corporation had 60,000 shares of common stock outstanding from January 1 to October 1, and 40,000 shares outstanding from October 1 to December 31. What is the weighted-average number of shares used for earnings per share calculations?
   a. 45,000 shares
   b. 50,000 shares
   c. 55,000 shares
   d. 100,000 shares

9. If retained earnings were $70,000 on January 1, 19xx, and $100,000 on December 31, 19xx, and if cash dividends of $15,000 were declared and paid during the year, net income for the year must have been
   a. $30,000.
   b. $45,000.
   c. $55,000.
   d. $85,000.

10. Which of the following would not appear in a statement of stockholders' equity?
    a. Conversion of preferred stock into common stock
    b. Dividends declared
    c. Extraordinary gains and losses
    d. Purchase of treasury stock

11. When a corporation has issued only one type of stock and wishes to compute book value per share, it needs all the information below except for
    a. retained earnings.
    b. current year's dividends.
    c. total contributed capital.
    d. total shares outstanding and subscribed.

12. Retained earnings is
    a. the same as cash.
    b. the amount invested by stockholders in a corporation.
    c. cumulative profits, less losses and dividends declared.
    d. unaffected by revenues and expenses.

Applying Your Knowledge

Exercises

1. For each of the following sets of facts, prepare
   the proper entry in the journal provided.

   Sept.   1   Patterson Corporation began operations
              by issuing 10,000 shares of $100 par value
              stock at $120 per share.

   Mar.   7   A 5 percent stock dividend is declared.
              The market price of the stock is $130 per
              share on March 7.

         30   This is the date of record for the stock
              dividend.

   Apr.   13   The stock dividend is distributed.

General Journal				
Date		Description	Debit	Credit

2. Quigley Corporation began operation on August 10, 19x1, by issuing 50,000 shares of $10 par value stock at $50 per share. As of January 1, 19x3, its capital structure was the same. For each of the following sets of facts for January of 19x3, prepare the proper entry in the journal provided. In all cases, assume sufficient cash and retained earnings.

Jan. 12 The corporation purchases 5,000 shares of stock from the stockholders at $60 per share.

20 The corporation reissues 2,000 shares of treasury stock at $65 per share.

27 The corporation reissues another 2,000 shares of treasury stock at $58 per share.

31 Retired the remaining 1,000 treasury shares.

General Journal				
Date		Description	Debit	Credit

3. Carter Corporation's balance sheet as of December 31, 19xx, includes the following information regarding stockholders' equity:

Contributed Capital	
Preferred Stock, $50 par value, 7% cumulative, 4,000 shares authorized, issued, and outstanding	$200,000
Common Stock, no-par, 30,000 shares authorized, issued, and outstanding	360,000
Paid-in Capital in Excess of Par Value, Preferred	40,000
Total Contributed Capital	$600,000
Retained Earnings	80,000
Total Stockholders' Equity	$680,000

Dividends in arrears total $28,000.

In the space that follows, compute book value per share of both preferred stock and common stock.

4. A company has $100,000 in operating income before taxes. It also had an extraordinary loss of $30,000 when lightning struck one of its warehouses. The company must pay a 40 percent tax on all items. Complete the partial income statement in good form.

Operating income before taxes	$100,000

5. Jamison Corporation had taxable income of $40,000, $40,000, and $80,000 in 19x1, 19x2, and 19x3, respectively. Its income for accounting purposes was $60,000, $30,000, and $70,000 for 19x1, 19x2, and 19x3, respectively. The difference between tax and accounting income was due to $30,000 in expenses that were deductible in full for tax purposes in 19x1, but were expensed one-third per year for accounting purposes. Make the correct journal entry to record income taxes in each of the three years. Assume a 40 percent tax rate.

	General Journal			
Date		**Description**	**Debit**	**Credit**

Crossword Puzzle
For Chapters 12 and 13

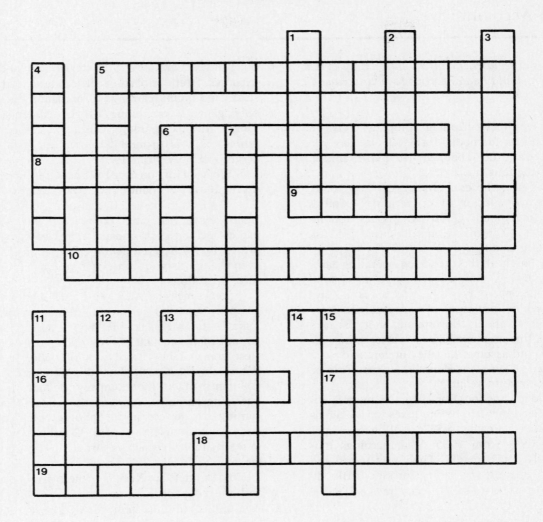

ACROSS

5. _____ income
7. Dividends in _____
8. Opposite of 13-Across
9. Corporate stock maneuver
10. Unusual and infrequent gain or loss
13. Legal capital amount
14. Fully _____ earnings per share
16. Common stock equity
17. Stock value for 8-Across
18. Callable
19. Net of _____

DOWN

1. Stock quantity
2. Financial statement reader
3. Negative retained earnings
4. Mutual _____
5. Capital structure type
6. _____ period adjustment
7. Restricted, as retained earnings
11. True stock value
12. Common dividend form
15. Sold to stockholders

Reading

Unreal Accounting

These days especially, paying attention only to the bottom line could be dangerous to your financial health.

Suppose your metal-bending company owns an old desk. It's on the books for $100. One day you discover the old desk belonged to Ben Franklin; Sotheby's auctions it off for $50,000.

Comes now the end of the year and you're calculating your company's operating earnings from bending metal. Question: Should you include the $49,900 profit from selling that old desk in "operating earnings"?

Don't laugh. In their reported operating earnings, lots of big companies include gains (and losses) from once-only events. As a result, says David Hawkins, professor of accounting at Harvard Business School, "investors cannot just take the bottom-line numbers before or after extraordinary items and assume that they understand what is going on." Doing so, Hawkins warns, "can be dangerous to your wealth."

Consider Time Inc. For 1986, the august publisher reported income, before taxes, of $626 million. Aftertax net came to $376 million, $5.95 per share, up 89% from 1985. With earnings momentum like that, maybe Time was worth the $100-plus a share it was selling for before Bloody Monday ripped it to $81. (It recovered to $88 two days later.)

But did Time's ongoing, operating businesses really earn $376 million? Is the figure a good basis from which to project 1987's earnings and buy its stock? Not necessarily.

Look at the $376 million reported profit, and you'll see it includes the equivalent of Ben Franklin's desk. To wit: In 1986, when the stock market was hot, Time sold 20% of a cable television subsidiary, American Television Communications Corp., to the public for a pretax gain of $318 million. Time booked this one-time gain as operating earnings—even though the only way it might realize a comparable gain next year would be to sell off yet another 20%.

Time also threw a $33 million profit on another investment, and $113 million in one-time expenses from relocating offices and reducing staff, into pretax earnings. Eliminate these once-only gains from selling off investments, and Time's aftertax operating earnings from ongoing businesses was around $129 million last year, down over 35% from 1985.

What's going on here? We called John Shank, professor of accounting at Dartmouth's Tuck School. Don't blame Time Inc., said Shank. Blame the accountants. Their rules make companies include such unusual items as stock sale profits and office relocation expenses in income, even though they are unrelated to current, or future, operations.

Sometimes the accounting rules understate a company's earnings from its ongoing businesses. Take Eastman Kodak. In 1985 Kodak decided to get out of the instant photography business, and close some plants. Total writeoff: $563 million. Where should Kodak show this amount? Its accountants made the company deduct it from operating earnings. As a result, Kodak reported earnings on its continuing photographic, copier and chemical businesses of $332 million, whereas in reality those businesses earned $597 million after tax.

Then, in 1986, Kodak wrote off more assets and sacked people, at a cost of $654 million. Again, this one-time item was deducted from operating earnings, with the result that Kodak reported earnings from ongoing operations of $374 million. But this time the charge made sense: The 1986 writeoff was, after all, associated with Kodak's ongoing businesses. The 1985 writeoff was on a business, instant photography, on which Kodak had irrevocably pulled the plug.

Why do accountants insist that companies report, as income from operations, gains or losses that will never recur? In essence, because they have come to the conclusion over the years that anything that produces income or expense in a given year must be dragged through the income statement in that year. If a metal-bending company earns $49,900 on an antique desk in 1986, that profit has to show up in 1986's net. Where else, argue the accountants, could it show up?

The accountants have been arguing this so-called dirty surplus problem for years. Back in the

Source: Article by Subrata N. Chakravarty. Reprinted by permission of *Forbes* magazine, November 16, 1987. © Forbes Inc., 1987.

Chapter 13

go-go accounting of the 1960s, companies had enormous latitude in reporting nonrecurring income and losses. The income they would usually report as income; the losses they would deduct from their retained earnings account, so as to manage earnings better. They could thus avoid acknowledging errors long enough until they could smoothly wipe them off the books. "So there was something called dirty surplus," recalls Dartmouth's John Shank, "which betrayed the bias of those who didn't like it."

The accounting rule writers quickly moved to solve that problem by encouraging companies to report nonrecurring income and loss on their income statements, but labeling them "Extraordinary Items." A new problem was born. "The practice [of reporting extraordinary items] created nothing but confusion because companies would take the good stuff into earnings and call the bad stuff extraordinary," explains Harvard's David Hawkins. The result was a new rule—Accounting Principles Board Opinion 30, issued 1973—which significantly tightened the definition of extraordinary items, defining them as events that were unrelated to the company's business and unlikely to recur. Under Opinion 30, any special event that did not qualify as an "extraordinary event" should be reported as an "unusual item."

Opinion 30 worked all right as long as there weren't too many unusual items. But then came the 1980s and widespread corporate restructuring—office closings, asset sales and all sorts of "unusual" items, some of which are related to operations and some of which are not.

So here the matter stands: By accounting rules, income from nonrecurring events—like selling the old desk, or selling off a part of a cable TV system—must be included as part of net income. So must items relating to errors and omissions of past years, even if their effect is to seriously distort current earnings with a one-time adjustment. If investors and other users of financial statements aren't clever enough to read all the explanatory footnotes to see how the company's ongoing businesses are doing—well, too bad for the investors.

The problem becomes more acute when you remember that Value Line, Standard & Poor's and other statistical services generally pick up only a single number—net income—to report a company's profitability.

This single, often meaningless number then gets reflected in return on equity, growth rate calculations, averages and the like.

"There are items that cause earnings to appear to be more volatile than they actually are on a continuing basis," says Hawkins. "But whether they make companies look better or worse, they are, in every case, a poor indicator of the companies' future earnings prospects." More relevant accounting, anyone?

Reading

"Rumpelstilzchen Accounting"

Has Standard Oil Co. (Ohio) Chairman Alton W. Whitehouse been rereading the story of Rumpelstilzchen, who spun straw into gold? In Sohio's fourth-quarter 1985 report, just out, Whitehouse says that Sohio's profit ($379 million) "would have increased 11%" over 1984's fourth quarter—only it didn't. Why not? A little matter of a $1.15 billion writeoff. And what's a writeoff among friends? Just a paper entry. An "extraordinary" charge.

Or is it "just" a paper entry? In Sohio's case the writeoff is a confession that Sohio blew well over $1 billion of shareholders' money when it decided to acquire Kennecott, the big copper-mining company. Sohio paid $1.8 billion for Kennecott five years ago. Did its value fall by $1 billion in a single quarter? No. It was a bad deal from the beginning, overpriced and ill-timed.

Hold it: Doesn't this suggest that Sohio was actually overstating its earnings over those five years that the Kennecott investment was deteriorating? Certainly it was evident well before Dec. 31, 1985 that the acquisition was a bad mistake.

Sohio portrays the writeoff as a brave and virtuous step. "We've streamlined the company," explains Sohio spokesman John Andes. "It gets us in shape to deal with the market and proceed as a very healthy company into 1986."

Past sin into future virtue. Bad judgment into praiseworthy realism.

David Hawkins, a finance professor at the Harvard Business School, isn't impressed. "The writedowns are usually taken well after the events actually occurred," says Hawkins, "which makes you think you can't believe any of the numbers over the last few years."

Rumpelstilzchen accounting, also known as Big Bath accounting, was used by dozens of businessmen in 1985's fourth quarter. It seemed a good time to take the hit. The stock market was strong enough to absorb the modestly bad news, and, besides, everyone was doing it.

Why do managers wait so long to take their medicine? Why are they so reluctant to write down assets on a regular basis? "Because it doesn't make them look like very good stewards of shareholders' interests," says a partner at Arthur Young & Co., who asked not to be identified, "particularly if they were the ones who said, 'Let's buy this business.' "

Avon Products' Chairman Hicks B. Waldron took the Big Bath. Waldron recently informed shareholders that he sold Avon's Mallinckrodt, Inc. division and booked a charge of $223 million in last year's fourth quarter. The charge washed fourth-quarter net income from $73.7 million in 1984 to a loss of $149 million in 1985.

Weren't Avon's pretax earnings then overstated by $223 million, up until the writedown? A reasonable question. But Waldron ignored that. Accentuating his "asset redeployment program," Waldron said he expected "earnings to improve steadily in 1986."

An immediate benefit, of course, of a Big Bath is to make your vital return on equity number look better. If you decrease the denominator faster than the numerator, the value of any fraction will grow to the sky.

When T. Boone Pickens was chasing after Unocal, for example, Fred Hartley stoutly defended Unocal's shale oil investment. With Pickens out of the way, Hartley wrote the investment off in last year's fourth quarter, at a cost of $250 million. The beauty of Big Bath accounting is that you decide when to face the music.

A modest proposal: Let managements take their Big Baths subjectively, but make them take the changes against *future* earnings, rather than bunching them up in one quarter's accounts as a special item. Since management overstated past earnings, why not make them understate future earnings to compensate? This is not allowed under current accounting rules, but say this for such a proposal: It would make managements pay for their mistakes where it really hurts.

Nothing wrong with admitting mistakes, but don't expect investors to forget that many of these same managements were responsible for the bad judgment in the first place.

Source: Article by Ben Weberman. Reprinted by permission of *Forbes* magazine, February 24, 1986. © Forbes Inc., 1986.

The Big Hit Parade

Herewith, some of 1985's more memorable writeoffs. In a few cases, sudden business reverses may have been behind the sudden writeoffs. But, in most cases, managements were simply washing the decks.

Company	Writeoff 1985	Net Income 1984 ($millions)	1985	Per Share book value 1984	writeoff 1985	net 1985	recent stock price (as of 2/3/86)
Cigna Corp	$1,200.0	$ 100.0	NA	$62.79	$16.60	NA	65 3/8
Sohio	1,150.0	1,488.0	$308.0	35.71	4.90	$1.31	47 3/4
Phillips Petroleum	342.0	810.0	418.0	14.28	1.23	1.44	10 7/8
Unocal	250.0	704.0	325.1	32.78	2.54	2.36	24
Avon Products	223.0	181.7	−59.9	18.55	2.82	−0.76	27 1/4
Crown Zellerbach	196.5	86.9	−26.8	36.91	7.14	−1.56	43 1/8
Gould	175.7	17.8	−175.7	19.59	3.58	−3.94	27 1/8
Koppers	150.0	28.8	−101.3	19.31	5.51	−3.72	23 5/8

NA: Not available

CHAPTER 14 THE STATEMENT OF CASH FLOWS

Reviewing the Chapter

OBJECTIVE 1: Describe the statement of cash flows, and define *cash* **and** *cash equivalents* **(pp. 689–690).**

1. The **statement of cash flows** is considered a major financial statement, as are the income statement, balance sheet, and statement of stockholders' equity. The statement of cash flows, however, provides much information and answers certain questions that the other three statements do not. It is a relatively new financial statement, and its presentation is required by the FASB.

2. The statement of cash flows shows the effects on **cash** and cash equivalents of the operating, investing, and financing activities of a company for an accounting period. **Cash equivalents** are short-term, highly liquid investments such as money market accounts, commercial paper (short-term notes), and U.S. Treasury bills. Short-term investments (marketable securities) are *not* considered cash equivalents.

OBJECTIVE 2: State the principal purposes and uses of the statement of cash flows (p. 690).

3. The principal purpose of the statement of cash flows is to provide information about a company's cash receipts and cash payments during an accounting period. This goal is in accordance with the FASB's "Statement of Financial Accounting Concepts No. 1," which states that financial statements should provide investors and creditors with information regarding the business's cash flows. The statement of cash flows' secondary purpose is to provide information about a company's operating, investing, and financing activities during the period.

4. Investors and creditors may use the statement of cash flows to assess such things as the company's ability to generate positive future cash flows, ability to pay its liabilities, ability to pay dividends, and need for additional financing. In addition, management may use the statement of cash flows (among other things) to assess the debt-paying ability of the business, determine dividend policy, and plan for investing and financing needs.

OBJECTIVE 3: Identify the principal components of the classifications of cash flows, and state the significance of noncash investing and financing transactions (pp. 691–695).

5. The statement of cash flows categorizes cash receipts and cash payments as operating, investing, and financing activities.
   a. **Operating activities** include receiving cash from customers from the sale of goods and services, receiving interest and dividends on loans and investments, and making cash payments for wages, goods and services purchased, interest, and taxes.
   b. **Investing activities** include purchasing and selling long-term assets and marketable securities (other than cash equivalents) as

well as making and collecting on loans to other entities.

c. **Financing activities** include issuing and buying back capital stock as well as borrowing and repaying loans on a short- or long-term basis (i.e., issuing bonds and notes). Dividends paid would also be included in this category, but repayment of accounts payable or accrued liabilities would not.

6. The statement of cash flows should include an accompanying schedule of **noncash investing and financing transactions.** Transactions such as the issuance of a mortgage for land or the conversion of bonds into stock represent simultaneous investing and financing activities that do not, however, result in an inflow or outflow of cash.

7. In the formal statement of cash flows, individual cash inflows from operating, investing, and financing activities are shown separately in their respective categories. To prepare the statement, one needs the assistance of a comparative balance sheet, the current income statement, and additional information about transactions affecting noncurrent accounts during the period. The four steps in statement preparation are (a) determining cash flows

from operating activities, (b) determining cash flows from investing activities, (c) determining cash flows from financing activities, and (d) presenting the information obtained in the first three steps in the form of a statement of cash flows.

OBJECTIVE 4a: Determine cash flows from operating activities using the direct method (pp. 696–702).

8. Cash flows from operating activities result from converting accrual-basis net income to a cash basis and may be determined using either the direct method or the indirect method. Under the **direct method,** Net Cash Flows from Operating Activities is determined by taking cash receipts from sales, adding interest and dividends received, and deducting cash payments for purchases, operating expenses, interest, and income taxes. See table below.

OBJECTIVE 4b: Determine cash flows from operating activities using the indirect method (pp. 696, 702–703).

9. Under the **indirect method,** Net Cash Flows from Operating Activities is determined by taking net income and adding or deducting items that do not affect cash flow from operations. Items to add include depreciation expense, amortization expense, depletion

---

Cash Receipts from Sales = Sales $\begin{cases} + \text{Decrease in Accounts Receivable} \\ \qquad\qquad \text{or} \\ - \text{Increase in Accounts Receivable} \end{cases}$

Cash Payments for Purchases = Cost of Goods Sold $\begin{cases} + \text{Increase in Inventory} \\ \qquad \text{or} \\ - \text{Decrease in Inventory} \end{cases}$ $\begin{cases} + \text{Decrease in Accounts Payable} \\ \qquad \text{or} \\ - \text{Increase in Accounts Payable} \end{cases}$

Cash Payments for Operating Expenses $=$ Operating Expenses $\begin{cases} + \begin{array}{l}\text{Increase in} \\ \text{Prepaid Expenses}\end{array} \\ \qquad \text{or} \\ - \begin{array}{l}\text{Decrease in} \\ \text{Prepaid Expenses}\end{array} \end{cases}$ $\begin{cases} + \begin{array}{l}\text{Decrease in} \\ \text{Accrued Liabilities}\end{array} \\ \qquad \text{or} \\ - \begin{array}{l}\text{Increase in} \\ \text{Accrued Liabilities}\end{array} \end{cases}$ $\begin{cases} - \begin{array}{l}\text{Depreciation and} \\ \text{Other Noncash Expenses}\end{array} \end{cases}$

Cash Payments for Income Taxes = Income Taxes Expense $\begin{cases} + \text{Decrease in Income Taxes Payable} \\ \qquad\qquad \text{or} \\ - \text{Increase in Income Taxes Payable} \end{cases}$

---

expense, losses, decreases in certain current assets (accounts receivable, inventory, and prepaid expenses), and increases in certain current liabilities (accounts payable, accrued liabilities, and income taxes payable). Items to deduct include gains, increases in certain current assets (see above), and decreases in certain current liabilities (see above). The direct and indirect methods produce the same results and are both considered GAAP. The FASB, however, recommends use of the direct method.

OBJECTIVE 5a: Determine cash flows from investing activities (pp. 704–707).

10. When determining cash flows from investing and financing activities, the objective is to explain the changes in the appropriate account balances from one year to the next. As previously stated, investing activities focus on the purchase and sale of long-term assets and short-term investments.
    a. Under the indirect approach, gains and losses from the sale of the above assets should be deducted from and added back to, respectively, net income to arrive at net cash flows from operating activities.
    b. Under the direct approach, gains and losses are simply ignored in determining net cash flows from operating activities.
    c. Under both approaches, the full cash proceeds are entered into the Cash Flows from Investing Activities section of the statement of cash flows.

OBJECTIVE 5b: Determine cash flows from financing activities (pp. 707–709).

11. Financing activities focus on certain liability and stockholders' equity accounts and include short- and long-term borrowing (notes and bonds) and repayment, issuance and repurchase of capital stock, and payment of dividends. Changes in the Retained Earnings account are explained in the statement of cash flows, for the most part, through analyses of net income and dividends declared.

OBJECTIVE 6: Prepare a statement of cash flows using the (a) direct and (b) indirect methods (pp. 709–711).

12. The only difference between the direct and indirect methods of preparing a statement of cash flows is in the structure of the cash flows from operating activities section. Exhibit 14–6 of your textbook presents a completed statement of cash flows that has incorporated the direct method.

13. Exhibit 14–7 of your textbook presents a completed statement of cash flows that has incorporated the indirect method. As already explained, the essence of the indirect approach is the conversion of net income into net cash flows from operating activities.

OBJECTIVE 7: Interpret the statement of cash flows (pp. 709–712).

14. When interpreting the statement of cash flows, it is important to examine the items *within* each section and to relate dollar amounts *between* sections. For example, cash flows from operating activities should normally be sufficient to cover dividend payments. In addition, the statement will disclose in what areas the company is expanding or contracting and how. Problems such as a drain of cash caused by overstocking goods might also be uncovered by the statement of cash flows. Finally, the schedule of noncash investing and financing transactions should never be overlooked in performing an analysis.

OBJECTIVE 8: Prepare a work sheet for the statement of cash flows (pp. 712–718).

15. A work sheet for preparing the statement of cash flows is especially useful in complex situations. Using the indirect approach, it essentially allows for the systematic analysis of all changes in the balance sheet accounts.

16. Exhibit 14–8 of your textbook presents the format of a completed work sheet. In preparing the work sheet, five steps should be followed.
    a. Enter all balance sheet accounts into the Description column, listing debit accounts before credit accounts.
    b. Enter all end-of-prior-period amounts and end-of-current-period amounts into the appropriate columns, and foot (add up).
    c. In the bottom portion of the work sheet, write Cash Flows from Operating Activities, Cash Flows from Investing Activities, and Cash Flows from Financing Activities, leaving sufficient space between sections to enter data.

d. Analyze the change in each balance sheet account, using the income statement and information on other transactions that affect noncurrent accounts during the period. Then enter the resulting debits and credits in the Analysis of Transactions columns, labeling each entry with a key letter corresponding to a reference list of changes.

e. Foot the top and bottom portions of the Analysis of Transactions columns. The top portion should balance immediately, but the bottom portion should balance only when the net increase or decrease in cash is entered (credited for an increase or debited for a decrease). The changes in cash entered into the top and bottom of the work sheet should equal each other and should be labeled with the same key letter.

Testing Your Knowledge

Matching

Match each term with its definition by writing the appropriate letter in the blank.

_____ 1. Statement of cash flows

_____ 2. Cash equivalents

_____ 3. Operating activities

_____ 4. Investing activities

_____ 5. Financing activities

_____ 6. Noncash investing and financing transactions

_____ 7. Direct method

_____ 8. Indirect method

a. The items placed at the bottom of the statement of cash flows in a separate schedule

b. The statement of cash flows section that most closely relates to net income (loss)

c. In determining cash flows from operations, the procedure that starts with the figure for net income

d. Short-term, highly liquid investments

e. The statement of cash flows section that deals mainly with stockholders' equity accounts and borrowing

f. The financial report that explains the change in cash during the period

g. The statement of cash flows section that deals with long-term assets and marketable securities

h. In determining cash flows from operations, the procedure that adjusts each income statement item from the accrual basis to the cash basis

Short Answer

Use the lines provided to answer each item.

1. Give two examples of noncash investing and financing transactions.

_____

_____

_____

_____

2. When the statement of cash flows is prepared under the indirect method, why are depreciation, amortization, and depletion expense added back to net income to determine cash flows from operating activities?

_____

_____

_____

_____

3. Which sections of the statement of cash flows are prepared identically under the direct and indirect methods?

_____

_____

_____

_____

4. List three examples of cash equivalents.

_____

_____

_____

True-False

Circle T if the statement is true, F if it is false. Please provide explanations for the false answers, using the blank lines at the end of the section.

T F   1. The statement of cash flows is a major financial statement required by the FASB.

T F   2. Payment on an account payable is considered a financing activity.

T F   3. The proceeds from the sale of investments would be considered an investing activity, whether the investments were classified as short-term or long-term.

T F   4. To calculate Cash Payments for Purchases, the figure for Cost of Goods Sold must be known, along with the changes in inventory and accounts payable during the period.

T F   5. Under the indirect method, a decrease in prepaid expenses would be added to net income in determining Net Cash Flows from Operating Activities.

T F   6. The Schedule of Noncash Investing and Financing Transactions might include line items for depreciation, depletion, and amortization recorded during the period.

T F   7. In the Analysis of Transactions columns of a statement of cash flows work sheet, Retained Earnings is credited and Dividends Paid debited for dividends paid during the period.

T F   8. In the Cash Flows from Operating Activities section of a statement of cash flows work sheet, the items that are credited in the Analysis of Transactions columns must be deducted from net income in the statement of cash flows.

T F   9. It is possible to suffer a net loss for the period but generate positive Net Cash Flows from Operating Activities.

T F 10. A net positive figure for Cash Flows from Investing Activities implies that the business is generally expanding.

T F 11. The issuance of common stock for cash would be disclosed in the financing activities section of the statement of cash flows.

T F 12. Under the indirect method, Loss on Sale of Buildings would be deducted from Net Income in the operating activities section of the statement of cash flows.

T F 13. To calculate Cash Payments for Operating Expenses, operating expenses must be modified by (among other accounts) depreciation, which is treated as an add-back.

T F 14. Cash obtained by borrowing would be considered a financing activity, whether the debt is classified as short-term or long-term.

T F 15. The purchase of land in exchange for the issuance of common stock in effect represents simultaneous investing and financing activities.

T F 16. It is possible for the direct and indirect methods to produce different net-change-in-cash figures on a statement of cash flows.

_____

_____

_____

_____

_____

_____

Multiple Choice

Circle the letter of the best answer.

1. How would Interest and Dividends Received be included in a statement of cash flows that employs the indirect method?
   a. Included as components of net income in the operating activities section
   b. Deducted from net income in the operating activities section
   c. Included in the investing activities section
   d. Included in the financing activities section
   e. Included in the Schedule of Noncash Investing and Financing Transactions

2. How would Gain on Sale of Investments be disclosed in a statement of cash flows that employs the indirect method?
   a. Added to the net income in the operating activities section
   b. Deducted from net income in the operating activities section
   c. Included in the investing activities section
   d. Included in the financing activities section
   e. Included in the Schedule of Noncash Investing and Financing Transactions

3. How would an increase in Accounts Payable be disclosed in a statement of cash flows that employs the indirect method?
   a. Added to net income in the operating activities section
   b. Deducted from net income in the operating activities section
   c. Included in the investing activities section
   d. Included in the financing activities section
   e. Included in the schedule of Noncash Investing and Financing Transactions

4. How would the purchase of a building by incurring a mortgage payable be disclosed in a statement of cash flows that employs the indirect method?
   a. Added to net income in the operating activities section
   b. Deducted from net income in the operating activities section
   c. Included in the investing activities section
   d. Included in the financing activities section
   e. Included in the Schedule of Noncash Investing and Financing Transactions

5. How would Dividends Paid be disclosed in a statement of cash flows that employs the indirect method?
   a. Added to net income in the operating activities section

   b. Deducted from net income in the operating activities section
   c. Included in the investing activities section
   d. Included in the financing activities section
   e. Included in the Schedule of Noncash Investing and Financing Transactions

6. How would Interest Paid be included in a statement of cash flows that employs the indirect method?
   a. Included as a component of net income in the operating activities section
   b. Deducted from net income in the operating activities section
   c. Included in the investing activities section
   d. Included in the financing activities section
   e. Included in the Schedule of Noncash Investing and Financing Transactions

7. How would an increase in inventory be disclosed in a statement of cash flows that employs the indirect method?
   a. Added to net income in the operating activities section
   b. Deducted from net income in the operating activities section
   c. Included in the investing activities section
   d. Included in the financing activities section
   e. Included in the Schedule of Noncash Investing and Financing Transactions

8. All of the following represent cash flows from operating activities except
   a. cash payments for income taxes.
   b. cash receipts from sales.
   c. cash receipts from issuance of stock.
   d. cash payments for purchases.

9. When net income is recorded (debited) in the Analysis of Transactions columns of a statement of cash flows work sheet, which item is credited?
   a. Cash
   b. Income Summary
   c. Net Increase in Cash
   d. Retained Earnings

10. Niemsky Corporation had cash sales of $30,000 and credit sales of $70,000 during the year, and the Accounts Receivable account increased by $14,000. Cash Receipts from Sales totaled
    a. $70,000.
    b. $86,000.
    c. $100,000.
    d. $114,000.

Applying Your Knowledge

Exercises

1. Use the following information to calculate the items below.

Accounts Payable, Jan. 1, 19xx	$ 47,000
Accounts Payable, Dec. 31, 19xx	54,000
Accounts Receivable, Jan. 1, 19xx	32,000
Accounts Receivable, Dec. 31, 19xx	22,000
Accrued Liabilities, Jan. 1, 19xx	17,000
Accrued Liabilities, Dec. 31, 19xx	11,000
Cost of Goods Sold for 19xx	240,000
Depreciation Expense for 19xx	20,000
Income Taxes Expense for 19xx	33,000
Income Taxes Payable, Jan. 1, 19xx	4,000
Income Taxes Payable, Dec. 31, 19xx	6,000
Inventory, Jan. 1, 19xx	86,000
Inventory, Dec. 31, 19xx	74,000
Operating Expenses for 19xx	70,000
Prepaid Expenses, Jan. 1, 19xx	2,000
Prepaid Expenses, Dec. 31, 19xx	3,000
Sales for 19xx	350,000

a. Cash Payments for Operating Expenses =

$ _____.

b. Cash Receipts from Sales =

$ _____.

c. Cash Payments for Income Taxes =

$ _____.

d. Cash Payments for Purchases =

$ _____.

e. Net Cash Flows from Operating Activities =

$ _____.

2. Use the following information to complete CLU Corporation's statement of cash flows work sheet on the next page for the year ended December 31, 19x9. Make sure to use the key letters in the Analysis of Transactions columns to refer to the following explanation list:

a. Net income for 19x9 was $22,000.

b-d. These key letters record changes in current assets and current liabilities.

e. Sold plant assets that cost $30,000 with accumulated depreciation of $10,000, for $24,000.

f. Purchased plant assets for $62,000.

g. Recorded depreciation expense of $26,000 for 19x9.

h. Converted bonds payable with a $10,000 face amount into common stock.

i. Declared and paid dividends of $12,000.

x. This key letter codes the change in cash.

		Analysis of Transactions for 19x9		
CLU Corporation Work Sheet for Statement of Cash Flows For the Year Ended December 31, 19x9				
Description	Account Balances 12/31/x8	Debit	Credit	Account Balances 12/31/x9
Debits				
Cash	35,000			29,000
Accounts Receivable	18,000			21,000
Inventory	83,000			72,000
Plant Assets	200,000			232,000
Total Debits	336,000			354,000
Credits				
Accumulated Depreciation	40,000			56,000
Accounts Payable	27,000			19,000
Bonds Payable	100,000			90,000
Common Stock	150,000			160,000
Retained Earnings	19,000			29,000
Total Credits	336,000			354,000
Cash Flows from Operating Activities				
Cash Flows from Investing Activities				
Cash Flows from Financing Activities				
Net Decrease in Cash				

Reading

The Savviest Investors Are Going with the Flow

Analyzing the "owner's earnings" of a company can uncover a stock's true worth

For most of the past two years, corporate profits looked pretty dreary, so Wall Street couldn't tantalize investors with stories about spectacular earnings gains. Instead, the Street pushed stocks in companies with lackluster profits but stupendous "cash flow"—roughly speaking, the earnings plus bookkeeping charges that don't involve current cash outlays (table). After all, the raiders were snapping up companies not for their earnings but for their cash flow. Now reported profits are back with a vengeance and should climb about 22% this year and more than 30% in 1988. Does cash flow still matter?

You bet it does. For one thing, the corporate takeover and leveraged buyout binge is far from over, and those deals are priced not by the target's earnings but its cash flow. And even if a company is an unlikely target or is never bought out, cash-flow analysis is a tool that peels away layers of accounting legerdemain and gets closer to the true worth of a company. "Earnings count, but it would be folly to look at earnings without looking at cash flow," says Lawrence Sondike, an analyst with Mutual Shares Corp., a fund manager that specializes in dissecting balance sheets.

"Cash flow is gaining as a valuation tool for investors," says E. Michael Metz, a market strategist for Oppenheimer & Co. That's a major change of sentiment for Wall Street, where the bells start ringing when the earnings numbers come out. Still, some investment pros dismiss cash-flow figures, which analysts derive from financial reports, as gimmickry to paper over bad earnings or to justify overpaying for a stock. "Paying 15 times cash flow doesn't sound as expensive as 25 times earnings," says Mark Tavel, president of Value Line Asset Management.

Cash-flow reporting should soon get some new respectability. The Financial Accounting Standards Board is expected to enact rules this fall that would standardize reporting of cash flow beginning with the 1988 annual reports. More uniform reporting should make it easier to assess stocks by cash flows.

No Leftovers

"The rise of the entrepreneurial investor" is what's behind the ascendancy of cash flow, says Oppenheimer's Metz. "Entrepreneurial investor" may sound like a euphemism for raider, but the term makes sense. To appraise a company by its cash flow—and there are numerous ways to figure it—is to think like an owner. Cash flow is sometimes called "owner's earnings" and for good reason. If you were the owner of a private company, would you care about reported profits? Of course not. In fact, your main concern would be that the company brings in enough money to meet the payroll, service debt, and maintain and expand the business. If, after all that, you still had money left over, it would be taxed as profits. So you would do everything you could to control the cash flow in a way that would leave as little as possible for the Internal Revenue Service to tax away.

That's why when entrepreneurial investors analyze a company's cash flow, they start with

---

Table 1

Three Kinds of Cash Flow

Cash Flow	Start with net income, then add back charges such as depreciation, amortization, and depletion, which reduce net income without taking cash out of the till.
Free Cash Flow	Start with cash flow, then deduct only those capital expenditures needed to maintain the company's business.
"Raider" Cash Flow	A raider wants the broadest measure of the cash available. So start with pretax income, add back interest expense, and deduct the necessary capital expenditures.

Source: Article by Jeffrey M. Laderman. Reprinted from September 7, 1987 issue of *Business Week* by special permission, copyright © 1987 by McGraw-Hill, Inc.

pretax—not aftertax—income. Next they add back all the noncash charges. To that sum, raiders will also add interest expense to get the broadest possible picture of the company's available cash. Then they see all the money that they could redirect, often in ways that minimize taxes. "Accountants just assume taxes have to be paid," says Mario J. Gabelli, a money manager, buyout specialist, and aficionado of cash-flow analysis long before it was fashionable. "But you don't have to pay taxes."

How so? Remember you're an owner-investor, not a passive shareholder, and you have control of the cash. You don't care about profit. So you take on a bundle of debt and devote the cash flow more toward servicing the debt than to producing taxable profits. And as you pay down the debt, your equity in the company automatically grows. The basic idea is no different than buying an income property with a small down payment and a large mortgage. Your cash flow—in this case, rental income—makes the monthly payments.

Forget about deal mania. Many argue that cash flow provides a better picture of earning power than reported profits, which may be distorted by accounting rules, the tax code, or financing decisions. Take, for example, "free cash flow," which includes net income and noncash charges but allows for enough capital expenditures to keep the company a viable enterprise. If the stock falls out of favor, a company can use its "free," or discretionary, cash flow to support the stock, perhaps by raising the dividend or buying back shares.

Quality Counts

Smart cash-flow analysis can help distinguish between a business losing money on its operations and losing money after the accountant's visits. Take, for example, Price Communications Corp., which owns broadcasting and newspaper publishing properties. According to its annual report, Price lost $24.6 million, or $2.45 a share, on net revenues of $87 million last year. Yet based on cash flow—which management defines as income before deductions for interest, amortization, depreciation, taxes, and certain one-time expenses— the company "earned" $2.19 a share. True, there's a lot of definitional leeway, but buyers of media companies in particular value properties on a multiple not of earnings but of cash flow. The stock is up 1,200% since its 1982 initial public offering— yet, in conventional terms, the company has never earned a dime.

Cash-flow profits need careful scrutiny, too. Tom Nourse, a San Diego–based analyst who provides cash-flow analyses to institutional investors, warns against "wildly optimistic" projections made about companies based on cash-flow numbers. Nourse compares cash flow with the company's growth in sales, a source of cash, and growth in investment, a use of cash, over a five-year period.

What's more, Nourse believes the "quality of cash flow" is as critical as the amount. "If most of the cash flow is coming from depreciation, it's not as good as a company where most is coming from income," says Nourse.

That's why the accounting standards board won't allow public companies to report cash flow per share as they do earnings per share. Where it comes from is as important as how much there is. Of course, you can say the same about reported earnings. The truth is, investors need both.

Reading

Now You See It . . .

Don't invest without checking into cash flow. Fine. But what's cash flow?

Cash flow is at least as important a measure of corporate health as reported earnings. But put a dozen investors in a room and you'll get almost as many different definitions of "cash flow" (*Forbes*, Apr. 7, 1986).

After grappling with the problem for more than six years, the Financial Accounting Standards Board has come up with the beginnings of a more precise definition. It would require all companies to use the same format to explain how cash and cash equivalents change from one reporting period to the next. The proposal still leaves companies with room for flexibility but will make investors' lives much easier. Why? Companies will have to show sources and uses of cash in three areas: operations, investing, financing.

Let's take a specific case: Lowe's Co., the North Carolina–based retailer of building materials. Last year Lowe's said in its annual report that cash flow amounted to $2.31 per share in 1985 as compared with $2.20 the year before. An investor looking at these numbers might have assumed Lowe's had plenty of cash left over for dividends and other purposes.

Not necessarily so. Although Lowe's used a generally accepted definition of cash flow, it was not a strict definition. It failed to subtract the cash absorbed by higher inventories and receivables. Lowe's ended the year with hardly more cash than it started the year, and its long-term debt almost doubled from 1984 to 1985—despite the positive cash flow.

Does it really matter how you measure cash flow? Very much. While Lowe's is healthy—the increased inventory and receivables simply reflect growth in revenues—there are situations where a company can go broke while reporting positive cash flow. How can this be? Simple.

Suppose inventories and receivables rise faster than sales—reflecting slow pay by customers and unsold goods. Under the simpler method of reporting cash flow (which would not include working capital components), such a company could report a positive cash flow even while it was fast running out of cash.

Endo-Lase was a horrifying example. A few years ago this distributor of medical lasers seemed to be going great guns. Its sales trebled in 1984, and cash flow—by the simplest measure—looked terrific, something like $3 million. Unfortunately, receivables mounted even faster than sales, rising 625%. What this means is that much of the reported increase in revenues took the form of IOUs. In the end, Endo-Lase had to go back and restate earnings for 1984, writing down receivables, writing up inventories and wiping out over 90% of the net profit. The company filed for Chapter 11 in 1986. Under the proposed rules, Endo-Lase's cash flow would have appeared negative.

Companies will be able to use either the direct or indirect method in calculating cash flow from operations. The direct method requires firms to list total cash receipts from sales, minus all cash payments to suppliers, employees, creditors and to the government for taxes. The bottom line would be actual cash balances from operations. The indirect method, on the other hand, starts with net income, then adjusts for depreciation, deferred taxes, gains and losses on sales of equipment or businesses and changes in working capital.

Of the two, the direct method is the most straightforward for assessing cash flows, since it is the least vulnerable to misinterpretation. Says Malcolm Murray Jr., president of Robert Morris Associates: "This all comes back to the fundamental premise that loans can be repaid only with cash."

When the smoke clears, investors will still need to do lots of homework. It's never enough to know just what the numbers are. You still have to figure out what the numbers mean. Again, Lowe's is an example. Even if it were forced to report a negative cash flow, it would still be a very healthy business; it would cease being one only if inventories and receivables increased faster than sales and the company's credit were deteriorating.

When it comes to some things, the more you try simplifying them, the more complicated they become.

Source: Article by Tatiana Pouschine. Reprinted by permission of *Forbes* magazine, February 9, 1987. © Forbes Inc., 1987.

CHAPTER 15 FINANCIAL STATEMENT ANALYSIS

Reviewing the Chapter

OBJECTIVE 1: Describe and discuss the objectives of financial statement analysis (p. 751).

1. Decision makers get spec.fic information from general-purpose financial statements by means of **financial statement analysis.**

2. The users of financial statements are classified as either internal or external. The main internal user is management. The main external users are creditors and investors. Both creditors and investors will probably acquire a **portfolio,** or group of loans or investments, because the risk of loss is far less with several investments than with one investment.

3. Creditors and investors use financial statement analysis to (a) assess past performance and the current position, and (b) assess future potential and the risk connected with that potential. Information about the past and present is very helpful in making projections about the future. Moreover, the easier it is to predict future performance, the less risk is involved. The lower risk means that the investor or creditor will require a lower expected return.

OBJECTIVE 2: Describe and discuss the standards for financial statement analysis (pp. 752-753).

4. Decision makers assess performance by means of (a) rule-of-thumb measurements, (b) analysis of past performance of the company, and (c) comparison with industry norms.

   a. Rule-of-thumb measurements for key financial ratios are helpful but should not be the only basis for making a decision. For example, a company may report high earnings per share, but may lack sufficient assets to pay current debts.

   b. The past performance of a company can help show trends. The skill lies in the analyst's ability to predict whether a trend will continue or will reverse itself.

   c. Comparing a company's performance with the performance of other companies in the same industry is helpful, but there are three limitations to using industry norms as standards. First, no two companies are exactly the same. Second, many companies, called **diversified companies** or **conglomerates,** operate in many unrelated industries, so that comparison is hard. (However, the recent requirement to report financial information by segments has been somewhat helpful.) Third, different companies often use different accounting procedures for recording similar items.

OBJECTIVE 3: State the sources of information for financial statement analysis (pp. 754-756).

5. The chief sources of information about publicly held corporations are published reports, SEC reports, business periodicals, and credit and investment advisory services.

a. A company's annual report provides useful financial information, and includes the following sections: (1) management's analysis of the past year's operations, (2) the financial statements, (3) footnotes, including the principal accounting procedures, (4) the auditor's report, and (5) a five- or ten-year summary of operations.

b. **Interim financial statements** may indicate significant changes in a company's earnings trend. They consist of limited financial information for less than a year (usually quarterly).

c. Publicly held corporations are required to file with the SEC an annual report (Form 10-K), a quarterly report (Form 10-Q), and a current report of significant events (Form 8-K). These reports are available to the public and are sources of valuable financial information.

d. Financial analysts obtain information from such sources as the *Wall Street Journal, Forbes, Barron's, Fortune,* the *Commercial and Financial Chronicle,* Moody's, Standard & Poor's, and Dun & Bradstreet.

OBJECTIVE 4: Identify the issues related to the evaluation of the quality of a company's earnings (pp. 756–759).

6. The most commonly used predictors of a company's performance are expected changes in earnings per share and in return on equity. Because net income is a component of both these ratios, the quality of earnings must be good if the measure is to be valid. The quality of earnings is affected by (a) the accounting estimates and procedures chosen when applying the matching principle, and (b) the nature of nonoperating items in the income statement. A different net income figure will result, for example, when different estimates and procedures for dealing with uncollectible accounts, inventory, depreciation, depletion, and amortization are chosen. In general, the method that produces a lower, or more conservative, figure will also produce a better quality of earnings. In addition, nonoperating and nonrecurring items, such as discontinued operations, extraordinary gains and losses, and the effects of accounting changes, can impair comparability if the financial analyst refers only to the bottom-line figure.

OBJECTIVE 5: Apply horizontal analysis, trend analysis, and vertical analysis to financial statements (pp. 759–766).

7. The most common tools and techniques of financial analysis are horizontal analysis, trend analysis, vertical analysis, and ratio analysis.

a. Comparative financial statements show the current and prior year's statements presented side by side to aid in financial statement analysis. In **horizontal analysis,** absolute and percentage changes in specific items from one year to the next are shown. The first of the two years being considered is called the **base year,** and the percentage change is computed by dividing the amount of the change by the base-year amount.

b. **Trend analysis** is the same as horizontal analysis, except that percentage changes are calculated for several consecutive years. For percentage changes to be shown over several years, **index numbers** must be used.

c. In **vertical analysis,** the percentage relationship of individual items on the statement to a total within the statement (for instance, cost of goods sold as a percentage of net sales) is presented. The result is a **common-size statement.** On a common-size balance sheet, total assets and total liabilities and shareholders' equity would each be labeled 100 percent. On a common-size income statement, sales would be labeled 100 percent. Common-size statements may be presented in comparative form to show information both within the period and between periods.

OBJECTIVE 6: Apply ratio analysis to financial statements in the study of an enterprise's liquidity, profitability, long-term solvency, and market tests (pp. 766–776).

8. In **ratio analysis,** certain relationships (ratios) between financial statement items are determined, then compared with those of prior years or other companies. Ratios provide information about a company's liquidity, profitability, long-run solvency, and market strength. The most common ratios are shown in the table on the next page.

Ratio	Components	Use or Meaning
Liquidity Ratios		
Current ratio	$$\frac{\text{Current assets}}{\text{Current liabilities}}$$	Measure of short-term debt-paying ability
Quick ratio	$$\frac{\text{Cash + marketable securities + receivables}}{\text{Current liabilities}}$$	Measure of short-term liquidity
Receivable turnover	$$\frac{\text{Net sales}}{\text{Average accounts receivable}}$$	Measure of relative size of accounts receivable balance and effectiveness of credit policies
Average days' sales uncollected	$$\frac{\text{Days in year}}{\text{Receivable turnover}}$$	Measure of average time taken to collect receivables
Inventory turnover	$$\frac{\text{Cost of goods sold}}{\text{Average inventory}}$$	Measure of relative size of inventory
Profitability Ratios		
Profit margin	$$\frac{\text{Net income}}{\text{Net sales}}$$	Net income produced by each dollar of sales
Asset turnover	$$\frac{\text{Net sales}}{\text{Average total assets}}$$	Measure of how efficiently assets are used to produce sales
Return on assets	$$\frac{\text{Net income}}{\text{Average total assets}}$$	Overall measure of earning power or profitability of all assets employed in the business
Return on equity	$$\frac{\text{Net income}}{\text{Average owners' equity}}$$	Profitability of owners' investment
Earnings per share	$$\frac{\text{Net income}}{\text{Weighted average outstanding shares}}$$	Means of placing earnings on a common basis for comparison
Long-Term Solvency Ratios		
Debt to equity ratio	$$\frac{\text{Total liabilities}}{\text{Owners' equity}}$$	Measure of relationship of debt financing to equity financing. A company with debt is said to be **leveraged.**
Interest coverage ratio	$$\frac{\text{Net income before taxes + interest expense}}{\text{Interest expense}}$$	Measure of protection of creditors from default on interest payments
Market Test Ratios		
Price/earnings (P/E) ratio	$$\frac{\text{Market price per share}}{\text{Earnings per share}}$$	Measure of amount the market will pay for a dollar of earnings
Dividends yield	$$\frac{\text{Dividends per share}}{\text{Market price per share}}$$	Measure of current return to investor
Market risk	$$\frac{\text{Specific change in market price}}{\text{Average change in market price}}$$	Measure of volatility (called **beta**) of the market price of a stock in relation to that of other stocks

Financial Statement Analysis

Testing Your Knowledge

Matching

Match each term with its definition by writing the appropriate letter in the blank.

_____ 1. Financial statement analysis

_____ 2. Portfolio

_____ 3. Diversified companies (conglomerates)

_____ 4. Interim financial statements

_____ 5. Horizontal analysis

_____ 6. Base year

_____ 7. Trend analysis

_____ 8. Index number

_____ 9. Vertical analysis

_____ 10. Common-size statement

_____ 11. Ratio analysis

_____ 12. Leverage

_____ 13. Beta

a. Debt financing
b. A group of investments or loans
c. A measure of market risk
d. A financial statement expressed in terms of percentages, the result of vertical analysis
e. Limited financial information for less than a year (usually quarterly)
f. The first year being considered when horizontal analysis is used
g. Getting specific information from general-purpose financial statements
h. A presentation of the percentage change in specific items over several years
i. A number used in trend analysis to show change in related items from one year to the next
j. A presentation of absolute and percentage changes in specific items from one year to the next
k. A presentation of the percentage relationships of individual items on a statement to a total within the statement
l. Companies that operate in many unrelated industries
m. The determination of certain relationships between financial statement items

Short Answer

Use the lines provided to answer each item.

1. Indicate five ratios that measure profitability.

2. Briefly distinguish between horizontal and vertical analysis.

3. List the three methods by which decision makers assess performance.

4. Why is it wiser to acquire a portfolio of small investments rather than one large investment?

True-False

Circle T if the statement is true, F if it is false. Please provide explanations for the false answers, using the blank lines at the end of the section.

T F **1.** Horizontal analysis is possible for both an income statement and a balance sheet.

T F **2.** Common-size financial statements show dollar changes in specific items from one year to the next.

T F **3.** A company with a 2.0 current ratio will experience a decline in the current ratio when a short-term liability is paid.

T F **4.** The figure for inventory is not used in computing the quick ratio.

T F **5.** Inventory turnover equals average inventory divided by cost of goods sold.

T F **6.** The price/earnings ratio must be computed before earnings per share can be determined.

T F **7.** When computing the return on equity, interest expense must be added back to net income.

T F **8.** When a company has no debt, its return on assets equals its return on equity.

T F **9.** The lower the debt to equity ratio, the riskier the situation.

T F **10.** Receivable turnover measures the time it takes to collect an average receivable.

T F **11.** A low interest coverage would be cause for concern for a company's bondholders.

T F **12.** A stock with a beta of less than 1.0 indicates a risk factor that is less than that of the market as a whole.

T F **13.** Dividends yield is a profitability ratio.

T F **14.** On a common-size income statement, net income is given a label of 100 percent.

T F **15.** Interim financial statements may serve as an early signal of significant changes in a company's earnings trend.

T F **16.** Probably the best source of financial news is the *Wall Street Journal*.

T F **17.** Return on assets equals the profit margin times asset turnover.

T F **18.** The quality of earnings would be affected by the existence of an extraordinary item in the income statement.

_____

_____

_____

_____

_____

_____

_____

_____

_____

_____

_____

_____

_____

_____

Multiple Choice

Circle the letter of the best answer.

1. Which of the following is a measure of long-term solvency?
   a. Current ratio
   b. Interest coverage
   c. Asset turnover
   d. Profit margin

2. Short-term creditors would probably be *most* interested in which ratio?
   a. Current ratio
   b. Earnings per share
   c. Debt to equity ratio
   d. Quick ratio

3. Net income is irrelevant in computing which ratio?
   a. Earnings per share
   b. Price/earnings ratio
   c. Asset turnover
   d. Return on equity

4. A high price/earnings ratio indicates
   a. investor confidence in high future earnings.
   b. that the stock is probably overvalued.
   c. that the stock is probably undervalued.
   d. little investor confidence in high future earnings.

5. Index numbers are used in
   a. trend analysis.
   b. ratio analysis.
   c. vertical analysis.
   d. common-size statements.

6. The main internal user of financial statements is
   a. the SEC.
   b. management.
   c. investors.
   d. creditors.

7. Comparing performance with industry norms is complicated by
   a. the existence of diversified companies.
   b. the use of different accounting procedures by different companies.
   c. the fact that companies in the same industry will usually differ in some respect.
   d. all of the above.

8. A low receivable turnover indicates that
   a. few customers are defaulting on their debts.
   b. the company's inventory is moving very slowly.
   c. the company is making collections from its customers very slowly.
   d. a small proportion of the company's sales are credit sales.

9. In a common-size income statement, net income will be given a label of what percentage?
   a. 0 percent
   b. The percentage that net income is in relation to sales
   c. The percentage that net income is in relation to operating expenses
   d. 100 percent

Applying Your Knowledge

Exercises

1. Complete the horizontal analysis for the comparative income statements shown here. Round percentages to the nearest tenth of a percent.

| | 19x1 | 19x2 | Increase or (Decrease) | |
			Amount	Percentage
Sales	$200,000	$250,000		
Cost of goods sold	120,000	144,000		
Gross margin	$ 80,000	$106,000		
Operating expenses	50,000	62,000		
Income before income taxes	$ 30,000	$ 44,000		
Income taxes	8,000	16,000		
Net income	$ 22,000	$ 28,000		

2. The following is financial information for Lassen Corporation for 19xx. Current assets consist of cash, accounts receivable, marketable securities, and inventory.

Average accounts receivable	$100,000
Average (and ending) inventory	180,000
Cost of goods sold	350,000
Current assets, Dec. 31	500,000
Current liabilities, Dec. 31	250,000
Market price, Dec. 31, on 21,200 shares	40/share
Net income	106,000
Sales	600,000
Average owners' equity	480,000
Average total assets	880,000

Compute the following ratios as of December 31. Round off to the nearest tenth of a whole number for a–i, to the nearest hundredth of a whole number in j–k.

a. The current ratio is _____ .

b. The quick ratio is _____ .

c. Earnings per share is _____ .

d. Inventory turnover is _____ .

e. Return on assets is _____ .

f. Return on equity is _____ .

g. Receivable turnover is _____ .

h. Average days' sales uncollected is _____ .

i. The profit margin is _____ .

j. Asset turnover is _____ .

k. The price/earnings ratio is _____ .

What Wall Street Sees When It Looks at Your P/E Ratio

The executive turned to the financial analyst and inquired why their company's price/earnings ratio was below those in their peer group. The analyst produced a graph of the historically up-and-down earnings pattern of the company and, indicating the lowest point on the graph, replied, "I think this is where we went wrong."

If you review the price/earnings ratio's relationship to the four principle [sic] methods of stock valuation, earnings emerge as a primary driver of a company's stock price. Earnings have many characteristics. Current and expected earnings, consistency, quality, momentum, sustainability, as well as the role of earnings in cash flow analysis, are all important aspects of the role of earnings in stock valuation.

Stock valuation models are used extensively by institutional researchers and investors to identify investment candidates. These models reflect four concepts: dividend discount, asset valuation, cash flow analysis, and relative valuation.

Model #1: Dividend Discount

The dividend discount model values a stock price as the present value of the stock's future dividend stream, discounted by the current interest rate. If an investor in an equity instrument expects to derive returns over the long term from the net income of a corporation in the form of dividend or asset accumulation, he has to look to the future for the expected return.

The tool most often used in determining the expected return is the P/E ratio. The P/E ratio is defined as the mechanism in which present earnings are capitalized. For example, if a company earns $1.50 per share for a given fiscal year and the stock price is $15 per share, the investor is willing to pay 10 times the current earnings to become an owner of the company.

If the company continues to earn $1.50 for a very long time, the investor will receive a 10-percent return on the original investment (earnings/price paid), which the company either distributes in dividends or uses to increase assets. However, if the earnings of the company grow by 10 percent

Source: Used by permission from *Financial Executive,* May/June 1990, copyright 1990, by Financial Executives Institute.

per year, everything else being equal, the company would earn $3.00 per share seven years later. The return on the original investment would actually be 20 percent. This example introduces the element of expected growth into the formula of determining the P/E multiple, the actual rate of the capitalization of earnings.

Current earnings and expected earnings, as illustrated in the previous example, are two of the three variables that influence the P/E ratio. Since companies do not operate in a vacuum, a third variable, the general market valuation, is introduced.

The general market valuation is the value of alternative investment opportunities. Alternative investment opportunities are driven by the prevailing level of interest rates. Even if management performs well, a stock price may languish because the discount factor investors apply to its dividend and earnings prospects may increase due to rising Treasury bond yields and the increased risk attributed to investors holding diversified portfolios of stocks.

The expected growth rate of earnings is worth more when interest rates are lower. As a general measure, with long-term Treasury rates at 10 percent, the market multiple would be about 10 times earnings; with Treasury rates at 8 percent, the multiple would be 12.5 times earnings. The Dow Jones P/E was a bit higher than 6 at the 1982 bear-market low, when interest rates fluctuated around 20 percent. The multiple did not decline to 5 or less perhaps because of the underlying book values and the relationship of the price to the net book value as discussed in the following section, return on net assets.

Conversely, companies' P/E multiples soared to 40 or more times earnings in 1968 and 1972, when interest rates were much lower. Interest rates at this time were 5 to 6 percent, but future growth expectations were very high.

There is also a strong inverse correlation between the long-term inflation trend and the P/E multiple. During inflationary periods, P/E ratios have ranged between 5 and 10. The ratio rises to between 15 and 20 in disinflationary or deflationary times.

A rule sometimes cited is that stock market conditions determine 50 percent to 55 percent of a stock's performance, the industry group determines 30 percent, and the company itself represents 15 to 20 percent. The 50 to 55 percent attributed to stock market conditions may be justified by the fact that the P/E reflects the market, which in turn reflects interest rates. Conversely, interest rates reflect the market, which is reflected by the P/E multiple. However, a flaw in the industry group theory, which determines 30 percent, is it incorrectly assumes a stock has no unique characteristics. An example is SmithKline Beecham and its Tagamet product for treating ulcers, which afforded it a multiple well above the average for the pharmaceutical group at the time the drug was introduced.

Data going back to the 1930s shows conclusively that stocks with low P/Es outperform stocks with high P/Es over the long term in virtually every period analyzed. More recent studies show similar results. Over the long term, a low P/E strategy enables investors to outperform the market and is valid regardless of the market performance at any particular time.

There are two reasons why this strategy works. First, a high P/E by definition has high expectations for earnings growth. Indeed, it discounts all good news and opens the door for a rapid adjustment in the price (and hence the multiple) to lower expectations when disappointing earnings are reported. Second, a low P/E stock may be relatively unknown and not yet have a strong analyst following. Chances are higher that a neglected stock is undervalued than that a popular issue is.

Low P/E multiples become high P/E multiples when expectations change. A good example is the telephone industry's traditionally low multiple, which changed as new technology (such as cellular telephones and fax machines) increased demand and deregulation enhanced earnings. Unless expectations change, however, a low P/E stock could retain its deserved low multiple.

Model #2: Return on Net Assets

The second major method of equity evaluation is return on net assets, including asset valuation. Asset valuation assumes the market price of a stock selling below its book value will rise toward this value if the book value reflects the true current value of the assets, whether appreciated or depreciated.

If the net assets (total assets minus total liabilities) per share are below the current market price, the assumption is that current management is failing to generate adequate returns from the company's assets. There are two approaches to this analysis.

First, by taking current net income and dividing by the net asset value (book value per share), a potential investor can figure the current return to shareholders, which could be below that offered through competitive financial instruments. Second, the valuation of the assets could have appreciated significantly beyond the depreciated (historical cost) basis. Thus, if the assets are marked to market and net income is divided by a larger base of net assets, the return may not be competitive. An inadequate return could be remedied by selling assets or better utilizing the assets in order to earn a higher return.

A Bear Stearns strategy paper entitled "Don't Earnings Matter Anymore?" states, "In this century, with the exception of the early 1930s, variations in price/earnings multiples have dominated the movements in stock prices. Anticipating shifts in P/E—the value of earnings—is the dominant investment consideration for the stock market."

Movement in the P/E indicates the capitalization rate is being changed. The willingness of investors to capitalize at a different rate changes due to the increased visibility of earnings (a long-term focus) or the certainty of earnings (in the short term).

Studies from Oxford University and the University of Chicago indicate that, except for the immediate future, past earnings growth is almost useless in predicting future earnings growth. Ironically, most analysts still extrapolate from the past into the future even though the margin for error is high. Indeed, a *Forbes* review found that, in mid 1985, the 1986 earnings growth that analysts projected for high-multiple companies was 73 percent higher than the actual results.

A Harvard Business School study of estimates for 1,250 companies for the five-year period ended in 1981 confirms this. The analysts' consensus estimates for less than 12 months in the future were off by an average of 30 percent. Yet it must be noted that past performance is the sole basis on which the impact of change can be intelligently forecast.

In the real world, forecasting is difficult. The more successful a company becomes, the more competition, government controls, and market saturation dampen its results. Cost increases that cannot be passed on to customers, economic vagaries, and new technology impact even the most stable companies.

In a study of the top 250 growth stocks between 1950 and 1980 to determine the characteristics of the best performing stocks, earnings momentum was found to be crucial to the stocks' performance, as was industry strength. The rate of growth in corporate earnings has a direct impact on the multiple: the higher the growth rate, the higher the multiple. As a general measure, the P/E should usually equal a company's expected rate of growth.

The expected sustainability of the growth rate is equally important. The stock market is risk averse and will provide a premium for dependability and predictability. Consistency through lower, but even, increments are [sic] worth more than two "down" and three "up" years in a five-year period.

A steady pattern of earnings growth is enhanced by management's openness in discussing the company's strategy. However, "want to do" and "can do" are two different concepts, and management must not say one when it means the other. A company may lose a hard-earned multiple if a strategy for growth, touted by management, falters and the financial community adopts a show-me attitude towards the stock. In a stable market, the price of the stock for a company caught in such an event can remain unchanged for one or two years until confidence is once again restored and a consistent earnings pattern for the stock is reestablished.

Quality-of-earnings analyses are used to determine the probability of earnings trends continuing and the extent to which earnings could represent distributable cash. High-quality earnings are defined as earnings that can be distributed in cash and are derived primarily from continuing operations that are not volatile from year to year. Conversely, low-quality earnings have only a small percentage of distributable cash and are derived primarily from non-operating sources.

Examples of low-quality earnings include changes to more liberal accounting estimates, a non-recurring item contributing significantly to results, an unusually large increase in deferred tax expense, or earnings that are cyclical (such as the earnings of commodity companies) or subject to wide variations due to uncontrollable forces such as weather. Companies with high-quality earnings command a higher P/E than companies with low-quality earnings even though these companies may be similar in other respects.

Model #3: Cash Flow Analysis

The third major method of evaluation is known as the cash on cash returns approach, or cash flow analysis. Under this method of evaluation, depreciation and other non-cash expenses are added to after-tax net income to project the pure cash flow of a company. (Some institutions use an alternate method known as a multiple of the EBDIT— earnings before depreciation, interest, and taxes.) Although net income could be depressed by a high depreciation expense, the company could generate very attractive cash flows.

Companies with a high figure as cash available for dividends or share repurchases usually are afforded a higher P/E relative to other companies in their peer industry group.

Model #4: Relative Valuation

The relative valuation approach dictates that the P/E multiple of a stock should have approximately the same relative relationship to the P/E multiple of some general market index as does the stock's earnings growth rate or return on equity. Relative P/E analysis is the most extensively used valuation approach.

However, because of its reliance on historical cost accounting (earnings per share and stockholders' equity), its value has been challenged in recent years as acquisitions, takeovers, and restructurings have increasingly reduced the comparability of historical data over time and between companies.

The P/E multiples of the S&P 500 or 400 are the usual barometers in evaluating a stock relative to the market. The relative valuation method compares a stock's current and past multiple to a current or past multiple for the market.

For each industry or security, charts display the P/E, ROE, dividend yield, price, and earnings per share for the current year, previous years, and the next year forecasted relative to the same data for the market (S&P 500 or 400 data). If the relationship between the current relative P/E ratio based on projected earnings and the projected relative return on equity differs substantially from the past relationship indicated on the charts, then a relative over- or undervaluation may exist and present a selling or buying opportunity.

There is a risk, however, to investing on a relative basis since the investor must make two forecasts: one for the company and one for the market level. For this reason, while this investment method can be successful, it may also sustain significant losses if the investor's estimates of either or both of the forecasts prove to be inaccurate.

The "E" of Earnings

A study was conducted of 300 institutional portfolio managers and analysts, most of whom manage more than $500 million for their own or client accounts. Of the respondents, 40 percent ranked the P/E ratio as the key factor in picking stocks (i.e., 40 percent would pay for earnings at a given price), while 35 percent rated present and near-term earnings potential as most important (i.e., 35 percent wanted earnings regardless of what they paid). Management strength was the key factor for 23 percent (and indeed management strength produces stronger earnings). Next in line were return on investment (13 percent), the earnings growth record (11 percent), and market share (10 percent). In effect, the majority of the participants considered earnings to be the most important component in selecting stocks, with 86 percent specifically citing the P/E (which contains the "E" of earnings), earnings potential, and earnings growth.

The P/E ratio enters into each of the major methods of stock evaluation because of the earnings component and, relative to the market, does not change unless expectations change. Corporate management must therefore focus on the quality and growth of current and future earnings and the consistency and reliability of those earnings. A wise man's words are well taken: "Expectations, both current and future, drive the P/E multiple. It's a bit like life."

Reading

How Industry Perceives Financial Ratios

There is some agreement on which ratios are important but a lack of consensus on how they should be computed.

Financial statements serve as the primary financial reporting mechanism of an entity, both internally and externally. These statements are the method by which management communicates financial information to stockholders, creditors, and other interested parties. An analysis of this financial information should include the computation and interpretation of financial ratios.

However, at present, comprehensive financial ratio analysis is hampered by the lack of standard computations. Currently, no regulatory agency such as the Securities & Exchange Commission or the Financial Accounting Standards Board gives guidance in this area, except for the computation of earnings per share. As this study will indicate, there is some agreement on which ratios are important, but there is a lack of consensus on the computational methodology of these ratios.

In order to get the views of financial executives on important issues relating to financial ratios, a questionnaire was sent to the controllers of the companies listed in Fortune's 500 Largest Industrials for 1979. Companies that were 100%-owned subsidiaries of another company were excluded, leaving 493 companies to be surveyed. One hundred and three usable responses were received which represents a response rate of 20.9%. Considering both the length of the questionnaire and the amount of detailed questions, the response rate was good.

There were 57 industries represented in the responses; however, three industries had a significantly greater number of responses than the others. These industries were petroleum (10), motor vehicle parts & accessories (8), and chemicals and allied products (9). The other industries were represented by three or less responses. A separate review of the responses of the more highly represented industries indicated that, in general, their responses were not appreciably different than the

Source: "How Industry Perceives Financial Ratios" by Charles H. Gibson, *Management Accounting,* April 1982. Copyright © 1982 by the Institute of Management Accountants (formerly National Association of Accountants).

summary of the overall responses. Any significant differences will be pointed out.

The questionnaire was designed to accomplish the following objectives: (1) to determine the primary measure that a particular ratio provides, (2) to arrive at the significance of a specific ratio as perceived by financial management, (3) to gather information on the computational methodology used, (4) to find out what use is being made of inflation accounting data in ratio analysis, and (5) to determine which financial ratios are included as corporate objectives and to whom these ratios are reported.

Primary Measure and Significance of Individual Ratios

The first section of the questionnaire was designed to determine the perceived importance of specific financial ratios and what the ratio primarily measured. For this purpose 20 specific ratios were used. Two of these ratios (degree of operating leverage, and degree of financial leverage) proved to be confusing to respondents as indicated by both their lack of response and their written comments. It appears the respondent was not familiar with these ratios; therefore, these two ratios were deleted from the summary.

The 20 ratios were selected based upon a review of textbooks, and discussion with financial executives, and a review of ratios reported in annual reports. It was not considered practical to list all possible ratios nor would it be practical to expect companies to complete an unreasonably long survey. In addition to the 20 specific ratios, the respondents were asked to list other ratios that their company computes.

To determine the primary measure that a particular ratio provides, we asked this question: "Do you perceive this ratio as a primary measure of liquidity, long-term debt paying ability, profitability, or other?" The "other" could be anything perceived by the firm. In all probability it would be a measure of activity, or a stock indicator.

Many ratios indicate several measures of a firm. For example, inventory turnover could be an indication of liquidity, profitability, and activity. This question was designed to determine the primary measure indicated by the ratio.

TABLE 1
Primary Measure and Significance of Specific Ratios

Ratio	Primary Measure					Significance	
	Liq.	Debt	Profit	Other	No. Responses	Avg. Rating	No. Responses
Days' sales in receivables	**68.0%**	1.0%	7.2%	23.8%	97	6.46	95
Accounts receivable turnover	**67.7%**	2.2%	6.5%	23.6%	93	5.05	88
Days' sales in inventory	**57.8%**	1.1%	12.2%	28.9%	90	5.31	93
Inventory turnover	**52.6%**	1.1%	17.9%	28.4%	95	6.52	91
Working capital	**91.0%**	2.0%	3.0%	4.0%	100	6.62	97
Current ratio	**94.0%**	3.0%	1.0%	2.0%	100	6.39	96
Times interest earned	7.4%	**71.3%**	12.8%	8.5%	94	6.14	96
Fixed charge coverage	7.9%	**69.7%**	15.7%	6.7%	89	5.44	89
Debt to assets	5.8%	**88.4%**	0.0%	5.8%	86	2.96	87
Debt to equity (or debt to capital)	6.2%	**85.6%**	2.1%	6.1%	97	7.48	95
Net profit margin	0.0%	˙0.0%	**100.0%**	0.0%	102	8.05	99
Total asset turnover	11.6%	2.3%	**51.2%**	34.9%	86	4.50	88
Return on investment (or capital)	0.0%	2.1%	**94.8%**	3.1%	96	8.52	94
Return on equity	1.1%	2.1%	**93.7%**	3.1%	95	8.07	94
Earnings per share	0.0%	0.0%	**98.0%**	2.0%	101	8.63	97
Price/earnings ratio	0.0%	1.1%	28.7%	**70.2%**	94	6.12	90
Dividend payout	6.4%	2.1%	9.6%	**81.9%**	94	6.47	95
Book value per share	0.0%	0.0%	4.2%	**95.8%**	96	5.17	96

To determine the perceived significance of a ratio, we asked: "How do you rate the significance of this ratio?"

0–2   low importance

3–6   average importance

7–9   high importance

A summary of the perceived primary measure and its significance rating for each of the 18 listed ratios (Table 1) indicates that there is a majority consensus on each ratio as to what the ratio primarily measures—an encouraging result that might help reduce some of the confusion about what a particular ratio is designed to measure. A number of the ratios that were rated primarily as an indication of liquidity were rated by approximately one-fourth of the companies as being a primary measure of something other than liquidity, for example, accounts receivable turnover. Ratios that received relatively high support in the "other" column often are listed in textbooks as activity ratios. Although they are an indication of

activity, in my opinion activity is not a logical end objective. Activity is an indication of liquidity, debt, or profitability, depending on the particular ratio. The results of this survey indicate that the financial executives agree that ratios which indicate activity are a primary measure of liquidity, debt, or profitability.

Three ratios—price/earnings, dividend payout, and book value per share—were indicated to have a primary measure other than liquidity, debt, or profitability. This result appears to be consistent with the widespread opinion that these ratios are primarily an indication of stock evaluation. A definite conclusion as to what these ratios measure cannot be made because the respondents were not asked to explain their interpretation of "other." This decision was a compromise in the design of the questionnaire in order to keep the response time reasonable.

Liquidity and Debt Ratios

Table 1 indicates the significance rating for each ratio. The significance rating given to the liquidity

TABLE 2
Additional Financial Ratios (by Financial Executives)

Ratio	Primary Measure					Significance	
	Liq.	Debt	Profit	Other	No. Responses	Avg. Rating	No. Responses
Return on assets	0.0%	3.8%	**96.2%**	0.0%	26	8.33	26
Gross margin	0.0%	0.0%	**100.0%**	0.0%	11	7.30	12
Quick ratio (acid test)	**80.0%**	0.0%	20.0%	0.0%	10	6.25	9
Cash flow/debt	10.0%	**80.0%**	0.0%	10.0%	10	6.75	9
Sales per employee	0.0%	0.0%	**75.0%**	25.0%	4	6.00	4

ratios is repeated below in order of their significance ratings.

Ratio	*Rating*
Working capital	6.62
Inventory turnover	6.52
Days' sales in receivables	6.46
Current ratio	6.39
Days' sales in inventory	5.31
Accounts receivable turnover	5.05

Note the range of significance does not appear to be material, which suggests that all of these ratios indicate some degree of liquidity. Probably all of these ratios need to be computed in order to get a reasonable view of liquidity based upon the interrelationship of these ratios. For example, accounts receivable turnover and inventory turnover indicate a degree of quality of receivables and inventory, respectively. The perceived quality of receivables and inventory would reflect as to what would be a reasonable current ratio. If the quality of receivables and/or inventory is low, then a higher current ratio would be necessary in order to compensate for a low quality segment that influences the ratio.

The companies responding in the petroleum industry gave three of the liquidity ratios a much lower rating than the overall rating received by the ratio. These ratios were days' sales in accounts receivable, accounts receivable turnover, and inventory turnover. These liquidity ratios were each given a rating of 2.50 by the firms in the petroleum industry. Days' sales in inventory was given a much higher rating of 7.00 by the chemicals and allied products than the overall rating of 5.31.

Working capital was rated 8.70 by the motor vehicle parts and accessories industry which was much higher than the 6.2 overall average.

Although it might be expected that some industries would rate certain ratios much higher or lower than other industries, there were not enough responses by industry to draw any definite conclusion on this point. It is noteworthy that material differences in rating by industry were not indicated for the debt or profitability ratios.

There is a wide range of perceived significance for the debt ratio, as noted below:

Ratio	*Rating*
Debt to equity (or debt to capital)	7.48
Times interest earned	6.14
Fixed charge coverage	5.44
Debt to assets	2.96

There are two views on a company's ability to carry debt. One relates to the balance sheet and the other relates to the income statement. The balance sheet view is concerned with how much debt the firm has in relation to funds provided by owners. The income statement view concentrates on the company's ability to service the outstanding debt. Both views are important and both need to be considered when drawing conclusions as to the company's ability to carry debt.

The balance sheet view is expressed with the ratio debt to equity (or debt to capital) and the debt to assets ratio. The debt to equity (or debt to capital) ratios were combined as one alternative because the pretesting of the questionnaire with financial executives and a review of annual reports indicated that there is agreement that a ratio which indicates the degree of debt carried on the balance sheet is needed. However, there is a great deal of disagreement as to the details of the computation. Usually a corporation will compute either the debt to equity or the debt to capital ratio, but not both. There are probably more than 15 different computations used to compute a ratio that indicates the degree of debt on the balance sheet.

The income statement view of debt is reflected by the firm's ability to meet fixed obligations in relation to income. Ratios that are designed to indicate a firm's ability to meet these fixed obligations are times interest earned, and fixed charge coverage. The difference between these ratios is that times interest earned only considers interest in relation to income while the fixed charge coverage considers interest plus other financing obligations a company considers fixed. An example of other fixed obligations would be the use of a portion of rent payments on operating leases.

The times interest earned coverage was rated to be moderately more significant than the fixed charge coverage. A firm probably should consider both these ratios to get an indication of its income ability to carry debt and related financing commitments.

Profitability and Other Ratios

Four of the profitability ratios received ratings over 8 out of a possible 9:

Ratio	Rating
Earnings per share	8.63
Return on investment (or capital)	8.52
Return on equity	8.07
Net profit margin	8.05
Total asset turnover	4.50

These ratios were rated the most significant of all of the ratios used in this study. This result seems to indicate that financial executives pay more attention to profitability than they do to liquidity or debt.

The one profitability ratio that was not given a high significance rating was the total asset turnover. Because the total asset turnover and the net profit margin are integral parts of the return on assets, they are both needed if a company wants to know why the return on assets is going up or down. Return on assets was not included in the list of ratios. It was excluded in an effort to minimize the list of ratios using the reasoning that if either or both net profit margin or total asset turnover were rated high, then the return on assets probably would be rated high.

It is probably necessary to compute all of the profitability ratios to get a reasonable view because each gives a different view of profitability.

As for the ratios rated primarily for other than an indication of liquidity, debt, or profitability, it was interesting that dividend payout (6.47) was rated to be more significant than the price/earnings ratio (6.12). This difference may have resulted because the survey's participants—financial managers—have placed more emphasis on their objective of dividend payout rather than the price/earnings ratio. A review of the financial ratios used in corporate objectives indicates this same point. Book value was rated 7.25 by the motor vehicle parts and accessories industry, which was materially higher than the overall rating for book value of 5.17.

The respondents were asked to list additional ratios that their company computes and to indicate the primary measure and significance of the ratio (Table 2). Many additional ratios were listed by less than four firms, but they are not included in Table 2 because they were not considered representative ratios.

The additional ratios indicate one more liquidity ratio, one more debt ratio, and three more profitability ratios. The liquidity ratio is the quick ratio (acid test), which is similar to the current ratio, except inventory has been removed from the current assets. The rating given to this ratio was approximately the same rating as was given the other liquidity ratios.

The additional debt ratio is the cash flow/debt ratio. The purpose of this ratio is to indicate the cash flow a company is generating in relation to the debt that it is carrying. This ratio first appeared in the literature in 1966 in a bankruptcy study conducted by W. H. Beaver.[1] In his study the cash flow/debt ratio came out as the ratio with the greatest predictive ability in terms of bankruptcy. The executives who listed this ratio in the survey gave it a relatively high rating of 6.75.

The additional profitability ratios were return on assets, gross margin, and sales per employee. The return on assets ratio was given a relatively high rating and was listed far more times than the other ratios added. The gross margin was listed by several firms as a profitability measure and it was given a relatively high rating by these executives. It appears that this ratio possibly should be considered as an important profitability ratio. The third profitability ratio added was sales per employee. Only four firms added this ratio, but they were all in the retail industry. This ratio is possibly an important profitability measure in the retail industry.

1. W. H. Beaver, "Financial Ratios as Predictors of Failure," Empirical Research in Accounting: Selected Studies, 1966. Supplement to Vol. 4, *Journal of Accounting Research*, 71–127.

Chapter 15

Computational Methodology

The same ratio may be computed in different ways in practice. This is particularly true of the profitability ratios and the debt ratios. These differences essentially are caused by differences of opinion on how to handle special income statement and special balance sheet items. There is a difference of opinion on how to handle these items on the income statement:

1. Unusual or infrequent items,
2. Equity income,
3. Minority share of earnings,
4. Discontinued operations,
5. Extraordinary items, and
6. Cumulative effect of change in accounting principle.

The special income statement items influence most of the profitability measures, and the times interest earned and fixed charge coverage in the debt ratios. To determine how financial management considers the special income statement items when computing these ratios, the question was asked for each special item in relation to a given ratio: "If your firm computes a given ratio, is the indicated special item included in net income in the numerator?" The firms were asked to assume that each item is material and is disclosed separately on the income statement.

Table 3 indicates that approximately 75% of the firms included unusual or infrequent items in the numerator. Whether to include unusual or infrequent items in the numerator is certainly a judgment decision.

A much higher percentage of firms included equity income in the numerator for the profitability ratios than they did for unusual or infrequent items. The percentage of firms that included equity income in the numerator when computing the times interest earned or fixed charge coverage dropped to approximately 70%. This drop in percentage probably was because equity income is a noncash flow item to the extent that actual cash dividends were not received.

There is a logically correct response when considering equity income. The net profit margin is the relationship between income and net sales. None of the investee's sales are included in the investor's income statement; therefore, equity income should not be included in the numerator. Return on assets expresses the relationship between income and total assets. Since the investment account is included in the total assets, the equity income should be included in the numerator. Return on investment expresses the relationship between income and long-term sources of funds. Therefore, equity income should be included in the numerator. Return on equity expresses the relationship between income and stockholders' equity. We would want to express the relationship between total income and stockholders' equity; therefore, the equity income should be included in the numerator. Times interest earned or fixed charge coverage ratio indicates the firm's ability to cover the interest or fixed charges; therefore, we would want to exclude the equity income from the numerator because it is a noncash flow item to the extent that actual cash dividends were not received.

Approximately 70% of the firms included minority share of earnings in the numerator when computing the given ratios. Is this a correct response? The new profit margin is the relationship between income and net sales. Since the sales of the subsidiary are consolidated with the parent company's sales, the minority share of earnings should be included with the parent company's income.

Return on assets expresses the relationship between income and total assets. Since subsidiary assets have been consolidated, the minority share of earnings should be included with the parent company's income. Return on investment expresses the relationship between income and long-term sources of funds; therefore, minority share of earnings should be included in the numerator. Return on equity expresses the relationship between income and stockholders' equity. Since the stockholders' equity does not include minority equity, the minority share of earnings should be excluded from the numerator. Times interest earned or fixed charge coverage indicates the firm's ability to cover the interest or fixed charge. The minority share of earnings is available for this coverage; therefore, we would want to include minority share of earnings in the numerator.

Discontinued operations were included in the numerator approximately 50% of the time; however, because discontinued operations are not recurring they should be excluded from the primary ratios. Approximately one-third of the time extraordinary items were included in the numerator. Again, extraordinary items are not recurring; therefore, they should be excluded from the numerator. A little less than 50% of the time firms included the cumulative effect of the change in accounting principle in the numerator, but this item also should be excluded from the numerator

TABLE 3
Percentage of Firms Including the Special Item in the Numerator

Special item

Ratio	Unusual or Infrequent Items	Equity Income	Minority Share of Earnings	Discontinued Operations	Extra-ordinary Items	Cumulative Effect of Change in Accounting Principle
Net profit margin	69.3%	81.2%	70.7%	41.0%	29.5%	44.0%
Return on assets	70.3%	85.7%	66.1%	47.6%	26.6%	46.8%
Return on investment	77.6%	90.1%	73.5%	55.1%	32.9%	45.7%
Return on equity	79.8%	91.8%	68.8%	56.2%	38.6%	51.3%
Times interest earned or fixed charge coverage	73.1%	70.1%	70.3%	46.9%	34.3%	48.4%

because it is not recurring and it applies to prior periods.

Balance Sheet Items

The balance sheet items in the survey were deferred taxes, minority interest, and leases. To determine how deferred taxes are handled, the executives were directed to concentrate on deferred taxes that are presented as liabilities other than short-term. When computing financial ratios, such as the debt to equity ratio (total liabilities divided by shareholders' equity), they were asked: "Are deferred taxes considered to be a long-term liability?" Forty-three out of 101 firms stated that they included deferred taxes as a liability when computing debt ratios such as debt to equity. Twenty-four firms ignored the amount entirely and excluded it from the ratio. Three companies considered the deferred tax amount in equity as a free source of funds. Of the 31 respondents who indicated they did not include deferred tax in liabilities, none explained adequately how they did consider the deferred tax item.

How deferred taxes should be handled is a difficult judgment decision. The deferred tax amount is not likely to result in a cash outlay. But part or all of the deferred tax amount may result in a cash outlay. To be conservative, the deferred tax amount should be included in liabilities. In terms of the probable cash outlay the deferred tax amount should be excluded from liabilities.

When a subsidiary is consolidated in a parent company that owns less than 100% of the stock,

an amount results on the balance sheet which is referred to as minority interest. This amount has alternative presentations including presentations with long-term liabilities and presentations between liabilities and stockholders' equity. The executives were asked to assume that they compute the debt to equity ratio. They were asked if the minority interest is included as part of debt, equity, or neither. Ninety-two responses were received on this question with 9.8% including it in debt, 17.4% in equity, and 72.8% not including it in the debt to equity computation.

FASB Statement No. 13 requires the capitalization of some leases on the balance sheet of the lessee. Operating leases are not capitalized but these commitments are disclosed in a footnote. The respondents were asked to consider capitalized leases which are presented as liabilities other than short-term. They were asked the question: "When computing financial ratios, such as the debt to equity ratio, are capitalized leases considered to be debt?" Ninety-two responses out of 97 considered capitalized leases to be part of debt while five did not.

The respondents were asked to consider operating (non-capitalized) leases. The question was: "Do you include the data on operating leases in ratio analysis?" Of the 101 responses, 18 companies indicated that they did include operating leases in ratio analysis. Most of the firms that included operating leases in ratio analysis do so by considering operating leases in the fixed charge coverage. How this is done varies by firm. Some examples of how operating leases are considered in a fixed charge computation are:

1. (a) Fixed charge coverage include 1/3
   (b) Total capital ratios include 7 x subsequent years' operating lease expenses
2. A portion of rent expense is included in the amount of fixed charges used in calculating fixed charge coverage.
3. An interest payment is imputed from the operating lease payment and this imputed interest is included as a fixed charge in determining the ratio of earnings to fixed charges.

One firm responded that operating leases are capitalized at the appropriate cost of debt after deducting implicit operating costs from the lease expense.

Inflation Accounting Data in Ratio Analysis

The respondents were asked if their firm uses any of the data called for in FAS No. 33, "Financial Reporting and Changing Prices," in ratio analysis. One hundred responses were received on this ques-

tion and 11 answered "yes." Examples of how this data is being used include:

1. Return on equity and return on capital employed are calculated using FAS No. 33 data and historical cost.
2. Income per share calculation only.
3. Ratios are computed on historical cost and inflation-adjusted amounts for comparison.
4. Inflation-adjusted assets are used in calculating the ratios:
   (a) Market value of stock over inflation-adjusted assets
   (b) Cash flow return on investment
5. Net income adjusted for general inflation (constant dollar) and changes in specific prices (current cost) is compared to net income on a historical cost basis.
6. When we measure such ratios as return on replacement cost of assets (for internal use only).

In light of the fact that only companies which report inflation accounting data were included in

TABLE 4
Key Financial Ratios Included as Corporate Objectives (100 Responses)

Ratio	No. Using This Ratio	Percentage Reported to:		
		Board	Key Employees	Stockholders
Return on equity	54	53%	51%	42%
Return on assets	53	49%	52%	13%
Net profit margin	43	41%	43%	24%
Earnings per share	38	38%	37%	32%
Return on capital	30	28%	30%	16%
Debt to capital	26	24%	23%	16%
Debt to equity	25	24%	24%	10%
Dividend payout	22	22%	19%	16%
Inventory turnover	18	15%	18%	2%
Days' sales in accounts receivable	13	10%	13%	2%
Current ratio	12	11%	12%	5%
Book value per share	10	10%	10%	9%
Earnings growth	9	9%	9%	6%
Working capital	9	8%	9%	8%
Fixed charge coverage	8	8%	7%	3%
Total asset turnover	7	6%	7%	0%
Accounts receivable turnover	6	4%	6%	0%
Days' sales in inventory	6	4%	5%	1%
Times interest earned	4	4%	4%	2%
Price/earnings ratio	4	3%	4%	2%
Operating margin	4	4%	4%	2%

Financial Statement Analysis

this survey, there does not appear to be much use made of the inflation accounting data in ratio analysis.

Key Financial Ratios as Corporate Objectives

Many firms have selected key financial ratios to be included as part of corporate objectives. Out of 100 respondents 93 indicated that their firms used financial ratios as part of their corporate objectives. Table 4 indicates the ratios that they use and to whom they are reported. Ratios reported by three or fewer firms are not listed.

In Table 4, the profitability ratios, which survey participants rated with the highest significance, were the same ratios used most frequently as corporate objectives. A couple of debt ratios were next in frequency of use. The most popular liquidity ratios were used less frequently than the most popular profitability or debt ratios.

The survey also indicates that a selected ratio is apt to be reported to both the board and to key employees, but a selected ratio is much less likely to be reported to stockholders.

In summary, financial ratios are an important tool in analyzing the financial results of a company and in managing a company. This survey of financial executives indicates the most significant ratios were rated to be profitability ratios. Overall, the debt and liquidity ratios were rated approximately the same.

The computational methodology used by the firms indicates that there is a need for guidance to enable them to compute more uniform ratios. This guidance probably should be provided by the Financial Accounting Standards Board.

Based on this survey, there does not appear to be much use made of inflation data in ratio analysis; however, the use of such data may improve as companies become more familiar with it.

Profitability ratios are those most likely to be used as corporate objectives. Ratios used as corporate objectives are as likely to be reported to the board as to key employees. It is much less likely that a key financial ratio will be reported to stockholders.

CHAPTER 16   INTERNATIONAL ACCOUNTING AND INTERCOMPANY INVESTMENTS

Reviewing the Chapter

OBJECTIVE 1: Define *exchange rate* **and record transactions that are affected by changes in foreign exchange rates (pp. 810–814).**

1. When businesses expand internationally (called **multinational** or **transnational corporations**), two accounting problems arise. (a) The financial statements of foreign subsidiaries involve different currencies. These must be translated into domestic currency by means of an **exchange rate.** (b) The foreign financial statements are not necessarily prepared in accordance with domestic generally accepted accounting principles.

2. Purchases and sales with foreign countries pose no accounting problem for the domestic company when the domestic currency is being used. However, when the transaction involves foreign currency, the domestic company should record an **exchange gain or loss.** This exchange gain or loss reflects the change in the exchange rate from the transaction date to the date of payment.

3. When financial statements are prepared between the transaction date and the date of payment, an unrealized gain or loss should be recorded if the exchange rate has changed.

OBJECTIVE 2: Describe the restatement of a foreign subsidiary's financial statements in U.S. dollars (pp. 814–815).

4. A foreign subsidiary that a parent company controls should be included in the parent company's consolidated financial statements. The subsidiary's financial statements must therefore be **restated** into the parent's **reporting currency.** The method of restatement depends on the foreign subsidiary's **functional** currency—that is, the currency with which it transacts most of its business.

5. Type I subsidiaries are self-contained within a foreign country. Their financial statements must be restated from the functional currency (local currency in this case) to the reporting currency. Type II subsidiaries are simply an extension of the parent's operations. Their financial statements must be restated from the local currency to the functional currency (which in this case is the same as the reporting currency).

6. When a Type I subsidiary operates in a country where there is hyperinflation (more than 100 percent cumulative inflation over three years), it should be treated as a Type II subsidiary, with the functional currency being the U.S. dollar.

OBJECTIVE 3: Describe progress toward international accounting standards (pp. 815–817).

7. At present, there are *some* recognized worldwide standards of accounting. To their credit, the International Accounting Standards Committee (IASC) and the International Federation of Accountants (IFAC) *have* made much progress in setting up these international accounting standards. Despite the efforts of these bodies, however, there are still serious inconsistencies in financial statements among countries, and comparison remains a difficult task. More and more countries, however, are recognizing the importance of uniform international accounting standards in conducting international trade.

OBJECTIVE 4: Apply the cost method and the equity method to the appropriate situations in accounting for long-term investments (pp. 818–823).

8. Corporations frequently invest in the securities of other corporations on a long-term basis. Some reasons for doing this are to obtain control over a desirable investee, to save time and money by investing in an existing company, to realize tax advantages, and to simply earn a return on the investment.

9. All long-term investments in the stock of other companies are recorded at cost. After purchase, the accounting treatment depends on the extent of influence exercised by the investing company. If the investing company can affect the operating and financing policies of the investee, even though it owns less than 50 percent of the investee's voting stock, it has **significant influence.** If the investing company can decide the operating and financing policies of the investee because it owns more than 50 percent of the investee's voting stock, it has **control.**

10. The extent of influence exercised over another company is often difficult to measure accurately. However, unless there is evidence to the contrary, long-term investments in stock are classified as (a) noninfluential and non-controlling (generally less than 20 percent ownership), (b) influential but noncontrolling (generally 20 to 50 percent ownership), and (c) controlling (over 50 percent ownership).

11. The cost method should be used in accounting for noninfluential and noncontrolling investments. The equity method should be used in accounting for all other (that is, influential or controlling) investments. In addition, consolidated financial statements should usually be prepared when a controlling relationship exists.
    a. Under the **cost method,** the investor records investment income as dividends are received. In addition, the securities are recorded on the balance sheet at the lower of cost or market. Unrealized Loss on Long-Term Investments is debited and Allowance to Reduce Long-Term Investments to Market is credited for the excess of total cost over total market. The debit appears in the owners' equity section of the balance sheet as a negative amount, and the credit appears in the asset section as a contra account to Long-Term Investments.
    b. Under the **equity method,** the investor records investment income as a debit to the Investment account and a credit to an Investment Income account. The amount recorded is the investee's periodic net income times the investor's ownership percentage. When the investor receives a cash dividend, the Cash account is debited and the Investment account is credited.
    c. When a company has a controlling interest in another company, the investor is called the **parent company** and the investee is called the **subsidiary.** Companies in such a relationship must prepare **consolidated financial statements** (combined statements of the parent and its subsidiaries). The purchase method (described below) or the pooling of interests method (the subject of a more advanced accounting course) is used.

OBJECTIVE 5: Explain when to prepare consolidated financial statements, and describe their uses (pp. 824–825).

12. Consolidated financial statements should be prepared when an investing company has legal and effective control over another company (usually more than 50 percent ownership). In the past, there were a handful of circumstances that precluded the preparation of consolidated financial statements even though control existed. However, a recent FASB pronouncement states that, with few exceptions, the financial statements of all majority-owned subsidiaries must now be consolidated with the parent company's financial statements for external reporting purposes. Consolidated financial statements are useful because they present a financial picture of the entire economic entity.

13. The **purchase method** of consolidation must be used when two conditions apply: The parent company owns more than 50 percent of the subsidiary's voting stock, and the acquisition was not through an exchange of stock.

14. When consolidated financial statements are prepared, **eliminations** must be made on the consolidating work sheet for intercompany items. Among those items that must be eliminated are intercompany receivables, payables, sales, purchases, interest income, and interest expense, as well as the investment in the subsidiary company. In addition, under the pur-

chase method, the entire stockholders' equity section of the subsidiary is eliminated.

OBJECTIVE 6a: Prepare consolidated balance sheets at acquisition date for purchase at book value (pp. 825–827).

15. Under the purchase method, the parent records the investment at the purchase cost.
    a. When the book value of the net assets purchased equals their cost, the assets and liabilities acquired should appear at cost on the consolidated balance sheet. No goodwill should be recorded.
    b. The stockholders' equity section of the subsidiary at acquisition is not included in the consolidated balance sheet.
    c. When less than 100 percent of the subsidiary has been purchased, the **minority interest** (outside ownership) must be disclosed on the consolidated balance sheet.

OBJECTIVE 6b: Prepare consolidated balance sheets at acquisition date for purchase at other than book value (pp. 827–830).

16. If the cost exceeds the book value of the net assets purchased, the extra amount should be allocated to the assets and liabilities acquired when consolidated financial statements are being prepared. The allocation should be based on fair market values at the date of acquisition. Any unassigned excess should be recorded as **goodwill** (or **goodwill from consolidation**) in the consolidated financial statements.

17. When the book value of the net assets purchased exceeds their cost, the book value of the assets should be reduced proportionately until the extra amount is eliminated.

OBJECTIVE 7: Prepare consolidated income statements for intercompany transactions (pp. 830–831).

18. Intercompany items must be eliminated when preparing a consolidated income statement. They are (a) intercompany purchases and sales, (b) intercompany income and expenses on loans, receivables, or bond indebtedness, and (c) other intercompany income and expenses.

Summary of Journal Entries Introduced in Chapter 16

A. (L.O. 1) Accounts Receivable, foreign company .... XX (amount billed)
        Sales .... XX (amount billed)
           Credit sale made, fixed amount billed in foreign
           currency

B. (L.O. 1) Cash .... XX (amount received)
        Exchange Gain or Loss .... XX (the difference)
           Accounts Receivable, foreign company .... XX (amount billed)
           Received payment in foreign currency, exchange loss
           arose from weakening of foreign currency in relation to
           U.S. dollar

C. (L.O. 1) Purchases .... XX (amount billed)
           Accounts Payable, foreign company .... XX (amount billed)
           Credit purchase made, fixed amount billed in foreign
           currency

D. (L.O. 1) Accounts Payable, foreign company .... XX (amount billed)
        Exchange Gain or Loss .... XX (the difference)
        Cash .... XX (amount paid)
           Made payment in foreign currency, exchange gain arose
           from weakening of foreign currency in relation to U.S.
           dollar

E. (L.O. 4) Long-Term Investments .... XX (purchase price)
        Cash .... XX (purchase price)
           Purchased long-term investment in stock, cost or equity
           method to be used

F. (L.O. 4) Unrealized Loss on Long-Term Investment .... XX (amount of decline)
        Allowance to Reduce Long-Term .... XX (amount of decline)
        Investment to Market
           Year-end adjustment for market decline in investment

G. (L.O. 4) Cash .... XX (amount received)
        Loss on Sale of Investment .... XX (the difference)
           Long-Term Investments .... XX (purchase price)
           To record sale of shares of stock (Note: had a gain on
           sale arisen, it would have been credited)

H. (L.O. 4) Cash .... XX (amount received)
        Dividend Income .... XX (amount received)
           Received cash dividend; cost method assumed

I. (L.O. 4) Allowance to Reduce Long-Term Investment to Market ... XX (amount of recovery)
        Unrealized Loss on Long-Term Investment .... XX (amount of recovery)
           To record partial recovery of market decline

J. (L.O. 4) Investment in XYZ Corporation .... XX (equity percentage)
        Income, XYZ Corporation Investment .... XX (equity percentage)
           Recognized percentage of income reported by investee;
           equity method assumed

K. (L.O. 4)   Cash   XX (amount received)
                Investment in XYZ Corporation   XX (amount received)
                     Cash dividend received; equity method assumed

L. (L.O. 6a)   Common Stock (subsidiary)   XX (current balance)
                Retained Earnings (subsidiary)   XX (current balance)
                     Investment in XYZ Corporation   XX (current balance)
                       Work sheet entry to eliminate intercompany investment at acquisition date, subsidiary wholly owned

M. (L.O. 6a)   Common Stock (subsidiary)   XX (current balance)
                Retained Earnings (subsidiary)   XX (current balance)
                     Investment in XYZ Corporation   XX (current balance)
                     Minority Interest   XX (equity percentage)
                     Work sheet entry to eliminate intercompany investment at acquisition date, subsidiary less than 100 percent owned

N. (L.O. 6b)   Other Long-Term Assets   XX (excess allocated)
                Goodwill   XX (excess allocated)
                Common Stock (subsidiary)   XX (current balance)
                Retained Earnings (subsidiary)   XX (current balance)
                     Investment in XYZ Corporation   XX (current balance)
                     Work sheet entry to eliminate intercompany investment at acquisition date; cost exceeds book value

O. (L.O. 6b)   Accounts Payable   XX (intercompany amount)
                Accounts Receivable   XX (intercompany amount)
                     Work sheet entry to eliminate intercompany receivables and payables

P. (L.O. 7)   Sales   XX (intercompany amount)
                Cost of Goods Sold (Purchases)   XX (intercompany amount)
                     Work sheet entry to eliminate intercompany sales and purchases

Q. (L.O. 7)   Interest Revenue (Other Revenue)   XX (intercompany amount)
                Interest Expense (Other Expense)   XX (intercompany amount)
                     Work sheet entry to eliminate intercompany interest

Testing Your Knowledge

Matching

Match each term with its definition by writing the appropriate letter in the blank.

_____ 1. Cost method

_____ 2. Equity method

_____ 3. Parent company

_____ 4. Subsidiary

_____ 5. Consolidated financial statements

_____ 6. Purchase method

_____ 7. Significant influence

_____ 8. Minority interest

_____ 9. Control

_____ 10. Eliminations

_____ 11. Restatement

_____ 12. Exchange rate

_____ 13. Reporting currency

_____ 14. Functional currency

_____ 15. Multinational (transnational) corporation

a. A business that operates in more than one country

b. The method used to account for noninfluential and noncontrolling investments

c. Outside ownership of a subsidiary

d. The consolidation method used when the parent owns more than 50 percent of the subsidiary's voting stock and did not acquire it through an exchange of stock

e. The type of money in which a given set of consolidated financial statements is presented

f. The method used to account for influential or controlling investments

g. A company that is controlled by another company

h. Expressing one currency in terms of another

i. A company that has a controlling interest in another company

j. Combined statements of the parent and its subsidiaries

k. Usually, ownership of 20 to 50 percent of another company's voting stock

l. Ownership of more than 50 percent of the voting stock of another corporation

m. The type of money with which a company transacts most of its business

n. Entries that appear on a consolidating work sheet

o. The value of one currency in terms of another

Use the lines provided to answer each item.

1. List the three classifications for long-term investments in stocks, as well as the method that should be used after purchase to account for each investment.

Classification

_____

_____

Method

_____

_____

_____

2. Briefly explain the accounting treatment for dividends received under the cost method and under the equity method.

_____

_____

_____

3. Under what circumstance should goodwill be recorded in a consolidated balance sheet?

_____

_____

_____

4. Why must certain items be eliminated when consolidated financial statements are prepared?

_____

_____

_____

_____

_____

5. Under what circumstances would a company record an exchange gain or loss?

_____

_____

_____

_____

True-False

Circle T if the statement is true, F if it is false. Please provide explanations for the false answers, using the blank lines at the end of the section.

T F 1. When one company has an influential but noncontrolling interest in another company, it would use the equity method to account for the investment.

T F 2. Under the cost method, the investor records investment income for a percentage (based on percentage ownership) of the investee's periodic net income.

T F 3. When one company owns at least 20 percent of another company, consolidated financial statements should be prepared.

T F 4. When consolidated financial statements are prepared, the parent's investment in the subsidiary must be eliminated.

T F 5. Under the purchase method of consolidation, the subsidiary's earnings for the entire year of acquisition are included in the consolidated financial statements.

T F 6. Under the equity method, the investor records a cash dividend by debiting Cash and crediting the investment account.

T F 7. A minority interest should be reported as an asset in the consolidated balance sheet.

T F 8. Goodwill from consolidation does not appear on the unconsolidated balance sheet of the parent or subsidiary, but may appear on the consolidated balance sheet.

T F 9. When Company A transacts business with foreign Company B in the currency of Company A, Company A will not record an exchange gain or loss even if the exchange rate has changed between the transaction date and the date of payment.

T F 10. Given the data in question 9, Company B should record an exchange gain or loss.

T F 11. When a given exchange rate remains constant over a period of time, no transaction involving the two currencies will result in an exchange gain or loss over that period.

T F 12. The calculation of net income should include any unrealized exchange gains and losses that arose during the period.

T F 13. When preparing consolidated financial statements, purchases of goods and services from outsiders should be eliminated.

T F 14. When the book value of the net assets purchased equals their cost, the assets and liabilities purchased should appear at cost on the consolidated balance sheet.

_____

_____

_____

_____

_____

_____

_____

_____

_____

_____

_____

_____

_____

_____

_____

_____

_____

_____

_____

_____

_____

_____

_____

_____

Multiple Choice

Circle the letter of the best answer.

1. The journal entry to record the receipt of a dividend under the cost method would include a
   a. debit to the investment account.
   b. credit to Dividend Income.
   c. debit to Goodwill.
   d. credit to the investment account.

2. When the book value of the net assets purchased exceeds their purchase cost,
   a. goodwill exists.
   b. the entire excess should appear as negative goodwill in the consolidated balance sheet.
   c. the subsidiary's long-term assets should be increased until the extra amount is eliminated.
   d. the subsidiary's long-term assets should be reduced until the extra amount is eliminated.

3. The elimination of an intercompany investment cannot include a
   a. debit to the investment account.
   b. debit to Goodwill.
   c. debit to Retained Earnings.
   d. credit to minority interest.

4. The unconsolidated financial statements of a parent company may not include
   a. purchases from its subsidiary.
   b. goodwill from consolidation.
   c. an account reflecting the investment in its subsidiary.
   d. purchases from outsiders.

5. Which of the following items would not be eliminated when consolidated financial statements are prepared, assuming that the subsidiary is 100 percent owned?
   a. The subsidiary's capital stock
   b. The parent's investment in the subsidiary
   c. Interest owed to the subsidiary from the parent
   d. Profit on goods sold by the subsidiary to outsiders

6. Morse Company uses the cost method to account for its three long-term investments. The total cost of the investments is $95,000, and the total market value of the investments at the end of 19xx is $60,000. The account Allowance to Reduce Long-Term Investments to Market has a credit balance of $10,000 before the 19xx adjusting entry is made. The year-end adjusting entry for 19xx would include a
   a. debit to Unrealized Loss on Long-Term Investments for $35,000.
   b. debit to Allowance to Reduce Long-Term Investments to Market for $10,000.
   c. credit to Allowance to Reduce Long-Term Investments to Market for $60,000.
   d. debit to Unrealized Loss on Long-Term Investments for $25,000.

7. The account Unrealized Loss on Long-Term Investments appears
   a. as a footnote only.
   b. on the balance sheet as a contra-asset account.
   c. on the income statement as a loss.
   d. on the balance sheet as a contra-owners' equity account.

8. When an American company purchases goods from France and the transaction involves francs, what would the American company record on the date of payment if the value of the franc declined relative to the dollar between the purchase date and the payment date?
   a. An unrealized exchange gain
   b. An exchange loss
   c. An exchange gain
   d. No exchange gain or loss

Applying Your Knowledge

Exercises

1. Weber Corporation purchased 80 percent of the common stock of Carter Corporation for $165,000. Carter's stockholders' equity included common stock of $60,000 and retained earnings of $90,000. On the lines provided, show the debits, credits, and amounts for the eliminating entry that would be made on the work sheet for consolidating the balance sheets of Weber and Carter. Assume that up to $10,000 of any excess of cost over carrying value is allocated to the building purchased.

Account Debited	Amount	Account Credited	Amount
_____	$ _____	_____	$ _____
_____	$ _____	_____	$ _____
_____	$ _____		
_____	$ _____		

2. Fairfax Corporation owns 15 percent of the voting stock of Andrews Company and 30 percent of the voting stock of Wilkins Company. Both are long-term investments. During a given year, Andrews paid total dividends of $80,000 and earned $110,000, and Wilkins paid total dividends of $50,000 and earned $65,000. In the journal, prepare Fairfax's entries to reflect the above facts. Leave the date column empty, as no dates have been specified.

	General Journal		
Date	Description	Debit	Credit

3. Randy Corporation, an American company, sold merchandise on credit to a Mexican company for 100,000 pesos. On the sale date, the exchange rate was $.05 per peso. On the payment date, the value of the peso had declined to $.045. Prepare the entries in the journal to record Randy Corporation's sale and receipt of payment. Leave the date column empty, as no dates have been specified.

General Journal				
Date		Description	Debit	Credit

Crossword Puzzle
For Chapters 14, 15, and 16

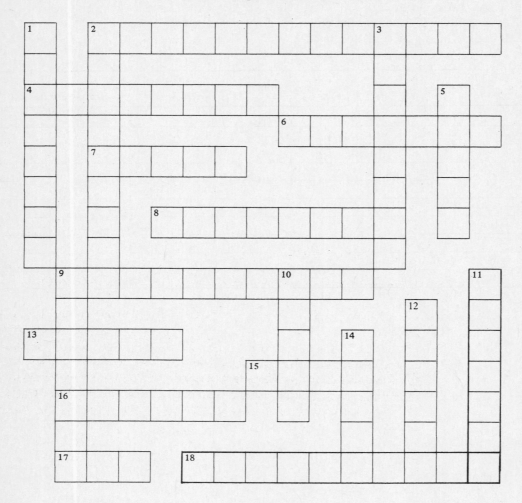

ACROSS

2. Ratio indicating investor confidence in a company (2 words)
4. Analysis resulting in 9-Across
6. Quarterly financial statement, e.g.
7. Statement of cash _____
8. Financial statement _____
9. Statement showing percentage relationships (hyphenated)
13. _____ analysis, a variation of horizontal analysis
15. Measure of market risk
16. Method to account for long-term investments
17. An operating-activity outflow
18. Analysis involving dollar and percentage changes

DOWN

1. Debt financing
2. Group of investments or loans
3. An operating-activity inflow or outflow
5. Dividends _____
9. With 14-Down, a measure of liquidity
10. Number used in 13-Across
11. Majority ownership of voting stock
12. Format for 7-Across
14. See 9-Down

Reading

How U.S. and European Accounting Practices Differ

Despite the efforts of the International Accounting Standards Committee (IASC), International Federation of Accountants (IFAC), the United Nations' Center for Transnational Corporations (UN:CTC), the European Economic Community (EEC), and the Organization for Economic Cooperation and Development (OECD) to harmonize accounting practices and certification requirements, differences in accounting practices still exist.

For example, British accounting systems are influenced by law. The French government can hold executives legally responsible for their firm's bankruptcy. The Netherlands has few mandatory accounting standards. Understanding these and other differences in foreign accounting practices can improve the multinational corporation's ability to do business abroad.

British Auditors May Own Client's Stock

Accounting in the United Kingdom is based on five Companies Acts that are laid out by Parliament and enforced by the secretary of state for trade. The U.K.'s accounting body, Accounting Standards Committee (ASC), resembles the old Accounting Principles Board of the United States. The ASC gives recommendations and issues exposure drafts and discussion papers but has no real power of enforcement. Its primary function is to standardize the accounting requirements as established by the Companies Acts. The U.K. system has no equivalent to the United States' Securities & Exchange Commission (SEC) or Financial Accounting Standards Board (FASB).

In comparing the financial statements and disclosure requirements, the U.K. tends to follow stricter guidelines than the U.S. does. They have four formats for the profit and loss accounts—a vertical and horizontal layout for each of the two forms. Form one is geared toward trading companies and arranges the accounts on an operational basis. Form two is for manufacturing companies and arranges the accounts according to their nature. The balance sheet has two formats and is laid out with specific references to Roman

Source: "How U.S. and European Accounting Practices Differ" by Roger K. Doost and Karen M. Ligon, *Management Accounting,* October 1986. Copyright © 1986 by Institute of Management Accountants (formerly National Association of Accountants).

and Arabic numerals. The law strictly spells out the exact format to be used for the U.K. statements. The actual statements required by law for public firms in the U.K. closely parallel the U.S. requirements and include the profit and loss statement, the balance sheet, the auditors' report, and the directors' report.

The reports of the U.K. are geared toward sophisticated users (shareholders) rather than regulatory bodies. The auditors judge whether the statements demonstrate a "true and fair view." The concept of "true and fair" can be compared with the U.S. concept of giving reasonable assurance about the statements according to GAAP. Although the "true and fair view" is broader than GAAP, it essentially means that the statements are correct according to the requirement as established by the Companies Acts. The auditors are responsible to the shareholders but as in the U.S. they are clients of the company. One major difference is that auditors may own stock in the client company even though this practice is discouraged.

How do the education requirements in the U.K. differ from those of the United States? The British system requires practical experience before candidates are allowed to take the qualifying exam. The three Chartered Institutes have a special training program for their candidates (three years for the university graduates and four years for other candidates). The other three institutes require experience in industry, commerce, or public service before candidates are eligible to take the examination. The U.K. does not require its qualified auditors to have university degrees. This practice contrasts with the United States where many state CPA boards require a degree of some type and allow candidates to take the exam before they have any practical experience.

In the area of price adjustments, the U.K. allows for historical cost or a modified historical cost. The historical cost method is similar to the method used in the U.S., but the modified historical cost approach allows for a revaluation of fixed assets and related depreciation accounts. This is not practiced in the United States.

The U.K. inflation accounting practices also differ from those of the United States. The U.K. requires supplemental information from all public companies on the "sacrifice value" (replacement cost). The statements may be shown in historical cost with supplemental information shown in the "sacrifice value," or the statements may be presented in "sacrifice value" with the supplemental information shown in historical cost. Adjustments must be made for depreciation, cost of sales, working capital, and gearing (write back of the other three items in proportion to the funds that have been borrowed). In contrast, the U.S. requires supplemental information using current cost and constant dollar (general price level adjustments), but the statements must be shown in historical cost.

France: No Double Taxation

The French have a very elaborate system based on tax law. The three types of taxes are direct, indirect, and successive or gift. Because of this system, the French do not have two sets of books nor do they have a provision for deferred taxes. The shareholders are not taxed on dividends and the problem of double taxation does not exist in France.

The French accounting system is promulgated by the ministry of economics and the system of taxation is upheld by the ministry for the budget. Following World War II, France created a professional organization to improve the accounting system in order to stimulate the economy. Over the years, the two ministries and the professional organization have created a 400-page document called the Chart that has models of the balance sheet and profit and loss statements, and detailed instructions on the preparation of the statements. The Chart has been designed to bring uniformity to the accounting statements. Because the economy primarily consists of small companies, it is essential that the statements are uniform to assist in comparability. The Chart is somewhat comparable to GAAP and all related pronouncements, bulletins, and statements. The major difference is that in France the government is involved in standard setting. In the U.S., the FASB does the majority of the work.

Revaluation in France is mandated by law during periods of high inflation. U.S. accounting rules require supplementary information with each set of financial statements regardless of the current inflation rate. The method used for valuation in France is a wholesale price index, and is similar to the method in the United States. Items that may be revalued include all tangible fixed assets, intangible assets, investments and securities in government obligations, and foreign currency

debts, receivables, and payables. In 1977 and 1978, depreciable and nondepreciable assets were added to the list of items to be revalued. These two new items are to be revalued according to their market values.

The French government puts pressure on business managers to perform well. For example, if a firm goes bankrupt, the business manager often is held liable and sometimes sent to jail.

As in most countries, France's requirements for qualified auditors are more stringent than in the U.S. Accounting students must pass an exam that covers accounting, economics, and law (unless they are a graduate of a university). Then, they take another series of exams after which they work as an apprentice for three years. While working as an apprentice, they specialize in one particular area and obtain an advanced certificate. Then they write a thesis. The candidates are not accepted until they are at least 25 years old. The U.S. requires a college education, one qualitative exam, and varying amounts of experience depending on the state. Also, there is no age limitation.

Because of France's involvement in the EEC, a few changes are being made in its system to assist the nation's accountants to become comparable with other European countries. France is considered very conservative because of its emphasis on taxes, but it is concerned with applying the "true and fair view" concept as promulgated by the British. Because of this desire, French accountants have started to adjust their statements when the tax laws prevent the statements from being realistic and representative.

Germans: Loyal to Historical Costs

The German accounting system is based on law and tax codes and is extremely conservative. The reporting system is geared to the workers and investors. It is greatly influenced by the German banks, because they provide the major investment and mandate the reporting requirements for many industries in Germany.

Evidence of the extreme conservatism is apparent in the financial statements. The amortization period for any intangible item is five years. In the United States, a maximum of 40 years is allowed.

Secondly, the stockholders' equity section of the German balance sheet includes numerous reserve accounts that are allowed to accumulate to 10% of capital stock, free reserves that accumulate up to 50% of profit from each period, and special reserves that are created from untaxed income. In addition to these three categories, tax laws often create more reserve accounts. Here the predominant valuation process is FIFO and items are valued at lower of cost or market or net realizable value. In the United States, there is no dependency on FIFO, and although lower of cost or market is practiced, most companies use LIFO method to minimize their tax liability.

The German income statement also uses an operational approach. Income is shown net of tax so there is no pretax income figure. However, unlike the U.S., Germany goes into great detail in listing expenses.

As in the U.S., dividends are not taken out in the calculation of income but are later subtracted from the retained earnings. Dividends in Germany are greatly constrained by law because of the provisions for extensive reserves.

Consolidation procedures in Germany differ slightly. Germany has three separate sets of statements; the world balance (domestic and foreign subsidiaries); parent statements; and the consolidated statements (domestic subsidiaries only). The parent and consolidated statements are the only ones required by law. In the U.S., only consolidated statements are required and special provisions are made for foreign subsidiaries. Parent statements often are prepared for parent company use.

Germany works at keeping inflation low and therefore does not have a requirement for supplemental information for changing prices. This loyalty to historical cost is another reflection of its conservative policies.

Along with the financial statements comes a management report that disclosed vast amounts of information about the firm. Information about the working environment, personnel, training, environmental responsibilities, and group activities in the industry is included in a section called social accounting. Emphasis on social reporting is not yet prevalent in the United States.

German auditors must have six years of experience before examination on various subjects. Candidates are usually college graduates but a degree is not required. Once they pass the exams they may be tax auditors or regular auditors. Two types of auditors are required because each business is specifically required to have a tax audit. In addition to external auditors, each company has a supervisory board that audits the company.

Germany has no equivalents to the SEC or FASB. It believes that these organizations cause a lack of emphasis on law in the accounting standards and procedures. This attitude reinforces their dependency on law, taxes, and conservatism. In fact, when individuals in other countries analyze the financial statements, they generally write up the figures because of the extreme conservatism of German policies and procedures.

Netherlands: Few Mandatory Accounting Standards

The Netherlands places a heavy emphasis on economics and applies an integral approach to the business environment. Dutch accountants are innovative and far from conservative in their accounting practices.

The integral approach means that the business environment should be studied as a whole and not as subparts. They desire one system to consummate all aspects of the business environment, and use economics as the center of study. The economic value theory is used for accounting in the Netherlands. This approach to accounting uses true economic value (replacement value) instead of historical cost.

The internal approach puts equal emphasis on profit and capital maintenance. As a result, the Dutch also place equal emphasis on the balance sheet and the income statement. In the U.S., there is more emphasis on the income statement because of the emphasis on profit.

One of the Dutch accountants' central theories is the concept of continuity and principle of going concern. In the Netherlands, the concept of going concern means keeping a constant flow of production, consumption, and capital maintenance. In the U.S., the going concern principle relates to the idea that a business has an unlimited life and this serves as a basis for a system that uses capitalization, accrual, and deferral.

Because of the Netherlands' economic value theory, there is a departure from the historical cost basis, and items are valued at their economic worth or replacement value. Holding gains are recognized because of the revaluation caused by the use of the economic value theory, and are listed in the stockholders' equity section of the balance sheet. In the U.S., gains are only recognized on the sale of items not merely from the holding of items.

The disclosure by companies is very good. Dutch executives attribute the country's strong economy to the freedom from strict accounting rules and procedures. There are very few mandatory accounting standards; and companies are basically allowed to determine how they will report their operating results. They voluntarily submit adequate disclosure for investors, creditors, and stockholders. The U.S. and most other countries have strict accounting rules and procedures that are created either by law or professional organizations.

Accountants and businessmen enjoy a reputation of excellent professionalism. One reason for this is the strong relationship between the educational process and the business world. The Dutch are very serious about education and this emphasis is reflected in their requirements for the education of auditors. There is a six-year university program that is comparable to the U.S. doctorate degree without the dissertation. This six-year program is followed by another two years of study. Many accountants choose an alternate route of an eight-year program given by the Education Bureau of the Dutch Institute of Public Accountants. Once the eight years of education have been acquired, the candidates must pass a final exam.

Another reflection of their professionalism can be seen in the auditors' report. In the Netherlands, financial statements are considered either clean or unclean. If there are reservations the statement is disclaimed. They have no equivalent to the United States "qualified audit."

Harmonization Is Vital

There are numerous reasons to work toward harmonization in accounting. It is important for mul-tinational corporations to be able to understand the policies of their host countries so that they can function comfortably in those environments. Harmonization also is important so that investors and creditors can arrange their business transactions with confidence in terms of valuation and earnings.

Even though harmonization is desirable in accounting, there are many obstacles standing in the way of progress in this area. Politics and nationalism is one major area of trouble. Everyone believes that his system is the best and is unwilling to change.

Another concern is the level of sophistication of accounting practices. Some countries are far advanced in business and accounting and they certainly would not want to regress to a simpler system. However, the less developed countries are not yet ready for a sophisticated system. Finally, there is no world enforcement agency to make sure the rules that are set are being followed.

Even with these obstacles, international standardization of accounting practices is a worthwhile goal. Understanding the differences and similarities that do exist is important to achieving this objective.

Reading

Valuing Global Securities: Is Accounting Diversity a Mountain or a Molehill?

The world is about to close the books on the 20th century amid a rapid-fire series of historic changes. Europe's markets are uniting. Eastern bloc countries are embracing capitalist values. The Japanese are aggressively investing abroad. Medium and small companies are scrambling for new international opportunities. And in the midst of all this, issuers, investors, and analysts around the world are grappling with some surprisingly fundamental accounting questions.

For example: If the price/earnings ratio of a Japanese company is dramatically higher than that of an otherwise comparable U.S. company, is it because the cost of funds in Japan is lower? Is it because real prices charged to Japanese customers are higher than those charged to non-Japanese customers in overseas markets, presumably resulting in higher profit margins? Or is it due to an accounting distortion? If so, to what degree? And which of the two markets—U.S., Japan, or both— is distorted?

Granted, the volume of international financial transactions has exploded in recent years and may grow much larger if the United States Securities and Exchange Commission (SEC) eases restrictions on the sale of foreign debt and equity in the U.S. to sophisticated buyers. But what effect has accounting diversity had on the global capital markets so far? And if the purpose of accounting is to portray economic reality, are the economics driving the accounting or vice versa?

To explore these questions, Arthur Andersen & Co. and Salomon Brothers Inc. commissioned a study[1] by New York University professors Frederick D. S. Choi and Richard M. Levich, who interviewed representatives of 52 institutions in Japan, the United Kingdom, Germany, Switzerland and the United States. Participants included corporate issuers, institutional investors, investment underwriters, market regulators, and rating agencies. Half the respondents stated that their capital market decisions are directly impacted by accounting diversity, but that's putting it mildly. The study revealed that almost all decisions are affected in some way.

Because accountants of the world are not united by a single language like Esperanto or measurement standard like the metric system, cross-border financial participants must translate a bewildering array of financial information with great dispatch and hope nothing important gets lost in the translation. As one executive of a major credit rating agency put it, "Ten years ago, our primary readership was a U.S. audience. Today, it is very much an international market because of the recent explosion in Eurobond and Euro-commercial paper offerings by companies in the U.S., Europe and Asia. And these international issuers are no longer brand names such as ICI or Siemens. It's a lot of companies that investors don't know, and frankly we're a little worried about this."

Some international companies bristle at the thought of painstaking disclosure to satisfy American regulators. But while that process can be very demanding, some companies believe it's worth the effort. Consider Mitsubishi Bank's listing of shares on the New York Stock Exchange last year. The fact that Mitsubishi was the first Japanese financial institution to open up its books to Wall Street was an important breakthrough.

Can there be a single standard of comparison? Definite answers are still elusive. The SEC, the U.S.-based Financial Accounting Standards Board (FASB) and many organizations outside the U.S., most significantly the International Accounting Standards Committee, have publicly stated that harmonization of international accounting standards is a priority. But others are more skeptical. As one issuer stated, "An international set of accounting standards would be a good idea, but we won't see it in our lifetimes."

Meanwhile, the world must cope with accounting diversity.

The Research Study

Accounting differences can affect the geographic spread of investments, the types of companies selected, the types of securities selected, the security valuation or expected returns and, to a lesser extent, information processing costs.

Source: Copyright © 1990 Arthur Andersen and Co., SC and Salomon Brothers. Reprinted with permission.

1. Frederick D. S. Choi (Leonard N. Stern School of Business, New York University) and Richard M. Levich (Leonard N. Stern School of Business, New York University, and National Bureau of Economic Research), *The Capital Market Effects of International Accounting Diversity* (New York, 1990).

Countries whose accounting principles proved most troublesome included Australia, France, Switzerland, West Germany and Japan. Specific measurement rules which were noted in the research study as a source of dissatisfaction include accounting for consolidated accounts, inventory valuation, foreign currency translation and transactions, provisions for bad debts, long-term contracts, contingencies, depreciation, goodwill, leases and marketable securities. For example, Japanese companies generally depreciate their fixed assets over shorter lives than in the United States and can establish certain discretionary reserves. That helps to explain, at least in part, why major Tokyo Stock Exchange issues recently sold for an average 60 times earnings versus the 13.8 price/earnings ratio for the Standard & Poor's 500.

Countries whose disclosure practices were found wanting included Switzerland, West Germany and Italy. Indeed, half of the respondents in the study reported being hindered by the absence of comparable disclosure standards. Items most frequently mentioned were segment information, methods of asset valuation, foreign operations disclosures, frequency and completeness of interim information, description of capital expenditures, hidden reserves, and off balance sheet items.

Then there were the respondents who argued that international accounting diversity does not matter to them. However, several explained how they changed their behavior when they encountered unfamiliar accounting, suggesting a greater impact than first meets the eye.

Issuer's Perspective

Issuers have many options. A non-U.S. issuer, for example, could go to the Eurobond market, rely on domestic bank or public financing, encourage foreign investors to come to their financial market, offer American Depository Receipts (receipts for shares held by a U.S. bank), or undertake a U.S. public or private placement. The decision would be based on several factors, including an analysis of the tradeoff between the costs of restatement versus the benefits of accessing non-local markets. One company decided several years ago to disclose more detailed financial information in line with U.S. norms. "Our P/E ratio is currently more than twice that of our major competitor," crowed one of the study participants, "and we feel it is due to our accounting and investor relations policy." Another company refuses to

issue any bonds or stock in the United States because of U.S. accounting principles and, perhaps more importantly, SEC requirements.

Conversely, most North American issuers report "no impact" of accounting diversity on their financial decisions, presumably because their expansive financial statements meet or exceed the expectations of global analysts.

Statistics on major stock exchanges in Europe, Japan and the United States reveal some curious anomalies. The New York Stock Exchange, for example, has listed only 89 foreign firms—almost none of them German or French—while almost three times that number are listed on the Amsterdam exchange, which is roughly 3% as large as the NYSE. The Frankfurt exchange stands out for requiring an issuer or lister to have a sponsoring bank. Meanwhile, foreign firms are almost totally absent from the Madrid, Milan, and Nordic exchanges.

What can be said about how shares are valued in different markets? While it is generally observed that the same security (e.g., a share of IBM) sells for nearly the same price on two exchanges when adjusted by the spot foreign exchange rate, there is considerable question as to whether the same general pricing formula is used to price different companies' shares on different markets. Some statistics that can be measured—such as the price/earnings ratio, the price/cash earnings ratio, and the price/book value ratio—reveal considerable variation across countries.

Many issuers have discovered that restatement made them appear less well off than before. One issuer complains that the accounting treatment for certain intangibles affects his company's reported net worth so much that it has not been able to get a credit rating from the major rating agencies. As a result, it has floated commercial paper in Europe rather than go to the U.S. market.

Stock Exchange Listings—1989

	Domestic	Foreign
American	896	64
Amsterdam	232	228
Frankfurt	809	474
London	1,993	587
Madrid	369	0
Milan	211	0
New York	1,604	89
Paris	459	217
Sydney	1,383	36
Tokyo	1,571	112
Toronto	858	103

Further, Arthur Andersen & Co. recently conducted an informal analysis of three years of earnings for foreign companies registering in the U.S. for the first time since 1986. The result was decreased net income in 114 of the 162 annual reporting periods examined. The biggest factor: The United Kingdom does not require companies to amortize goodwill, a fact that may have influenced some prodigious Anglo-American takeover activity in the last several years. As one respondent in the research study put it, "The impact of national differences in the accounting treatment of purchased goodwill has given U.K. companies an advantage over U.S. companies in bidding for merger candidates." This view is widely shared.

Despite this, many other companies' operating income increases from restatement to U.S. principles due to the more conservative accounting principles in their home countries.

Increasingly, companies are accepting the fact that their cost of capital is impacted by market factors beyond their own borders. Thus, a financing analysis limited to domestic options is frequently viewed as incomplete. In fact, the most sophisticated issuers are developing multinational reporting capabilities that satisfy a number of rating scales, quickly and economically.

Accounting Diversity and Underwriter Decisions

Underwriters cope with diversity of accounting principles and disclosure requirements in a variety of ways: soliciting only the top-tier firms in a given industry, relying on credit ratings, and accessing foreign capital via private placements. Alternatively, they may examine rates of change in original accounting data or instruct their clients to restate their accounts. But one underwriter does not stop there. "Restatement is helpful but not sufficient," he said. "Accounts which are prepared by accountants are true but they may not be all the truth. It is important to understand the local cultural and business norms as a basis for properly interpreting the restated numbers."

One of the sharpest comments in the study dealt with the myriad hurdles a foreign company must clear before it can raise money publicly in the U.S. "I think any company should think five times before getting caught with a U.S. quote and the requirement to produce quarterly [statements]," says one underwriter. "Damned expensive! And there is no benefit at all because the few U.S. investors who invest internationally won't be interested whether it is quoted in New York or not. I would always advise my clients not to have a quote in New York unless you're prepared to spend a huge amount of money. If you want to produce quarterly reports, that's fine. But the opinion of the rest of the world is that production of quarterly reports is not helpful; half-yearly is quite enough."

At any rate, the number of companies worldwide that supplemented domestic equity issues with international offerings jumped 17% last year, and all of the underwriters interviewed by Professors Choi and Levich plan to increase international activity in the future. One of the more innovative deals took place last December when Rhone-Poulenc, the state-owned French chemical company, issued a new class of securities with features that appealed to foreigners. This will help the company pay for its recent acquisitions in the U.S. and elsewhere. And with at least a dozen other state-owned companies strapped for cash, the Rhone-Poulenc deal could serve as a paradigm, says New York–based *Corporate Finance Magazine*.

One underwriter argues that the U.S. and U.K. are so oversupplied with information that it is difficult to use information to outperform the market. Elsewhere, however, it is a different story. "In the international market, you can enjoy much higher returns [from] information. Accounting differences, in this context, provide underwriters with an opportunity because they act as a barrier to entry."

Of course, this underwriter was referring to how some organizations can exploit undervalued situations around the world more easily and economically than others. "The thing that's nice about international fund management is that the boutiques can't do it," he says. "The range of skills that is required . . . linguistic skills, accounting skills and the like, are too expensive for many to compete. The number of countries and companies to monitor is immense."

The Investor Perspective

Institutional investors in the U.S. are finding it harder and harder to beat the overall average market returns. Many are turning to overseas markets where the competition with other U.S. investors is scarce and the opportunities for larger returns are more abundant. Hence, the clamor for improved databases on foreign companies and a narrowing of accounting differences.

"Would I purchase a global database in which company accounts were restated to U.S. GAAP or some third-country GAAP if it were available? Very definitely," said one money manager.

"This is what we are all waiting for," his colleague added. "Indeed, if such data were available we would seriously consider organizing ourselves along industry lines as we were in the early years. . . . For me, it would be very interesting to see what a company like Nestle would look like if it reported according to U.S. accounting standards."

The fact remains that a lot of people remain leery of international securities, despite predictions that harmonized standards will not only make analysts' lives a littler easier but also enlarge investor interest.

"Comparisons are more feasible for a U.S. company, a U.K. company or an Australian company," said one money manager. "Scandinavia is improving. The Japanese companies are a nightmare. In Europe, even within countries, there may be significant differences in reporting. As a general rule, in Europe, the closer you get to Switzerland, the worse the financial reporting becomes."

Comparisons between Japanese and non-Japanese companies are especially difficult. In most cases, analysts only have access to public data, which is usually insufficient to make accurate restatements. "Accounting differences which affect the 'E' in the P/E ratio partly explain why we are underweighted in Japan," grouses one investor.

In the case of Korea, one investor complained that many companies there are using straight-line depreciation while the majority of Japanese companies employ the declining balance method. "While cash flow analysis can provide you with some answers, in order for us to give an accurate picture of the companies in each country, some adjustments must be made for accounting differences," he said. "While this is easy to say, it is difficult to implement."

Some investors responsible for building prudent international portfolios rely on original financial statements and a well-developed knowledge of foreign accounting practices and financial market conditions. "You cannot compare very easily across markets," says one money manager. "You can't use the same stock picking, the same valuation techniques. The kind of political risks you see in Hong Kong you don't see in West Germany and vice versa. In almost every single market in the world, local investors predominate and control the valuation system. These local investors are parochial beings, and they don't necessarily know or care how valuation systems work elsewhere in the world. They have their own way and they've been doing it for quite a long time."

Five investors said they dealt with diverse accounting principles informally by mentally adjusting for major differences in accounting measurements. Others compared the rate of change of a company's performance over time, used a dividend discount model as opposed to a discounted earnings framework, or relied solely on macroeconomic variables to make asset allocations by country, then invested in a diversified portfolio of securities within each country. Then there was an investor who relied primarily on "sociological trends"—monitoring the direction of consumer preferences and investing in industry leaders which are expected to capitalize on those trends.

Accounting diversity also prompted the adoption of different investment strategies. One large investor chose to limit his exposure to foreign equities in favor of government or quasi-government bonds. The equities he did purchase were limited to countries whose accounting principles were not very different from his own.

Another institutional investor coped by adopting a top-down approach to foreign investments. "So far we don't attempt to compare results between countries," he said. "This does not mean that we do not want to do it. But thus far, we do not have the capability to do it. We have tried it in the past and have had disappointing results. . . . I think that if the investor could be convinced that there is more reliable information available he would take a more active approach and rely on individual companies. At present, this is not the case and may be why so many investors have taken a passive approach and just invest in the index. . . . With a country, if no reliable information is provided, then we stick to the well-known companies in that country and do not consider second- or third-tier companies."

What is common to these diverse experiences is that investor behavior changes when accounting data is different or lacking. It is noteworthy that many investors in the research study admitted that they changed their analytical methods for foreign companies, apparently in contradiction of their prior assertion that accounting diversity did *not* influence their decisions.

Of course, some participants in these circumstances feel that they profit from their special or scarce capabilities. "We don't care if accounting differences are great if you can buy the foreign stock at a cheap enough price," declared one investor. Another said, "Make a big effort to understand the company and you may make a lot of money, especially if other participants in the market have not done as much analysis."

Meanwhile, interest in overseas investments

continues to grow. The best examples may be country funds, which have become popular despite what critics say are the hefty premiums. According to Lipper Analytical Services, Inc., the top closed-end funds in the U.S. last year were the Mexico, Asia Pacific, Brazil, Thai and Taiwan funds. Their average return was 76%.

Regulators' Perspective

Most of the regulators interviewed expected an increase in their oversight of international securities. A 1989 Arthur Andersen study of European capital markets[2] confirmed that the impact of the changing regulatory environment will be considerable as the structure of capital markets changes. Greater regulation will raise the cost of doing business and squeeze profitability. And higher capital requirements could lower returns on equity. Nonetheless, the Arthur Andersen study cited a growing trend of internationalization, with more than 250 European companies expected to list beyond their borders over the next five years. At the same time, the recent surge in leveraged buyouts and merger and acquisition activities is reducing the number of domestic shares that are listed or traded on domestic exchanges. That further opens the door to listings and new capital market issues from the international arena.

But while Europe's move to integrate its capital markets by 1992 has already had a demonstrable effect, regulators are divided on international accounting standards proffered by the International Accounting Standards Committee. One regulator prefers the notion of reciprocity to harmonization—reciprocity meaning that each securities exchange or regulatory body agrees to accept the accounting, financial disclosure and audit practices of the foreign issuer's home country. Another preferred to have each country strengthen its national standards rather than conform to some arbitrary norm which generally reflects some minimum acceptable standard.

No matter what develops, the SEC has become increasingly hospitable toward foreign registrants. In 1982, for example, the Commission adopted a disclosure system under which eligible foreign issuers file a less onerous Form 20-F and are exempt from proxy and insider reporting requirements. And if proposed rules governing large, sophisticated investors are any indication, the Commission may rely more on market forces

2. Arthur Andersen & Co. and The Economist Publications, *European Capital Markets, A Strategic Forecast* (London: The Economist Publications, 1989).

to deal with the issue of international accounting diversity. The eagerly awaited Rule 144A, for example, will lift restrictions on the trade of unregistered securities and very likely spur trading of foreign debt and equity in the U.S. Some U.S. investment bankers have gone on record saying that Rule 144A could be the most important change since the shelf registration provisions of Rule 415 transformed the debt markets in recent years.

Should Accountants of the World Unite?

Accounting rule differences present an imposing barrier to the comparison of industry leaders in Europe, Japan and the U.S. There is little doubt that automobile enthusiasts on Wall Street would find a comparative analysis of Daimler-Benz, Nissan and Ford interesting. However, today's analysis, blurred by accounting ambiguity, may be further complicated by national macroeconomic, tax, regulatory and cultural differences.

Intuitively, harmonization of international accounting rules is a sensible and appealing course of action. Who would dispute the logic of a global language for business? But while the International Accounting Standards Committee and professional accounting organizations around the world have enacted a number of changes along these lines, progress has been slow.

The real issue, though, is whether the world has put the cart before the horse. The effect of troublesome differences in accounting standards on the capital markets must be better understood before the true costs and benefits of harmonization can be known. Only then will the path toward harmonization be clear.

Hurtling Toward the Millennium

The decade of the Eighties has produced profound changes to the international capital markets.

- The international equity market, when measured by secondary turnover, reached US $1,212.6 billion in 1988.
- The largest net investors in international equities in 1988 were Europeans (including U.K. investors), who accounted for 73% of the total.
- The international equity market has grown in value by an average rate of 36.6% per annum compounded since 1979.
- In volume (number of shares traded), the international equity market has grown by an average 17.9% per annum compounded since 1979.

• European equity markets (including the U.K.) were the major recipients of net (new money) international equity flows in 1988, attracting 82% of the total.

The Nineties promise to be even more dramatic as capital-raising opportunities proliferate amid the confluence of financial ingenuity, mind-boggling technology and political reforms.

Indeed, companies doing business cross-border will have to navigate through a maze of international complexity. The costs these businesses incur to finance their operations must be compared to costs of all alternate means of financing to determine whether they are optimizing their funding decisions. Overseas funds may be cheaper as MCA, the U.S. entertainment conglomerate, found last year when it sold $200 million in 5.5% convertible subordinated debentures through a Euromarket syndicate led by Salomon Brother International Ltd.

There is little agreement today on what to do about international accounting diversity, but it is certain that companies doing cross-border business will be affected by it. So it is imperative that more hard data be gathered and a greater effort put forth to understand how diversity affects capital market transactions. More and better information will make for better decisions.

It will help investors to judge whether a foreign company's share prices are consistent with intrinsic value. Issuers could better decide whether a premium yield must be paid to induce foreign investors to buy their paper. Better data would also shed light on the factors that drive the cost of capital, and perhaps suggest strategies for raising future capital more efficiently or cheaply.

Included research will create a better understanding of the information that really counts in making investment decisions. The international environment is complex and, like it or not, everyone will be affected by the changes now underway. Business people will have to change the way they operate. But those who commit themselves to a better understanding of these issues will have an advantage in the global capital markets.

Reading

Mishmash Accounting

Did you know that General Electric's assets have ballooned to $110 billion as of Dec. 31, up from $40 billion at the end of 1987? Or that General Motors' debt is now 47% of capitalization, up from 10% at the end of 1987?

No, these blue chips have not turned into speculative plays. What's going on is just the sort of nonsense that the critics predicted from the Financial Accounting Standards Board rule on consolidation. Under this rule, approved after much contention in October 1987, all majority-owned subsidiaries must be folded into the parent's financial statements, no matter what business the subs are in. Before the rule took effect with 1988 annual reports, companies with subsidiaries outside their core business—such as finance, insurance or leasing subs—were not forced to fold the subs' assets and liabilities into the parent's consolidated balance sheet. That made sense because manufacturing and finance companies use capital so differently that their balance sheets are not really comparable.

Justification for the rule was that companies could bury liabilities in their subsidiaries. But the cure is worse than the disease. "Now GM looks like a finance company with a car division," quips Normal Strauss, a partner at Ernst & Young.

The old rule wasn't so terrible for investors. A company could exclude a subsidiary from its main balance sheet only if it also reported a balance sheet for the subsidiary. If there's any reforming to be done it should take place in Europe. In Germany a public company can bury so much in unreported subsidiaries that its true profit remains a secret.

Finance companies typically have huge receivables, huge liabilities and relatively small revenues. So investors measure their performance by standards quite different from those of manufacturing companies.

What irks Robert Richter, vice president of administration of Dana Corp., is the thought of all those investors who for stocks using financial ratios: return of assets, operating margins, debt-to-equity and the like. When Dana was forced to consolidate its finance sub, virtually all

Source: Article by Dana Wechsler. Reprinted by permission of *Forbes* magazine, November 27, 1989. © Forbes Inc., 1989.

of its ratios changed, even though the fundamentals did not. Someone spending a fair amount of time with the annual report would be able to figure this out. But an investor using a computer to filter for investment candidates would never get this far.

"A year ago, any list of companies with less than 50% debt would have had Dana on it," says Richter. "We should be there now, but we aren't."

What's more, ratios are only helpful when one can draw comparisons across similar companies. "After you lump financial services with the manufacturing operations, what companies is it comparable to?" asks Richter. "What's the appropriate debt-to-equity ratio, or interest coverage? There aren't any answers because there aren't any comparables."

Securities analysts don't like the change any more than the companies do. Their instinct is to evaluate a company piecemeal—whence all the talk these days about breakup value. Now that job is much tougher.

"I had one fellow pleading with me to tell him what was long-term debt," says Eugene Flegm, assistant controller of GM. "I went back to the traditional number and gave it to him. He said, 'That's it!' like he'd found an old friend."

He goes on: "Try to find one person who uses the new data. So what are we giving it to them for?"

Indeed, many companies with finance subsidiaries now feel compelled to present the numbers both ways, the old and the new. General Electric added 33 pages to the financial section of its annual report. "We felt we had to," explains Bernard Doyle, manager of corporate accounting services. "Otherwise the old GE would have disappeared."

In some cases, the consolidated number for liabilities is downright misleading. Dana's 1988 balance sheet shows $3.7 billion of liabilities. But the company is on the hook for only $1.8 billion; the remaining $1.9 billion represents liabilities of Dana's finance sub, Diamond Financial Holdings, for which the parent is not liable. Lenders who extend credit to Diamond generally rely on Diamond's own financial statements. If Diamond failed, Dana's shareholders would likely be out only $128 million, their equity in the subsidiary.

GM, which used to release its earnings figures three weeks after the end of each quarter, now needs four weeks to compile the results. All calculations have to be made twice. What's the cost to GM in man-hours? "No one is impressed if it costs GM another few hundred thousand dollars," replies Flegm. "But if the benefit is zero, I don't even want to spend $10 on it."

The new consolidation rule has been one resounding flop. The solution is simple: Repeal it.

APPENDIX A ACCOUNTING FOR UNINCORPORATED BUSINESSES

Reviewing the Appendix

OBJECTIVE 1: Record the basic transactions affecting the owner's equity of a sole proprietorship (pp. Ap-1–Ap-2).

1. A **sole proprietorship** is a business owned by one person. In accounting, it is considered an entity separate from its owner, but for legal purposes, the owner and proprietorship are considered one and the same (that is, the owner is personally liable for all debts of the business). A cash investment is recorded as a debit to Cash and a credit to the owner's capital account. A cash withdrawal is recorded as a debit to the owner's withdrawals account and a credit to Cash. Closing entries for a sole proprietorship are the same as for a corporation, except that Income Summary is closed to the owner's capital account, as is the owner's withdrawals account (an account that does not exist for a corporation).

OBJECTIVE 2: Identify the major characteristics of a partnership (pp. Ap-2–Ap-4).

2. According to the Uniform Partnership Act, a **partnership** is "an association of two or more persons to carry on as co-owners of a business for profit." Its chief characteristics are as follows:
   a. Voluntary association: Partners choose each other when they form their business.
   b. **Partnership agreement:** Partners may have either an oral or a written agreement.
   c. **Limited life:** Certain events may dissolve the partnership.
   d. **Mutal agency:** Each partner may bind the partnership to outside contracts.
   e. **Unlimited liability:** Each partner is personally liable for all debts of the partnership.
   f. Co-ownership of partnership property: Business property is jointly owned by all partners.
   g. Participation in partnership income: Each partner shares income and losses of the business.

OBJECTIVE 3: Identify the advantages and disadvantages of a partnership, and compare it to other forms of business (p. Ap-4).

3. A partnership has several advantages. It is easy to form and to dissolve. It is able to pool capital resources and individual talents. It avoids the corporation's tax burden. It gives freedom and flexibility to its partners' actions.

4. The disadvantages of a partnership are limited life, mutual agency, unlimited liability, capital limitation, and difficulty of transferring ownership interest.

OBJECTIVE 4: Record investments of cash and of other assets by the partners in forming a partnership (pp. Ap-4–Ap-6).

5. The owners' equity section of a partnership's balance sheet is called **partners' equity,** and separate capital and withdrawals accounts must be maintained for each partner. When a partner makes an investment, the assets contributed are debited at their fair market value, and the partner's capital account is credited.

OBJECTIVE 5: Compute the profit or loss that partners share, based on a stated ratio, a capital investment ratio, and salaries and interest to partners (pp. Ap-6–Ap-10).

6. The method of distributing partnership income and losses should be specified in the partnership agreement. The most common methods base distribution on (a) a stated ratio only, (b) a capital investment ratio only, and (c) a combination of fixed salaries, interest on each partner's capital, and the stated ratio. Net income is distributed to partners' equity by debiting Income Summary and crediting each partner's capital account; the reverse is done for a net loss.

7. When income and losses are based on a stated ratio only, partnership income or loss for the period is multiplied by each partner's ratio (stated as a fraction or percentage) to arrive at each partner's share.

8. When income and losses are based on a capital investment ratio only, partnership income or loss for the period is multiplied by each partner's proportion of (a) total capital invested at the beginning of the period or (b) average capital during the period.

9. When income and losses are based on salaries, interest, and a stated ratio, a certain procedure must be followed. First, salaries and interest must be allocated to the partners regardless of the net income figure for the period. Then, any net income left over after the salary and interest must also be allocated to the partners, in the stated ratio. On the other hand, if the salary and interest are greater than net income, then this excess must be deducted from each partner's allocation, in the stated ratio.

OBJECTIVE 6: Record the admission of a new partner (pp. Ap-10–Ap-12).

10. When a partnership is legally dissolved, it loses the authority to continue business as a going concern. **Dissolution** of a partnership

occurs upon the (a) withdrawal of a partner, (b) bankruptcy of a partner, (c) incapacity of a partner, (d) death of a partner, (e) admission of a new partner, (f) retirement of a partner, or (g) expiration of the partnership agreement.

11. A new partner may be admitted into a partnership by either (a) purchasing an interest in the partnership from one or more of the original partners or (b) investing assets into the partnership.
    a. When a new partner purchases an interest from another partner, the selling partner's capital account is debited and the buying partner's account is credited for the interest in the business sold. The purchase price is ignored in making this entry.
    b. When a new partner invests his or her own assets into the partnership, the contributed assets are debited and the new partner's capital account is credited. The amount of the debit and credit may or may not equal the value of the assets. It depends on the value of the business and the method applied. When the partners feel that the business is worth more than its net assets indicate, they will probably ask the entering partner to pay them a bonus. Under the opposite set of circumstances, a partnership may give the new partner a greater interest in the business than the value of the assets contributed.

OBJECTIVE 7: Describe the implications of the withdrawal or death of a partner and of the liquidation of a partnership (pp. Ap-13–Ap-14).

12. A partner may withdraw from (leave) a partnership in one of two ways. (a) The partner may take assets from the partnership that are greater than, less than, or equal to his or her capital investment. (b) The partner may sell his or her interest to new or existing partners. In addition, when a partner dies, the partnership is thereby dissolved. Accordingly, certain immediate steps must be taken to settle with the heirs of the deceased partner.

13. **Liquidation** of a partnership is the process of (a) selling partnership assets, (b) paying off partnership liabilities, and (c) distributing the remaining assets to the partners.

Testing Your Knowledge

Matching

Match each term with its definition by writing the appropriate letter in the blank.

_____ 1. Sole proprietorship

_____ 2. Partnership

_____ 3. Voluntary association

_____ 4. Partnership agreement

_____ 5. Limited life

_____ 6. Mutual agency

_____ 7. Unlimited liability

_____ 8. Dissolution

_____ 9. Liquidation

_____ 10. Partners' equity

a. The sale of partnership assets, and payment to creditors and owners
b. The fact that any change in partners will cause the business to dissolve
c. The power of each partner to enter into contracts that are within the normal scope of the business
d. The balance sheet section that lists the partners' capital accounts
e. A business owned by one person
f. An association of two or more persons to carry on as co-owners of a business for profit
g. Creditors' claim to the partners' personal assets if the partnership cannot pay its debts
h. The end of a partnership as a going concern
i. The specifics of how the partnership is to operate
j. The partners' consent to join one another in forming a partnership

Applying Your Knowledge

Exercises

1. Partners A, B, and C each receive a $10,000 salary, as well as 5 percent interest on their respective investments of $60,000, $40,000, and $50,000. If they share income and losses in a 3:2:1 ratio, how much net income or loss would be allocated to each under the following circumstances?

   a. A net income of $40,500

   A = $ _____

   B = $ _____

   C = $ _____

   b. A net income of $25,500

   A = $ _____

   B = $ _____

   C = $ _____

   c. A net loss of $4,500

   A = $ _____

   B = $ _____

   C = $ _____

2. Partners G, H, and I have capital balances of $10,000 each, and share income and losses in a 2:2:1 ratio. They agree to allow J to purchase a one-third interest in the business. If they use the bonus method to record the transaction, provide the proper journal entry under each of the following assumptions:
   a. J contributes $12,000 in cash.
   b. J contributes $15,000 in cash.
   c. J contributes $21,000 in cash.

General Journal				
Date		Description	Debit	Credit

APPENDIX B OVERVIEW OF GOVERNMENTAL AND NOT-FOR-PROFIT ACCOUNTING

Reviewing the Appendix

OBJECTIVE 1: Explain and differentiate some basic concepts related to governmental and not-for-profit accounting (p. Ap-19).

1. Appendix B deals with accounting for state and local governments, colleges and universities, hospitals, and voluntary health and welfare organizations. The first four learning objectives relate to accounting for state and local governments, and the last paragraph relates to accounting for the other not-for-profit groups listed above.

2. The development of governmental accounting standards is currently the responsibility of the Governmental Accounting Standards Board (GASB). Formerly, it was the responsibility of the National Council on Governmental Accounting (NCGA). These standards are developed, not to measure profit, but to measure the changes in the funds available for governmental activities. Of primary importance is the control the governmental unit exercises over the funds made available, many for specific purposes. In governmental accounting, a **fund** is defined as a fiscal and accounting entity, and it is generally based on **modified accrual accounting** (defined in paragraph 5).

OBJECTIVE 2: Describe the types of funds used in governmental accounting (pp. Ap-19–Ap-20).

3. State and local governments use a variety of funds, each of which must show (a) the finan-

cial position and results of operations for the period, and (b) compliance with legal provisions of state and local government.

a. The **general fund** accounts for financial resources, such as police, fire, and sanitation, that are not accounted for in any other fund.

b. **Special revenue funds** account for revenues that are legally restricted to specific purposes.

c. **Capital projects funds** account for the acquisition and construction of major capital projects, such as buildings, highways, and sewer systems.

d. The **debt service fund** accounts for resources to pay principal and interest on long-term debt.

e. **Enterprise funds** account for activities, such as golf courses and utilities, that charge the public for goods or services.

f. **Internal service funds** account for goods or services that one governmental agency provides to another (within the same governmental unit).

g. **Trust and agency funds** account for assets held for individuals, private organizations, or other funds.

4. The funds discussed in paragraph 3a–d are described as **governmental funds;** the enterprise and internal service funds are described as **proprietary funds;** and trust and agency funds are described as **fiduciary funds.** State

and local governments also use a **general fixed assets account group** and a **general long-term debt group** to account for fixed assets and long-term liabilities, respectively, that are not related to specific proprietary or trust funds.

OBJECTIVE 3: Explain the modified accrual basis of accounting used by state and local governments (pp. Ap-20–Ap-23).

5. Modified accrual accounting differs from accrual accounting in (a) the method of measuring and recognizing revenues and expenditures, (b) the incorporation of the budget into the accounting records, and (c) the use of **encumbrances** to account for purchases. In governmental accounting, **revenues** are increases in fund resources (other than from interfund transactions or proceeds of long-term debt), and are recognized when measurable and available. **Expenditures** are decreases in fund resources (other than from interfund transfers). Whereas business accounting emphasizes the matching of revenues and expenses to obtain net income, governmental accounting focuses on the inflows and outflows of fund resources. Examples of general fund journal entries follow.
   a. The budget is incorporated into the accounts with a debit to Estimated Revenues, a credit to Appropriations, and a credit to Fund Balance (assuming that revenues are expected to exceed expenditures). The Appropriations account will enable the governmental unit to exercise control over its expenditures. Also, the Fund Balance occupies the equity section of governmental and nonprofit balance sheets.
   b. When a governmental unit purchases an asset that is to be received in several weeks or months, the general fund debits Encumbrances and credits Reserve for Encumbrances. This entry will ensure that the governmental unit adheres to its spending limit.
   c. When the above asset is received, two entries are made into the general fund. First, the encumbrance entry is reversed. Second, a debit to Expenditures and a credit to Cash or Vouchers Payable are made. The encumbered amount will not necessarily be equal to the amount of the expenditure.

OBJECTIVE 4: Describe the financial reporting system used in governmental accounting (p. Ap-23).

6. Financial statements of a governmental unit include (a) a combined balance sheet, (b) two types of combined statements of revenues, expenditures, and changes in fund balances, (c) a combined statement of revenues, expenses, and changes in retained earnings (or equity), and (d) a combined statement of changes in financial position.

OBJECTIVE 5: Provide a brief introduction to other types of not-for-profit accounting (pp. Ap-23–Ap-25).

7. Not-for-profit organizations such as colleges and hospitals are similar to governmental units in their use of several types of funds and in the absence of the profit motive. However, they differ in their use of full accrual accounting and in their inability to impose a tax as a source of revenue. Also, many of the funds obtained by not-for-profit organizations are restricted to specific purposes by the donors.
   a. Colleges and universities use an unrestricted current fund, a restricted current fund, loan funds, endowment funds, annuity and life income funds, plant funds, and agency funds. In addition, they prepare (1) a statement of current revenues, expenditures, and other changes, and (2) a statement of changes in fund balances.
   b. Not-for-profit hospitals use an unrestricted fund, a specific purpose fund, and endowment funds. In hospital accounting, revenues are classified by source, and expenses by function. Statements prepared are the balance sheet, statement of revenues and expenses, statement of changes in fund balances, and statement of cash flows.
   c. Voluntary health and welfare organizations, such as the American Cancer Society and the Sierra Club, use funds like those used by colleges and universities. In addition, they prepare a statement of support, revenues and expenses, and changes in fund balances, as well as a balance sheet. As a rule, revenues are classified as public support revenue and revenue from charges for goods and services. Similarly, expenses are classified as program services and supporting services.

Testing Your Knowledge

Matching

Match each term with its definition by writing the appropriate letter in the blank.

_____ 1. Fund

_____ 2. Modified accrual accounting

_____ 3. Governmental Accounting Standards Board (GASB)

_____ 4. General fund

_____ 5. Special revenue funds

_____ 6. Capital projects funds

_____ 7. Debt service fund

_____ 8. Endowment funds

_____ 9. Enterprise funds

_____ 10. Internal service funds

_____ 11. Trust and agency funds

_____ 12. Proprietary funds

_____ 13. Fiduciary funds

_____ 14. Revenues

_____ 15. Expenditures

_____ 16. Appropriations

_____ 17. Fund balance

_____ 18. Encumbrances

_____ 19. Unrestricted fund

_____ 20. Restricted fund

a. Funds to account for gifts and bequests

b. A fund to account for resources to pay principal and interest on long-term debt

c. The body responsible for developing governmental GAAP

d. The budgetary account used to control or limit expenditures for the period

e. Funds to account for goods or services that one governmental agency provides to another

f. Decreases in fund resources (other than from interfund transfers)

g. Funds to account for services or public improvements to special properties

h. A descriptive term for trust and agency funds

i. The account to reflect anticipated expenditures on the books

j. A fiscal and accounting entity

k. A fund for general operating activities

l. Funds to account for assets held for individuals, private organizations, or other funds

m. The fund to account for financial resources that are not accounted for in any other fund

n. Funds to account for activities that resemble private business activities

o. Increases in fund resources (other than from interfund transactions or proceeds of long-term debt)

p. A descriptive term for the enterprise and internal service funds

q. The basis of accounting for governmental units

r. In fund accounting, the equity section of the balance sheet

s. Funds to account for the acquisition and construction of buildings, streets, etc.

t. A fund to be used only for a specific purpose

Applying Your Knowledge

Exercise

1. Transactions for the year ended December 31, 19xx, for the town of Sharon are presented here. For each, prepare the journal entry that would appear in Sharon's General Fund. Omit explanations.

    a. On January 1, the town adopted its budget for the year with estimated revenues of $950,000 and appropriations of $935,000.

    b. On March 15, property taxes of $900,000 were levied. It is estimated that 1% will prove uncollectible.

    c. On March 25, goods were ordered for an estimated cost of $50,000.

    d. On May 9, a new bus was purchased for $30,000 cash.

    e. By June 15, property tax collections totaled $893,000. The remaining $7,000 was written off as uncollectible.

    f. On June 27, the goods ordered on March 25 were received. The supplier's invoice was for $51,000. A voucher was prepared, to be paid next week.

    g. On July 5, the voucher of June 27 was paid.

    h. By December 31, actual revenues totaled $955,000 and actual expenditures totaled $947,000. No encumbrances existed at year-end.

	General Journal		
Date	Description	Debit	Credit

Reading

Crunched Numbers

Government's system of accounting comes under rising criticism

The problem with the federal government, Rep. Joseph J. DioGuardi says, is that it has too many lawyers and too few accountants.

Mr. DioGuardi is an accountant. Last year, after a career spent poring over the books of private corporations, he won a seat in Congress and began studying the books of the federal government. "I'm appalled at the way we account for government spending around here," he says, his voice rising with indignation. "We're using a Mickey Mouse, cash-basis accounting system."

The New York Republican is more emphatic than most of his fellow accountants, but he isn't alone in his critique. The government's top accountant, Comptroller General Charles A. Bowsher, agrees. So do various other accountants, budget officials and economists both inside and out of government. Federal budget-accounting procedures "would be illegal if they were practiced by publicly traded private corporations," says Michael Boskin, a Stanford University economist.

Policy Affected

Bad accounting methods, critics say, can produce bad government policy. Because Washington focuses primarily on the cash it spends and gets each year—and the difference, or deficit, between them—its drive to cut immediate outlays can lead to actions that turn out to be penny-wise and pound-foolish. For example, the federal government often leases buildings to avoid the big cash outlay of a purchase even though leasing costs more in the long run.

The Gramm-Rudman plan to balance the budget is creating new pressure to slash the deficit and its concentrating attention on the strengths and weaknesses of the government's accounting methods. "I think Gramm-Rudman may bring this whole accounting issue to the forefront," Mr. Bowsher says. "When people try to wrestle with this thing, I think there will be a lot of interest in

Source: "Crunched Numbers" by Alan Murray, *The Wall Street Journal,* February 3, 1986. Reprinted by permission of *The Wall Street Journal,* © 1986 Dow Jones & Company, Inc. All Rights Reserved Worldwide.

getting a more streamlined, easier-to-understand accounting system."

Right now, White House officials say they are considering compilation of a "capital budget" in addition to the annual cash-based budget. The proposed budget would account separately for the government's long-term investments in real estate, computers, warships and other weapons and would attempt to estimate the rate at which such assets are wearing out. That's important, accountants say, because it helps the government keep track of the eventual costs of repairing or replacing those assets. The proposal, however, wouldn't exempt capital investments from the Gramm-Rudman deficit-cutting ax.

Budget Proposals

An example of the importance of accounting conventions will be evident in the Reagan administration's fiscal 1987 budget, to be unveiled Wednesday. That budget will include proposals to sell billions of dollars of federal assets, including the Naval Petroleum Reserve, the Bonneville Power Administration and part of the government's loan portfolio.

Under accounting methods used by private companies, such asset sales wouldn't necessarily increase net incomes. And if the assets were sold for less than the amount invested in them, they could result in a loss.

Under government accounting conventions, in contrast, the cash raised by those asset sales would help meet the new budget law's deficit target, regardless of the sale prices. "It's like selling your house to pay for your current spending," Mr. Boskin says.

Costs Confused

The problem with that cash-in, cash-out accounting, critics say, is that it doesn't give sufficient attention to actual costs. For instance, the administration, as part of its budget proposal, is likely to lean more heavily on government loan guarantees rather than direct loans. But although loan guarantees might not require any cash outlays over the next few years, they could prove very costly in the long term if loans go bad.

Of course, the Generally Accepted Accounting Principles used by corporations have their own problems and often can be employed to cloud as well as to reveal a company's financial picture. What's more, sometimes the rules are bent. "When you're in Chapter 11, you manage for cash and to hell with all this other nice gobbledygook," says Donald Moran, a former Reagan administration budget official who currently is a vice president of ICF Incorporated, a Washington consulting firm. But accountants say the shortcomings of business accounting pale in comparison with the government's methods.

"Basically, the government is like someone who uses only a checkbook," says Morton Egol, a New York partner in Arthur Andersen & Co., a big accounting firm. "That's not a complete picture of its financial affairs. It doesn't reflect assets, liabilities, commitments in the future. How can you run a trillion-dollar business without knowing what its financial position is?"

Administration budget officials emphatically deny that they ignore the underlying costs of government programs. "Everybody here is very conscious of those things," says Edwin Dale, the spokesman for the Office of Management and Budget. He also notes that increasing emphasis on three-year and five-year budget projections helps lawmakers focus on longer-run costs. Along with framing the budget in terms of annual outlays, both Congress and the budget office also state spending in terms of budgetary "authority," which sometimes allows agencies to obligate funds over several years. And other defenders of the current accounting system contend that government accounts don't lend themselves to corporate-style ledgers.

Nevertheless, the combination of Gramm-Rudman's deficit-reduction goals and a simple cash accounting system may drive the administration and Congress to embrace proposals this year that will help raise cash or cut spending in the short run but increase costs over the long run. Consider these examples:

—Faced with pressure to reduce spending, the Pentagon will try to stretch out weapons programs instead of cutting them outright. Under government accounting, that will slow spending and lower the deficit in the short run, but "the delays will make total program costs and total funding costs go up," says David Smith, a defense analyst at Sanford G. Bernstein & Co., a New York investment firm.

—As emphasis on the deficit increases, getting approval to buy or construct federal office space has become nearly impossible. "We haven't done any major construction since the Nixon years," says Raymond A. Fontaine, the comptroller for the General Services Administration. As a result, the government's rent bill runs about a billion dollars a year. Mr. Fontaine argues that because the government pays lower interest rates than private builders do and because it is almost certain to need the office space indefinitely, it would usually save money by owning rather than leasing. "The way it is now, at the end of 20 years you end up with nothing but a bunch of canceled rent checks," he complains.

—Getting approval to make new investments in computers and other equipment that might improve government productivity in the long run—but costs lots of money in the short run—is also increasingly difficult. "Anything that has a future payoff is really going to get hurt" under the new budget law, says Frederick Wolf, the director of the GAO's accounting and financial management division.

Such examples illustrate why Mr. Bowsher, Mr. DioGuardi and others believe that reforming government accounting is critical. "My colleagues tell me to take my green eyeshade off," Mr. DioGuardi says, "but I tell them I won't trade my green eyeshade for blinders."

Grimmer Picture

A comprehensive balance sheet listing all the government's assets and liabilities might help focus attention on true costs, the reformers believe. Such a system of accounting, Mr. DioGuardi contends, would also show that the government is much further in the red than commonly supposed.

"When you hear about $2 trillion in accumulated deficits, that's the good news," he says. "That's what's on the books. You wouldn't believe what is off the books."

Mr. Egol estimates that if accrued, but unfunded, Social Security liabilities are included, the government's liabilities exceed its assets by approximately $3.4 trillion, "more than the value of all stocks listed on the New York Stock Exchange." On this expanded basis, he argues, the fiscal 1984 deficit was more than $300 billion rather than the $185 billion commonly reported.

Stanford's Mr. Boskin is working on a similar calculation and, like Mr. Egol, has concluded that the government is "several trillion dollars" in the red. And a "prototype" financial statement prepared by the Treasury Department for fiscal 1984 found government liabilities of $4.74 trillion, offset by only $937.3 billion in assets.

Many Problems

Such calculations are fraught with problems, however. A key question, for instance, is how to treat Social Security. Mr. Boskin, Mr. Egol and the Treasury all choose to view it as a pension program. As a result, Social Security obligations stretching far into the future must be recorded on the liability side of the balance sheet. That decision alone adds $1.9 trillion to the government's liabilities in 1984. If the program is treated as a transfer-payment program financed annually and not a pension program, that huge liability disappears.

There are other problems as well. For instance, how do you calculate the annual depreciation of missiles, bombs or tanks? How do you account for investments in public education? And what about the federal government's one asset that no private company can match: the power to tax?

"At the high level of accounting theory, this all sounds intriguing," ICF's Mr. Moran says. "But it makes no sense because government is different than any other form of enterprise." Trying to put together a comprehensive financial statement for the federal government, Mr. Moran adds, would be "fabulously expensive."

David Nathan, a budget official at the Commerce Department, comments: "The government deals in assets that are unlike anyone else's. There is no bottom line. How much is it worth, for example, to be the only one in town allowed to print money?"

The proposal to establish a separate capital-expenditures budget, long pushed by a variety of accountants and economists, contemplates a budget that would look at the cost of an investment over its entire life. By paying more attention to such a budget, proponents say, the government would be less likely to adopt costly stretchouts of military purchases, to delay investments that might save money in the long run or to sell capital assets to reduce operating deficits.

"We equate a dollar going into salaries with a dollar going into a building that will last 15 years," the GAO's Mr. Wolf says. "That idea has been rejected by nearly everyone else." A capital budget would help policy makers make such distinctions, he adds.

Mr. Boskin says: "If you were a counsel to private industry, you would advise that they know whether their money is in new plant and R&D or whether it's going to pay their secretary. We don't do that. There is a real potential for making ill-advised long-term government decisions by not having a separate capital account."

More Pork?

Despite the advantages of such a separate account, many OMB officials argue that a capital budget would encourage "pork-barrel" spending on federal buildings, highways and canals. Mr. Bowsher says that he discussed the idea with David Stockman last year and that the former budget director responded that a capital budget would simply give big spenders in Congress an opportunity "to rebuild every bridge in America." Capital budgeting, Mr. Moran agrees, creates "a serendipitous interaction between the theoretical leanings of accountants and the practical leanings of politicians."

Whatever the merits of arguments for accounting reform, they don't seem to be carrying the day in Washington. Mr. DioGuardi is trying to rally the support of all the accountants in Congress, but so far he has found only three others. "I can't identify more than a handful in the entire history of Congress!" he exclaims.

And at any rate, says Mr. Nathan of the Commerce Department, accounting changes aren't likely to alter the way Washington works. "The budget is politics," he says, "and people want to make new decisions every year. No one has ever been able to demonstrate to me that accounting methods are going to change the way decisions are made."

Reading

What Users Want in Government Financial Reports

Annual reports prepared according to the standards of the Governmental Accounting Standards Board often contain more than 30 pages of notes —one recent report contains 70 pages. . . . Although due process procedures are intended to ensure that each required disclosure specified in GASB standards is needed, the cumulative volume of information raises these questions:

- Do current GASB standards require note disclosures that no longer serve a useful purpose?
- Are there disclosure needs that current GASB standards don't meet?

A Reader Survey

To answer these questions, the GASB sponsored a research study on note disclosures in 1987–88. A series of interviews was held with representatives of important user groups: debt rating agencies, debt insurers, underwriters, investment bankers, bond attorneys, legislative and oversight officials, public finance researchers and citizen advocate and information groups. A sample set of notes to financial statements was sent to each interviewee before the interview. A total of 55 individuals representing 28 organizations were interviewed.

In every interview, the main interest of serious readers—persons whose occupations require regular use of government financial reports—was on *major individual operating funds and enterprise funds with material amounts of outstanding debt*. However, data presented in the general purpose financial statements are aggregated by fund type. This finding should be of special interest to auditors and their clients because only the general financial statement and its notes usually are covered by the independent auditor's report.

Disclosures Considered Important

Although the objectives of users in each category differed, there was general agreement that notes to financial statements should be *concise presenta-*

Source: Article by Leon E. Hay and James F. Antonio. Reprinted with permission from the *Journal of Accountancy,* Copyright © 1990 by American Institute of Certified Public Accountants, Inc. Opinions of the authors are their own and do not necessarily reflect policies of the AICPA.

tions of essential information. Interviewees had very little interest in

- General policy statements.
- Recitations of financial reporting standards.
- Lengthy explanations of unessential details.

If a reporting entity followed accounting policies not in conformity with generally accepted accounting principles—particularly policies relating to revenue recognition and expense or expenditure recognition—interviewees said notes should disclose this. Also, the entity should disclose situations in which its accounting policies differed from those used during the previous year. To the extent policy statements are needed, respondents indicated they should be presented with the appropriate note or notes explaining the items appearing in the financial statements.

Also considered useful were disclosures regarding

- Events of noncompliance with laws, regulations and agreements.
- Material contingent liabilities.
- Significant effects of subsequent events.

Although these disclosures are useful as they are now presented, respondents suggested they would be even more useful if they were expanded.

More Disclosure Wanted

Rather than present a financial picture at one given point in time, respondents wanted to know whether balance sheets are representative of an entity's financial position during the fiscal year. Also, they wanted to know whether the revenues and expenditures reported for the year fit the trend of revenues and expenditures over time and whether events have occurred, or are expected to occur, that may affect revenue streams or expenditures materially.

Interviewees didn't expect annual forecasts but they wanted reports to contain information that would help them develop their own evaluations of financial position and results of operations of individual funds—not fund types.

Disclosures of Subsequent Events

Specifically, serious readers wanted disclosures of events or actions that may materially affect financial data after the balance sheet date. These include

Events of noncompliance. Although Statement on Auditing Standards no. 63, *Compliance Auditing Applicable to Governmental Entities and Other Recipients of Governmental Financial Assistance,* now provides guidance to independent auditors on this subject, it hadn't been promulgated at the time of the study. Nevertheless, interviewees asked for note disclosure of violations of laws, regulations, contracts, debt covenants or other agreements that could materially affect the financial statements. Examples are failure to comply with restrictions on the use of revenue and other financing sources, expenditures in excess of appropriations, expenditures for unauthorized purposes and failure to meet the reporting requirements of higher jurisdictions. Interviewees added disclosures should include a brief statement of actions taken, or to be taken, to prevent recurrence of the violations. If no action has been taken and none is planned, the note should say as much.

Contingencies, including litigation. Interviewees want to be informed of potential material liabilities.

Events presaging financial stress. Readers wanted to know about events occurring, or expected to occur, that would be likely to cause the government to incur large capital outlays or increased operating expenditures in advance of future revenues. Examples include the development of a major resort, theme park or factory.

Budget Disclosures

The laws of a number of jurisdictions mandate that revenues and expenditures be budgeted on a basis other than GAAP. GASB standards require these differences be reconciled on the face of the financial statements or in accompanying notes. Interviewees said their information needs would be better served if GASB required several additional disclosures.

Material differences between original budget and final amended budget. Respondents wanted disclosure of material differences between revenues (by source) and appropriations (by function) in the budget approved at the beginning of the year and they wanted the revenues (by source) and appropriations (by function) in the final amended budget for the year. They also asked for explanations of any material differences.

Budget/GAAP reporting differences. If the budget and GAAP reporting differences aren't reconciled on the face of the financial statements, readers indicated the notes should set forth only *material* differences.

More Specific Revenue and Expenditure/Expense Disclosures

GASB standards currently require an entity to present a combined statement of revenues, expenditures and changes in fund balances for all government fund types and a combined statement of revenues, expenses and changes in retained earnings for proprietary fund types. The standards require note disclosure of policies for accounting recognition of revenues, expenditures and expenses but interviewees didn't consider these useful. Instead of the current general policy statements, the interviewees requested additional information.

Revenues. Respondents recommended disclosure for each major fund, for the current and four preceding years, about actual property tax rates compared with maximum statutory property tax rates; amounts of levies, collections and delinquencies as a percentage of levies; sales tax rates and collections; income tax rates and collections; and similar data for each major revenue source. Notes, they said, also should describe threats of material interruption of revenue streams.

Expenditures/expenses. Respondents wanted five years of data for each significant function, program or other category for each major fund.

More Specific Asset, Liability and Equity Disclosures

Current GASB standards specify the notes to the financial statements disclose details about each major category of assets, liabilities and fund equity. Interviewees offered several additional disclosures for the GASB's consideration.

Assets

Cash. Notes should include a cash flow statement discussing short-term borrowing and repayment during the year.

Investments. Disclosures should contain a brief statement of investment restrictions set by state law and local laws, a brief statement of the entity's investment policies and a summary of activity during the year—not just yearend balances

Receivables (all categories including interfund receivables). Users again wanted to know about activity during the year—not just yearend balances. They also asked for the ages of receivables and any other useful information for evaluating the adequacy of allowances for uncollectibles.

Capital assets. Interviewees as a group said they had little interest in disclosures about capital assets at yearend or changes in such assets during the year, unless the relationship of the changes to the entity's capital improvement program was made clear. This suggestion has been instrumental to GASB's ongoing capital assets reporting project.

Liabilities

Short-term debt. Short-term debt incurred and repaid during the year should be disclosed, respondents said. Also, the notes should disclose anything unusual or significant about the debt.

Long-term debt. Readers said notes should disclose the amounts of required interest payments and principal payments for tax-supported debt; special assessment debt; and revenue debt, by enterprise, for the year following the balance sheet date. Interviewees said they would be satisfied if the note summarized total interest and principal payments required for subsequent years until maturity and if it specified the amount and year of maximum annual debt service. Any other unusual or significant facts relating to long-term debt also should be disclosed.

Pension plan obligations and other employee benefits. Interviewees requested disclosure of the portion of the government's resources used, and to be used, for benefits. Moreover, actions to be taken in order to cover any unfunded liability also should be disclosed.

Construction and other commitments. Readers asked for a description of the entity's ultimate commitments for construction and other projects and the time span before the commitments are extinguished. The relation of current construction to the government's capital improvement program, if one exists, also should be disclosed.

Fund Equity

Assuming reservations are disclosed on the face of the statements, respondents said the notes need disclose only material equity transfers and other major changes.

Implications for the GASB Agenda

Although the GASB technical project agenda for the remainder of 1990 is already set, a separate project on note disclosure will be started as soon as time permits. Such a project is expected to reexamine disclosures in their entirety and delete those that duplicate one another or are marginally useful. Those notes that are useful will be reorganized or expanded.

The research report already has had a beneficial effect by raising the sensitivity of the GASB to the practical limits of voluminous note disclosures. Thus, in ongoing GASB projects, each potential disclosure is being examined in the light of this study. Copies of the report, *A Study of the Usefulness of Disclosures Required by GASB Standards,* are available for $10 from the GASB Order Department, P.O. Box 30784, Hartford, Connecticut 06150.

APPENDIX C SPECIAL-PURPOSE JOURNALS

Reviewing the Appendix

OBJECTIVE 1: Explain the objectives and uses of special-purpose journals (pp. Ap-30–Ap-31).

1. Companies using manual data processing (keeping handwritten accounting records) record an entry in one or more journals. A company can record all its transactions in the general journal. However, companies with a large number of transactions also use **special-purpose journals** to save time, effort, and money.

2. Most business transactions fall into one of four types, and are recorded in one of four special-purpose journals, as follows:
   a. Sales of merchandise on credit are recorded in the sales journal.
   b. Purchases of merchandise on credit are recorded in the purchases journal.
   c. Receipts of cash are recorded in the cash receipts journal.
   d. Disbursements of cash are recorded in the cash payments journal.

OBJECTIVE 2: Construct and use the following types of special-purpose journals: sales journal, purchases journal, cash receipts journal, cash payments journal, and others as needed (pp. Ap-31–Ap-45).

3. The **sales journal** saves time because (a) each entry requires only one line; (b) account names need not be written out, since frequently occurring accounts are used as column headings; (c) an explanation is not needed; and (d) only total sales for the month

are posted to the Sales account, not each individual sale. Postings are made daily, however, to customer accounts (in the accounts receivable subsidiary ledger). Similar time-saving principles apply to the other special-purpose journals.

4. The **purchases journal** is used to record purchases on credit. A single-column purchases journal records the purchases of merchandise only. However, a multicolumn purchases journal will accommodate purchases of more than just merchandise. Only total purchases for the month are posted to the Purchases account; however, postings are made daily to creditor accounts (in the accounts payable subsidiary ledger).

5. All receipts of cash are recorded in the **cash receipts journal**. Typically, a cash receipts journal would include debit columns for Cash and Sales Discounts and credit columns for Sales, Accounts Receivable, and "Other Accounts." Postings to customer accounts and "Other Accounts" are made on a daily basis. All column totals, except for Other Accounts, are posted to the general ledger at the end of the month.

6. All payments of cash are recorded in the **cash payments journal**. Typically, a cash payments journal would include debit columns for "Other Accounts" and Accounts Payable, and credit columns for Cash and Purchases Discounts. Postings to creditor accounts and Other Accounts are made daily. All column

totals, except for Other Accounts, are posted to the general ledger at the end of the month.

7. Transactions that cannot be recorded in a special-purpose journal, such as the purchase of office equipment on credit (assuming a single-column purchases journal), are recorded in the general journal. Closing entries and adjusting entries are also made in the general journal. Postings are made at the end of each day, and in the case of Accounts Receivable and Accounts Payable, postings are made to both the controlling account and the subsidiary account.

8. Special-purpose journals of businesses may differ slightly from those used in the textbook, because the types of transactions may vary. However, an understanding of the general concepts and mechanics of special-purpose journals makes adapting to a different system relatively easy.

OBJECTIVE 3: **Explain the purposes and relationships of controlling accounts and subsidiary ledgers (pp. Ap-32–Ap-34).**

9. Most companies that sell to customers on credit keep an accounts receivable record for each customer. In this way the company can determine how much a given customer owes at any time. All customer accounts are filed alphabetically in the accounts receivable **subsidiary ledger.**

10. The general ledger, however, contains an Accounts Receivable **controlling** or **control account.** The controlling account is updated at the end of each month and keeps a running total of *all* accounts receivable. Its balance should equal the sum of all the accounts in the accounts receivable subsidiary ledger.

11. Most companies also use an Accounts Payable controlling account and subsidiary ledger, which function much like the Accounts Receivable controlling account and subsidiary ledger.

Testing Your Knowledge

Matching

Match each term with its definition by writing the appropriate letter in the blank.

_____ 1. Special-purpose journal

_____ 2. Subsidiary ledger

_____ 3. Subsidiary account

_____ 4. Controlling account

_____ 5. Schedule of accounts receivable or accounts payable

a. Any journal except the general journal
b. A formal listing of customers or creditors
c. The record of a customer or creditor in a subsidiary ledger
d. Where the customer or creditor accounts are kept
e. Any general ledger account that has a related subsidiary ledger

Applying Your Knowledge

Exercises

1. In the spaces provided, indicate the symbol of the journal that should be used by Targum Appliance Store.

    S = Sales journal
    P = Purchases journal (single-column)
  CR = Cash receipts journal
  CP = Cash payments journal
    J = General journal

___ a. Goods that had been purchased by Targum on credit are returned.
___ b. Goods that had been purchased by Targum for cash are returned for a cash refund.
___ c. Toasters are purchased on credit by Targum.
___ d. The same toasters are paid for.
___ e. A blender is sold on credit.
___ f. The electric bill is paid.
___ g. Adjusting entries are made.
___ h. Office furniture is purchased by Targum on credit.
___ i. Closing entries are made.
___ j. Targum pays for half of the office furniture.
___ k. A customer pays a bill and receives a discount.

2. Enter the following transactions of Riley Liquidators, Inc., into the cash receipts journal provided. Complete the Post. Ref. column as though the entries had been posted daily. Also, make the proper posting notations in the journal as though the end-of-month postings had been made. Accounts Receivable is account no. 114, Sales is account no. 411, Sales Discounts is account no. 412, and Cash is account no. 111.

Feb. 3 Received payment of $500 less a 2 percent discount from Frank Simpson for merchandise previously purchased on credit.

9 Sold equipment (account no. 135) for $8,000 cash.

14 Issued $10,000 more in common stock (account no. 311).

23 Stanley Hall paid Riley $150 for merchandise he had purchased on credit.

28 Cash sales for the month totaled $25,000.

Cash Receipts Journal								
					Credits		Debits	
Date		Account Credited	Post. Ref.	Other Accts.	Accts. Receiv.	Sales	Sales Disc.	Cash

3. A page from a special-purpose journal is provided below.

Date	Ck. no.	Payee	Other Account Debited	Post. Ref.	Debits Other Accounts	Debits Accounts Payable	Credits Purchases Discounts	Credits Cash
May 1	114	Vincennes Supply Co.		✔		800	16	784
7	115	Jeppson Bus. Equip.	Office Equipment	167	2000			2000
13	116	Daily Planet	Advertising Expense	512	350			350
19	117	Olsen Motors		✔		420		420
					2350	1220	16	3554
					(315)	(211)	(413)	(111)

The following questions relate to this journal.

a. What type of journal is this? _____

b. What error was made in the preparation of this journal? _____
_____
_____

c. Provide an explanation for the four transactions.

May 1 _____
_____

May 7 _____
_____

May 13 _____
_____

May 19 _____
_____

d. Explain the following:

1. The checks in the Post. Ref. column
_____
_____

2. The numbers 167 and 512 in the Post. Ref. column _____
_____

3. The numbers below the column totals
_____
_____
_____
_____
_____
_____

APPENDIX D INTRODUCTION TO PAYROLL ACCOUNTING

Reviewing the Appendix

OBJECTIVE 1: Identify and compute the liabilities associated with payroll accounting (pp. Ap-53–Ap-55).

1. The three general types of liabilities associated with payroll accounting are (a) liabilities for employee compensation, (b) liabilities for employee payroll withholding, and (c) liabilities for employer payroll taxes. An employee is under the direct supervision and control of the company. An independent contractor (such as a lawyer or a CPA) is not, and is therefore not accounted for under the payroll system.

2. **Wages** are hourly or piecework pay. **Salaries** are the monthly or yearly rates paid generally to administrative or managerial employees.

3. The employer is required by law to withhold certain taxes from the employee's wages and to remit those taxes to government agencies. The employer also makes other withholdings for the employee's benefit.
   a. FICA taxes provide for retirement and disability benefits, survivor's benefits, and medical benefits.
   b. Federal income taxes depend on (1) the amount that the employee earns, and (2) the number of exemptions claimed on the employee's W-4 form (Employee's Withholding Exemption Certificate). The amount that the employer withholds and remits to the government should be close to the employee's actual federal income tax liability. State income taxes require similar withholding procedures.
   c. Withholdings may also be made for pension plans, insurance premiums, union dues, and savings plans.

OBJECTIVE 2: Record transactions associated with payroll accounting (pp. Ap-56–Ap-59).

4. An employee's take-home pay equals his or her gross earnings less total withholdings. To help make payroll procedures easier, the company must keep a separate **employee earnings record** for each employee, listing all payroll data (earnings, deductions, and payment). Each year, the firm must inform the employee of his or her yearly earnings and withholdings on a W-2 form (Wage and Tax Statement). The employee uses this form to complete the individual tax return.

5. The **payroll register** is a detailed listing of the company's total payroll each payday. Each employee's name, regular and overtime hours, gross earnings, deductions, net pay and payroll classification are listed for that payroll period. The journal entry for recording the payroll is based on the column totals of the payroll register.

6. Independent of the employee's taxes, the employer must pay (a) FICA tax, (b) federal unemployment insurance taxes (FUTA), and

(c) state unemployment compensation taxes. These taxes are considered operating expenses, and require a debit to Payroll Tax Expense and a credit to each of the three tax liabilities.

7. To pay salaries, many companies use a special payroll bank account against which payroll checks are drawn. In addition, monthly or quarterly payments for withholdings must be made to the proper agencies.

Testing Your Knowledge

Matching

Match each term with its definition by writing the appropriate letter in the blank.

_____ 1. Wages

_____ 2. Salaries

_____ 3. Withholdings

_____ 4. FICA tax

_____ 5. W-2 form

_____ 6. W-4 form

_____ 7. Take-home pay

_____ 8. Employee earnings record

_____ 9. Payroll register

_____ 10. Payroll tax expense

a. A listing of payroll data for all employees for one payday

b. A tax paid by both the employer and the employee

c. Monthly or yearly pay to (usually) a manager or administrator

d. Gross earnings less total withholdings

e. A portion of earnings retained by the employer and remitted to appropriate agencies

f. A statement listing exemptions claimed

g. A yearly statement of earnings and withholdings

h. FICA and unemployment taxes levied on the employer

i. A record containing all payroll data for one employee

j. Hourly or piecework pay to an employee

Applying Your Knowledge

Exercise

1. Frank Nelson, an office worker who is paid $6.50 per hour, worked 40 hours during the week of May 7. FICA taxes are 7.65 percent, union dues are $5, state taxes withheld are $8, and federal income taxes withheld are $52. In addition, Nelson's employer must pay (on the basis of gross earnings) FICA taxes of 7.65 percent, federal unemployment taxes of 0.8 percent, and state unemployment taxes of 5.4 percent. Prepare journal entries that summarize Nelson's earnings for the week and that record the employer's payroll taxes. Round off amounts to the nearest cent.

General Journal				
Date		Description	Debit	Credit

APPENDIX E ACCOUNTING FOR BOND INVESTMENTS

Reviewing the Appendix

OBJECTIVE 1: Account for the purchase of bonds between interest dates (pp. Ap-64–Ap-65).

1. When bonds are purchased as long-term investments, the investment account is debited at cost (which includes broker's commission). Accrued Interest Receivable is debited for accrued interest since the last interest date, and Cash is credited for cash paid.

OBJECTIVE 2: Amortize the premium or discount of a bond (pp. Ap-65–Ap-67).

2. When interest is received on a bond investment, Cash is debited for cash received, Bond Interest Earned is credited for cash received plus the amortization of a bond discount or minus the amortization of a bond premium,

and the investment account is debited (when there is a discount) or credited (when there is a premium) to balance the entry. Prior entries to accrue interest may slightly alter the above entry. Under this method of amortization, a bond discount or bond premium account is not used.

OBJECTIVE 3: Account for the sale of bonds (p. Ap-67).

3. At the maturity date, the bond investment account should equal the maturity value. However, if the bonds are sold prior to maturity, a gain or loss should be recorded for the difference between cash received and the bonds' carrying value.

Applying Your Knowledge

Exercise

1. On March 1, 19x1, Alt Company purchased ten $1,000 Pamco bonds at 94 plus a broker's commission of $200 plus accrued interest. The bonds had a face interest of 8 4/10 percent and paid interest each January 1 and July 1. In the journal provided, prepare Alt Company's journal entries based on the following facts (advice: keep a running T account for Investment in Bonds):

March 1, 19x1	Purchased the bonds.
July 1, 19x1	Received the interest and amortized the discount or premium. Assume a 9 percent effective interest rate.
Dec. 31, 19x1	Recorded accrued interest and amortized the discount or premium.
Jan. 1, 19x2	Received the interest.
March 1, 19x2	Sold all ten bonds at 95 less a $200 commission.

General Journal			
Date	Description	Debit	Credit

SPECIMEN FINANCIAL STATEMENTS: COCA-COLA ENTERPRISES INC.

Source: Excerpts from the 1990 Annual Report of Coca-Cola Enterprises Inc. are reprinted with permission.

Specimen Financial Statements

The Financial Report from the 1990 Annual Report of Coca-Cola Enterprises Inc. is provided as a real example of the financial statement section of a major, well-known corporation. This complete set of financial statements, management's discussion and analysis, notes to the financial statements, report of the independent accountants, and other information are provided for students to see the end product of the accounting process. They may be used by instructors and students for discussion and illustration of the concepts, techniques, and statements presented in *Financial Accounting,* Fourth Edition.

1990 FINANCIAL REPORT

SELECTED FINANCIAL DATA

COCA-COLA ENTERPRISES INC.

(In thousands except per share data)

	1990[B]	1989[C]	1988[D]	1987[E]	Pro Forma 1986[F]	1986[G]
Summary of Operations					(unaudited)	
Net operating revenues	$4,034,043	$3,881,947	$3,874,445	$3,329,134	$3,191,418	$1,951,008
Cost of sales	2,359,267	2,313,032	2,268,038	1,916,724	1,872,304	1,137,720
Gross profit	1,674,776	1,568,915	1,606,407	1,412,410	1,319,114	813,288
Selling, general and administrative expenses	1,339,928	1,258,848	1,225,238	1,075,290	1,024,790	645,218
Provision for restructuring	9,300	–	27,000	–	–	–
Operating income	325,548	310,067	354,169	337,120	294,324	168,070
Interest income	6,566	6,564	8,505	11,566	10,485	6,327
Interest expense	(206,648)	(200,163)	(210,936)	(171,466)	(198,090)	(82,526)
Other income (deductions) – net	(519)	10,463	12,183	(4,445)	(8,626)	(7,101)
Gain on sale of operations	59,300	11,000	103,800	–	–	–
Income before income taxes	184,247	137,931	267,721	172,775	98,093	84,770
Provision for income taxes	90,834	66,207	115,120	84,403	77,344	56,978
Net income	93,413	71,724	152,601	88,372	20,749	27,792
Preferred stock dividend requirements	16,265	18,217	9,882	–	–	–
Net income available to common shareholders	$ 77,148	$ 53,507	$ 142,719	$ 88,372	$ 20,749	$ 27,792
Other Operating Data						
Depreciation expense	$ 149,434	$ 148,145	$ 143,160	$ 122,900	$ 107,663	$ 68,203
Amortization expense	$ 86,109	$ 80,874	$ 82,437	$ 71,633	$ 65,244	$ 24,095
Share and Per Share Data						
Average common shares outstanding	119,217	129,768	138,755	140,036	140,000	76,705
Net income per common share	$ 0.65	$ 0.41	$ 1.03	$ 0.63	$ 0.15	$ 0.36
Dividends per common share	$ 0.05	$ 0.05	$ 0.05	$ 0.05	$ –	$ –
Year-end Financial Position						
Property, plant and equipment – net	$1,372,747	$1,286,345	$1,179,737	$1,038,134	$ 849,537	$ 849,537
Goodwill and other intangible assets	3,046,871	2,878,928	2,935,334	2,690,950	2,460,569	2,460,569
Total assets	5,020,596	4,731,946	4,669,207	4,250,024	3,811,019	3,811,019
Long-term debt, excluding current maturities	1,960,164	1,755,626	2,062,022	2,091,089	1,779,796	1,779,796
Shareholders' equity	1,626,479	1,680,137	1,808,377	1,526,147	1,447,524	1,447,524
Total capital[H]	4,498,281	4,251,245	4,240,437	3,836,319	3,391,424	3,391,424

[A] Fiscal years presented are the 52-week periods ended December 28, 1990, December 29, 1989, December 30, 1988 and January 1, 1988; and the 53-week period ended January 2, 1987. All acquisitions and divestitures have been included in or excluded from (as the case may be) the consolidated operating results of the Company from their respective transaction dates.

[B] In February 1990, the Company sold its food service vending operations in Memphis, Tennessee. The Company acquired the Coca-Cola Bottling Company of the Islands and the A&W franchise rights for Monroe and Dade Counties in Florida in March 1990. In June 1990, the Company acquired the Coca-Cola Bottling Company of Arkansas and sold its majority interest in Coca-Cola Bottling Company of Ohio and its 100% ownership interest in Portsmouth Coca-Cola Bottling Company, Inc. In December 1990, the Company acquired Fort Myers Coca-Cola Bottling Company.

[C] In February 1989, the Company sold its wholly owned subsidiaries, Goodwill Bottling Ltd. and Goodwill Bottling North Ltd. (the "Goodwill Bottlers"). The outstanding common stock of the West Georgia Coca-Cola Bottlers,Inc. ("West Georgia CCBC") and the assets of the Coca-Cola Bottling Company of West Point-LaGrange ("CCBC of West Point-LaGrange") were acquired in April 1989. The Palestine Coca-Cola Bottling Company ("Palestine CCBC") was acquired in July 1989 and the Coca-Cola Bottling Company of Greenville, Inc. ("Greenville CCBC") was acquired in October 1989.

[D] The Coca-Cola Bottling Company of Memphis, Tenn. ("Memphis CCBC"), the Florida operations of The Coca-Cola Bottling Company of Miami, Inc. ("Miami CCBC"), and all of the Maryland and a portion of the Delaware operations of Delaware Coca-Cola Bottling Company, Inc. ("Delaware CCBC") were acquired in January 1988. In December 1988, the Company sold a wholly owned subsidiary, The Coca-Cola Bottling Company of Mid-America, Inc. ("Mid-America").

[E] Five Coca-Cola bottling companies, acquired from The Coca-Cola Company in July 1987 (the "Rainwater Bottlers"), and McAllen Coca-Cola Bottling Company and Brownsville Coca-Cola Bottling Company (the "Valley Bottlers"), were acquired in August 1987.

[F] The pro forma summary of operations gives effect to 1986 acquisitions as though they had been completed at the beginning of 1986.

[G] The Louisiana Coca-Cola Bottling Company, Ltd. ("Louisiana CCBC") and four bottling companies owned by the Barron family (the "Barron Companies") were acquired in February 1986 and July 1986, respectively. The JTL Affiliated Coca-Cola Bottling Companies (the "JTL Bottlers") and BCI Holdings Corporation (the "Beatrice Bottlers") were acquired in September 1986.

[H] Total capital includes total debt (net of cash and cash equivalents), long-term deferred income taxes and shareholders' equity.

18

MANAGEMENT'S DISCUSSION AND ANALYSIS OF FINANCIAL CONDITION AND RESULTS OF OPERATIONS

COCA-COLA ENTERPRISES INC.

Description of Business

Coca-Cola Enterprises Inc. (the "Company") produces, packages and distributes soft drink products of The Coca-Cola Company and other companies through exclusive and perpetual rights to approximately 40% of the United States population. The business of the Company includes the operations of certain soft drink bottlers contributed to the Company by The Coca-Cola Company in 1986 combined with subsequent acquisitions. The Company was a wholly owned subsidiary of The Coca-Cola Company until November 21, 1986, at which time 51% of the Company's common shares were sold by the Company in a public offering. Since such date, The Coca-Cola Company has owned approximately 49% of the Company's outstanding common shares.

The Company seeks to manage its business to enhance long-term cash flow from operations through balancing growth in sales volume, net price and cost. The Company also seeks to utilize financial leverage and cash flow generated from operations to support capital expenditures and possible future acquisitions. The Company intends to acquire additional bottling businesses that offer the Company an acceptable rate of return on such long-term investments and an opportunity to effectively continue to implement its operating strategies.

Operating Results

Net Operating Revenues and Operating Income

Net operating revenues for 1990 increased by 4% over 1989 primarily due to a unit volume increase of approximately 3% and improvements in net pricing for case sales to retailers of approximately 3%. Assuming that the acquisition of the Arkansas operations had occurred at the beginning of 1989, volume would have increased by approximately 4% for fiscal year 1990. Revenues other than from case sales to retailers in 1990 decreased primarily as a result of (i) reduced fountain syrup delivery program activity and (ii) the sale of the Company's Memphis food service vending operations. Net operating revenues for 1989 approximated that of 1988 due to an approximate 1% decrease in unit volume offset by an approximate 1% increase in net revenues per unit. Assuming that the sale of Mid-America had occurred at the beginning of 1988, volume would have increased by approximately 4% for fiscal year 1989.

The Company's increases in constant territory unit volume of 4% in 1990 and 1989 exceeded industry averages

in both years. The Company's long-term strategy will be to continue (i) to seek volume gains greater than those enjoyed by both its principal competitor and the soft drink industry as a whole; (ii) to maintain or increase its market share; and (iii) to attain appropriate price increases in the market while remaining price competitive. Management believes that these strategies are important to the development of the Company and in the long term will maximize operating cash flow (operating income before depreciation and amortization).

Operating cash flow and operating income in 1990 increased over 1989 by approximately 4.1% and 5.0%, respectively, primarily due to favorable pricing and unit volume experienced during the year. While per unit cost of sales increased approximately 1% in 1990 over 1989, the increases in both unit volume and pricing more than offset the aggregate dollar increase in cost of sales. Operating results for 1990 include certain one-time selling, general and administrative charges discussed below that had the effect of reducing comparisons to 1989.

The Company realized reduced operating cash flow and operating income in 1989 compared to 1988 primarily due to (i) the sale of Mid-America, (ii) increased per unit selling, general and administrative expenses and (iii) increased cost of sales per unit.

Selling, General and Administrative Expenses

Selling, general and administrative expenses on a per unit basis increased in 1990 over 1989 primarily due to (i) a $12 million one-time charge related to replacement and repair of certain underground fuel storage tanks expected to be incurred during the next several years; (ii) incremental reserves of $10 million established for potentially uncollectible trade accounts receivable; (iii) a $9.3 million restructuring charge; and (iv) increased marketing costs (net of support from soft drink licensors). Unit volume related net marketing costs paid by the Company increased in 1990 compared to 1989 by an amount approximately equal to 1% of related net sales income. Such marketing efforts support growth in unit volume while allowing the Company to attain increased net price realization. Selling, general and administrative expenses on a per unit volume basis increased in 1989 compared to 1988 primarily as a result of greater marketing costs (net of support from soft drink licensors).

The Company owns and operates more than 17,000 vehicles that include delivery trucks, vans and automobiles

19

used in the sale and distribution of its products. While the Company is subject to fluctuations in the price of fuel, management does not believe such fluctuations will have a significant effect on results of operations.

In December 1990, the Financial Accounting Standards Board issued Statement of Financial Accounting Standards No. 106, "Employers' Accounting for Postretirement Benefits Other Than Pensions." This Statement, which requires adoption by 1993, will change the Company's current practice of accounting for postretirement benefits to require accrual of the costs of such benefits for Company employees during the years such employees render service to the Company. The Company is evaluating the effects of the adoption of this Statement.

Environmental Issues

During 1990, the Company finalized review of a multiyear plan for remediation and maintenance of its underground fuel storage tanks. The Company estimates that an aggregate $71 million will be incurred by the Company from 1990 to 1993 for expenditures related to Federal and State requirements for maintenance and use of such underground tanks. Of such amount, an aggregate $16 million represents capital expenditures during 1990 and approximately $43 million is estimated to represent capitalized expenditures during 1991, 1992 and 1993. The remaining amount of $12 million relates to costs which are noncapitalized expenditures the Company anticipates to incur during the four-year program. The Company recognized such $12 million during 1990 as a one-time charge against earnings, classifying such amount as selling, general and administrative expenses. Except for the depreciation costs attributable to capitalized expenditures, the Company does not anticipate any material expense in future years relating to this issue.

Provision for and Effects of Restructuring

The Company recognized a $9.3 million provision for restructuring in 1990 principally to provide for the planned standardization of the Company's information systems operations. A $27 million provision for restructuring was also recognized in 1988 principally to provide for costs related to consolidation and relocation of certain manufacturing and administrative facilities and the write-down of certain property, plant and equipment and other assets.

The consolidation and restructuring of the Company's operations has resulted in (i) beneficial cost trends for certain packaging and raw materials; (ii) increased operating efficiency and productivity; (iii) increased ability to attain net price realization; and (iv) substantial opportunities to realize future operating economies. These beneficial effects are expected to continue through 1991 and into the foreseeable future.

Interest Expense

Net interest expense increased in 1990 over 1989 primarily due to higher average debt balances partially offset by the effects of lower average interest rates in 1990. The higher debt balances in 1990 reflect the costs of financing capital expenditures, share repurchases and the June 1990 acquisition of the Arkansas operations, which were partially offset by the benefit obtained from applying the proceeds of the June 1990 divestiture of the Company's Ohio operations. Net interest expense decreased in 1989 over 1988 primarily due to lower average debt balances partially offset by the effects of higher average interest rates in 1989. The lower debt balances in 1989 reflect the use of proceeds from the sale of Mid-America in December 1988 and the issuance of $250 million of variable rate preferred stock in May 1988. Favorable interest rate comparisons between 1990 and 1989 acted to offset the incremental debt incurred to finance the Company's share repurchase program. The Company's blended borrowing rates for 1990 and 1989 were approximately 8.4% and 8.9%, respectively. Management believes the Company's blended borrowing rate for 1991 will be between 8% and 8.5%.

Other Income (Deductions)

Other income (net) in 1990 includes an approximate $2.5 million gain on the repurchase of certain of the Company's outstanding Notes and Debentures. Such amounts in 1989 included (i) an approximate $7 million gain on the repurchase of an aggregate $90 million in face value of certain of the Company's outstanding Notes, Debentures, Medium-Term Notes and Eurobonds; (ii) an approximate $5.9 million gain on the sale-leaseback of certain real property; and (iii) an aggregate $6.5 million benefit resulting from the favorable resolution of certain liabilities initially established for acquisitions made by the Company.

Sale of Operations

In February 1990, the Company completed the sale of its food service vending operations in Memphis, Tennessee for $11 million, resulting in a pretax gain of approximately $3.7 million. In June 1990, the Company completed the sale

20

of its majority interest in its Ohio operations for approximately $122 million, resulting in a pretax gain of approximately $55.6 million. In February 1989, the Company completed the sale of the Goodwill Bottlers for approximately $27 million, resulting in a pretax gain of approximately $11 million. In December 1988, the Company sold a wholly owned bottler, Mid-America, for approximately $282.3 million, resulting in a pretax gain of approximately $103.8 million. The Ohio operations and Mid-America were sold to The Johnston Coca-Cola Bottling Group Inc. The Coca-Cola Company owns an approximate 22% interest in such purchaser and has representation on its Board of Directors.

Income Taxes

The Company's effective tax rates for 1990, 1989 and 1988 were 49.3%, 48% and 43%, respectively. The higher effective rates for 1990 and 1989 reflect lower pretax earnings as compared to 1988. Since a portion of the Company's goodwill amortization is nondeductible for tax purposes, the effective tax rate increases as lower pretax earnings are recognized. Acquisitions, divestitures and State income tax effects have also contributed to the fluctuations in the Company's effective tax rate.

The Financial Accounting Standards Board issued in 1987, Statement of Financial Accounting Standards No. 96, "Accounting for Income Taxes." The Financial Accounting Standards Board is currently considering certain amendments to this Statement including a delay in the required adoption date to 1993. The Company continues to evaluate the effects of the adoption of this Statement, which it currently expects to adopt in 1993.

Other Factors

The Company has participated in arrangements with The Coca-Cola Company since 1987 whereby the Company purchases substantial amounts of its high fructose corn syrup requirements from The Coca-Cola Company. This arrangement has been extended through 1991. The Company has also contracted with The Coca-Cola Company to manufacture through 1991, in selected locations, syrup from the Company's concentrate and sweeteners for a fee.

Effective January 1, 1990 and January 1, 1991, respectively, The Coca-Cola Company increased prices of its concentrates and syrups sold to the Company under the Bottle Contracts by approximately 3.5% and 3.9% and the prices of its concentrates

and syrups sold to the Company under post-mix distributorship appointments by approximately 9% and 6%. These 1990 price changes increased by approximately $22 million the amount the Company paid to The Coca-Cola Company in 1990 for comparable volumes of concentrate and syrup purchased in 1989 under the Bottle Contracts and by approximately $12 million the amount the Company paid to The Coca-Cola Company in 1990 for comparable volumes of syrup and concentrate purchased in 1989 under the post-mix distributorship appointments. The 1991 price changes will increase by approximately $24 million the amount the Company will pay to The Coca-Cola Company in 1991 for comparable volumes of concentrate and syrup purchased in 1990 under the Bottle Contracts and by approximately $8 million the amount the Company will pay to The Coca-Cola Company in 1991 for comparable volumes of syrup and concentrate purchased in 1990 under the post-mix distributorship appointments. Under the Bottle Contracts, The Coca-Cola Company has no rights to establish the resale prices at which any of the Company bottlers sell their products.

Financial Position

At December 28, 1990, total cash and cash equivalents amounted to $0.5 million, a decrease of $9.2 million compared to December 29, 1989. The Company's primary sources of cash in 1990 consisted of (i) funds provided from operations ($332.1 million); (ii) proceeds from the sale of certain operations ($92.9 million); and (iii) the issuance by the Company of certain long-term debt ($1,076.2 million). The Company's primary uses of cash in 1990 consisted of (i) costs associated with additions to property, plant and equipment ($259.2 million); (ii) acquisition of bottling companies ($267.9 million); (iii) the purchase of common stock for treasury ($134.4 million); and (iv) payments on long-term debt ($848.6 million).

The Company's commercial paper program is supported by a revolving bank credit agreement, which is in effect until February 18, 1992. Maximum borrowing capacity under the agreement is $550 million. There are no borrowings currently outstanding under this agreement; however, under the commercial paper program supported by this agreement, there was $438.1 million outstanding at December 28, 1990.

In 1990, the Company repurchased approximately $54.1 million in face amount of certain of its outstanding long-term debt. These transactions resulted in an aggregate pretax gain of approximately $2.5 million.

21

COCA-COLA ENTERPRISES INC.

In June 1990, the Company acquired Coca-Cola Bottling Company of Arkansas from The Coca-Cola Company for approximately $250 million. The Company also acquired two other bottling operations and certain franchise rights for purchase prices aggregating approximately $32 million. The Company intends to maintain a program of acquisitions that satisfies its strategic objectives of providing an acceptable rate of return on such long-term investments and an opportunity to effectively continue to implement its operating strategies.

The percentage of total debt (net of cash and cash equivalents) to total capital was 56% and 54% at December 28, 1990 and December 29, 1989, respectively. Total capital is defined by the Company as total debt, long-term deferred income taxes and shareholders' equity.

In December 1990, the Company announced a share repurchase program of up to 15 million shares of its common stock. Shares will be repurchased by the Company over time and the timing for execution of such repurchase transactions will be a function of relative share price and debt to total capital ratios. When the Company's debt to total capital ratio is below 55%, resources will be allocated to share repurchase after discretionary capital expenditures and strategic acquisitions. When the debt to capital ratio is at 55% or above, shares will only be repurchased if they are trading at what is considered to be a significantly attractive multiple of operating cash flow. Approximately equal numbers of shares will be repurchased from the public and The Coca-Cola Company in order to maintain The Coca-Cola Company's current 49% ownership interest in the Company.

Also in December 1990, the Company completed a 25 million share repurchase program initiated in December 1988. Under this program, the Company repurchased approximately 8.9 million shares in 1990, 10.8 million shares in 1989 and 5.3 million in 1988, at a cost, (including commissions) of $134.4 million, $176.9 million and $88.9 million, respectively.

The increase in investments and other long-term assets is principally due to an aggregate $40 million of notes receivable obtained as partial proceeds from the sale of the Company's Ohio operations. Construction in progress increased during 1990 over 1989 primarily due to increased purchases of information systems equipment and activity related to the remediation of the Company's underground fuel storage tanks. Goodwill and other intangible assets increased during 1990 over 1989 primarily due to the acquisition of the Arkansas operations partially offset by amortization and the effects from divestitures. Increases in accrued compensation and accrued advertising were the primary components of the change in accounts payable and accrued expenses in 1990 compared to 1989. Accounts payable to The Coca-Cola Company decreased primarily as a result of timing of the receipt of marketing support payments. Other long-term obligations increased primarily due to additional insurance reserves established in 1990. The increase in long-term debt reflects funding for the acquisition of the Arkansas operations, partially offset by proceeds from the sale of the Ohio operations.

Management of the Company believes that, in addition to current financial resources available (cash and cash equivalents and the Company's commercial paper program), adequate capital resources are available to satisfy the Company's capital expenditure and acquisition programs. Such sources of capital would include, but not be limited to, domestic and foreign bank borrowings and the issuance of public or privately placed debt or certain equity securities. Management believes that the Company is able to generate sufficient cash flow to maintain its current operations.

22

CONSOLIDATED STATEMENTS OF INCOME

COCA-COLA ENTERPRISES INC.

(In thousands except per share data)		Fiscal Year	
	1990	1989	1988
Net Operating Revenues	**$4,034,043**	$3,881,947	$3,874,445
Cost of sales	**2,359,267**	2,313,032	2,268,038
Gross Profit	**1,674,776**	1,568,915	1,606,407
Selling, general and administrative expenses	**1,339,928**	1,258,848	1,225,238
Provision for restructuring	**9,300**	–	27,000
Operating Income	**325,548**	310,067	354,169
Nonoperating income (deductions):			
Interest income	**6,566**	6,564	8,505
Interest expense	**(206,648)**	(200,163)	(210,936)
Other income (deductions) – net	**(519)**	10,463	12,183
Gain on sale of operations	**59,300**	11,000	103,800
Income Before Income Taxes	**184,247**	137,931	267,721
Provision for income taxes	**90,834**	66,207	115,120
Net Income	**93,413**	71,724	152,601
Preferred stock dividend requirements	**16,265**	18,217	9,882
Net Income Available to Common Shareholders	**$ 77,148**	$ 53,507	$ 142,719
Average Common Shares Outstanding	**119,217**	129,768	138,755
Net Income Per Common Share	**$ 0.65**	$ 0.41	$ 1.03

The accompanying Notes to Consolidated Financial Statements are an integral part of these statements.

Coca-Cola Enterprises Inc.

CONSOLIDATED BALANCE SHEETS

Coca-Cola Enterprises Inc.

(In thousands except share data)	**December 28, 1990**	December 29, 1989
ASSETS		
Current		
Cash and cash equivalents, at cost (approximates market)	**$ 507**	$ 9,674
Trade accounts receivable, less allowances of $18,754 and $13,472, respectively	**296,822**	297,098
Inventories	**128,450**	127,880
Prepaid expenses and other assets	**69,562**	58,735
Total Current Assets	**495,341**	493,387
Investments and Other Long-Term Assets	**105,637**	73,286
Property, Plant and Equipment		
Land	**157,008**	129,591
Buildings and improvements	**453,100**	427,206
Machinery and equipment	**1,302,938**	1,243,969
Containers	**37,238**	34,830
	1,950,284	1,835,596
Less allowances for depreciation	**723,856**	665,999
	1,226,428	1,169,597
Construction in progress	**146,319**	116,748
	1,372,747	1,286,345
Goodwill and Other Intangible Assets	**3,046,871**	2,878,928
	$5,020,596	$4,731,946

The accompanying Notes to Consolidated Financial Statements are an integral part of these balance sheets.

24

LIABILITIES AND SHAREHOLDERS' EQUITY

Current

Accounts payable and accrued expenses	$ **456,765**	$ 395,069
Accounts payable to The Coca-Cola Company	**21,396**	51,657
Loans and notes payable and current maturities of long-term debt	**576,630**	549,396
Total Current Liabilities	**1,054,791**	996,122
Long-Term Debt	**1,960,164**	1,755,626
Deferred Income Taxes	**335,008**	266,086
Other Long-Term Obligations	**44,154**	33,975

Shareholders' Equity

Preferred stock, $1 par value		
Authorized — 100,000,000 shares;		
Issued and outstanding — 2,500 shares, at aggregate liquidation preference	**250,000**	250,000
Common stock, $1 par value		
Authorized — 500,000,000 shares;		
Issued — 140,471,081 shares and 140,363,166 shares, respectively	**140,471**	140,363
Paid-in capital	**1,262,755**	1,262,288
Reinvested earnings	**382,243**	311,198
Common stock in treasury, at cost 25,636,358 shares and 17,317,010 shares, respectively	**(408,990)**	(283,712)
	1,626,479	1,680,137
	$5,020,596	$4,731,946

Coca-Cola Enterprises Inc.

25

CONSOLIDATED STATEMENTS OF SHAREHOLDERS' EQUITY

COCA-COLA ENTERPRISES INC.

(In thousands except per share data)

Three Fiscal Years ended December 28, 1990	Number of Shares — Common Stock	Preferred Stock	Treasury Stock	Amount — Common Stock	Preferred Stock	Paid-in Capital	Reinvested Earnings	Treasury Stock	Total Shareholders Equity
Balance January 1, 1988	140,260	–	472	$140,260	$ –	$1,264,965	$127,513	$ 6,591	$1,526,147
Forfeit of awards under stock award plan	–	–	10	–	–	–	–	154	(154)
Purchase of common stock for treasury	–	–	7,327	–	–	–	–	106,341	(106,341)
Issuance of shares to employee savings investment plan	–	–	(430)	–	–	350	–	(5,995)	6,345
Sale of preferred stock in public offering	–	2	–	–	250,000	(4,501)	–	–	245,499
Dividends on preferred stock (per share - $3,512.72)	–	–	–	–	–	–	(8,782)	–	(8,782)
Dividends on common stock (per share - $0.05)	–	–	–	–	–	–	(6,938)	–	(6,938)
Net income	–	–	–	–	–	–	152,601	–	152,601
Balance December 30, 1988	140,260	2	7,379	140,260	250,000	1,260,814	264,394	107,091	1,808,377
Issuance of shares to employee savings investment plan	–	–	(819)	–	–	1,339	–	(12,127)	13,466
Issuance of shares under stock award plan	103	–	–	103	–	1,749	–	–	1,852
Unamortized cost of restricted shares	–	–	–	–	–	(1,614)	–	–	(1,614)
Purchase of common stock for treasury	–	–	10,757	–	–	–	–	176,944	(176,944)
Adjusting payment under share repurchase program	–	–	–	–	–	–	–	11,804	(11,804)
Dividends on preferred stock (per share - $7,389.08)	–	–	–	–	–	–	(18,473)	–	(18,473)
Dividends on common stock (per share - $0.05)	–	–	–	–	–	–	(6,447)	–	(6,447)
Net income	–	–	–	–	–	–	71,724	–	71,724
Balance December 29, 1989	140,363	2	17,317	140,363	250,000	1,262,288	311,198	283,712	1,680,137
Purchase of common stock for treasury	–	–	8,944	–	–	–	–	134,406	(134,406)
Issuance of shares to employee savings investment plan	–	–	(625)	–	–	185	–	(9,128)	9,313
Exercise of employee stock options	21	–	–	21	–	279	–	–	300
Issuance of shares under stock award plan	87	–	–	87	–	1,181	–	–	1,268
Unamortized cost of restricted shares	–	–	–	–	–	(1,178)	–	–	(1,178)
Dividends on preferred stock (per share - $6,569.73)	–	–	–	–	–	–	(16,424)	–	(16,424)
Dividends on common stock (per share - $0.05)	–	–	–	–	–	–	(5,944)	–	(5,944)
Net income	–	–	–	–	–	–	93,413	–	93,413
Balance December 28, 1990	140,471	2	25,636	$140,471	$250,000	$1,262,755	$382,243	$408,990	$1,626,479

The accompanying Notes to Consolidated Financial Statements are an integral part of these statements.

26

Specimen Financial Statements

CONSOLIDATED STATEMENTS OF CASH FLOWS

COCA-COLA ENTERPRISES INC.

(In thousands)		Fiscal Year	
	1990	1989	1988
Cash Flows From Operating Activities			
Net Income	**$ 93,413**	$ 71,724	$152,601
Adjustments to reconcile net income to net cash provided by operating activities:			
Depreciation	**149,434**	148,145	143,160
Amortization	**86,109**	80,874	82,437
Deferred income taxes	**76,332**	50,902	96,701
Decrease (increase) in current assets and current liabilities	**(10,257)**	50,631	(15,166)
Gain on sale of operations	**(59,300)**	(11,000)	(103,800)
Decrease (increase) in other noncurrent assets	**4,179**	(12,836)	(4,104)
Decrease in deferred income taxes	**–**	–	(8,938)
Gain on repurchase of debt	**(2,480)**	(7,048)	(8,489)
Other nonoperating cash flows	**(5,338)**	(24,326)	(26,336)
Net cash provided by operating activities	**332,092**	347,066	308,066
Cash Flows From Financing Activities			
Proceeds from the issuance of loans and notes payable	**250,000**	–	–
Proceeds from the issuance of long-term debt	**826,166**	505,699	387,796
Purchase of common stock for treasury	**(134,406)**	(188,748)	(106,341)
Payments on long-term debt	**(848,646)**	(408,471)	(426,338)
Sale of common stock	**300**	204	–
Reissuance of treasury stock	**9,313**	13,466	6,345
Issuance of preferred stock	**–**	–	245,499
Dividends on common and preferred stock	**(22,368)**	(24,920)	(15,720)
Net cash provided by (used in) financing activities	**80,359**	(102,770)	91,241
Cash Flows From Investing Activities			
Capital expenditures	**(259,195)**	(273,059)	(273,121)
Proceeds from the sale of property, plant and equipment	**12,553**	31,779	19,459
Acquisitions of companies, net of cash acquired	**(267,895)**	(21,833)	(461,542)
Proceeds from the sale of operations	**92,919**	28,329	304,762
Net cash used in investing activities	**(421,618)**	(234,784)	(410,442)
Net increase (decrease) in cash and cash equivalents	**(9,167)**	9,512	(11,135)
Cash and cash equivalents at beginning of year	**9,674**	162	11,297
Cash and cash equivalents at end of year	**$ 507**	$ 9,674	$ 162

The accompanying Notes to Consolidated Financial Statements are an integral part of these statements.

27

Ownership and Reorganization

The Company operates in a single industry segment, which encompasses the manufacture, distribution and marketing of soft drink products. The Company is the successor to Coca-Cola Bottling Enterprises, Inc., which transferred substantially all of its assets to the Company in September 1986, in a corporate reorganization. The Company was a wholly owned subsidiary of The Coca-Cola Company until November 21, 1986, at which time 51% of the Company's common shares were sold by the Company in a public offering. Since such date, The Coca-Cola Company has owned approximately 49% of the Company's outstanding common shares.

Principal Accounting Policies

The significant accounting policies and practices followed by the Company and its subsidiaries are as follows:

Basis of Presentation

The consolidated financial statements include the accounts of the Company, its wholly owned subsidiaries, and its majority-owned subsidiary (Coca-Cola Bottling Company of Ohio) through the date of its sale by the Company in June 1990. Minority interests related to partially owned subsidiaries are not material.

All significant intercompany accounts and transactions are eliminated in consolidation. The fiscal years presented are the 52-week periods ended December 28, 1990, December 29, 1989 and December 30, 1988. Certain reclassifications have been made to 1989 and 1988 amounts to conform to the 1990 presentation.

Cash Equivalents

Cash equivalents include all highly liquid debt instruments purchased with a maturity of less than three months.

Inventories

Inventories are valued at the lower of cost or market. Cost is computed principally on the last-in, first-out (LIFO) method.

Property, Plant and Equipment

Property, plant and equipment is stated at cost, less allowance for depreciation. Depreciation expense is determined principally by the straight-line method. The annual rates of depreciation are 2% to 5% for buildings and improvements; 5% for land improvements; and 7% to 34% for machinery and equipment. The Company capitalizes, as land improvements, certain environmental contamination treatment costs which improve the condition of the property as compared with the condition when constructed or acquired.

Goodwill and Other Intangible Assets

Goodwill and other intangible assets are stated on the basis of cost and are amortized, principally on a straight-line basis, over the estimated future periods to be benefited (primarily 40 years). Accumulated amortization amounted to $334.8 million and $253.2 million at December 28, 1990 and December 29, 1989, respectively.

Interest Rate Hedging Agreements

In the management of its interest rate exposure, the Company is party to a variety of interest rate swaps, short positions in interest rate futures and has sold debt warrants deemed as interest rate hedges. For interest rate swap agreements, the interest differential is recognized as an adjustment of interest expense. Realized and unrealized gains and losses on all financial instruments designated and effective as hedges of interest rate exposure are deferred and recognized as increases or decreases to interest expense over the lives of the hedged liabilities.

Deferred Income Taxes

Deferred income taxes are provided on timing differences at the tax rates in effect upon origination. The Company has not elected early adoption of Financial Accounting Standards Board Statement of Financial Accounting Standards No. 96, ("Accounting for Income Taxes"). The Company continues to evaluate the effects on the Company of this Statement, which is scheduled for adoption in 1993.

Acquisitions and Divestitures

In June 1990, the Company acquired the outstanding common stock and business of Coca-Cola Bottling Company of Arkansas from The Coca-Cola Company in a transaction accounted for under the purchase method of accounting. The purchase price approximated $250 million in cash and debt. In separate transactions in 1990, the Company also acquired (i) the assets and business of Coca-Cola Bottling Company of the Islands located in Massachusetts; (ii) the A&W franchise rights for Monroe and Dade Counties in Florida; and (iii) the outstanding common stock of Fort Myers Coca-Cola Bottling Company in Florida. These acquisitions, which were accounted for under the purchase method of

28

accounting, were acquired for an aggregate purchase price of approximately $32 million in cash and notes. The territories acquired include portions of Arkansas, Florida, Louisiana, Massachusetts and Texas. The operating results for the companies acquired in 1990 have been included in the Company's consolidated statements of income from their respective dates of acquisition and did not significantly affect the Company's operating results for the year.

Also in 1990, the Company sold in separate transactions (i) its food service vending operations in Memphis, Tennessee for approximately $11 million in cash and (ii) its majority ownership interest in Coca-Cola Bottling Company of Ohio and 100% ownership interest in Portsmouth Coca-Cola Bottling Company, Inc. for approximately $122 million in cash and notes. These transactions resulted in pretax gains of approximately $3.7 million and $55.6 million, respectively. The Coca-Cola Company owns an approximate 22% equity ownership interest in the purchaser of the Ohio operations and has representation on its Board of Directors.

In separate transactions in 1989, the Company acquired (i) the outstanding common stock of the Coca-Cola Bottling Company of Greenville, Inc.; (ii) the assets and business of Palestine Coca-Cola Bottling Company; (iii) the outstanding common stock of West Georgia Coca-Cola Bottlers, Inc.; and (iv) the assets and business of the Coca-Cola Bottling Company of West Point-LaGrange. These acquisitions, which were accounted for under the purchase method of accounting, were acquired for an aggregate purchase price of $24.5 million in cash and notes. The territories acquired include portions of Alabama, Georgia and Texas. The operating results for the acquired companies have been included in the Company's consolidated statements of income from their respective dates of acquisition and did not significantly affect the Company's operating results for the year.

In February 1989, the Company sold its wholly owned subsidiaries, Goodwill Bottling Ltd. and Goodwill Bottling North Ltd. (the "Goodwill Bottlers"), for approximately $27 million in cash, resulting in a pretax gain of approximately $11 million. The Goodwill Bottlers' territories include Vancouver Island and portions of Northern British Columbia, Canada. The Coca-Cola Company owns an approximate 49% equity ownership interest in the purchaser and has representation on its Board of Directors.

In January 1988, the Company acquired Memphis

CCBC, Miami CCBC and a portion of Delaware CCBC in a transaction accounted for under the purchase method of accounting. These operations were purchased from The Coca-Cola Company for approximately $518 million in cash and debt. The acquired territories include portions of Arkansas, Delaware, Florida, Maryland, Mississippi and Tennessee. Also during 1988, the Company acquired substantially all of the assets of a bottling company in Texas and the license rights to produce and distribute various Barq's beverages in a portion of Louisiana for an aggregate purchase price of $9.2 million in cash and notes.

In December 1988, the Company sold a wholly owned bottler, Mid-America, for approximately $282.3 million in cash, resulting in a pretax gain of approximately $103.8 million. The Coca-Cola Company owns an approximate 22% interest in the purchaser and has representation on its Board of Directors.

Inventories are comprised of the following (in thousands):

	December 28, 1990	December 29, 1989
Finished goods	$ 88,411	$ 83,808
Raw materials	34,714	35,509
Other	13,348	15,474
	136,473	134,791
Less LIFO reserve	(8,023)	(6,911)
	$128,450	$127,880

Accounts Payable and Accrued Expenses are comprised of the following (in thousands):

	December 28, 1990	December 29, 1989
Trade accounts payable	$234,873	$219,087
Deposits on containers and shells	21,247	17,580
Accrued advertising payable	45,781	25,182
Accrued compensation payable	51,550	33,447
Accrued insurance payable	25,567	26,366
Accrued interest payable	34,311	33,972
Other accrued expenses	43,436	39,435
	$456,765	$395,069

29

COCA-COLA ENTERPRISES INC.

Long-Term Debt consists of the following (in thousands):

	December 28, 1990	December 29, 1989
Commercial Paper	$ 438,121	$ 691,159
8.25% Notes, due 1990	–	98,787
8.85% Notes, due 1990	–	100,000
Floating Rate Notes, due 1991 (7.82% at December 28, 1990)	250,000	–
8.50% Notes, due 1991	150,337	150,906
8.75% Notes, due 1992	150,674	151,013
8.00% Notes, due 1993	249,808	–
8.20% Notes, due 1993	249,047	–
U.S. Dollar Equivalent Floating Rate Australian Notes, due 1993 (7.82% at December 28, 1990)	47,885	–
8.35% Notes, due 1995	248,811	–
7.875% Notes, due 1997	249,623	253,040
8.75% Debentures, due 2017	153,320	173,193
Notes with weighted average interest rates of 8.35% maturing within one year	161,700	338,350
Notes with weighted average interest rates of 8.53% maturing within one to three years	71,680	179,700
Notes with weighted average interest rates of 9.44% maturing within three to twenty-eight years	60,750	114,430
9.55% Senior Promissory Notes, due in varying annual installments from 1991 to 1995 (total face value of $9,818 with stated interest rate of 15.136%)	10,569	12,350
Capital lease obligations	8,825	11,955
Other long-term debt and notes payable	35,644	30,139
	2,536,794	2,305,022
Less current maturities	576,630	549,396
	$1,960,164	$1,755,626

Maturities of long-term debt and capital leases for the five fiscal years subsequent to December 28, 1990, are as follows (in thousands): 1991 – $576,630; 1992 – $616,026; 1993 – $611,307; 1994 – $33,099; and 1995 – $258,617.

The Company's commercial paper program is supported by a revolving bank credit agreement (the "1987 Credit Agreement") in effect until February 18, 1992. The borrowing capacity available under the 1987 Credit Agreement at December 28, 1990 was $550 million. There are no borrowings currently outstanding under this agreement; however, under the commercial paper program supported by this agreement there was $438 million outstanding at December 28, 1990. The weighted average interest rates of borrowings through the commercial paper program, including the effects of hedging activities, were approximately 7.9% and 9.1% for fiscal years 1990 and 1989, respectively. The Company had hedged a significant amount of its floating interest rate exposure for 1991 through short positions in Eurodollar futures.

At December 28, 1990, the Company had outstanding four interest rate swap agreements with banks relating to certain of its long-term debt other than commercial paper. Two of these agreements for contract amounts aggregating $100 million relate to its floating rate Medium-Term Notes. Another swap in the amount of $250 million relates to the Floating Rate Notes due in 1991. The remaining agreement for a contract amount of approximately $47.9 million relates to the Company's 14% Australian dollar notes due in 1993. The interest rate swap agreements effectively change the Company's interest rate exposure on $100 million floating rate Medium-Term Notes due in 1991 to fixed rates averaging 8.4% and the interest rate exposure on $250 million Floating Rate Notes due in 1991 to a LIBOR based floating rate, which averaged 8.1% during 1990. The swap agreement converts the 14% fixed rate Australian dollar obligation to a LIBOR based floating rate, which averaged 8.1% during 1990.

The Company also has outstanding an interest rate swap agreement with a bank for a contract amount of $150 million under which the Company pays fixed rates averaging 8.5%. This swap hedges a portion of the Company's floating rate commercial paper program through at least 1992.

In separate January 1990 transactions, the Company issued $250 million of 8% Notes due January 1993 and $100 million (Australian) of 14% Notes due January 1993. Simultaneously with these respective transactions, the Company (i) sold warrants to purchase debt, the effect of which, if any, will permit the extension of the maturity of the 8% Notes and (ii) entered into a currency and interest rate exchange agreement which hedged the Company's Australian dollar liability, creating a U.S. dollar liability at a floating interest rate less than the Company's unhedged commercial paper borrowing rates. In April 1990, the Company issued $250 million of Floating Rate Notes due April 1991.

In June 1990, the Company issued $250 million of

30

8.35% Notes due June 1995. In conjunction with the issuance of the 8.35% Notes, the Company sold debt warrants, the effect of which will permit the extension of the maturity of the 8.35% Notes on a zero-coupon basis for five or twenty-five additional years. The warrants also grant to their holders the right to a one-time cash payment in 1995 by the Company in lieu of exercise if the senior debt securities of the Company are rated noninvestment grade and if long-term interest rates have declined significantly.

In August 1990, the Company filed a registration statement with the Securities and Exchange Commission enabling the Company to issue to the public up to $1 billion of debt, warrants to purchase debt, and currency warrants. In November 1990, the Company issued $250 million of 8.2% Notes due November 1993 with warrants to purchase an additional $250 million of 8.2% three-year Notes due July 1994.

The Company's 8.75% Notes due 1992 and 8.5% Notes due 1991 were issued outside of the United States and are redeemable at the Company's option under certain conditions pertaining to changes in United States and foreign tax laws.

In 1990, the Company repurchased approximately $23.5 million in face amount certain of its outstanding fixed rate long-term debt. Such debt included Notes and Debentures with maturities ranging from 1997 to 2017 and bearing a weighted average interest rate of approximately 8.6%. These transactions resulted in an aggregate pretax gain of approximately $2.3 million.

In addition, the Company repurchased approximately $39 million (Australian) in face amount of the Australian Notes resulting in a pretax gain of approximately $0.2 million. Concurrently the Company terminated currency and interest rate exchange agreements associated with such debt.

In 1989, the Company repurchased approximately $90 million in face amount of certain of its outstanding long-term debt. Such debt included Notes, Debentures, Medium-Term Notes and Eurobonds with an average maturity (excluding sinking fund requirements) of 2016 and bearing a weighted average interest rate of approximately 9%. These transactions were initially funded by borrowings under the Company's commercial paper program and resulted in an aggregate pretax gain of approximately $7 million.

In 1988, the Company repurchased for cash and 9.55% Senior Promissory Notes certain of its outstanding debt. These transactions resulted in a pretax gain of approximately $8.5 million.

Approximately 64% of the Company's debt (net of cash and cash equivalents) at December 28, 1990 was at rates fixed at least through 1991.

The Company is exposed to credit losses for the periodic settlements of amounts due under interest rate swaps and foreign exchange contracts. Amounts due the Company under these contracts were not material at December 28, 1990.

Terms of the 1987 Credit Agreement and/or the outstanding Notes and Debentures include various provisions which, among other things, require the Company to (i) maintain defined consolidated net worth and coverage ratios and (ii) limit the incurrence of certain liens or encumbrances in excess of defined amounts. None of these restrictions are presently significant to the Company.

Leases

The Company leases office and warehouse space, computer hardware and machinery and equipment under lease agreements which expire at various dates through 2019. At December 28, 1990, future minimum lease payments under capital and noncancellable operating leases were as follows (in thousands):

Fiscal Year	Capital Leases	Operating Leases
1991	$ 2,910	$11,863
1992	2,730	8,037
1993	1,488	4,925
1994	704	3,359
1995	582	1,245
Later years	3,627	9,504
Total minimum lease payments	12,041	$38,933
Less amount representing interest	3,216	
Present value of net minimum lease payments	$ 8,825	

Rent expense, including operating leases, was approximately $26 million, $24 million and $28 million during 1990, 1989 and 1988, respectively.

Preferred Stock

In May 1988, the Company issued 2,500 shares of variable dividend rate nonvoting preferred stock at a purchase price of $100,000 per share. The holders are entitled to cumulative dividends at a rate determined by an auction approxi-

31

COCA-COLA ENTERPRISES INC.

mately every forty-nine days. The weighted average dividend rate of the preferred stock was 6.5% and 7.3% during 1990 and 1989, respectively.

The preferred stock is subject to redemption at the Company's option, at any time, at $101,000 per share (plus accrued dividends) through May 4, 1991 and at $100,000 per share (plus accrued dividends) thereafter.

Holders of the preferred stock are permitted to elect two additional directors to the Company's Board of Directors if the Company is in arrears for the equivalent of six quarterly dividend payments. The Company is current on all preferred dividend payments.

Stock Options and Other Stock Plans

The Company's 1986 Stock Option Plan (the "Stock Option Plan") provides for the granting of nonqualified stock options to certain key employees. The Stock Option Plan provides that 3 million shares of the Company's common stock may be granted prior to the plan's expiration in October 1991. In addition, the Company adopted, in February 1990, the 1990 Management Stock Option Plan (the "Management Option Plan"), which provides for the granting of nonqualified stock options to certain key management employees. The Management Option Plan provides that options for 2 million shares of the Company's common stock may be granted. Options awarded under the Stock Option Plan and the Management Option Plan are generally granted at prices which equate to fair market value on the date of grant, become exercisable proportionally over three years and expire ten years subsequent to award. Further information relating to these plans follows:

	1990	1989
Options outstanding at beginning of year	1,923,134	1,016,800
Options granted	2,134,800	939,500
Options exercised	(20,415)	(13,166)
Options cancelled	(282,960)	(20,000)
Options outstanding at end of year	3,754,559	1,923,134
Options exercisable at end of year (Option price – $14.50 to $16.125 per share)	1,446,394	738,972
Shares available for future grant	1,245,441	1,076,866

In 1988, the Company adopted the Stock Appreciation Rights Plan (the "SAR Plan") whereby certain officers and other key employees have been awarded 1,212,700 Stock Appreciation Rights ("units"). The SAR Plan provides for an aggregate 1.5 million units to be awarded to qualified participants prior to the SAR Plan's expiration in April 1993. Each unit entitles the holder to receive cash based on the difference between the market value of one share of the Company's common stock on the date of award and the fair market value of such stock on the date of exercise. During 1990, an aggregate 41,699 units were forfeited and none were exercised. During 1989, an aggregate 28,750 units were forfeited and 2,916 units were exercised. At December 28, 1990, an aggregate 1,093,335 units were outstanding and 403,749 units were available for future award.

In 1986, each of the seven directors who was not an officer of the Company or The Coca-Cola Company was awarded an option to acquire up to 1,500 shares of common stock at $16.50 per share (the initial public offering price). In 1990, a new director who is not an officer of the Company or The Coca-Cola Company was awarded an option to acquire up to 1,500 shares of common stock at $16.50 per share. In addition, in 1986, certain officers of the Company were granted options to purchase 245,000 shares of the Company's common stock at $16.50 per share. Except for 46,500 options that have been cancelled, these options are currently exercisable and will expire in November 1996. No options resulting from these grants have been exercised.

The 1986 Restricted Stock Award Plan (the "Stock Award Plan") provides for awards to certain officers and other key employees of the Company of up to 1 million shares of the Company's common stock. Each award vests when a participant dies, retires or becomes disabled, or when the Compensation Committee of the Board of Directors elects, in its sole discretion, to remove certain restrictions. Such awards also entitle the participant to full dividend and voting rights. The market value of the shares at the date of grant is charged to operations ratably over the vesting periods. In 1990, 87,500 shares were granted under the Stock Award Plan, resulting in an aggregate 427,500 shares being granted since 1986.

Pension and Certain Benefit Plans

The Company sponsors various pension plans, participates in certain multiemployer pension plans and through December 30, 1988, participated in a pension plan sponsored by The Coca-Cola Company (the "Master Pension Plan"). Effective

32

January 1, 1989, the Company adopted the Coca-Cola Enterprises Inc. Employees' Pension Plan and Trust (the "CCE Pension Plan"), a qualified defined benefit plan to cover substantially all salaried and certain nonunion hourly employees. Most of these employees were previously covered by other company-sponsored plans or the Master Pension Plan. The CCE Pension Plan assumed all liabilities with respect to current employees of the Company who were active participants in the Master Pension Plan on December 31, 1988. In addition to the liabilities assumed, assets were transferred to the CCE Pension Plan from the Master Pension Plan based upon the present value of accrued benefits of active Company employees compared to the present value of accrued benefits of all participants in the Master Pension Plan. The Company's pension plans cover substantially all of the Company's employees. The Company's funding policy is to contribute amounts to the plans sufficient to meet the minimum funding requirements set forth in the Employee Retirement Income Security Act of 1974, plus such additional amounts as management may determine to be appropriate consistent with applicable legal limits. The benefits related to company-sponsored plans are based on years of service and compensation earned during years of employment.

Pension expense amounted to approximately $11.9 million (including $4.8 million for noncompany-sponsored plans) in fiscal year 1990, $10.4 million (including $5.2 million for noncompany-sponsored plans) in fiscal year 1989 and $7.1 million (including $5.3 million for noncompany-sponsored plans) in fiscal year 1988.

Net pension costs for company-sponsored pension plans for 1990, 1989 and 1988 included the following components (in thousands):

	Fiscal Year		
	1990	1989	1988
Service cost — benefits earned during the period	$9,398	$8,035	$6,698
Interest cost on projected benefit obligation	20,538	18,588	14,479
Actual return on assets	12,229	(34,399)	849
Net amortization and deferral	(35,105)	13,017	(20,162)
Net pension cost	$7,060	$5,241	$1,864

The following table sets forth the plans' funded status and amounts recognized in the Company's Consolidated Balance Sheets as of the most recent actuarial valuation dates, October 1, 1990 and October 1, 1989 (in thousands):

	1990		1989	
	Plans Whose Assets Exceed Accumulated Benefits	Plans Whose Accumulated Benefits Exceed Assets	Plans Whose Assets Exceed Accumulated Benefits	Plans Whose Accumulated Benefits Exceed Assets
Actuarial present value of benefit obligations:				
Vested benefit obligation	$(143,673)	$ (6,980)	$(126,476)	$(2,460)
Accumulated benefit obligation	$(171,089)	$ (7,246)	$(152,237)	$(2,532)
Projected benefit obligation	$(218,246)	$(13,152)	$(211,061)	$(7,736)
Plan assets at fair value, primarily listed stocks and U.S. bonds	229,714	4,876	265,867	271
Plan assets in excess of (less than) projected benefit obligation	11,468	(8,276)	54,806	(7,465)
Unrecognized net (gain) loss	20,391	(982)	(14,522)	(990)
Unrecognized prior service cost	2,526	1,045	3,518	53
Unrecognized net transition (asset) liability	(16,613)	2,967	(19,939)	3,674
Valuation adjustment for estimated tax effects	(4,444)	–	(6,772)	–
Plan contributions made from October 1 through year-end	121	–	1,622	–
Prepaid pension cost included in the balance sheet	$ 13,449	$ (5,246)	$ 18,713	$(4,728)

33

COCA-COLA ENTERPRISES INC.

The weighted average discount rate and rate of increase in future compensation utilized in determining the actuarial present value of the projected benefit obligation as of the respective valuation dates were 9.5% and 5.5%, in 1990 and 1989 respectively. The expected long-term rate of return on plan assets was 9% in 1990 and 1989.

The Company sponsors a Saving Investment Plan which covers all employees who are 21 years of age with one or more years of service. The Company matches, with equivalent value of Company stock, 100% of the voluntary contributions up to a maximum of 3% of a participant's compensation. The Company's 1990 and 1989 contribution expenses, were approximately $8.5 million and $8.1 million, respectively.

The Company participates in various plans that provide postretirement health care and life insurance benefits to virtually all nonunion employees who retire with a minimum period of service. The cost of these benefits is expensed as claims are incurred. This annual cost is not significant to the Company. In December 1990, the Financial Accounting Standards Board issued Statement of Financial Accounting Standards No. 106, "Employers' Accounting for Postretirement Benefits Other Than Pensions." This Statement, which requires adoption by 1993, will change the Company's current practice of accounting for such postretirement benefits to require accrual of the costs of such benefits for Company employees during the years such employees render service to the Company. The Company is evaluating the effects of the adoption of this Statement.

Provision for Restructuring

In the second quarter of 1990, the Company recognized a $9.3 million restructuring charge relating primarily to the planned standardization of the Company's information systems operations. In the fourth quarter of 1988, the Company recognized a $27 million restructuring charge which principally provided for costs related to consolidation and relocation of certain manufacturing and administrative facilities and the write-down of certain property, plant and equipment and other assets.

Income Taxes

The provision for income taxes consists of the following (in thousands):

Fiscal Year ended	Federal	State & Local	Total
December 28, 1990			
Current	$ 3,250	$11,250	$14,500
Deferred	71,741	4,593	76,334
December 29, 1989			
Current	$ 7,153	$ 8,152	$15,305
Deferred	48,853	2,049	50,902
December 30, 1988			
Current	$ 8,419	$10,000	$18,419
Deferred	90,993	5,708	96,701

During 1987, the Company filed elections under Section 338 of the Internal Revenue Code, which related to various bottling companies acquired in 1986. Tax operating loss carryforwards aggregating approximately $417 million have arisen from the additional tax deductions resulting from such elections. These carryforwards are available to offset future Federal taxable income through their expiration in the amount of $146 million in the year 2001, $93 million in 2002, $68 million in 2004 and $110 million in 2005. Realization of these carryforwards for income tax purposes will not affect financial statement reported income in future years. Income taxes recoverable of $6.9 million and $11.8 million were included in prepaid assets at December 28, 1990 and December 29, 1989, respectively.

A reconciliation of the statutory Federal rate to the Company's effective rates follows:

	Fiscal Year		
	1990	1989	1988
Statutory rate	34.0%	34.0%	34.0%
State income taxes — net of Federal benefit	5.7	4.9	3.9
Amortization of goodwill	5.4	6.2	3.1
Acquisition adjustments	0.7	0.7	0.1
Other, net	3.5	2.2	1.9
	49.3%	48.0%	43.0%

34

Deferred income taxes are provided for the differences in timing of recognizing certain items for financial reporting and income tax purposes. Deferred income taxes consist principally of the following (in millions):

	Fiscal Year	
	1990	1989
Depreciation	$30.0	$27.4
Amortization	69.7	64.7
Tax net operating losses	(38.0)	(27.7)
Installment gain election for sale of Ohio operations	12.4	–
Accrual to cash adjustments	1.2	(9.1)
Alternative minimum tax	(2.0)	(5.2)
Other, net	3.0	0.8
	$76.3	$50.9

The Financial Accounting Standards Board issued in 1987 Statement of Financial Accounting Standards No. 96, "Accounting for Income Taxes." The Financial Accounting Standards Board is currently considering certain amendments to this Statement including a delay in the required adoption date to 1993. The Company continues to evaluate the effects of the adoption of this Statement, which it currently expects to adopt in 1993.

Related Party Transactions

The Company and its subsidiaries are licensed bottlers of soft drink products of The Coca-Cola Company. The Company and The Coca-Cola Company have entered into several transactions and agreements related to their respective businesses. Several significant transactions and agreements entered into between the Company and The Coca-Cola Company are disclosed in the accompanying financial statements and related notes. In addition, the following represent other material transactions between the Company and The Coca-Cola Company during 1990 and 1989:

Share Repurchase

In December 1990, the Company completed the 25 million share repurchase program. During 1990, the Company repurchased approximately 4 million shares from The Coca-Cola Company at an aggregate purchase price of approximately $60.3 million. During 1989, the Company repurchased 3.0 million shares from The Coca-Cola

Company for an aggregate purchase price of approximately $48.8 million. The price paid for shares repurchased from The Coca-Cola Company on a per share basis, approximately equates to the average price paid for shares repurchased during the year from the Company's public shareholders.

Product Ingredient Purchases

In the ordinary course of business, the Company purchases sweeteners, soft drink syrups and concentrates from The Coca-Cola Company. The Company paid The Coca-Cola Company approximately $919.6 million and $922.1 million for sweetener, syrup and concentrate purchases, during 1990 and 1989, respectively.

Fountain Syrup and Package Product Sales

Certain of the Company's operations sell fountain syrup to The Coca-Cola Company and deliver on behalf of The Coca-Cola Company such syrup to certain major or national accounts of The Coca-Cola Company. In addition, the Company sells bottle/can products to The Coca-Cola Company at prices that equate to amounts charged by the Company to its major customers. During 1990 and 1989, The Coca-Cola Company paid the Company approximately $132.5 million and $157.7 million, respectively, for fountain syrups, bottle/can products and delivery and billing services.

Antitrust Indemnity Agreement

During 1990 and 1989, The Coca-Cola Company paid the Company approximately $4.8 million and $6.6 million, respectively, pursuant to an agreement which indemnifies the Company for certain costs, settlements and fines arising out of alleged antitrust violations which occurred prior to the acquisition of certain bottlers by the Company.

Marketing Support Arrangements

The Coca-Cola Company engages in a variety of marketing programs, local media advertising and other similar arrangements to promote the sale of products of The Coca-Cola Company in territories operated by the Company. For 1990 and 1989, total direct marketing support provided to the Company by The Coca-Cola Company was approximately $186.3 million and $184.6 million, respectively. In addition, the Company paid an additional $43 million and $41.8 million in 1990 and 1989, respectively, for local media and marketing program expense pursuant to a cooperative advertising arrangement with The Coca-Cola Company.

35

COCA-COLA ENTERPRISES INC.

Legal Proceedings

Since its formation in 1986, bottling company subsidiaries of the Company entered guilty pleas to Federal charges of conspiring to violate the Sherman Antitrust Act and paid fines aggregating approximately $4.8 million. Approximately 20 civil actions, some of them purported class actions, have been prosecuted in Federal and State courts relating to these charges. Only three of such suits are currently pending. The remainder have all been settled, but two of those settled cases await court approval. The Company has paid approximately $25 million in settlements and fees in connection with the above described criminal and civil proceedings. The conduct which was the predicate for the offenses charged occurred prior to the acquisition of the bottling companies by the Company. A substantial portion of the fines, penalties, judgements, settlements, costs, expenses and other liabilities related to these and similar proceedings are reimbursed to the Company pursuant to various indemnity agreements, including one with The Coca-Cola Company.

Therefore, none of the fines or settlements had, individually or in the aggregate, nor will any related judgements or settlements have, a material adverse effect on the financial position or results of operations of the Company. The Company is also involved in various other claims and legal proceedings, the resolution of which management believes will not have a material adverse effect on the financial condition or results of operations of the Company.

Commitments and Contingent Liabilities

The Company is contingently liable for guarantees of the indebtedness owed by manufacturing cooperatives of approximately $6 million and $3 million at December 28, 1990 and December 29, 1989, respectively.

Under the Company's insurance programs, coverage is obtained for catastrophic exposures as well as those risks required to be insured by law or contract. It is the policy of the Company to retain a significant portion of certain expected losses related primarily to workers' compensation, physical loss to property, business interruption resulting from such loss and comprehensive general, product and vehicle liability. Provisions for losses expected under these programs are recorded based upon the Company's estimates of the aggregate liability for claims incurred. Such estimates utilize certain actuarial assumptions followed in the insurance industry. The Company has provided letters of credit aggregating approximately $59 million in connection with certain insurance programs.

Federal, State and local laws and regulations govern the Company's operation of underground fuel storage tanks. The Company has a significant number of storage tanks that will require removal, replacement or modification to satisfy regulations which go into effect in varying stages through 1998. The Company estimates total environmental expenditures related to storage tanks beginning in 1990 will aggregate approximately $71 million. Of this amount, approximately $59 million represents capital expenditures. Of such amount, an aggregate $16 million represents capital expenditures during 1990 and approximately $43 million is estimated to represent capitalized expenditures during 1991, 1992 and 1993. The remaining amount of $12 million has been accrued as an operating expense in 1990. The Company does not currently expect any additional material expenses in future years associated with storage tanks (other than depreciation of amounts capitalized). Therefore, the Company's remediation of environmental contamination resulting from storage tanks is not expected to have a material adverse effect on results of operations or financial condition of the Company.

Supplemental Disclosures of Cash Flow Information

Changes in assets and liabilities net of effects from acquisitions and divestitures of companies were as follows (in thousands):

	1990	1989	1988
Trade accounts receivable	$ (6,683)	$ (2,448)	$(21,701)
Inventories	(863)	(2,520)	(1,821)
Prepaid expenses and other assets	(11,320)	8,147	3,031
Accounts payable and accrued expenses	7,333	59,683	5,325
Accrued income taxes	1,276	(12,231)	—
Decrease (increase)	$(10,257)	$ 50,631	$(15,166)

36

Cash payments during the year were as follows (in thousands):

	1990	1989	1988
Interest (net of capitalized amount)	$206,309	$203,177	$205,386
Income taxes	$ 7,861	$ 14,654	$ 26,335

In conjunction with the acquisitions of bottling companies, liabilities were acquired as follows (in thousands):

	1990	1989	1988
Fair value of assets acquired	$319,316	$ 24,876	$566,214
Cash paid	267,895	21,833	461,542
Liabilities acquired	$ 51,421	$ 3,043	$104,672

Quarterly Financial Data

(Unaudited; in millions except per share data):

	Net Operating Revenues		Gross Profit	
	1990	1989	1990	1989
First Quarter	$ 906.4	$ 859.6	$ 376.3	$ 359.3
Second Quarter	1,124.9	1,088.5	471.0	435.8
Third Quarter	1,067.3	1,022.1	435.8	402.0
Fourth Quarter	935.4	911.7	391.7	371.8
Fiscal Year	$4,034.0	$3,881.9	$1,674.8	$1,568.9

	Net Income		Net Income Available to Common Shareholders	
	1990	1989	1990	1989
First Quarter	$ 8.0	$ 13.5	$ 3.9	$ 8.8
Second Quarter	55.3	38.8	51.2	34.0
Third Quarter	19.0	12.7	15.0	8.3
Fourth Quarter	11.1	6.7	7.0	2.4
Fiscal Year	$ 93.4	$ 71.7	$ 77.1	$ 53.5

	Net Income Per Common Share	
	1990	1989
First Quarter	$ 0.03	$ 0.07
Second Quarter	0.42	0.26
Third Quarter	0.13	0.06
Fourth Quarter	0.06	0.02
Fiscal Year	$ 0.65*	$ 0.41

Each quarter presented includes thirteen weeks.

* Due to the timing of share repurchases by the Company and the method used in calculating per share data as prescribed by Accounting Principles Board Opinion No. 15, the quarterly per share data for 1990 does not sum to the per share data as computed for the year.

37

Through the first three quarters of 1990, the Company recognized charges of approximately $2.4 million, $2.8 million and $4.1 million, respectively, related to environmental remediation issues including the replacement and repair of certain underground fuel storage tanks owned by the Company. Such charges have been previously reported as other deductions, a nonoperating expense. In the fourth quarter, the Company recognized an additional $2.7 million environmental remediation charge, resulting in a full-year aggregate charge of $12 million ($0.06 per share). Such charge has been reclassified and reported in the Company's financial statements for the quarters and fiscal year as a component of selling, general and administrative expense, an operating expense.

In the first quarter of 1990, the Company sold its food service vending operations in Memphis, Tennessee, recognizing a pretax gain of approximately $3.7 million ($0.01 per share).

In the second quarter of 1990, the Company (i) sold its majority interest in its Ohio operations and 100% ownership interest in the Portsmouth operations, recognizing an aggregate pretax gain of approximately $55.6 million ($0.26 per share); (ii) established a pretax restructuring reserve for planned standardization of the Company's information systems operations aggregating $9.3 million ($0.05 per share); and (iii) established incremental reserves for potentially uncollectible trade accounts receivable resulting in a pretax charge of approximately $10 million ($0.05 per share).

In the first quarter of 1989, the Company (i) sold the Goodwill Bottlers, recognizing a pretax gain of $11 million ($0.04 per share); (ii) repurchased certain of the Company's outstanding debt resulting in an aggregate pretax gain of $2.6 million ($0.01 per share); and (iii) recognized an aggregate $4.4 million pretax benefit ($0.02 per share) resulting from the favorable resolution of certain liabilities established for acquisitions previously made by the Company.

In the second quarter of 1989, the Company recognized (i) a $5.9 million pretax gain ($0.02 per share) resulting from the sale-leaseback of certain real property and (ii) repurchased certain of the Company's debt which resulted in an aggregate pretax gain of $4.4 million ($0.02 per share).

In the fourth quarter of 1989, the Company established certain incremental reserves for potentially uncollectible trade accounts receivable resulting in a pretax charge of approximately $6 million ($0.02 per share).

38

COCA-COLA ENTERPRISES INC.

Management is responsible for the preparation and integrity of the consolidated financial statements appearing in this Annual Report. The financial statements were prepared in conformity with generally accepted accounting principles appropriate in the circumstances and, accordingly, include some amounts based on management's best judgments and estimates. Financial information in this Annual Report is consistent with that in the consolidated financial statements.

Management is responsible for maintaining a system of internal accounting controls and procedures to provide reasonable assurance, at an appropriate cost/benefit relationship, that assets are safeguarded and that transactions are authorized, recorded and reported properly. The internal accounting control system is augmented by a program of internal audits and appropriate reviews by management, written policies and guidelines, careful selection and training of qualified personnel and a written Code of Business Conduct adopted by the Board of Directors, applicable to all employees of the Company and its subsidiaries. Management believes that the Company's internal accounting controls provide reasonable assurance that assets are safeguarded against material loss from unauthorized use or disposition and that the financial records are reliable for preparing financial statements and other data and maintaining accountability for assets.

The Audit Committee of the Board of Directors, composed solely of Directors who are not officers of the Company or The Coca-Cola Company, meets with the independent auditors, management and internal auditors periodically to discuss internal accounting controls, auditing and financial reporting matters. The Committee reviews with the independent auditors the scope and results of the audit effort. The Committee also meets with the independent auditors and the Company's Director of Internal Audit without management present to ensure that the independent auditors and the Company's Director of Internal Audit have free access to the Committee.

The independent auditors, Ernst & Young, are recommended by the Audit Committee of the Board of Directors, selected by the Board of Directors, and that selection is ratified by the Company's shareholders. Ernst & Young is engaged to audit the consolidated financial statements of Coca-Cola Enterprises Inc. and subsidiaries and conduct such tests and related procedures as Ernst & Young deems necessary in conformity with generally accepted auditing standards. The opinion of the independent auditors, based upon their audit of the consolidated financial statements, is contained in this Annual Report.

Brian G. Dyson
President and Chief Executive Officer

Lawrence R. Cowart
Executive Vice President and Chief Financial Officer

Atlanta, Georgia
January 30, 1991

39

REPORT OF ERNST & YOUNG, INDEPENDENT AUDITORS

COCA-COLA ENTERPRISES INC.

Board of Directors
Coca-Cola Enterprises Inc.

We have audited the accompanying consolidated balance sheets of Coca-Cola Enterprises Inc. and subsidiaries as of December 28, 1990 and December 29, 1989, and the related consolidated statements of income, shareholders' equity, and cash flows for each of the three years in the period ended December 28, 1990. These financial statements are the responsibility of the Company's management. Our responsibility is to express an opinion on these financial statements based on our audits.

We conducted our audits in accordance with generally accepted auditing standards. Those standards require that we plan and perform the audit to obtain reasonable assurance about whether the financial statements are free of material misstatement. An audit includes examining, on a test basis, evidence supporting the amounts and disclosures in the financial statements. An audit also includes assessing the accounting principles used and significant estimates made by management, as well as evaluating the overall financial statement presentation. We believe that our audits provide a reasonable basis for our opinion.

In our opinion, the financial statements referred to above present fairly, in all material respects, the consolidated financial position of Coca-Cola Enterprises Inc. and subsidiaries at December 28, 1990 and December 29, 1989, and the consolidated results of their operations and their cash flows for each of the three years in the period ended December 28, 1990, in conformity with generally accepted accounting principles.

Ernst & Young

Atlanta, Georgia
January 30, 1991

40

DIRECTORS OF CCE

COCA-COLA ENTERPRISES INC.

John L. Clendenin
Chairman of the Board of Directors,
President and Chief Executive Officer
of BellSouth Corporation

Johnnetta B. Cole
President of Spelman College

Lawrence R. Cowart
Executive Vice President and
Chief Financial Officer of
Coca-Cola Enterprises Inc.

Brian G. Dyson
President and Chief Executive Officer
of Coca-Cola Enterprises Inc.

T. Marshall Hahn, Jr.
Chairman of the Board of Directors
and Chief Executive Officer of
Georgia-Pacific Corporation

Claus M. Halle
International Consultant to The Coca-Cola
Company; Retired Senior Executive of The
Coca-Cola Company

John E. Jacob
President and Chief Executive Officer of the
National Urban League, Inc.

Robert A. Keller
Senior Vice President and Corporate
Counsel of The Coca-Cola Company

Donald R. Keough
Chairman of the Board of Directors
of Coca-Cola Enterprises Inc.;
President and Chief Operating Officer
of The Coca-Cola Company

Wilton D. Looney
Honorary Chairman of the Board of
Directors of Genuine Parts Company

Jack L. Stahl
Senior Vice President and Chief
Financial Officer of The Coca-Cola
Company

Francis A. Tarkenton
Chairman of the Board of Directors
and Chief Executive Officer of
KnowledgeWare, Inc.

Joel R. Wells, Jr.
Chairman of the Board of Directors
of SunTrust Banks, Inc.
(Deceased)

CCE TERRITORIES

CCE's exclusive territories include portions
of 26 states, the District of Columbia and
the U.S. Virgin Islands. We are the principal
bottler of the products of The Coca-Cola
Company in the five states with the largest
gains in population during the 1980's.

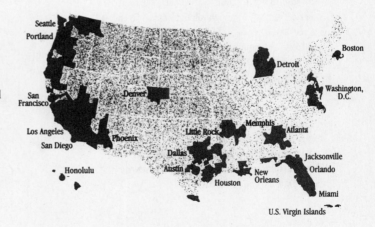

41

COCA-COLA ENTERPRISES INC.

Common Stock

Trading symbol: CCE
Number of shares issued and outstanding as of year-end: 114,834,723
Number of shareholders of record as of year-end: 10,836

Stock Exchanges

Listed and traded: New York Stock Exchange
Traded: Boston, Cincinnati, Midwest, Pacific, Philadelphia

Annual Meeting

Shareholders are cordially invited to attend our Annual Meeting of Shareholders at 9:00 a.m., local time, April 10, 1991, at the Hotel du Pont, 11th and Market Streets, Wilmington, Delaware.

Dividends

CCE typically pays quarterly dividends on or about the first day of January, April, July and October.

Shareholder Investment Plan

All shareholders of record are invited to participate in the Shareholder Investment Plan. The Plan provides a convenient, economical and systematic method of acquiring additional shares of the Company's common stock. The Plan permits shareholders of record to reinvest dividends from Company stock in shares of CCE. Shareholders also may purchase Company stock through voluntary cash investments of up to $60,000 per year.

All costs and commissions associated with joining and participating in the Plan are paid by the Company.

The Plan's administrator, First Chicago Trust Company of New York, purchases stock for voluntary cash investments on or about the first day of each month, and for dividend reinvestment on or about the first of April, July, October and January.

At year-end, 18% of shareholders of record were participants in the Plan. In 1990, shareholders invested $13,857 in dividends and $110,806 in cash in the Plan.

Stock Prices

Listed below is a two-year summary of New York Stock Exchange Composite prices for CCE common stock.

1990	High	Low	Close
Fourth quarter	16 1/8	12 5/8	15 1/2
Third quarter	16 7/8	12 1/4	13
Second quarter	16 3/8	14	16
First quarter	16 1/2	13 3/4	15 1/2

1989	High	Low	Close
Fourth quarter	18 1/4	15 1/4	16
Third quarter	18 1/2	15 3/4	17 1/4
Second quarter	18 3/4	15 7/8	17 1/8
First quarter	17	14 3/4	16 5/8

Company Information

The following information will be regularly furnished to shareholders: Annual Report, Quarterly Report, Proxy Statement, Notice of Annual Meeting of Shareholders.

This information and the following publications are available on request at no charge from the Shareholder Relations Department: Annual Report on Form 10-K, Quarterly Report on Form 10-Q, Shareholder Handbook, Shareholder Investment Plan brochure.

Printed on recycled paper

42

ANSWERS

Chapter 1

Matching

1. h	**7.** s	**13.** u	**19.** d
2. f	**8.** c	**14.** e	**20.** g
3. o	**9.** j	**15.** l	**21.** a
4. r	**10.** v	**16.** q	**22.** p
5. w	**11.** i	**17.** m	**23.** k
6. n	**12.** b	**18.** t	

Short Answer

1. (L.O. 8) Management accounting, public accounting, government and other not-for-profit accounting, and accounting education
2. (L.O. 7) Alpha Corporation
   Income Statement
   For the Year Ended June 30, 19xx
3. (L.O. 1) Bookkeeping deals only with the mechanical and repetitive recordkeeping process. Accounting involves bookkeeping as well as the design of an accounting system, its use, and the analysis of its output.
4. (L.O. 1) Set a goal, consider alternatives, make the decision, take action, evaluate the results
5. (L.O. 8)
   a. *Integrity*—The accountant is honest, regardless of consequences.
   b. *Objectivity*—The accountant is impartial in performing his or her job.
   c. *Independence*—The accountant avoids all relationships that could impair his or her objectivity.

   d. *Due care*—The accountant carries out his or her responsibilities with competence and diligence.
6. (L.O. 2) Management, outsiders with a direct financial interest, outsiders with an indirect financial interest
7. (L.O. 2) To earn a satisfactory profit to hold investor capital; to maintain sufficient funds to pay debts as they fall due
8. (L.O. 7)
   Statement
   a. Balance sheet
   b. Income statement
   c. Statement of cash flows
   d. Statement of retained earnings
   Purpose
   a. Shows financial position at a point in time
   b. Measures net income during a certain period
   c. Discloses operating, financing, and investing activities during the period
   d. Shows how retained earnings changed during the period

True-False

1. F (L.O. 7) It is the balance sheet that shows financial position.
2. F (L.O. 3) The IRS interprets and enforces tax laws.
3. T (L.O. 1)
4. T (L.O. 6)
5. T (L.O. 6)
6. F (L.O. 6) It indicates that the company has one or more debtors.
7. T (L.O. 6)
8. F (L.O. 4) The measurement stage refers to the recording of business transactions.
9. F (L.O. 7) Dividends are a deduction in the statement of retained earnings.
10. T (L.O. 3)
11. T (L.O. 5)
12. T (L.O. 7)
13. T (L.O. 7)
14. F (L.O. 3) That is the GASB's responsibility.
15. F (L.O. 5) A corporation is managed by its board of directors.

16. F (L.O. 3) Internal auditing is an aspect of management accounting, not public accounting.
17. T (L.O. 3)
18. F (L.O. 6) Net assets equal assets *minus* liabilities.
19. F (L.O. 7) Balance sheets do not include revenues and expenses.
20. F (L.O. 4) Nonexchange transactions, such as the accumulation of interest, do exist.
21. T (L.O. 1)
22. T (L.O. 7)
23. T (L.O. 4)
24. F (L.O. 8) The status of CMA (certified management accountant) is sought mainly by management accountants.
25. F (L.O. 2) Economic planners have an indirect financial interest in accounting information.
26. T (L.O. 6)
27. T (L.O. 8)

Multiple Choice

1. a (L.O. 7) The answer "Wages Expense" is correct because it is the account title, of the possible choices, that would appear on the income statement. The income statement is the financial statement that reports revenues and expenses.
2. c (L.O. 3) The SEC (Securities and Exchange Commission) is the organization that regulates financial trading. Its role is to help protect the public from incomplete information. The SEC requires that certain financial information be made available so that the public will be able to make informed investment decisions.
3. b (L.O. 5) The stock of a corporation is easily transferred from one investor to another. Corporations are owned through ownership of shares of stock.
4. b (L.O. 3) Management accounting is a term that refers to the types of reports and uses of accounting data internal to an organization. Public accounting is the type of accounting that dictates the proper preparation of reports and financial statements for users external to the firm.
5. b (L.O. 7) The balance sheet is a "snapshot" of the business, in a financial sense, on a given date. The account balances, as they

appear on the balance sheet, are a report of the ultimate effect of financial transactions during an accounting period, not a report of the actual transactions.
6. a (L.O. 8) An audit is used to verify the information presented by the management of a firm in its financial statements. The term "fairness" refers to the ability of users of the financial statements to rely on the information as presented.
7. d (L.O. 6) Collection on an account receivable is simply an exchange of one asset (the account receivable) for another asset (cash). As a result, there is no effect on the accounting equation.
8. d (L.O. 5) The partners *are* the partnership. There is no separate legal entity in this form of organization. When a partner leaves the partnership, the original partnership is dissolved, although a new partnership may be formed by replacing the exiting partner.
9. a (L.O. 7) "Assets" is a major heading found in the balance sheet. Accounts Receivable is merely a type of asset.
10. c (L.O. 6) The payment of a liability will reduce both sides of the accounting equation equally. The transaction is a reduction

in assets and a reduction in liabilities in equal amounts.

11. c (L.O. 8) Financial accounting is a broad term that applies to all facets of recording and reporting a business entity's transactions.

12. d (L.O. 6) The purchase of an asset for cash is an exchange of one asset for another. It is an increase and a decrease, in equal amounts, to one side of the accounting equation. Therefore, it has no effect on total assets, liabilities, or owners' equity.

Exercises

1. (L.O. 2, 7)
   a. Potential investors need all recent financial statements to assess the future profitability of a company and thus whether they should invest in it.
   b. The principal goal of the SEC is to protect the public. Insisting that Lindlay make its statements public as well as examining the statements for propriety will certainly aid the public in making decisions regarding Lindlay.
   c. The bank will have difficulty in determining Lindlay's ability to repay the loan if it does not have access to Lindlay's most recent financial statements.
   d. Present stockholders will wish to see the statements in order to decide whether to sell, maintain, or increase their investments.
   e. Management will want to see the statements because the statements should help them pinpoint the weaknesses that caused the year's loss.

2. (L.O. 6) $35,000

3. (L.O. 7)

Acme TV Repair Corporation
Balance Sheet
December 31, 19xx

Assets

Cash	$ 950
Accounts Receivable	1,500
Equipment	850
Land	1,000
Building	10,000
Truck	4,500
	$18,800

Liabilities

Accounts Payable	$ 1,300

Stockholders' Equity

Common Stock	14,500
Retained Earnings	3,000
	$18,800

---

4. (L.O. 6)

Transaction	Assets				Liabilities	Stockholders' Equity	
	Cash	Accounts Receivable	Supplies and Equipment	Trucks	Accounts Payable	Common Stock	Retained Earnings
a	+ $20,000					+ $20,000	
b	−650		+ $650				
c				+ $5,200	+ $5,200		
d	+ 525						+ $525
e	−2,600				−2,600		
f		+ $150					+ 150
g	−250						−250
h	+ 150	−150					
i		+ 20	−20				
j	−200						−200
Balance at end of month	$16,975	$20	$630	$5,200	$2,600	$20,000	$225

Solution to Crossword Puzzle
(Chapter 1)

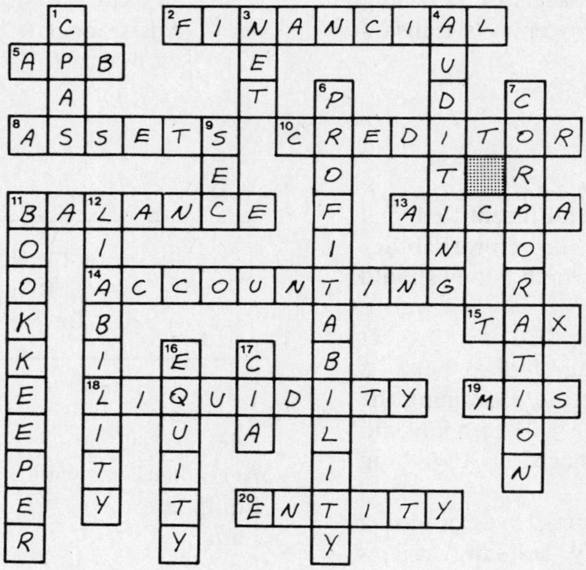

Crossword grid solution:

Across:
- 2. FINANCIAL
- 5. APB
- 8. ASSETS
- 10. CREDITOR
- 11. BALANCE
- 13. AICPA
- 14. ACCOUNTING
- 15. TAX
- 18. LIQUIDITY
- 19. MIS
- 20. ENTITY

Down:
- 1. CA...
- 3. NET
- 4. AUDIT
- 6. PROFIT
- 7. CRR
- 9. SE
- 11. BOOKKEEPER
- 12. LIABILITY
- 13. ANG
- 16. EQUITY
- 17. CABLY
- Corporation (AICPA column): AICPA / CORPORATION

Chapter 2

Matching

1. k   7. a   13. e   19. d
2. f   8. m   14. n
3. q   9. l   15. p
4. o   10. s   16. h
5. b   11. j   17. c
6. g   12. r   18. i

Short Answer

1. (L.O. 5, 6, 8) Journalize transactions, post journal entries to the ledger accounts, prepare a trial balance
2. (L.O. 1)
   a. July 14
   b. $150
   c. Cash and Accounts Receivable
3. (L.O. 4) Two examples are the purchase of any asset for cash and collection on an account receivable.
4. (L.O. 6) One example is payment on an account payable.

True-False

1. F (L.O. 1) A sale should be recorded when it takes place.
2. T (L.O. 1)
3. T (L.O. 2)
4. F (L.O. 4) The credit side of an account does not imply anything favorable or unfavorable.
5. F (L.O. 4) Only those accounts with zero balances will have equal debits and credits.
6. F (L.O. 6) One quickly determines cash on hand by referring to the ledger.
7. T (L.O. 2)
8. F (L.O. 3) Notes Payable is the proper account title; the liability is evidenced by the existence of a promissory note.
9. T (L.O. 3)
10. T (L.O. 4)
11. F (L.O. 4) It is possible to have all increases or all decreases in a journal entry.
12. F (L.O. 6) Journal entries are made before they are posted to the ledger.
13. F (L.O. 6) Liabilities and owners' equity accounts are indented only when credited.
14. T (L.O. 6)
15. T (L.O. 7)
16. T (L.O. 7)
17. T (L.O. 6)
18. F (L.O. 2) It is a table of contents to the general ledger.
19. F (L.O. 3, 4) Unearned Revenues has a normal credit balance.
20. F (L.O. 3) Retained earnings is not cash and should be shown in the stockholders' equity section.
21. T (L.O. 3)

Multiple Choice

1. c (L.O. 1) Summarization of accounting data occurs at the end of the accounting cycle. Journal entries are prepared throughout the accounting period.

2. d (L.O. 5) When a liability is paid, each side of the accounting equation is reduced in equal proportion. The transaction results in a reduction in an asset and a corresponding reduction in a liability.

3. c (L.O. 6) The explanation accompanying a journal entry is a brief statement as to the reason for the entire transaction. Debits and credits are elements of the recorded transaction. The explanation is entered after all debit and credit entries have been made.

4. d (L.O. 7) The final step in the posting process is the transfer of the ledger account number to the Post. Ref. column of the general journal. This last step is an indication that all other steps in the process are complete.

5. c (L.O. 8) If only part of a journal entry has been posted, the omitted information would usually be either a debit or a credit. As a result, total debits would not equal total credits in the general ledger accounts. Therefore, the trial balance would be out of balance.

6. b (L.O. 4) In the transaction described, the receipt of cash in payment of an account receivable, an exchange of one asset for another has occurred. Therefore, total assets would remain unchanged.

7. a (L.O. 4) The Dividends account ultimately causes a reduction in Retained Earnings, a stockholders' equity account. A decrease in stockholders' equity is recorded with a debit.

8. b (L.O. 3) Of the accounts listed, Prepaid Rent is the only one that is classified as an asset. Unearned Revenue is a liability, Retained Earnings is a stockholders' equity account, and Fees Earned is a revenue account.

9. a (L.O. 3) Of the accounts listed, only Interest Payable would represent an amount owing.

10. b (L.O. 5) Unearned Rent would represent a liability on the accounting records of the *lessor.* The question refers to the possible entries of the *lessee,* which include entries into Prepaid Rent, Rent Payable, and Rent Expense.

11. c (L.O. 4) Sales is a revenue account. Revenues increase with a credit entry, and therefore Sales is referred to as having a *normal credit balance.* Revenues ultimately cause an increase in Retained Earnings, which also has a normal credit balance.

Exercises

1. (L.O. 6)

		General Journal		
Date		**Description**	**Debit**	**Credit**
May	2	Cash	28,000	
		Common Stock		28,000
		To record the stockholders' original investment		
	3	Prepaid Rent	900	
		Cash		900
		Paid 3 months' rent in advance		
	5	Printing Press	10,000	
		Photographic Equipment	3,000	
		Cash		2,000
		Accounts Payable		11,000
		Purchased a press and equipment from Irvin Press, Inc.		
	8	No entry		
	9	Cash	1,200	
		Unearned Revenue		1,200
		Received payment in advance from Doherty's Department Store for brochures to be printed		
	11	Office Supplies	800	
		Notes Payable		800
		Purchased paper from Pulp Supply Co.		
	14	Cash	250	
		Accounts Receivable	250	
		Revenue from Services		500
		Completed job for Sullivan Shoes		
	14	Salaries Expense	200	
		Cash		200
		Paid the pressman his weekly salary		
	15	Accounts Payable	1,000	
		Cash		1,000
		Payment on account owed to Irvin Press, Inc.		
	18	Cash	250	
		Accounts Receivable		250
		Sullivan Shoes paid its debt in full		
	20	Dividends	700	
		Cash		700
		The board of directors declared and paid a $700 cash dividend		
	24	Utilities Expense	45	
		Accounts Payable		45
		To record electric bill		
	30	Accounts Payable	45	
		Cash		45
		To record payment of electric bill		

2. (L.O. 4)
   a. $1,750 debit balance
   b. $1,000 credit balance
   c. $14,600 debit balance

3. (L.O. 7)

General Journal				Page 7
Date	**Description**	**Post. Ref.**	**Debit**	**Credit**
Apr. 3	Cash	11	1,000	
	Revenue from Services	41		1,000
	Received payment from Malden Company for services			
5	Accounts Payable	21	300	
	Cash	11		300
	Paid Douglas Supply Company for supplies purchased on March 31 on credit			

Cash						Account No. 11	
						Balance	
Date	**Item**	**Post. Ref.**	**Debit**	**Credit**		**Debit**	**Credit**
Apr. 3		7	1,000			1,000	
5		7		300		700	

Accounts Payable						Account No. 21	
						Balance*	
Date	**Item**	**Post. Ref.**	**Debit**	**Credit**		**Debit**	**Credit**
Apr. 5		7	300			300	

Revenue from Services						Account No. 41	
						Balance	
Date	**Item**	**Post. Ref.**	**Debit**	**Credit**		**Debit**	**Credit**
Apr. 3		7		1,000			1,000

*Previous postings have been omitted, resulting in an improbable debit balance in Accounts Payable.

Chapter 3

Matching

1. i	**6.** q	**11.** a	**16.** j
2. d	**7.** f	**12.** h	**17.** b
3. n	**8.** k	**13.** m	**18.** g
4. r	**9.** e	**14.** p	**19.** t
5. c	**10.** o	**15.** l	**20.** s

Short Answer

1. (L.O. 4) Dividing recorded expenses among two or more accounting periods; dividing recorded revenues among two or more accounting periods; recording unrecorded expenses; recording unrecorded revenues

2. (L.O. 2, 3) The matching rule means that revenues should be recorded in the period in which they are earned, and that all expenses related to those revenues should also be recorded in that period.

3. (L.O. 5) Depreciation is the allocation of the cost of a long-lived asset to the periods benefiting from the asset.

4. (L.O. 4, 5) Prepaid expenses are expenses paid for in advance; they are initially recorded as assets. Unearned revenues represent payment received in advance of providing goods or services; they are initially recorded as liabilities.

5. (L.O. 7) The steps should be numbered as follows: 3, 6, 1, 4, 2, 5.

True-False

1. T (L.O. 1)
2. T (L.O. 1)
3. F (L.O. 2) A calendar year lasts specifically from January 1 to December 31.
4. T (L.O. 2)
5. F (L.O. 2) Under accrual accounting, the timing of cash exchanges is irrelevant in recording revenues and expenses.
6. F (L.O. 3) Adjusting entries are made before the financial statements are prepared.
7. T (L.O. 5)
8. F (L.O. 5) It would be debited for the amount available during the period less ending inventory.

9. F (L.O. 5) Accumulated Depreciation (a contra account) will have a credit balance, even though it appears on the left side of the balance sheet.
10. T (L.O. 5)
11. F (L.O. 5) Unearned Revenues is a liability account.
12. F (L.O. 5) The credit is to a liability account.
13. T (L.O. 6)
14. F (L.O. 5) If payment has not yet been received, the debit is to Accounts Receivable.
15. T (L.O. 5)

Multiple Choice

1. c (L.O. 1) Nominal accounts are those that would appear on an income statement. They are also referred to as temporary accounts.

2. b (L.O. 5) The use of office supplies is recorded as an expense. Adjustments to Office Supplies are the result of reconciling the ending inventory of office supplies to a cumulative total in the Office Supplies account. This cumulative total is a result of the addition of office supplies to the beginning office supplies inventory balance throughout the accounting period.

3. b (L.O. 5) Unearned Fees is used to record the firm's liability for amounts received and not yet earned. The use of this system of recognition is required so that revenue amounts will be properly represented and allocated in the appropriate accounting period. As the revenues are earned, the

proper amounts are transferred from liabilities to revenues. Between the time those future revenues are received and the time they are actually earned, one accounting period may have ended and another accounting period begun.

4. a (L.O. 5) Depreciation is the spreading of the cost of an asset over the expected useful life of that asset. The matching rule requires this gradual recovery of the cost while the asset is in use in the revenue-generating activities of a firm.

5. c (L.O. 6) Net income is the result of the calculation that nets revenues and expenses. The adjusted trial balance contains summary balances of each general ledger account, after adjustments.

6. d (L.O. 5) The adjustment debiting Interest Receivable and crediting Interest Income is required so that interest income for the period is properly allocated, even though payment of the interest is not required as yet. This income recognition is necessary for compliance with the matching rule.

7. a (L.O. 2) Estimates are involved in the preparation of account balances used to report net income. An example of such an estimate is the recording of depreciation expense. Although not exact, the reported net income of one accounting period can be compared with the net income of other accounting periods, providing a basis for conclusions regarding the firm.

8. d (L.O. 5) Until such time as Prepaid Rent is expired, and through adjustments is recorded as an expense, it remains an asset on the books of a firm.

9. b (L.O. 4) The Cash account balance represents a dollar amount at the time of the preparation of the balance sheet. Cash will *never* be involved in the end-of-period adjustments.

10. c (L.O. 7) The final step in the accounting cycle is the preparation of closing entries, which serve to transfer income or loss (as well as dividends) into Retained Earnings and to "zero out" all temporary accounts.

Exercises

1. (L.O. 5)

Gotham Bus Company
Partial Balance Sheet
December 31, 19x3

Assets

Cash		$5,000
Accounts Receivable		3,000
Company Vehicles	$24,000	
Less Accumulated Depreciation	9,000	15,000
Total Assets		$23,000

2. (L.O. 5)
   a. $970
   b. $1,750
   c. $450

3. (L.O. 4, 5)

	General Journal			
Date*		**Description**	**Debit**	**Credit**
a.		Supplies Expense	125	
		Supplies		125
		To record supplies consumed during the period		
b.		Wages Expense	2,000	
		Wages Payable		2,000
		To record accrued wages		
c.		Unearned Revenue	600	
		Revenue from Services		600
		To record earned revenue		
d.		Depreciation Expense, Building	4,500	
		Accumulated Depreciation, Building		4,500
		To record depreciation on building		
e.		Advertising Expense	2,000	
		Prepaid Advertising		2,000
		To record advertising used up during the year		
f.		Insurance Expense	250	
		Unexpired Insurance		250
		To record insurance expired during the year		
g.		Accounts Receivable	2,200	
		Revenue from Services		2,200
		To record revenue earned for which payment has not been received		
h.		Interest Expense	52	
		Interest Payable		52
		To record accrued interest on notes payable		
i.		Income Taxes Expense	21,700	
		Income Taxes Payable		21,700
		To record accrued income tax expense		

*In reality, all of the adjusting entries would be dated December 31.

Solution to Crossword Puzzle
(Chapters 2 and 3)

Chapter 4

Matching

1.	d	**4.**	b	**7.**	c
2.	g	**5.**	h	**8.**	a
3.	i	**6.**	f	**9.**	e

Short Answer

1. (L.O. 5) Revenue accounts, expense accounts, Income Summary, Dividends
2. (L.O. 1) Trial Balance, Adjustments, Adjusted Trial Balance, Income Statement, Balance Sheet
3. (L.O. 7) Assets, liabilities, and owners' equity accounts will appear. Revenue and expense accounts, Income Summary, and the Dividends account will not appear.
4. (L.O. 8) Reversing entries enable the bookkeeper to continue making simple, routine journal entries rather than more complicated ones.

True-False

1. T (L.O. 1)
2. T (L.O. 2)
3. T (L.O. 1)
4. T (L.O. 3)
5. F (L.O. 5) Income Summary does not appear in any statement.
6. F (L.O. 5) Only nominal accounts are closed.
7. T (L.O. 6)
8. F (L.O. 6) The Dividends account is closed to Retained Earnings.
9. F (L.O. 6) When there is a net loss, Income Summary will be credited.
10. T (L.O. 8)
11. F (L.O. 1) The work sheet is never published.
12. F (L.O. 1) The key letter is in the *Adjustments* columns to relate debits and credits of the same entry.
13. T (L.O. 1)
14. F (L.O. 7) It will not include the Dividends account, because that account will have a zero balance.

Multiple Choice

1. c (L.O. 7) Of the accounts listed, Retained Earnings is the only account that remains open after the closing procedures are complete at the end of the accounting cycle. The post-closing trial balance is a listing of such accounts, along with their account balances.
2. d (L.O. 2) Of the choices given, this is the only sequence that it is possible to complete in order. In the proper sequence of steps in the accounting cycle, during the end-of-period process, the financial statements are prepared prior to entering the closing entries in the general journal.
3. b (L.O. 8) Reversing entries "undo" some of the effects of certain adjusting entries. Therefore, they could be referred to as "opposite to" adjusting entries.
4. a (L.O. 1) The amount used to reconcile the Income Statement columns of the work sheet and the Balance Sheet columns of the work sheet is the net income or loss. When the entry that is required to bring the Balance Sheet columns into balance on the work sheet is an entry to the credit column, there must have been a net income. The corresponding entry to bring the Income Statement columns into balance will be to the debit column.
5. a (L.O. 6) Of the accounts listed, Unearned Commissions is the only choice that is not involved in the closing process. Unearned

Commissions is a permanent account, a balance sheet account, and will remain open from one period to the next if it contains a balance.

6. b (L.O. 6) When, in the closing process (after revenues and expenses have been closed), Income Summary has a debit balance (expenses have exceeded revenues), the account will be closed by a credit entry equal to the debit balance. The corresponding debit will be an entry to Retained Earnings, reducing the balance of that account by an amount equal to the net loss for the period.

7. c (L.O. 5) The closing entries occur after the adjusting entries, during the end-of-period steps in the accounting cycle. The purpose of the adjusting entries is to update the revenue and expense accounts.

8. a (L.O. 3) All the components of a statement of retained earnings have been provided, except for net income or loss. A net income figure of $55,000 will correctly complete the statement.

Exercises

1. (L.O. 6)

General Journal				
Date		Description	Debit	Credit
July	*31*	Revenues from Services	4,700	
		Income Summary		4,700
		To close revenue accounts		
	31	Income Summary	700	
		Rent Expense		500
		Telephone Expense		50
		Utility Expense		150
		To close the expense accounts		
	31	Income Summary	4,000	
		Retained Earnings		4,000
		To close Income Summary account		
	31	Retained Earnings	2,500	
		Dividends		2,500
		To close the dividends account		

2. (L.O. 3)

Barrett's Fix-it Services, Inc.
Statement of Retained Earnings
For the Month Ended July 31, 19xx

Retained Earnings, July 1, 19xx	$3,000
Add Net Income for July	4,000
Subtotal	$7,000
Less Dividends declared in July	2,500
Retained Earnings, July 31, 19xx	$4,500

3. (L.O. 1)

Steve's Maintenance, Inc.
Work Sheet
For the Year Ended December 31, 19xx

Account Name	Trial Balance Debit	Trial Balance Credit	Adjustments Debit	Adjustments Credit	Adjusted Trial Balance Debit	Adjusted Trial Balance Credit	Income Statement Debit	Income Statement Credit	Balance Sheet Debit	Balance Sheet Credit
Cash	2,560				2,560				2,560	
Accounts Receivable	880		(e) 50		930				930	
Prepaid Rent	750			(a) 550	200				200	
Lawn Supplies	250			(c) 150	100				100	
Lawn Equipment	10,000				10,000				10,000	
Accum. Deprec., Lawn Equip.		2,000		(b) 1,500		3,500				3,500
Accounts Payable		630				630				630
Unearned Landscaping Fees		300	(f) 120			180				180
Common Stock		5,000				5,000				5,000
Retained Earnings		1,000				1,000				1,000
Dividends	6,050				6,050				6,050	
Grass-Cutting Fees		15,000		(e) 50		15,050		15,050		
Wages Expense	3,300		(d) 280		3,580		3,580			
Gasoline Expense	140				140		140			
	23,930	23,930								
Rent Expense			(a) 550		550		550			
Depreciation Expense			(b) 1,500		1,500		1,500			
Lawn Supplies Expense			(c) 150		150		150			
Landscaping Fees Earned				(f) 120		120		120		
Wages Payable				(d) 280		280				280
Income Taxes Expense			(g) 1,570		1,570		1,570			
Income Taxes Payable				(g) 1,570		1,570				1,570
			4,220	4,220	27,330	27,330	7,490	15,170	19,840	12,160
Net Income							7,680			7,680
							15,170	15,170	19,840	19,840

4. (L.O. 4, 6, 8)

		General Journal		
Date		**Description**	**Debit**	**Credit**
Dec.	*1*	Cash 　Notes Payable 　　To record 90-day bank note	20,000	20,000
	31	Interest Expense 　Interest Payable 　　To record accrued interest on note	200	200
	31	Income Summary 　Interest Expense 　　To close interest on note	200	200
Jan.	*1*	Interest Payable 　Interest Expense 　　To reverse adjusting entry for interest	200	200
Mar.	*1*	Notes Payable Interest Expense 　Cash 　　To record payment of note plus interest	20,000 600	20,600

Chapter 5

Matching

1. c	**5.** l	**9.** i	**13.** f	**17.** t
2. h	**6.** k	**10.** d	**14.** p	**18.** o
3. j	**7.** s	**11.** m	**15.** n	**19.** q
4. e	**8.** g	**12.** a	**16.** r	**20.** b

Short Answer

1. (L.O. 1) Revenues from sales (net sales)
   - Cost of goods sold
   = Gross margin from sales
   - Operating expenses
   = Income before income taxes
   - Income taxes
   = Net income
2. (L.O. 3) Merchandise inventory, beginning
   + Net purchases
   = Goods available for sale
   - Merchandise inventory, ending
   = Cost of goods sold
3. (L.O. 4) (Gross) purchases
   - Purchases returns and allowances
   - Purchases discounts
   = Subtotal
   + Freight in
   = Net purchases
4. (L.O. 2) Gross sales
   - Sales returns and allowances
   - Sales discounts
   = Revenues from sales (net sales)
5. (L.O. 7) Income Summary is debited and Merchandise Inventory credited for the beginning balance. Merchandise Inventory is debited and Income Summary credited for the ending balance. Both entries are treated as adjusting entries, independent of the closing entries.
6. (L.O. 9)
   a. *Control environment*—The overall attitude, awareness, and actions of the owners and management of a business
   b. *Accounting system*—The methods and records established to accomplish the objectives of internal control.
   c. *Control procedures*—Actual steps taken to safeguard the business's assets and ensure the reliability of its records.
7. (L.O. 9) Required authorization for certain transactions
   Recording of all transactions
   Design and use of adequate documents
   Limited access to assets
   Periodic, independent verification of records
   Separation of duties
   Sound personnel procedures
8. (L.O. 11) (Any six of the following would answer the question)
   Separate the authorization, recordkeeping, and custodianship of cash
   Limit access to cash
   Designate a person to handle cash
   Use banking facilities and minimize cash on hand
   Bond employees with access to cash
   Protect cash on hand with safes, cash registers, etc.
   Conduct surprise audits of cash on hand
   Record all cash receipts promptly
   Deposit all cash receipts promptly
   Make all cash payments by check

True-False

1. F (L.O. 3) It will result in an understated net income.
2. F (L.O. 2) It means that payment is due 10 days after the end of the month.
3. T (L.O. 3)
4. F (L.O. 5) The dealer is more likely to use the perpetual inventory system.
5. T (L.O. 4)
6. T (L.O. 7)
7. F (L.O. 2) It is a contra account to *gross sales*.
8. T (L.O. 5)
9. T (L.O. 3)
10. T (L.O. 5)
11. T (L.O. 5)
12. F (L.O. 8) It is closed with a debit.
13. F (L.O. 2) It normally has a debit balance.
14. F (L.O. 4) It requires a debit to Office Supplies, because it is not merchandise.
15. T (L.O. 1)
16. T (L.O. 1)
17. F (L.O. 5) Both are done at the end of the period.
18. F (L.O. 2) 2/10, n/30 is a sales discount, offered for early payment. A trade discount is a percentage off the list or catalog price.
19. F (L.O. 4) Title passes at the shipping point.
20. F (L.O. 9) It increases the probability of accuracy but will not guarantee it.
21. T (L.O. 10)
22. F (L.O. 11) This procedure could easily lead to theft.
23. F (L.O. 11) The supplier is sent a purchase *order*.
24. F (L.O. 9) Rotating employees is good internal control because it might uncover theft.

Multiple Choice

1. d (L.O. 4) Using the gross method of accounting for purchases, the discounts are taken at the time of payment. As a result, the discount of $10, in this example (after allowing for the purchase returns), would be entered as a credit to balance the journal entry, which would also include a debit to Accounts Payable for the balance due ($500) and a credit to Cash for the balance due less the discount ($490).

2. c (L.O. 4) Purchase Returns and Allowances is a contra account to the Purchases account. Purchases has a normal debit balance. Its corresponding contra accounts have a normal credit balance.

3. d (L.O. 3) Counting ending inventory at a larger amount than actually exists would result in a larger adjustment from goods available for sale. This would result in an understatement of cost of goods sold.

4. b (L.O. 3) Freight out is a selling expense. It is not considered to be an element of the cost of obtaining goods.

5. d (L.O. 4) Using the net method to account for purchases, the firm would record the account payable using the assumption that discounts would be taken. The original entry would be a credit to Accounts Payable for the purchase net of the discount, in this case $98. When that account is paid, the entry to record that transaction would include a debit to Accounts Payable for $98.

6. c (L.O. 8) Beginning inventory is eliminated with a credit through the adjusting and closing process. Purchases Returns and Allowances and Sales, on the other hand, are closed with debits. Income Summary is closed with a debit *or* a credit, depending upon whether a net income or a net loss has resulted.

7. d (L.O. 11) The purchase requisition is the initial demand for goods. The purchase requisition is prepared by the individual who ultimately needs the inventory for sale or production. The requisition is then authorized by the appropriate person before the process of purchasing begins.

8. a (L.O. 11) Proper internal control procedures separate the functions of handling of assets and recordkeeping in hopes of preventing employee theft.

9. a (L.O. 6) Freight Out is considered a selling expense within the operating expenses section of the income statement. Sales Discounts appears as a contra account to Gross Sales, whereas Freight In and Purchases appear within the cost of goods sold section.

10. a (L.O. 8) Under the closing entry method, beginning inventory is placed on the debit side of the Income Statement columns. This procedure has the effect of adding beginning inventory to net purchases to arrive at goods available for sale.

Exercises

1. (L.O. 2, 4)

Date		Description	Debit	Credit
		General Journal		
May	*1*	Purchases	500	
		Accounts Payable		500
		Purchased merchandise on credit, terms 2/10, n/60		
	3	Accounts Receivable	500	
		Sales		500
		Sold merchandise on credit, terms 2/10, 1/20, n/30		
	4	Freight In	42	
		Cash		42
		Paid for freight charges		
	5	Office Supplies	100	
		Accounts Payable		100
		Purchased office supplies on credit		
	6	Accounts Payable	20	
		Office Supplies		20
		Returned office supplies of May 5 purchase		
	7	Accounts Payable	50	
		Purchases Returns and Allowances		50
		Returned merchandise from May 1 purchase		
	9	Accounts Receivable	225	
		Sales		225
		Sold merchandise on credit, terms 2/10, 1/15, n/30		
	10	Accounts Payable	450	
		Purchases Discounts		9
		Cash		441
		Paid for purchase of May 1		
	14	Sales Returns and Allowances	25	
		Accounts Receivable		25
		The customer of May 9 returned merchandise		
	22	Cash	198	
		Sales Discounts	2	
		Accounts Receivable		200
		The customer of May 9 paid		
	26	Cash	500	
		Accounts Receivable		500
		The customer of May 3 paid for merchandise		

2. (L.O. 8)

General Journal				
Date		Description	Debit	Credit
Dec.	31	Sales	100,000	
		Interest Income	150	
		Merchandise Inventory	8,000	
		Purchases Discounts	500	
		Purchases Returns and Allowances	500	
		Income Summary		109,150
		To close out nominal accounts with credit balances, and to establish the ending inventory		
	31	Income Summary	86,280	
		Advertising Expense		5,000
		Freight In		2,000
		Freight Out		4,000
		Merchandise Inventory		10,000
		Rent Expense		3,000
		Sales Returns and Allowances		200
		Sales Discounts		300
		Wages Expense		7,000
		Purchases		50,000
		Income Taxes Expense		4,780
		To close nominal accounts with debit balances, and to close out beginning inventory		
	31	Income Summary	22,870	
		Retained Earnings		22,870
		To close out the Income Summary account		
	31	Retained Earnings	12,000	
		Dividends		12,000
		To close out Dividends account		

3. (L.O. 6)

Jefferson Merchandising Company Partial Income Statement For the Year 19xx			
Gross Sales			$100,000
Less: Sales Discounts		$ 300	
Sales Returns and Allowances		200	500
Net Sales			$ 99,500
Less Cost of Goods Sold			
Merchandise Inventory, Jan. 1		$10,000	
Purchases	$50,000		
Less: Purchases Discounts	500		
Purchases Returns and Allowances	500		
	$49,000		
Add Freight In	2,000		
Net Purchases		51,000	
Goods Available for Sale		$61,000	
Less Merchandise Inventory, Dec. 31		8,000	
Cost of Goods Sold			53,000
Gross Margin from Sales			$ 46,500

Note: See Chapter 6 for placement of interest income in this type of income statement.

4. (L.O. 7)

General Journal				
Date		Description	Debit	Credit
Dec.	31	Income Summary	10,000	
		Merchandise Inventory		10,000
		To remove beginning balance of Merchandise Inventory and		
		transfer it to Income Summary		
	31	Merchandise Inventory	8,000	
		Income Summary		8,000
		To establish ending balance of Merchandise Inventory and deduct		
		it from goods available for sale in Income Summary		

Mammoth Mart, Inc.
Work Sheet
For the Month Ended March 31, 19xx

Account Name	Trial Balance Debit	Trial Balance Credit	Adjustments Debit	Adjustments Credit	Adjusted Trial Balance Debit	Adjusted Trial Balance Credit	Income Statement Debit	Income Statement Credit	Balance Sheet Debit	Balance Sheet Credit
Cash	1,000				1,000				1,000	
Accounts Receivable	700				700				700	
Merchandise Inventory	400				400		400	620	620	
Prepaid Rent	750			(a) 250	500				500	
Equipment	4,200				4,200				4,200	
Accounts Payable		900				900				900
Common Stock		3,000				3,000				3,000
Retained Earnings		1,200				1,200				1,200
Sales		9,800				9,800		9,800		
Sales Discounts	300				300		300			
Purchases	3,700				3,700		3,700			
Purchases Returns and Allowances		150				150		150		
Freight In	400				400		400			
Salaries Expense	3,000		(b) 500		3,500		3,500			
Advertising Expense	600				600		600			
	15,050	15,050								
Rent Expense			(a) 250		250		250			
Salaries Payable				(b) 500		500				500
Depreciation Expense			(c) 375		375		375			
Accumulated Depreciation, Equipment				(c) 375		375				375
Income Taxes Expense			(e) 180		180		180			
Income Taxes Payable				(e) 180		180				180
			1,305	1,305	16,105	16,105	9,705	10,570	7,020	6,155
Net Income							865			865
							10,570	10,570	7,020	7,020

Solution to Crossword Puzzle
(Chapters 4 and 5)

Chapter 6

Matching

1. g	**6.** s	**11.** q	**16.** b
2. n	**7.** m	**12.** l	**17.** k
3. r	**8.** d	**13.** j	**18.** f
4. t	**9.** o	**14.** a	**19.** p
5. i	**10.** h	**15.** e	**20.** c

Short Answer

1. (L.O. 5)

Business Organization	Name for Owners' Equity Section
Sole Proprietorship	Owners' Equity
Partnership	Partners' Equity
Corporation	Stockholders' Equity

2. (L.O. 7) *Profit margin*—Shows net income in relation to net sales.

Asset turnover—Shows how efficiently assets are used to produce sales.

Return on assets—Shows net income in relation to average total assets.

Return on equity—Shows net income in relation to owners' investment.

Debt to equity ratio—Shows the proportion of a business financed by creditors and that financed by owners.

3. (L.O. 7) *Working capital*—Current assets minus current liabilities.

Current ratio—Current assets divided by current liabilities.

4. (L.O. 3) *Consistency and comparability*—Applying the same accounting procedures from one period to the next.

Materiality—The relative importance of an item or event.

Cost-benefit—The cost of providing additional accounting information should not exceed the benefits gained from it.

Conservatism—Choosing the accounting procedure that will be least likely to overstate assets and income.

Full disclosure—Showing all relevant information in the financial statements or in the footnotes.

True-False

1. F (L.O. 5) They are considered current assets if collection is expected within the normal operating cycle, even if that cycle is more than one year.

2. F (L.O. 4) Accounting is best described as an information system that is circular and continuous.

3. T (L.O. 6)

4. F (L.O. 6) Operating expenses are made up of selling expenses and general and administrative expenses only.

5. T (L.O. 2)

6. T (L.O. 7)

7. F (L.O. 5) Short-term investments in stock should be included in the current assets section of the balance sheet.

8. F (L.O. 7) *Liquidity* is what is being defined.

9. F (L.O. 5) The operating cycle can be less than one year.

10. F (L.O. 5) Net worth is merely another term for owners' equity, and does not necessarily equal net asset worth.

11. T (L.O. 6)

12. F (L.O. 6) The net income figures will be the same, although they are arrived at differently.

13. F (L.O. 8) It is the accountants' report that is divided into scope and opinion sections.

14. F (L.O. 7) Working capital equals current assets *minus* current liabilities.

15. T (L.O. 7)

16. F (L.O. 2) *Reliability* is what is being described.

17. T (L.O. 8)

18. F (L.O. 6, 8) Financial statements are condensed when they contain little detail; they are consolidated when they combine parent and subsidiary information.

Multiple Choice

1. c (L.O. 5) The conversion of inventories to cash is the basis for a firm's operations. This conversion cycle (called the normal operating cycle) is frequently less than 12 months. However, if it is *greater* than 12 months, the inventory by definition is still classified as a current asset.

2. c (L.O. 6) The single-step income statement does not isolate gross margin from sales. Instead, cost of goods sold is combined with other operating expenses and then subtracted from net sales to calculate income from operations.

3. b (L.O. 7) The current ratio gives management information about a firm's liquidity. Liquidity is important for anticipation of a company's capability to cover operations and current liabilities.

4. d (L.O. 5) The owner's capital account would appear on the balance sheet of a sole proprietorship or partnership only.

5. a (L.O. 8) An accountant's (auditor's) job is to examine the financial statements of a client firm to determine the fairness of the presentation of the accounting data. That determination is set forth as an "opinion" within the independent auditor's report.

6. a (L.O. 7) The ratio described is the profit margin, which describes the relationship between the outcome of operations and total revenues.

7. c (L.O. 6) "Operating expenses" is a broad term referring to expenses of running a company *other than the cost of goods sold.*

8. c (L.O. 3) Conservatism requires that losses experienced by a firm should be recognized in the period of the decline. Since inventories and short-term investments are subject to fluctuations in value, losses are recorded to reflect a negative economic impact on a firm from market conditions.

9. c (L.O. 6) The Retained Earnings account is increased by net income and decreased by dividends declared. The only amount that would reflect these facts is $13,000.

10. d (L.O. 1) Each choice except *d* describes an objective of FASB *Statement of Financial Accounting Concepts No. 1.* The FASB statement described is not a source of information to be used as an addendum to an accountant's report.

Exercises

1. (L.O. 5)

1. d	5. a	9. f	13. X
2. e	6. c	10. e	14. a
3. c	7. a	11. d	15. e
4. g	8. b	12. a	

2. (L.O. 7)

a. $40,000	d. 12.5%
b. 3:1	e. 16⅔%
c. 10%	f. 1.25 times

3. (L.O. 6)

a.
Confrey Corporation
Income Statement (Multistep)
For the Year Ended December 31, 19xx

Net Sales	$200,000
Less Cost of Goods Sold	150,000
Gross Margin from Sales	$ 50,000
Less Operating Expenses	30,000
Income from Operations	$ 20,000
Add Interest Revenues	2,000
Income before Taxes	$ 22,000
Less Income Tax Expense	5,000
Net Income	$ 17,000
Earnings per Share	$4.86/share

b.
Confrey Corporation
Income Statement (Single-Step)
For the Year Ended December 31, 19xx

Revenues		
Net Sales	$200,000	
Interest Revenues	2,000	$202,000
Expenses		
Cost of Goods Sold	$150,000	
Operating Expenses	30,000	
Income Tax Expense	5,000	185,000
Net Income		$ 17,000
Earnings per Share		$4.86/share

Chapter 7

Matching

1. s	6. j	**11.** a	**16.** o	**21.** k
2. c	7. f	**12.** l	**17.** b	
3. g	8. t	**13.** i	**18.** h	
4. q	9. p	**14.** u	**19.** d	
5. m	10. e	**15.** r	**20.** n	

Short Answer

1. (L.O. 3, 4) Percentage of net sales method, accounts receivable aging method, direct charge-off method
2. (L.O. 5, 6) It means that the original payee who discounts a note receivable must make good on the note if the maker does not pay at maturity.
3. (L.O. 3) There would be a debit balance when more accounts are written off (in dollar amounts) than have been provided for in the adjusting entries for estimated uncollectible accounts.

4. (L.O. 5)
Principal
\+ Interest
= Maturity value
− Discount
= Proceeds from discounting
5. (L.O. 7) Bank service charge, a customer's NSF check, and an error in recording a check (only if underrecorded)

True-False

1. T (L.O. 4)
2. F (L.O. 3) It does follow the matching principle.
3. F (L.O. 3) The balance must be taken into account.
4. T (L.O. 2)
5. T (L.O. 4)
6. T (L.O. 4)
7. F (L.O. 5) The computation is .05 × 700 × 90/360.
8. T (L.O. 2)
9. F (L.O. 5) The payee must make good if the maker defaults.
10. F (L.O. 5) It has a duration of 62 days.
11. T (L.O. 5)
12. F (L.O. 3) Total assets will remain the same.

13. T (L.O. 5)
14. F (L.O. 3) The debit is to Allowance for Uncollectible Accounts.
15. T (L.O. 6)
16. T (L.O. 2)
17. F (L.O. 8) The reverse is true.
18. T (L.O. 7)
19. F (L.O. 7) No adjsuting entries are made for outstanding checks.
20. F (L.O. 7) It will begin with September 30 balances.
21. T (L.O. 7)
22. F (L.O. 1) Accounts receivable is a short-term liquid asset, but not a cash equivalent.
23. F (L.O. 4) Major credit cards involve factoring *without* recourse.

Multiple Choice

1. d (L.O. 4) The credit card company would deduct the 5 percent charge before remitting cash to the company.

2. b (L.O. 5) Principal × time × rate for *b* equals $12. Each of the other choices results in $6.

3. c (L.O. 3) Using the percentage of net sales method of calculating adjustments for Allowance for Uncollectible Accounts, the amount of the Uncollectible Accounts Expense is based upon the sales of the period. Therefore, it is not netted with an existing balance in the allowance account.

4. a (L.O. 6) Since the discounting bank has the right to extract funds from a firm's account if a note is dishonored, the firm carries that liability until such time as the note is paid to the bank. Once the note is paid off, the contingent liability is eliminated.

5. d (L.O. 4) With the direct charge-off method of accounting for uncollectible accounts, no allowance account is used. Therefore, each account, as it becomes uncollectible, is written off directly, recording both the expense and the reduction in Accounts Receivable.

6. c (L.O. 3) When an allowance account has been established to record anticipated uncollectible accounts, the expense was recorded at the time the allowance was made. As a result, when the actual uncollectible account is known and written off, the allowance account is reduced, and Accounts Receivable is reduced by the amount of the uncollectible subsidiary ledger account balance.

7. a (L.O. 5) The discount rate is used as an adjustment to the maturity value of a note to calculate the proceeds upon discounting that note to the bank. The details of a note would not include the discount rate, since it is unknown at the time the note is originated. Additionally, whether a note is to be discounted or not is irrelevant in determining the note arrangements.

8. b (L.O. 4) The direct charge-off method of handling uncollectible accounts often postpones the Uncollectible Accounts Expense of a given accounting period to subsequent accounting periods. Usually, a significant period of time elapses between a credit sale and the determination that the corresponding receivable is uncollectible.

9. c (L.O. 1) Inventory is not considered a short-term liquid asset. The ability of a firm to convert its inventory to cash is the basis for the firm's operations. Short-term liquid assets, by definition, are those assets that can be quickly converted to cash (or are cash or near cash) to cover operating expenses and immediate cash requirements.

10. c (L.O. 1) Using the conservatism principle, losses resulting from changing market position are to be acknowledged on the books of a firm. Therefore, the lower of cost or market is used to revalue marketable securities for fair presentation of the actual financial position of a company.

11. c (L.O. 8) When a petty cash fund is replenished, the various expenditures are debited and Cash is credited; the Petty Cash account is neither debited nor credited.

12. a (L.O. 7) By definition, the bank is not aware of a deposit in transit at the bank statement date. The company must therefore add the amount to the balance per bank statement to reflect the proper cash balance.

Exercises

1. (L.O. 5)
  a. $16.00
  b. $910.00
  c. $43.17
  d. $4.00

2. (L.O. 7)
  1. d   **3.** b   **5.** a
  2. c   **4.** d   **6.** d

3. (L.O. 8) $87.50

4. (L.O. 3, 4, 5, 6)

\	\	General Journal		
Date		**Description**	**Debit**	**Credit**
Dec.	*31*	Interest Receivable	75	
		Interest Income		75
		To record accrued interest on Notes Receivable		
	31	Uncollectible Accounts Expense	24,000	
		Allowance for Uncollectible Accounts		24,000
		To record estimated bad debts		
Jan.	*3*	Notes Receivable, Kohn	10,000	
		Accounts Receivable, Kohn		10,000
		Ms. Kohn substituted a 30-day, 6% note for her debt		
	8	Allowance for Uncollectible Accounts	1,000	
		Accounts Receivable, O'Brien		1,000
		To write off Mr. O'Brien's account		
	14	Accounts Receivable, MasterCard	3,800	
		Credit Card Discount Expense	200	
		Sales		4,000
		To record credit card sales; discount fee is 5 percent		
	18	Cash	10,020	
		Notes Receivable, Kohn		10,000
		Interest Income		20
		To record discount of Kohn's note		
	24	Cash	3,800	
		Accounts Receivable, MasterCard		3,800
		Received check from MasterCard		
	25	Accounts Receivable, O'Brien	600	
		Allowance for Uncollectible Accounts		600
		To reinstate O'Brien's account		
	28	Cash	200	
		Accounts Receivable, O'Brien		200
		Received $200 from O'Brien		
Feb.	*2*	Accounts Receivable, Kohn	10,060	
		Cash		10,060
		To record payment on Kohn's dishonored note (maturity value plus protest fee)		

Solution to Crossword Puzzle
(Chapters 6 and 7)

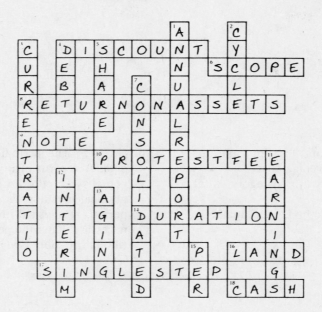

Chapter 8

Matching

1. m	5. j	9. c	13. k
2. h	6. a	10. l	
3. d	7. f	11. e	
4. g	8. i	12. b	

Short Answer

1. (L.O. 2) First-in, first-out; last-in, first-out; specific identification; average-cost
2. (L.O. 6) Item-by-item, major category, total inventory
3. (L.O. 7) Gross profit method, retail method

4. (L.O. 5) The periodic system does not keep detailed records of inventory, whereas the perpetual system does. Under the periodic system, physical inventory is taken at the end of each period. A physical inventory is not absolutely necessary under the perpetual inventory system (though it should be done).

True-False

1. T (L.O. 1)
2. T (L.O. 1)
3. T (L.O. 1)
4. T (L.O. 1)
5. F (L.O. 1) They belong in the buyer's ending inventory if the buyer has title to the goods.
6. T (L.O. 4)
7. F (L.O. 3) Not necessarily. The actual flow of goods is not known, although flow of costs is assumed.
8. F (L.O. 3) It will result in the highest income.
9. F (L.O. 7) Items sold are recorded only at retail.

10. F (L.O. 7) Cost of goods sold is estimated by subtracting the gross margin percentage of sales from total sales.
11. T (L.O. 5)
12. F (L.O. 3) Average cost will result in a higher net income.
13. F (L.O. 5) Subsidiary files are kept under the perpetual method.
14. F (L.O. 3) The requirement is for LIFO, not FIFO.
15. F (L.O. 1) The consignee has possession, but not title.

Multiple Choice

1. b (L.O. 2) The cost to store goods is normally considered too difficult to trace to specific inventory items, so it is expensed when incurred. The other costs listed are more closely related to the acquisition cost of the inventory.
2. a (L.O. 4) Under rising prices, the FIFO inventory method will result in the matching of current selling prices with the oldest, least expensive costs. Of the inventory methods listed, this method will result in the highest taxable income, and therefore the highest tax liability.

3. c (L.O. 1) Forgetting to inventory a warehouse will result in an understated ending inventory, which will in turn produce an overstated cost of goods sold. An overstated cost of goods sold will produce an understated net income and therefore an understated owner's equity.
4. c (L.O. 3) With low-volume, high-priced goods, it is especially necessary to match the selling price of a particular item with its cost in order to avoid the financial statement distortion that otherwise might arise. Only specific identification will accomplish this direct matching.

5. b (L.O. 7) In performing the retail inventory calculation, freight in is incorporated at cost, not at retail. The other choices provided are included as stated.

6. a (L.O. 1) The matching rule states that a cost must be expensed in the period in which that cost helps to generate revenue. Therefore, the cost of inventory is expensed in the period in which the inventory is sold.

7. d (L.O. 1) By definition, inventory should appear on the balance sheet of the company that has title to the goods (though not necessarily possession of them).

8. c (L.O. 5) Under the perpetual inventory system, when goods are sold, entries must be made both to record the sale and to update the Cost of Goods Sold and Inventory accounts. This practice is in accordance with the matching rule.

Exercises

1. (L.O. 3)
   a. $6,600; $8,800
   b. $7,200; $8,200
   c. $6,820; $8,580

2. (L.O. 7)

	Cost	Retail	
Beginning Inventory	$70,000	$125,000	
Net Purchases	48,000	75,000	
Freight In	2,000	—	
Cost/Retail	$120,000 ·	$200,000	= 60%
— Sales		156,000	
Estimated Ending Inventory at Retail		44,000	
		x 60%	
Estimated Ending Inventory at Cost		$26,400	

3. (L.O. 7)

Beginning Inventory	$150,000
Net Purchases	120,000
Goods Available for Sale	$270,000
— Estimated Cost of Goods Sold ($300,000 x 80%)	240,000
Estimated Cost of Ending Inventory	$ 30,000

4. (L.O. 5)

Date	Purchased			Sold			Balance		
	Units	Cost	Total	Units	Cost	Total	Units	Cost	Total
May 1							100	10.00	1,000.00
4	60	12.00	720.00				100 60	10.00 12.00	1,720.00
8				50	12.00	600.00	100 10	10.00 12.00	1,120.00
17	70	11.00	770.00				100 10 70	10.00 12.00 11.00	1,890.00
25				70 10 20	11.00 12.00 10.00	1,090.00	80	10.00	800.00

5. (L.O. 5)

\multicolumn{5}{c}{General Journal}

Date		Description	Debit	Credit
May	17	Merchandise Inventory	770	
		Accounts Payable		770
		To record purchase of inventory		
	25	Cash	2,000	
		Sales		2,000
		To record cash sales		
	25	Cost of Goods Sold	1,090	
		Merchandise Inventory		1,090
		To record cost of merchandise sold		

Chapter 9

Matching

1. e	**7.** r	**13.** u	**19.** i
2. w	**8.** h	**14.** c	**20.** d
3. n	**9.** q	**15.** k	**21.** p
4. s	**10.** j	**16.** m	**22.** f
5. l	**11.** v	**17.** g	**23.** b
6. t	**12.** o	**18.** a	

Short Answer

1. (L.O. 6) An addition adds to the physical layout, as a new building wing. A betterment merely improves the existing layout, as a new air-conditioning system.
2. (L.O. 7) When cash received equals the carrying value of the asset sold.
3. (L.O. 9) Cost of oil well. Estimated residual value of oil well. Estimated barrels to be extracted over life of well. Actual barrels extracted and sold during that year.
4. (L.O. 6) Ordinary repairs merely maintain the asset in good operating condition, as a paint job or tune-up. Extraordinary repairs, however, increase the asset's estimated residual value or useful life, as a complete overhaul.
5. (L.O. 1) Amortization, depreciation, depletion
6. (L.O. 3) Physical deterioration, obsolescence

True-False

1. T (L.O. 3)
2. T (L.O. 7)
3. T (L.O. 1)
4. F (L.O. 3) Depreciation is a process of allocation, not of valuation.
5. F (L.O. 3) The wearing out of a machine is irrelevant in computing depreciation.
6. T (L.O. 2)
7. T (L.O. 5)
8. T (L.O. 4)
9. F (L.O. 4) Depreciation expense will be $1,000 in the second year also.
10. T (L.O. 5)
11. T (L.O. 8)
12. F (L.O. 4) It will result in more net income.
13. F (L.O. 3) Depreciable cost equals cost minus residual value.
14. F (L.O. 4) The carrying value will theoretically never reach zero under this method.
15. T (L.O. 5)
16. F (L.O. 10) A *trademark* is a name or symbol that may be used only by its owner.
17. T (L.O. 6)
18. F (L.O. 6) A betterment is a capital expenditure.
19. F (L.O. 6) The carrying value increases, because the Accumulated Depreciation account is decreased (debited).
20. F (L.O. 7) The Accumulated Depreciation account is always *debited* when a depreciable asset is sold.
21. F (L.O. 6) An expenditure refers to the *purchase* of an asset, whereas an expense refers to the expiration of asset cost, through its use.
22. T (L.O. 8)
23. F (L.O. 7) Depreciation expense should be brought up to date prior to sale.
24. T (L.O. 10)
25. T (L.O. 4)
26. T (L.O. 10)
27. F (L.O. 10) Research and development costs should normally be charged as expense in the year incurred.
28. T (L.O. 9)

Multiple Choice

1. c (L.O. 2) Since the relative values of the lump-sum purchase are known, a ratio can be determined and applied to the purchase price of both assets. Total value assigned to the land and building is $80,000. Of that $80,000, $20,000, or 25 percent, is apportioned to the land. 25 percent of the purchase price for both assets is $16,500.

2. a (L.O. 3) The expired cost of an asset is its total accumulated depreciation to date. Depreciation is the allocation of the cost of an asset over its useful life.

3. d (L.O. 4) An accelerated method of depreciation would result in greater depreciation expense in the first year that an asset is put into service. However, additional data are required to determine which method would be the most accelerated for a specific asset.

4. c (L.O. 5) This change in accounting estimate would result in an adjustment to the depreciation schedule of the asset. The remaining depreciable cost would be spread over the remaining (new) estimated useful life of the machine.

5. c (L.O. 10) Although the life of an intangible asset may be difficult to estimate, GAAP has set a "reasonable" limit on how long a firm may amortize the costs associated with intangible assets.

6. b (L.O. 2) While land is not a depreciable asset, improvements to land are. This could include buildings, street lights, pavement, etc. Each improvement has an estimable useful life over which the costs will be recovered. Land does not have an estimable useful life, and therefore is not subject to depreciation.

7. a (L.O. 5) The entry described is an adjusting entry. During the accounting period, purchases of spare parts are recorded as debits to that asset account. As spare parts are used, there is no journal entry to record the reduction in the account balance. At the period end, a physical inventory reveals the amount remaining, and the adjustment must be made to record the expense of the use of spare parts.

8. d (L.O. 7) In order to eliminate the asset from the company's accounting records, existing accounts pertaining to the asset must be removed from the books as part of the transaction. Since the book value of the machine was $2,000 and the original cost was $9,000, accumulated depreciation must have been $7,000 (credit balance). To eliminate that account, a debit of $7,000 should be recorded to Accumulated Depreciation.

9. b (L.O. 6) The new roof has an economic life of more than a year. Therefore, the expenditure for that new roof is considered a capital expenditure.

10. d (L.O. 6) Understatement of net income results from expensing a capital expenditure. By definition, capital expenditures should be spread over the useful life of the acquisition (more than one period). If the entire cost is put into one period, expenses for that period will be overstated.

11. b (L.O. 9) Depletion costs assigned to a given period are the result of calculations based upon expected total output over the life of the oil well. Total costs divided by total expected units of output provides the depletion cost per unit. If expected units of output is overestimated, unit cost will be less.

12. a (L.O. 10) Up to the point at which the software is technologically feasible, its costs are treated as research and development, and therefore must be expensed.

13. d (L.O. 10) Research and development costs are considered revenue expenditures and are recognized in the period incurred. It is a difficult problem to estimate the useful life of research and development.

Exercises

1. (L.O. 4)

	Depreciation Expense	Accumulated Depreciation	Carrying Value
a.	$4,800	$ 9,600	$16,400
b.	$6,400	$14,400	$11,600
c.	$6,240	$16,640	$ 9,360

2. (L.O. 4)

$$\$2,250 \left(\frac{\$35,000 - \$5,000}{100,000 \text{ toys}} \times 7,500 \text{ toys} \right)$$

3. (L.O. 6)

a. C	d. C	f. R	h. C
b. R	e. C	g. C	i. R
c. R			

4. (L.O. 8)

General Journal				
Date		Description	Debit	Credit
Jan.	1	Machinery (new)	23,000	
		Accumulated Depreciation, Machinery	17,000	
		Loss on Trade-in of Machinery	500	
		Cash		15,500
		Machinery (old)		25,000
		To record trade-in of machine, following GAAP		
	1	Machinery (new)	23,500	
		Accumulated Depreciation, Machinery	17,000	
		Cash		15,500
		Machinery (old)		25,000
		To record trade-in of machine, following income tax rulings*		

*For income tax purposes, neither gains nor losses are recognized on the exchange of similar assets.

5. (L.O. 9)

General Journal				
Date		Description	Debit	Credit
Dec.	31	Depletion Expense	40,000	
		Accumulated Depletion, Coal Mine		40,000
		To record depletion of coal mine for 19xx		

Solution to Crossword Puzzle
(Chapters 8 and 9)

Chapter 10

Matching

1. n	**4.** d	**7.** o	**10.** j	**13.** e
2. k	**5.** l	**8.** g	**11.** h	**14.** i
3. f	**6.** m	**9.** c	**12.** a	**15.** b

Short Answer

1. (L.O. 2) Definitely determinable liabilities, estimated liabilities

2. (L.O. 3) Some examples of contingent liabilities are pending lawsuits, tax disputes, discounted notes receivable, the guarantee of another company's debt, and failure to follow government regulations.

3. (L.O. 2) Income taxes payable, estimated warranty expense, vacation pay. (There are others.)

4. (L.O. 2) Some examples of definitely determinable liabilities are trade accounts payable, short-term notes payable, dividends payable, sales tax payable, excise tax payable, current portion of long-term debt, accrued liabilities, payroll liabilities, and deferred revenues.

5. (L.O. 1) A financial instrument is a contract that results in an asset in one entity's records and a liability in another's.

True-False

1. F (L.O. 2) A deferred revenue is a liability on the balance sheet representing an obligation to deliver goods or services.

2. T (L.O. 2)

3. T (L.O. 1)

4. T (L.O. 2)

5. F (L.O. 2) Sales Tax Payable is a definitely determinable liability.

6. F (L.O. 2) A warranty is an estimated liability.

7. T (L.O. 6)

8. T (L.O. 5) Payments associated with an ordinary annuity are made at the *end* of each period.

9. F (L.O. 6) The higher the interest rate, the *lower* the present value.

10. T (L.O. 3)

11. F (L.O. 2) The account is associated with notes whose interest is included in the face amount.

12. F (L.O. 2) An estimate should be recorded for Product Warranty Expense in year 1, the year of the sale.

Multiple Choice

1. c (L.O. 2) Property tax bills are not available to a firm until months after the liability actually exists. Therefore, the accountant must estimate the property taxes due for the accounting period, and enter that estimate onto the books as a liability. Upon receipt of the actual tax bill, adjustments will be made. This method is required by the matching rule, which allows for estimates when perfect information is not available, to match expenses of a period to that accounting period.

2. d (L.O. 2) Pending lawsuits, and the settlement thereof, would be recorded as contingent liabilities, but only if the outcome against the company is estimable and probable.

3. c (L.O. 2) Under the matching rule, estimated liabilities for vacation pay as a result of current employee status must be recorded as an expense of the current period. Therefore, by the time the employee exercises the right to a paid vacation, the expense has been recorded by the use of an allowance account, Estimated Liability for Vacation Pay. As the liability expires, it is reduced by a debit entry. This credit entry is to Cash for the disbursement of pay to the employee.

4. d (L.O. 2) The entry to record payment in advance of the property tax bill would be a debit to the Prepaid Property Tax account and a credit to Cash. Then, as each monthly share of the prepaid amount expires, the entry would be a debit to Property Tax Expense and a reduction (credit entry) to the corresponding prepaid (asset) account.

5. b (L.O. 5) When interest is calculated on a semiannual basis, the annual interest rate is cut in half, but the number of years must be doubled to arrive at the correct number of semiannual periods.

6. d (L.O. 6) To calculate the present value of a single sum due in the future, one must multiply the future amount by the present value of a single sum factor, using the assumed discount rate and number of periods.

7. c (L.O. 5, 6) One way to calculate the future value of a single sum invested now is to divide the single sum by the appropriate present value of a single sum factor.

8. a (L.O. 7) Even though the problem states that there is no interest borne by the note, a rate must be applied. The method for doing so would be to record the note, discounted at an appropriate rate. The principal of the note less the discount is the actual "cost" of the equipment to Marina Pools, Inc.

9. b (L.O. 2) With the passage of time, Discount on Notes Payable will be changed into Interest Expense, in accordance with the matching rule.

Exercises

1. (L.O. 2)

General Journal				
Date		Description	Debit	Credit
Dec.	31	Product Warranty Expense	525	
		Estimated Product Warranty Liability		525
		To record estimated warranty expense for washing machines		
Apr.	9	Estimated Product Warranty Liability	48	
		Parts, Wages Payable, etc.		48
		To record the repair of a washing machine		

2. (L.O. 5, 6) **a.** $747 ($1,000 × .747)
   b. $4,122 ($1,000 × 4.122)
   c. $1,126 ($1,000 × 1.126)
   d. $1,745.81 ($100,000/57.28)

3. (L.O. 7) Present value = $2,000 × 4.494 = $8,988

The purchase should not be made because the present value of future cash savings is less than the initial cost of the equipment.

4. (L.O. 7)

a. Equipment ($10,000 × .826)   8,260
   Discount on Notes Payable   1,740
       Notes Payable   10,000

b. Interest Expense ($8,260 × .1)   826
       Discount on Notes Payable   826

c. Interest Expense ($1,740 − $826)   914
   Notes Payable   10,000
       Discount on Notes Payable   914
       Cash   10,000

Chapter 11

Matching

1. i	6. s	11. m	16. n
2. d	7. j	12. l	17. p
3. q	8. f	13. b	18. h
4. a	9. c	14. g	19. k
5. o	10. e	15. r	20. t

Short Answer

1. (L.O. 1) A debenture is an unsecured bond, whereas an indenture is the contract between the bondholder and the corporation.
2. (L.O. 2) A premium would probably be received when the bond's interest rate is higher than the market rate for similar bonds at the time of the issue.
3. (L.O. 2) Interest = principal × rate × time
4. (L.O. 3) Present value of periodic interest payments; present value of maturity value

True-False

1. T (L.O. 1)
2. T (L.O. 1)
3. F (L.O. 1) Bond interest must be paid on each interest date. It is not something that the board of directors declares.
4. T (L.O. 2)
5. F (L.O. 4) It will be less than the cash paid.
6. T (L.O. 4)
7. F (L.O. 5) Bond Interest Expense is credited.
8. T (L.O. 4)
9. F (L.O. 4) It equals interest payments *plus* the bond discount.
10. T (L.O. 6)
11. F (L.O. 4) The premium amortized will increase in amount each year.
12. T (L.O. 4)
13. T (L.O. 7)
14. T (L.O. 7)
15. T (L.O. 6)
16. T (L.O. 2)
17. T (L.O. 7)

Multiple Choice

1. d (L.O. 5) When bonds are issued between interest dates, the amount the investor pays for the bond includes the accrued interest as of the date of issue. On the interest date, the full interest due for the entire period is paid out to each bondholder, including those who have held a bond for only a partial period. The issuing firm maintains the abnormal balance in the Bond Interest Expense account until the interest is paid to the bondholders.

2. a (L.O. 7) Interest expense on a mortgage is based upon the unpaid balance. Over time, as the principal of the mortgage is reduced, the interest portion of a fixed payment becomes less. Therefore, the portion of the payment attributable to the reduction of the unpaid balance increases.

3. d (L.O. 2) Bonds issued at a premium have a carrying value above the face value. As the premium is amortized, the carrying value is reduced. As long as there is an unamortized bond premium on the books, the bonds will have a carrying value of more than the face value. This information is presented on the balance sheet as a long-term liability.

4. c (L.O. 5) Interest expense for the period must be recorded as an adjustment at year-end. In recording interest expense for bonds that were sold at a discount, the calculation includes a reduction in Unamortized Bond Discount, which has a normal debit balance.

5. b (L.O. 4) Using the effective interest method, the calculation for interest expense is based upon the current carrying value of the bonds. As the bond discount is amortized, that carrying value increases. As a result, the interest expense per period also increases.

6. b (L.O. 7) The lease described in answer *b* does not meet the requirements for a capital lease. The arrangement does not resemble a sale. It is therefore an operating lease.

7. c (L.O. 6) Early retirement of bonds is considered an extraordinary occurrence. Therefore, when a gain or loss results from the transaction, the results will be presented on the income statement as an extraordinary item. In the transaction described, the company paid $204,000 ($200,000 x 102%) for bonds outstanding with a carrying value of $195,000. The difference between the carrying value and the amount paid ($9,000) is a loss.

8. c (L.O. 6) The carrying value of the bonds is $612,000. If one-third of the bonds are converted, the carrying value of the bonds payable will be reduced by $204,000 ($612,000/3).

Exercises

1. (L.O. 2, 4)
   a. $9,000 ($600,000 − $591,000)
   b. $21,000 ($600,000 x 7% x $\frac{1}{2}$)
   c. $21,450 $\left(\$21,000 + \dfrac{\$9,000}{20}\right)$
   d. $593,700 ($600,000 − $6,300)
2. (L.O. 2, 4)
   a. $550,000 ($500,000 x 110%)
   b. $17,500 ($500,000 x 7% x $\frac{1}{2}$)
   c. $16,500 ($550,000 x 6% x $\frac{1}{2}$)
   d. $1,000 ($17,500 − $16,500)
   e. $549,000 ($550,000 − $1,000)
3. (L.O. 2)

Interest payments ($600,000 x 8% x 10)	$480,000
Premium on bonds payable ($600,000 x 6%)	36,000
Total interest costs	$444,000 ($44,400/year)

4.

		General Journal		
Date		**Description**	**Debit**	**Credit**
Dec.	31	Cash	50,000	
		Notes Payable		50,000
		Borrowed $50,000 at 10% on 5-year note		
Dec.	31	Notes Payable	10,000	
		Interest Expense	5,000	
		Cash		15,000
		Made first installment payment		
Dec.	31	Notes Payable	10,000	
		Interest Expense	4,000	
		Cash		14,000
		Made second installment payment		

5.

		General Journal		
Date		**Description**	**Debit**	**Credit**
Dec.	31	Cash	50,000	
		Notes Payable		50,000
		Borrowed $50,000 at 10% on 5-year note		
Dec.	31	Notes Payable	8,190	
		Interest Expense	5,000	
		Cash		13,190
		Made first installment payment		
Dec.	31	Notes Payable	9,009	
		Interest Expense	4,181	
		Cash		13,190
		Made second installment payment		

Solution to Crossword Puzzle
(Chapters 10 and 11)

```
 ¹P  E  N  S  I  O  N  P ²L  A  N      ³S
  R              E              E         ⁴R
  E    ⁵F  A ⁶C  E     A     ⁷I  R        E
  M        O    ⁸D ⁹S  I  N  K  I  N  G   G
¹⁰I  N ¹¹D  E  N  T  U  R  E  S     T     A     I
  U    E     T        E        E     L        S
  M    F     I    ¹²I     ¹³T  E  R ¹⁴M        T
       I     N        N        S        O        E
¹⁵A    N     G        C    ¹⁶F           T        D
¹⁷N  E  T     E        O     U           T
  U    ¹⁸E  S  T  I  M  A  T  E  D        G
  I    L              E     U    ¹⁹C  A  L  L
  T    Y              R              G
  Y    ²⁰S  I  M  P  L  E     ²¹Z  E  R  O
```

Chapter 12

Matching

1. f	6. m	11. d	16. q
2. k	7. g	12. h	17. i
3. p	8. a	13. c	18. r
4. l	9. o	14. s	19. j
5. e	10. n	15. t	20. b

Short Answer

1. (L.O. 1) Separate legal entity, limited liability, ease of capital generation, ease of transfer of ownership, lack of mutual agency, continuous existence, centralized authority and responsibility, professional management
2. (L.O. 1) Government regulation, double taxation, limited liability, separation of ownership and control
3. (L.O. 3) Contributed capital, retained earnings
4. (L.O. 5) Upon dividend declaration, upon corporate liquidation

True-False

1. T (L.O. 1)
2. T (L.O. 6)
3. T (L.O. 1)
4. F (L.O. 2) Organization costs are normally amortized over the early years of a corporation's life.
5. T (L.O. 3)
6. T (L.O. 6)
7. F (L.O. 5) It may.
8. T (L.O. 5)
9. F (L.O. 3) Par value has no necessary relation to market value (worth).
10. F (L.O. 7) Stockholders' equity remains the same when cash is received.
11. F (L.O. 5) No stockholders are ever guaranteed dividends.
12. F (L.O. 3) Common stock is considered the residual equity of a corporation.
13. F (L.O. 8) The amount of compensation is measured on the *grant* date.
14. F (L.O. 4) Total assets and total liabilities decrease.
15. F (L.O. 5) Dividends (in arrears) are not a liability until declared. Any arrearage normally appears as a footnote.

Multiple Choice

1. d (L.O. 7) Subscriptions Receivable is an asset account and will appear in the asset section of the balance sheet.
2. a (L.O. 7) When a stock subscription has been fully paid, the stock will be issued. Each time common stock is issued, the Common Stock account will be credited. The debit entry will be to Common Stock Subscribed.
3. c (L.O. 3) Authorized shares is the maximum number of shares a corporation will be able to issue. Until such time as shares are issued, they are considered unissued. Outstanding shares are those shares that are issued and in the hands of stockholders (as opposed to in the treasury of the corporation). Treasury stock is considered to be issued.

4. d (L.O. 5) Since the preferred stock is non-cumulative, there are no dividends in arrears. The current dividend declared will be distributed to preferred stockholders based upon 7 percent of the par value of $100. Of the declaration, therefore, $7,000 will be distributed to the preferred stockholders (.07 × $100 × 1000 shares). The remaining $33,000 will be distributed, pro rata, to the common stockholders.

5. d (L.O. 1) Stockholders of a corporation are protected from unlimited liability. Under most circumstances, their liability (or potential for loss) is limited to the amount of the stockholder's investment.

6. d (L.O. 4) The declaration of a cash dividend requires a journal entry to record the liability and to reduce retained earnings by the amount of the declared dividend. On the date of payment of the dividend, a journal entry is required to record the elimination of the liability created on the date of declaration and the reduction in cash as a result of the payment. The date of record is a data-gathering date, and no journal entry is required.

7. b (L.O. 4) If stock is purchased after the date of record, the new owner has no rights to the dividends not yet distributed.

8. d (L.O. 5) The call feature on stock specifies an amount for which the corporation can buy back the stock. It is binding to the stockholder and to the issuing corporation in spite of possible differences between the call price and the market value at the time the stock is called.

Exercises

1. (L.O. 5) Preferred stockholders receive:
   $18,000 (1,000 × $100 × 6% × 3 years).
   Common stockholders receive:
   $33,000 ($51,000 − $18,000).

2. (L.O. 7)

	General Journal				
Date		**Description**		**Debit**	**Credit**
May	*1*	Subscriptions Receivable, Common		70,000	
		Common Stock Subscribed			50,000
		Paid-in Capital in Excess of Par Value, Common			20,000
		Accepted subscriptions for 1,000 shares of $50 par value common stock at $70 per share			
	1	Cash		14,000	
		Subscriptions Receivable, Common			14,000
		Collected 20% down payment on stock subscriptions			
June	*3*	Cash		28,000	
		Subscriptions Receivable, Common			28,000
		Collected 40% installment on stock subscriptions			
	18	Cash		28,000	
		Subscriptions Receivable, Common			28,000
		Collected remaining 40% on stock subscriptions			
	18	Common Stock Subscribed		50,000	
		Common Stock			50,000
		Issued 1,000 shares of $50 par value common stock			

Chapter 13

Matching

1. j	6. b	11. p	16. h
2. c	7. n	12. d	17. f
3. r	8. g	13. o	18. q
4. s	9. i	14. a	19. e
5. m	10. l	15. k	20. t

Short Answer

1. (L.O. 1) Net loss from operations, cash dividend declaration, stock dividend declaration, certain prior period adjustments, and certain treasury stock transactions

2. (L.O. 2) A stock split changes the par or stated value, whereas a stock dividend does not. A stock dividend transfers retained earnings to contributed capital, whereas a stock split does not.

3. (L.O. 9) It must be unusual in nature. It must occur infrequently.

4. (L.O. 3) Treasury stock is stock that has been both issued and repurchased by the corporation. Unissued stock has never been issued.

True-False

1. F (L.O. 9) The net of taxes amount is *less* than $20,000.
2. F (L.O. 4) Restricted Retained Earnings is not a cash account.
3. T (L.O. 6)
4. F (L.O. 2) Each stockholder owns the same percentage as before.
5. T (L.O. 2)
6. F (L.O. 2) Its main purpose is to increase marketability by causing a decrease in the market price. The decrease in par value is more a byproduct of a stock split.
7. T (L.O. 3)
8. F (L.O. 3) Paid-in Capital, Treasury Stock Transactions should be recorded for the excess of issue price over cost.

9. F (L.O. 3) Treasury stock is listed in the stockholders' equity section, as a deduction.
10. F (L.O. 9) It does not because it is not an unusual and infrequently occurring event.
11. F (L.O. 9) Extraordinary items should appear on the income statement.
12. T (L.O. 9)
13. F (L.O. 2) It is classified as part of contributed capital.
14. T (L.O. 10)
15. T (L.O. 8)
16. T (L.O. 1)
17. F (L.O. 10) Common stock equivalents are always included, provided they are not antidilutive.

Multiple Choice

1. a. (L.O. 2) A stock split simply requires replacing the number of shares outstanding prior to the split with the number of shares outstanding subsequent to the split. There is no other adjustment to stockholders' equity.

2. c (L.O. 2) They distributed a stock dividend of 1,000 shares (10% of 10,000 shares). The 11,000 shares outstanding after the stock dividend were then split into 4 shares for each 1 share (11,000 x 4), resulting in total shares outstanding of 44,000.

3. d (L.O. 4) A restriction on retained earnings is simply an indication of the intended use of the balance. The restricted amount remains in the stockholders' equity section of the balance sheet, but may be identified separately to identify the amounts unavailable for dividends.

4. c (L.O. 2) On the date of distribution of a stock dividend, Common Stock is credited and Common Stock Distributable is debited. Retained Earnings was adjusted on the date of declaration.

5. d (L.O. 3) When a company is dealing in its own stock, losses are never recognized. What would otherwise be considered a loss is recorded as a reduction in stockholders' equity. The exact nature of the transaction in this case is unknown, because of the lack of detail.

6. b (L.O. 3) Treasury stock is considered issued. For the purpose of cash dividends, however, treasury stock is *not* considered to be outstanding.

7. a (L.O. 9) Extraordinary items appear on the income statement to indicate the overall economic impact of the financial event upon the company. Extraordinary items will be presented after income (loss) from operations and after income (loss) from discontinued operations.

8. c (L.O. 10) For EPS calculations, 40,000 shares were outstanding for the entire year.

An additional 20,000 shares were outstanding for 9/12 of the year. 20,000 × 9/12 = 15,000 shares. 40,000 shares + 15,000 shares is 55,000 average shares outstanding for the year.

9. b (L.O. 1) There was a $30,000 increase in retained earnings during the year, even after a $15,000 cash dividend. Therefore, net income for the year must have been $45,000 ($30,000 + 15,000).

10. c (L.O. 5) Extraordinary gains and losses are presented in the income statement.

11. b (L.O. 10) If a corporation has only one type of stock, it would be common stock. Book value per share would be calculated by dividing total stockholders' equity by the number of shares issued. The current year's dividends would have already reduced retained earnings and total stockholders' equity. Dividend information would be irrelevant to finding book value per share.

12. c (L.O. 1) Retained earnings accumulates over time as a result of undistributed income of the corporation. Each accounting period that earnings are not entirely distributed to the stockholders through dividends, retained earnings will increase. Accounting periods in which losses occur result in a reduction in retained earnings. Dividends declared are taken from retained earnings.

Exercises

1. (L.O. 2)

General Journal				
Date		Description	Debit	Credit
Sept.	*1*	Cash	1,200,000	
		Common Stock		1,000,000
		Paid-in Capital in Excess of Par Value		200,000
		To record issuance of stock		
Mar.	*7*	Retained Earnings	65,000	
		Common Stock Distributable		50,000
		Paid-in Capital in Excess of Par Value		15,000
		To record declaration of stock dividend		
	30	No entry		
Apr.	*13*	Common Stock Distributable	50,000	
		Common Stock		50,000
		To record distribution of stock dividend		

2. (L.O. 3)

		General Journal		
Date		Description	Debit	Credit
Jan.	12	Treasury Stock, Common	300,000	
		Cash		300,000
		To record purchase of treasury stock		
	20	Cash	130,000	
		Treasury Stock, Common		120,000
		Paid-in Capital, Treasury Stock Transactions		10,000
		To record reissue of treasury stock		
	27	Cash	116,000	
		Paid-in Capital, Treasury Stock Transactions	4,000	
		Treasury Stock, Common		120,000
		To record reissue of treasury stock		
	31	Common Stock	10,000	
		Paid-in Capital in Excess of Par Value	40,000	
		Retained Earnings	10,000	
		Treasury Stock, Common		60,000
		To record retirement of treasury stock		

3. (L.O. 6)

Total stockholders' equity		$680,000
Less:		
Par value of outstanding		
preferred stock	$200,000	
Dividends in arrears	28,000	
Equity allocated to		
preferred shareholders		228,000
Equity pertaining to		
common shareholders		$452,000

Book value per share:

Preferred stock = $228,000/4,000 shares = $57 per share

Common stock = $452,000/30,000 shares = $15.07 per share

4. (L.O. 9)

Operating income before taxes		$100,000
Less income tax expense		40,000
Income before extraordinary item		$ 60,000
Extraordinary lightning loss	$ 30,000	
Less applicable tax	(12,000)	18,000
Net income (loss)		$ 42,000

5. (L.O. 8)

		General Journal		
Date		Description	Debit	Credit
19x1		Income Tax Expense	24,000	
		Deferred Income Taxes		8,000
		Current Income Taxes Payable		16,000
		To record income taxes for 19x1		
19x2		Income Tax Expense	12,000	
		Deferred Income Taxes	4,000	
		Current Income Taxes Payable		16,000
		To record income taxes for 19x2		
19x3		Income Tax Expense	28,000	
		Deferred Income Taxes	4,000	
		Current Income Taxes Payable		32,000
		To record income taxes for 19x3		

Solution to Crossword Puzzle
(Chapters 12 and 13)

Chapter 14

Matching

1. f   3. b   5. e   7. h
2. d   4. g   6. a   8. c

Short Answer

1. (L.O. 3) Issuing capital stock to retire long-term debt
   Purchasing a long-term asset by incurring long-term debt
2. (L.O. 4) Because they represent noncash expenses that have been legitimately deducted in arriving at net income. Adding them back effectively cancels out the deduction.

3. (L.O. 6) Cash flows from investing activities
   Cash flows from financing activities
   Schedule of noncash investing and financing transactions
4. (L.O. 1) Money market accounts
   Commercial paper (short-term notes)
   U.S. Treasury bills

True-False

1. T (L.O. 1)
2. F (L.O. 3) It is considered an operating activity.
3. T (L.O. 5)
4. T (L.O. 4)
5. T (L.O. 4)
6. F (L.O. 4, 5) Depreciation, depletion, and amortization would be found in the operating activities section.
7. F (L.O. 8) The reverse is true.
8. T (L.O. 8)
9. T (L.O. 7)

10. F (L.O. 7) It implies that the business is generally contracting.
11. T (L.O. 5)
12. F (L.O. 4) It would be added to net income.
13. F (L.O. 4) Depreciation must be *deducted* from operating expenses in this case.
14. T (L.O. 5)
15. T (L.O. 5)
16. F (L.O. 6) A change in methods will not produce a different net-change-in-cash figure.

Multiple Choice

1. a (L.O. 4) Cash receipts from sales, interest, and dividends are used to calculate cash inflows from operating activities. Under the indirect method, they are simply components of the net income figure presented.

2. b (L.O. 4) Net income in the operating activities section of the statement of cash flows includes the gain on sale of investments. That amount needs to be backed out of the operating activities section to avoid duplication of cash inflow data.

3. a (L.O. 4) An increase in Accounts Payable indicates an increase in cash available to the firm. To reflect the absence of that cash outflow, the amount by which the payables have increased will be added to the cash from operating activities section under the indirect method of preparing a statement of cash flows.

4. e (L.O. 5) The purchase of a building by incurring a mortgage payable does not involve any cash inflow or outflow. The investing and financing activity will be disclosed in the schedule of noncash investing and financing transactions.

5. d (L.O. 5) The payment of dividends is a cash outflow and would be disclosed in the financing activities section of the statement of cash flows. Investments made in a corporation by the stockholders through the purchase of stock are considered a source of financing by the corporation.

6. a (L.O. 4) Interest paid is a component of operating activities and would be recorded as a cash outflow.

7. b (L.O. 4) The increase in inventory represents a cash outflow and would be deducted from net income in the operating activities section of the statement of cash flows. The counter-entry is the adjustment for changing levels of accounts payable.

8. c (L.O. 4, 5) Cash payments from the issuance of stock are a cash inflow from financing activities. No adjustment to net income is required, since the sale and issuance of stock is not recorded as a revenue and is not presented on the income statement.

9. d (L.O. 8) In the analysis of transactions for the preparation of the statement of cash flows, each operating, financing, and investing activity of the period is reconstructed. Net income results in an increase in retained earnings, and the analysis begins with a credit entry to that account.

10. b (L.O. 4) Total sales were $100,000. Of that amount, $14,000 was diverted by an increase in Accounts Receivable. $100,000 less $14,000 equals $86,000 in cash receipts from cash sales and Accounts Receivable.

Exercises

1. (L.O. 4)
   a. $57,000 ($70,000 operating expenses + $1,000 increase in Prepaid Expenses + $6,000 decrease in Accrued Liabilities − $20,000 in Depreciation Expense)
   b. $360,000 ($350,000 Sales + $10,000 decrease in Accounts Receivable)
   c. $31,000 ($33,000 Income Taxes Expense − $2,000 increase in Income Taxes Payable)
   d. $221,000 ($240,000 Cost of Goods Sold − $12,000 decrease in Inventory − $7,000 increase in Accounts Payable)
   e. $51,000 (b − a − c − d above)

2. (L.O. 8)

CLU Corporation
Work Sheet for Statement of Cash Flows
For the Year Ended December 31, 19x9

Description	Account Balances 12/31/x8	Analysis of Transactions for 19x9 Debit	Analysis of Transactions for 19x9 Credit	Account Balances 12/31/x9
Debits				
Cash	35,000		(x) 6,000	29,000
Accounts Receivable	18,000	(b) 3,000		21,000
Inventory	83,000		(c) 11,000	72,000
Plant Assets	200,000	(f) 62,000	(e) 30,000	232,000
Total Debits	336,000			354,000
Credits				
Accumulated Depreciation	40,000	(e) 10,000	(g) 26,000	56,000
Accounts Payable	27,000	(d) 8,000		19,000
Bonds Payable	100,000	(h) 10,000		90,000
Common Stock	150,000		(h) 10,000	160,000
Retained Earnings	19,000	(i) 12,000	(a) 22,000	29,000
Total Credits	336,000	105,000	105,000	354,000
Cash Flows from Operating Activities				
Net Income		(a) 22,000		
Increase in Accounts Receivable			(b) 3,000	
Decrease in Inventory		(c) 11,000		
Decrease in Accounts Payable			(d) 8,000	
Gain on Sale of Plant Assets			(e) 4,000	
Depreciation Expense		(g) 26,000		
Cash Flows from Investing Activities				
Sale of Plant Assets		(e) 24,000		
Purchase of Plant Assets			(f) 62,000	
Cash Flows from Financing Activities				
Dividends Paid			(i) 12,000	
		83,000	89,000	
Net Decrease in Cash		(x) 6,000		
		89,000	89,000	

Chapter 15

Matching

1. g	**5.** j	**8.** i	**11.** m
2. b	**6.** f	**9.** k	**12.** a
3. l	**7.** h	**10.** d	**13.** c
4. e			

Short Answer

1. (L.O. 6) Profit margin, asset turnover, return on assets, return on equity, earnings per share
2. (L.O. 5) Horizontal analysis presents absolute and percentage changes in specific financial statement items from one year to the next. Vertical analysis, on the other hand, presents the percentage relationship of individual items on the statement to a total within the statement.
3. (L.O. 2) Rule-of-thumb measures, analysis of past performance of the company, comparison with industry norms
4. (L.O. 1) The risk of total loss is far less with several investments than with one investment because only a rare set of economic circumstances could cause several different investments to suffer large losses all at once.

True-False

1. T (L.O. 5)
2. F (L.O. 5) Common-size financial statements show relationships between items in terms of percentages, not dollars.
3. F (L.O. 6) The current ratio will increase.
4. T (L.O. 6)
5. F (L.O. 6) It equals the cost of goods sold divided by average inventory.
6. F (L.O. 6) The reverse is true, because the price/earnings ratio depends upon the earnings per share amount.
7. F (L.O. 6) Interest is not added back.
8. T (L.O. 6)
9. F (L.O. 6) The higher the debt to equity ratio, the greater the risk.
10. F (L.O. 6) Receivable turnover measures how many times, on the average, the receivables were converted into cash during the period.
11. T (L.O. 6)
12. T (L.O. 6)
13. F (L.O. 6) It is a market test ratio.
14. F (L.O. 5) Sales would be labeled 100 percent.
15. T (L.O. 3)
16. T (L.O. 3)
17. T (L.O. 6)
18. T (L.O. 4)

Multiple Choice

1. b (L.O. 6) Interest coverage is a measure of security that a creditor may use to gauge a company's ability to cover interest payments on loans extended to the firm.
2. d (L.O. 6) The quick ratio measures a company's ability to cover immediate cash requirements for operating expenses and short-term payables.
3. c (L.O. 6) Asset turnover is calculated using sales as the numerator and average assets as the denominator. It is a measure of the efficient use of a company's assets.
4. a (L.O. 6) A high price/earnings ratio indicates optimism about a company's future. That positive outlook may be due to anticipated increases in earnings and growth of the company.

5. a (L.O. 5) Index numbers are calculated to reflect percentage changes over consecutive periods of time. The base year will be assigned the value of 100%, then changes from that base will be assigned a percentage so that adjustments to subsequent amounts can be compared with base amounts. This method is used to identify trends, eliminating differences resulting from universal changes, such as inflation.

6. b (L.O. 1) Management uses financial statements to make decisions about the future of the company. Management also uses financial statements to analyze variances between actual results and budgeted results of operations. By using financial statements, management is better able to plan and control major functions of management. Each of the other choices listed is an external user of financial statements.

7. d (L.O. 2) Each of the factors listed in choices *a* through *c* contributes to the complications of comparing a company with the industry in which it operates.

8. c (L.O. 6) The turnover of receivables is the number of times receivables are collected in relation to sales in an accounting period. If the number is low, average accounts receivable balances are presumed to be high and credit policy is presumed to be weak.

9. b (L.O. 5) Net income will be given a percentage in relation to sales, as will all other components of the income statement. Sales will equal 100%.

Exercises

1. (L.O. 5)

| | 19x1 | 19x2 | Increase (or Decrease) | |
			Amount	Percentage
Sales	$200,000	$250,000	%50,000	25%
Cost of goods sold	120,000	144,000	24,000	20%
Gross margin	$ 80,000	$106,000	26,000	32.5
Operating expenses	50,000	62,000	12,000	24%
Income before income taxes	$ 30,000	$ 44,000	14,000	46.7%
Income taxes	8,000	16,000	8,000	100%
Net Income	$ 22,000	$ 28,000	6,000	27.3%

2. (L.O. 6)

a. 2.0 ($500,000/$250,000)

b. 1.3 $\left(\dfrac{\$500,000 - \$180,000}{\$250,000}\right)$

c. $5 ($106,000/21,200)

d. 1.9 times ($350,000/$180,000)

e. 12.0% ($106,000/$880,000)

f. 22.1% ($106,000/$480,000)

g. 6.0 ($600,000/$100,000)

h. 60.8 days (365/6.0)

i. 17.7% ($106,000/$600,000)

j. .68 (%600,000/$880,000)

k. 8 times ($40/$5)

Chapter 16

Matching

1. b	5. j	9. l	13. e
2. f	6. d	10. n	14. m
3. i	7. k	11. h	15. a
4. g	8. c	12. o	

Short Answer

1. (L.O. 4)

Classification	Method
Noninfluential and noncontrolling	Cost
Influential but noncontrolling	Equity
Controlling	Equity (also, consolidate)

2. (L.O. 4) Under the cost method, Dividend Income is recorded when dividends are received. Under the equity method, the Investment account is credited (decreased).

3. (L.O. 6) When the cost exceeds the book value of the net assets purchased, any excess that is not assigned to specific assets and liabilities should be recorded as goodwill.

4. (L.O. 5) Intercompany items are eliminated to avoid misleading consolidated financial statements. For example, if intercompany receivables and payables were (incorrectly) included in consolidated financial statements, that portion would represent the amount that the combined companies owed themselves.

5. (L.O. 1) When the exchange rate changes between the transaction date and the payment date, and foreign currency is involved, the domestic company would record an exchange gain or loss.

True-False

1. T (L.O. 4)
2. F (L.O. 4) The investor would do that under the equity method.
3. F (L.O. 4) Over 50 percent is the requirement for consolidated financial statements.
4. T (L.O. 6)
5. F (L.O. 7) The subsidiary's earnings are included from the date of acquisition only.
6. T (L.O. 4)
7. F (L.O. 6) A minority interest should be reported in the stockholders' equity section.
8. T (L.O. 6)
9. T (L.O. 1)
10. T (L.O. 1)
11. T (L.O. 1)
12. T (L.O. 1)
13. F (L.O. 7) Purchases of goods and services from outsiders should not be eliminated.
14. T (L.O. 6)

Multiple Choice

1. b (L.O. 4) Under the cost method of accounting for investments, dividends received are recorded as a source of income. The dividends are not used to adjust the value of the investment.

2. d (L.O. 6) The book value of each long-term asset will be reduced in proportion to the value of each asset relative to the whole. Each asset will maintain its value relative to the other assets, but the total book value will be reduced to the purchase price.

3. a (L.O. 6) The investment in the subsidiary company will be credited in making eliminations to prepare consolidated financial statements of the parent and subsidiary companies.

4. b (L.O. 6) Goodwill is used as a plug figure on the consolidation of the parent and subsidiary companies. Goodwill does not appear on the unconsolidated financial statements of the parent company.

5. d (L.O. 7) Profit on goods sold by the subsidiary to outsiders is an income item that is part of the total income of the parent and subsidiary upon consolidation. It will not be eliminated during consolidation.

6. d (L.O. 4) The adjustment required to recognize a loss on long-term investments includes a debit to Unrealized Loss on Long-Term Investments and a credit to Allowance to Reduce Long-Term Investments to Market. Since the market value of the investment is $35,000 below the cost, and since the allowance account has a credit balance of $10,000, the adjustment for the current period will be an additional $25,000.

7. d (L.O. 4) So that the users of financial statements will get a fair picture of the value of the company, Unrealized Loss on Long-Term Investments appears as a reduction in owners' equity. The corresponding allowance account is a contra-asset account and is used to revalue the investment account to the lower of cost or market. Upon disposal of the long-term investment, the unrealized loss may be realized, and appear on the income statement.

8. c (L.O. 1) Since fewer francs were required to satisfy the payment for the asset, the company has experienced a gain in reporting the transaction in dollars. At the payment date, more francs were required to equal one dollar.

Exercises

1. (L.O. 6)

Account Debited	Amount	Account Credited	Amount
Common Stock (Carter)	$60,000	Investment in Carter Corporation	165,000
Retained Earnings (Carter)	90,000	Minority Interest	30,000
Building	10,000		
Goodwill	35,000		

2. (L.O. 4)

		General Journal		
Date		Description	Debit	Credit
		Cash	12,000	
		Dividend Income		12,000
		To record cash dividend from Andrews*		
		Cash	15,000	
		Investment in Wilkins Company		15,000
		To record cash dividend from Wilkins		
		Investment in Wilkins Company	19,500	
		Income, Wilkins Company Investment		19,500
		To recognize 30% of income reported by Wilkins Company		

*Andrews' earnings of $110,000 are irrelevant, since Fairfax is using the cost method to account for the investment.

3. (L.O. 1)

		General Journal		
Date		Description	Debit	Credit
		Accounts Receivable, Mexican Company	5,000	
		Sales		5,000
		To record sale of merchandise		
		Cash	4,500	
		Exchange Gain or Loss	500	
		Accounts Receivable, Mexican Company		5,000
		To record receipt of payment		

Solution to Crossword Puzzle
(Chapters 14, 15, and 16)

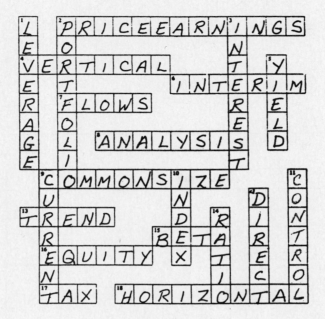

Appendix A

Matching

1. e	**5.** b	**8.** h
2. f	**6.** c	**9.** a
3. j	**7.** g	**10.** d
4. i		

Exercises

1. (L.O. 5)
  a. A = $14,500 (10,000 + 3,000 + 1,500)
   B = $13,000 (10,000 + 2,000 + 1,000)
   C = $13,000 (10,000 + 2,500 + 500)
  b. A = $7,000 (10,000 + 3,000 − 6,000)
   B = $8,000 (10,000 + 2,000 − 4,000)
   C = $10,500 (10,000 + 2,500 − 2,000)
  c. A = ($8,000) (10,000 + 3,000 − 21,000)
   B = ($2,000) (10,000 + 2,000 − 14,000)
   C = $5,500 (10,000 + 2,500 − 7,000)

2. (L.O. 6)

		General Journal			
Date		**Description**		**Debit**	**Credit**
a.		Cash		12,000	
		G, Capital		800	
		H, Capital		800	
		I, Capital		400	
		J, Capital			14,000
		To record purchase of one-third interest by J			
b.		Cash		15,000	
		J, Capital			15,000
		To record purchase of one-third interest by J			
c.		Cash		21,000	
		G, Capital			1,600
		H, Capital			1,600
		I, Capital			800
		J, Capital			17,000
		To record purchase of one-third interest by J			

Appendix B

Matching

1. j	**8.** a	**15.** f
2. q	**9.** n	**16.** d
3. c	**10.** e	**17.** r
4. m	**11.** l	**18.** i
5. g	**12.** p	**19.** k
6. s	**13.** h	**20.** t
7. b	**14.** o	

Exercise

1. (L.O. 3)

General Journal				
Date		**Description**	**Debit**	**Credit**
Jan.	*1*	Estimated Revenues	950,000	
		Appropriations		935,000
		Fund Balance		15,000
Mar.	*15*	Property Taxes Receivable	900,000	
		Revenue		891,000
		Estimated Uncollectible Property Taxes		9,000
	25	Encumbrances	50,000	
		Reserve for Encumbrances		50,000
May	*9*	Expenditures	30,000	
		Cash		30,000
June	*15*	Cash	893,000	
		Estimated Uncollectible Property Taxes	7,000	
		Property Taxes Receivable		900,000
	27	Reserve for Encumbrances	50,000	
		Encumbrances		50,000
	27	Expenditures	51,000	
		Vouchers Payable		51,000
July	*5*	Vouchers Payable	51,000	
		Cash		51,000
Dec.	*31*	Revenues	955,000	
		Estimated Revenues		950,000
		Fund Balance		5,000
	31	Appropriations	935,000	
		Fund Balance	12,000	
		Expenditures		947,000

Appendix C

Matching

1. a
2. d
3. c
4. e
5. b

Exercises

1. (L.O. 2)
a. J	**d.** CP	**g.** J	**j.** CP
b. CR	**e.** S	**h.** J	**k.** CR
c. P	**f.** CP	**i.** J	

2. (L.O. 2)

				Credits			**Debits**	
Date		**Account Credited**	**Post. Ref.**	**Other Accts.**	**Accts. Receiv.**	**Sales**	**Sales Disc.**	**Cash**
Feb.	*3*	Frank Simpson	✔		500		10	490
	9	Equipment	135	8,000				8,000
	14	Common Stock	311	10,000				10,000
	23	Stanley Hall	✔		150			150
	28	Sales				25,000		25,000
				18,000	650	25,000	10	43,640
				(✔)	(114)	(411)	(412)	(111)

3. (L.O. 2)

a. Cash payments journal

b. The "Other Accounts" total should have a check (not an account number) below it to signify that it is not posted at the end of the month.

c. May 1 Paid Vincennes Supply Co. for $800 of supplies previously purchased. Paid within the discount period, receiving a $16 discount.

May 7 Purchased for cash $2,000 of office equipment from Jeppson Business Equipment.

May 13 Paid for ad placed in the *Daily Planet.*

May 19 Paid Olsen Motors for $420 of items previously purchased. Did not pay within the discount period.

d. 1. The amounts in the Accounts Payable column were posted to the accounts payable subsidiary accounts (Vincennes Supply and Olsen Motors).

2. The amounts in the Other Accounts column were posted to the general ledger accounts (Office Equipment and Advertising Expense).

3. The 315 is an error, as already explained. The other numbers refer to the postings of column totals to the general ledger accounts.

Appendix D

Matching

1. j	**5.** g	**8.** i
2. c	**6.** f	**9.** a
3. e	**7.** d	**10.** h
4. b		

Exercises

1. (L.O. 2)

	General Journal			
Date	**Description**	**Debit**	**Credit**
May 11	Office Salaries Expense	260.00	
	FICA Tax Payable		19.89
	Union Dues Payable		5.00
	State Income Tax Payable		8.00
	Federal Income Tax Payable		52.00
	Salaries Payable		175.11
	To record payroll liabilities and salaries expense for Frank Nelson		
11	Payroll Taxes Expense	36.01	
	FICA Tax Payable		19.89
	Federal Unemployment Taxes Payable		2.08
	State Unemployment Taxes Payable		14.04
	To record payroll taxes on Nelson's earnings		

Appendix E

Exercises

1. (L.O. 1–3)

General Journal				
Date		**Description**	**Debit**	**Credit**

Mar.	*1*	Investment in Bonds
		Accrued Interest Receivable
		   Cash
		      To record purchase of bonds
			9,600.00
			140.00
				
				9,740.00

July	*1*	Cash
		Investment in Bonds $288 − 280)
		   Accrued Interest Receivable
		   Interest Earned ($9600 x 9% X 4/12)
		      To record semiannual interest and amortization of discount
			420.00
			8.00
				
				140.00
				288.00

Dec.	*31*	Accrued Interest Receivable
		Investment in Bonds
		   Interest Earned
		      To record accrued interest and amortization of discount
			420.00
			12.36
				
				432.36

Jan.	*1*	Cash
		   Accrued Interest Receivable
		      To record receipt of interest
			420.00	
				420.00

Mar.	*1*	Investment in Bonds*
		   Interest Earned
		      To amortize 2 months' interest
			4.31	
				4.31

	1	Cash ($9500 − 200 + 140)
		Loss on Sale of Investments
		   Investment in Bonds
		   Interest Earned
		      To record sale of bonds
			9,440.00
			324.67
				
				9,624.67
				140.00

		*$9,620.36 x 9% x 1/6 = $144.31
		  10,000 x 8.4% x 1/6 = 140.00
		                     $ 4.31		